EDUCATION AND THE LABOUR MOVEMENT
1870-1920

By the same author

A Student's View of the Universities (1943)
Intelligence Testing and the Comprehensive School (1953)
Education in the New Poland (1954)
The Common Secondary School (1955)
Studies in the History of Education, 1780–1870 (1960)

Psychology in the Soviet Union (1957) (Editor)
New Trends in English Education (1957) (Editor)
The Challenge of Marxism (1963) (Editor)
Educational Psychology in the U.S.S.R. (1963) (Editor, with Joan Simon)
Non-Streaming in the Junior School (1964) (Editor)

STUDIES IN THE HISTORY OF EDUCATION

EDUCATION AND THE LABOUR MOVEMENT 1870-1920

by

BRIAN SIMON

1965
LAWRENCE & WISHART
LONDON

Printed in Great Britain by
The Camelot Press Ltd., London and Southampton

CONTENTS

LIST OF ILLUSTRATIONS

ACKNOWLEDGMENTS

The author and publishers gratefully acknowledge the following permissions to quote from copyright material: Ernest Benn Ltd., *Imperialism and the Rise of Labour* by E. Halévy; A. and C. Black Ltd., *Lads' Clubs* by C. E. B. Russell; The Clarendon Press, Oxford, *The Silent Social Revolution* by G. A. N. Lowndes; Wm. Collins Sons & Co., *Youth Will be Led* by Alicia C. Percival; Constable & Co. Ltd., *The Education Department and After* by G. W. Kekewich; Mr. S. J. Curtis, *Education in Britain since 1900*; J. M. Dent & Sons Ltd., *Men, Movements and Myself* by Lord Snell; Hodder & Stoughton Ltd., *The Life of Sir George Williams* by J. E. Hodder-Williams; Macmillan & Co. Ltd., *Sir Robert Morant* by B. M. Allen and *The Origins of the Labour Party* by Henry Pelling; Methuen & Co. Ltd., *Public Schools and British Opinion since 1860* by E. C. Mack; George Newnes Ltd., *My Life's Battles* by Will Thorne; John Murray Ltd., *Canon Barnett, His Life, Work and Friends* by Dame S. A. Barnett; Routledge and Kegan Paul Ltd., *Parity and Prestige in English Education* by O. Banks, *From School Board to Local Authority* by Eric Eaglesham and *Adult Education, a Comparative Study* by R. Peers; University of London Press Ltd., *Making Men* by W. McG. Eager and *A History of English Elementary Education* by Frank Smith.

Acknowledgment is due to the following publishers and organisations for permission to reproduce illustrations: the Radio Times Hulton Picture Library for photographs of Annie Besant, Charles Bradlaugh, Canon and Mrs. Barnett, A. J. Balfour, Will Thorne and a Free Church demonstration in 1902, and for contemporary drawings showing free dinners to poor children (1890), a penny dinner to Board School children (1885), the London School Board (1882) and a London School Board capture (1871); the British Museum Newspaper Library for cartoons from *The Sun* (19.2.1895) and *Justice* (1.5.1896); Curtis Brown Ltd. for a photograph of the Norwich Branch of the Socialist League; Routledge & Kegan Paul Ltd., for a drawing of Wortley Working Men's Institute; the National Adult School Union for an Adult School handbill; B. T. Batsford Ltd., for a drawing of the Stanley Road Higher Grade School, Nottingham and a drawing of a pupil teachers' centre at Brentwood; the Central Office of Information for two photographs of Uppingham School; John Murray Ltd., for a drawing of West Street School, London Fields; the Bursar of Wellington College for a photograph of the Wellington College governors; the Hutchinson Publishing Group for photographs of a march against Birrell's Bill of 1906 and of Bishop Knox; George Newnes Ltd., for a cartoon by Walter Crane; the City of Leicester Museums and Art Gallery for Henry Payne's School Board Election address; the National Magazine Co., Ltd. for a "Spy" cartoon of the Duke of Devonshire from *Vanity Fair*.

INTRODUCTION

THIS book covers some aspects of educational development in the half-century following the Education Act of 1870, seen from the standpoint of the working-class movement, which began at this period to develop a socialist perspective. Looked at from this angle the measures of the time tend to take on a changed complexion; for example, the Education Act of 1902, represented in most textbooks as a far-sighted measure of reform, appeared to many at the time as a betrayal of the principles on which educational advance should be based.

To understand why this is so it is necessary briefly to recall earlier struggles and the close connection between educational policies and wider political developments. In my *Studies in the History of Education, 1780-1870* it was argued that the period 1850 to 1870 might be seen as a crucial "moment of change" in English education. During these twenty years, with the aid of a series of Royal Commissions followed by Acts of Parliament, the ancient universities and public schools were reformed to meet the needs of the Victorian upper middle class, while steps were taken to remodel the endowed grammar schools on three grades to serve three different social levels or occupational groupings. In effect these years saw the structuring of an hierarchical system of education in which each type of school played its allotted role in the social order.

The crown of these developments was the Education Act of 1870 which established a universal system of elementary schools for the working class. The fact that this measure was passed only three years after the Franchise Act of 1867 underlined the connection between the idea of mass popular education on the one hand, and the extension of the franchise on the other. This conception had been fundamental to the thinking of the "philosophic radicals", Jeremy Bentham and James Mill, who had been concerned, in the period up to 1832, to oust the landed aristocracy from political power. Education was to be the means by which the mass of the people, the "labouring poor", would be brought to understand their identity of interest with capital. Hence the Benthamite "democratic model", which envisaged government by Parliamentary representatives of the middle class, elected on a universal franchise by an "educated" and so "enlightened" working class. By this means the self-interested rule of the landed aristocracy would be overthrown, and a government, based on the willing franchise of the people, and concerned with the interests of all, would be substituted.

The Reform Act of 1832 did not, of course, enfranchise the working class; that of 1867, however, brought approximately a million artisans on to the voting registers and, in terms of the Benthamite creed, made universal education a political necessity. From the standpoint of the working class, which had fought strongly for the extension of the franchise and for popular education, however, both these measures had positive aspects. While the full demands of the most advanced working-class bodies were not won in 1870, elected School Boards were established on which it became possible to gain representation and these gave scope for further advances. The issue, therefore, became that of the direction in which popular education would develop.

This question, of great importance for the working class, was now to be determined in new circumstances. This is the age of imperialism on the one hand, and on the other, of the beginnings of social welfare legislation and of social reform generally. Partly as a result of the Education Act of 1870 and the increasing literacy and "involvement" of the working class, upper and middle-class aims in education are less openly stated than formerly, though remaining fundamentally the same as at an earlier period. Working-class aims, however, now begin to be much more clearly formulated in the light of socialist ideas, differing markedly from the utopian socialism of the age of Owen. At the same time conscious efforts are now made to extend and transform education, both among adult workers and in the system of schools that had now come into being. It is with these, often opposite, tendencies that this volume is concerned.

Part One describes the growth of independent political organisation and of socialist ideas during the period 1870 to 1900, concentrating on the educative aspects of a social movement of deep significance; it outlines the measures, partly educational, partly social, which were developed to some extent as a response to this movement, and analyses the increasing polarisation of education itself during this period. The educational aspirations of the working class, and the campaigns undertaken to improve conditions and widen opportunity, are also delineated.

The Education Act of 1902 is seen as a turning point, an attempt to resolve a number of pressing political, social and religious issues almost, one might say, at the expense of the educational interests of those for whom the elementary school system was established. Part Two is, then, concerned largely with the three years 1900 to 1902, years when education became a matter of primary political importance, and when a new direction was given to the educational system as a whole. Part Three then carries the story of pressure and counter-pressure, of new educational initiatives both in the school system and in adult education, up to the close of the First World War.

No attempt is made, therefore, to cover the whole story of educational developments at this time; many important aspects are necessarily left aside—the slow evolution, for instance, of a system of technical education and, related to this, the beginnings of the modern universities in the provincial cities. Attention is concentrated rather on those areas in which working-class opinion and activity made itself felt in the new conditions of political democracy. Since education played a crucial role in the Democratic Model, the general struggles of the time found their reflection in the field of education, both in policies advanced for the schools and in action in the sphere of adult education.

My particular thanks are due to Joan Simon, with whom the problems dealt with in this book have been fully discussed and who has once more assisted greatly with the final draft; to James Klugmann who has generously given time and energy to discuss the planning of the book and reading the manuscript; to Lionel Munby and Frank Jackson who have read particular chapters, and to W. W. Craik whose own book on the Central Labour College was being drafted at the same time as this, and who kindly allowed me to see his chapters as they were written. I owe a debt also to W. P. McCann whose unpublished thesis "Trade Unionist, Co-operative and Socialist Organisations in relation to Popular Education, 1870-1902", covers part of the ground of this book, particularly Chapter 4 and parts of Chapters 6 and 7, as also to higher degree students whose work with me has bordered on this field. My debt to the work of Elie Halévy will once more be obvious, as also to the more specific pioneering work of Professor Eaglesham on the administrative events surrounding the 1902 Act. I have to thank the librarians of the Leicester School of Education, the University of Leicester, the Trades Union Congress, the British Museum Newspaper Library, the Marx Memorial Library, and the Department of Education and Science for assistance over a considerable period. To Miss Langton and Mrs. Goodrich, who deciphered and typed succeeding drafts of the manuscript, I am also most grateful.

September 1964

BRIAN SIMON

PART I

DEMOCRACY
AND
EDUCATION
1870–1900

CHAPTER I

THE RISE OF SOCIALISM AND ITS EDUCATIONAL IMPLICATIONS

THE formation of new socialist groups in the 1880s marked a decisive break in working-class politics—the beginnings of a new move towards independent political organisation and activity which had repercussions in the field of trade union organisation and considerable educational implications. The twenty years following 1850 were years of prosperity, of rapid industrial development and colonial expansion, with Britain supplying manufactured goods to Europe, America and further afield on a quite new level. These years had seen the growth of what Bronterre O'Brien, the Chartist leader, called a "labour aristocracy", embracing particularly the skilled crafts in engineering and building. In contrast to the militancy of the Chartist period, the trade union outlook could now be summarised in the slogan "a fair day's wage for a fair day's work". The working class in general formed the tail of the great Liberal party.

Nevertheless active participation particularly in the struggle for the Franchise Act (1867) and for the Education Act three years later marked a new phase in political activity. At the same time the consolidation brought about by the formation of the Trades Union Congress in 1868, and by the holding of the first Co-operative Congress in modern times in the same year, indicated that the level, power and influence of working-class organisation was reaching a new stage. By 1870 factory production had become the rule throughout industry; the working class itself had greatly increased in size, become more homogeneous and therefore more united. Through trade unionism and co-operation it had fashioned weapons for the defence of its interests. Through the Franchise Act an important section had won their rights as citizens. These were the forces that came into play in widespread industrial struggles when prosperity gave place to the "Great Depression" which, starting in 1876, lasted for twenty years.

It was during this latter period that socialist organisations came into being which adopted a Marxist outlook, so far as it was then understood. The Social Democratic Federation, established as such in

B

1884, stood for social ownership of the means of production and exchange and saw the winning of political power by the working class as the essential means to achieving this end. The formation in the late 1880s of the great unions of the unskilled took place under socialist leadership and so there began to develop that connection between political activity and industrial organisation which had been so signally lacking in the days of the Chartists and early socialists. At the same time the new socialist groups embarked on a programme of propaganda and education which brought a new conception of the potentialities of living and new hope to the more advanced sections of the working class. It was particularly William Morris, originally profoundly influenced by Ruskin and Carlyle and later by Marx, who brought this new vision to the working-class movement—a vision of a society in which labour would be pleasurable and education the right of all.

The general move towards independent organisation and political activity, the specific aims now advanced by socialists, involved a break with liberalism, with acceptance of a *status quo* in which the working class played the subservient role allotted to it in the democratic model. This whole movement was, therefore, educative in the widest sense. Socialist educational programmes aimed directly to change the workers' outlook, to develop a new conception of the dignity of man. In this sense the importance of the early socialist movement, as Morris insisted, was primarily educational. But the ideas propagated also influenced the day-to-day struggles. Before men could develop their human capacities they must win the right to be men—leisure to think, to read, to educate themselves. If new ideas were to be spread widely there must be freedom of speech and assembly, halls and meeting places, newspapers representing the new outlook. All these needs were pursued as a background to more specific educational demands which also challenged the established democratic model. We may look here at various strands in this movement—efforts at self-education, the development of clubs, the scope and role of the working-class press, the policies of the new unionism, all of which contributed towards the enlightenment of a developing working-class movement.

1. SOCIALIST PIONEERS, PROPAGANDA AND TEACHING

There were precursors to the new socialist groups which prepared the way for the new political alignment and fresh educational efforts.

The year 1870 had seen a massive republican agitation led by Chamberlain, Dilke and Bradlaugh, which developed with the overthrow of Napoleon III and the establishment of the Third Republic in France. This radical-liberal movement won wide support among the workers and led to the establishment of Republican Clubs in the main cities. There was also a development of local groupings under the auspices of the National Secular Society in which Bradlaugh and Annie Besant were the leading figures. Bradlaugh's radical and secularist propaganda, presented in popular terms, exercised an ever-increasing influence among the working class—an influence that reached its height in the years 1880-5 during the long struggle he conducted to take his seat in Parliament without taking the oath. Though himself a strong individualist and anti-socialist, Bradlaugh represented a centre of political opposition to the Church and Tory party, to those "dominating parish, school and town"; carrying on the rationalist tradition of Paine, Godwin, Shelley and Owen, he became the "rallying point for all the half-expressed political revolt of the workers".[1]

This revolt became more clearly apparent in the movement to win a further extension of the franchise in the early 1880s, a movement arising from the mounting disillusion of advanced workers with Liberal and Tory governments alike, both for legislating entirely in the interest of the middle class and for pursuing reactionary policies abroad. In Northumberland and Durham the miners formed County Political Associations in support of a new measure, while the agricultural workers, led by Joseph Arch, were also extremely active. The movement culminated in mass meetings and demonstrations throughout the country, while the passage of the Act in 1884, despite obstruction in the House of Lords, laid the basis for independent working-class representation in Parliament.

As a result of these campaigns on matters in which the working class was interested—republicanism, secularism, extension of the franchise—there was a wide development of working-class clubs. The most important were undoubtedly the Radical Clubs formed in connection with the Liberal party but often and increasingly pursuing independent political aims. But there were also the branches of the National Secular Society and many other discussion clubs where the issues of the day were hotly debated, successors of a long line going back to the days of the Corresponding Societies of the 1790s. No assessment of the influence of these clubs can be made but their number

[1] Dona Torr, *Tom Mann and his Times* (1956), 49-50.

and variety can be gauged by a glance at the lecture lists in the National Secular Society's *The National Reformer*. As well as branches of the Secular Society all over the country, and various Radical Clubs— for instance the Towers Hamlet Radical Club, the Marylebone Radical Reform Association (which was organised into branches)— there figure a number of societies such as the London Dialectical Society, the Camden Debating Society, the Claremont Eclectic Debating Society, and the well-known Stratford Dialectical and Radical Club which was the earliest to adopt a socialist standpoint.

With this background, of organisation and a ferment of discussion, it is not surprising that Henry George's propaganda for a "single tax" on rent had so phenomenal a success; his *Progress and Poverty* achieved a circulation of some 100,000 and he had "a triumphant lecture tour" in Britain in 1882. George's proposals for land reform were not socialism but they marked an important step in that direction, taking up an issue which had long been of central concern to the Labour movement. Land reform became the issue of the hour and Henry George's influence brought many to take the first steps towards becoming socialists.

It was, however, life itself that laid the foundations for acceptance of socialist ideas and welcoming of the socialist perspective, as is illustrated by the recollections of many socialist pioneers. Forced by economic necessity to start work at the age of seven or eight, denied education beyond the merest rudiments, many of the men who led the working-class struggles of the 1880s and '90s had bitter memories of hardships. The conditions under which agricultural workers lived throughout the century are vividly evoked in the autobiographies of Joseph Arch, born in 1826, and Harry Snell, born in 1865. Both began work between the ages of eight and nine—scaring crows. Both had the very minimum of schooling. Life for all in the village was a "fierce and unbroken struggle for food and shelter".[1] Both carried bitter memories of their childhood. The people were kept in "poverty and serfdom . . . dependence and wretchedness," writes Arch. "The horrors of those times are clearly and vividly before my mind's eye even now. It is as if they had been burned and branded into me. I cannot forget them."[2] "The memory of the privations and the social indignities that I saw and experienced as a child," writes Snell, "still

[1] Lord Snell, *Men, Movements and Myself* (1936), 6.
[2] Joseph Arch, *Joseph Arch, The Story of his Life* (Ed. Countess of Warwick, 3rd edn. n.d.), 11, 14.

arouses in me an unabated resentment, and I am thankful that long before I knew the cause of and possible remedies for the suffering around me, I hated the system which produced and defended it, with an intensity which has never diminished."[1]

Others working in industry had similar experiences. Keir Hardie (born 1856) was forced out to work at the age of seven as a result of hardship caused by a ship-building strike—he was taught to read by his parents despite the desperate plight of the family. At ten he was sent down the mines as a trapper, working a ten hour day. These childhood experiences, according to his biographer, "left an indelible mark on (his) character. . . . It was a period of his life to which in after years he seldom referred, but always with bitterness."[2]

The miners' leader, Robert Smillie (born 1857) was looked after by his grandmother because of the death of both of his parents; he attended an infant school for a short time "but got little beyond the alphabet" and at nine was working as an errand boy "to ease to some extent the struggle we were continually waging for a bare existence". He went to school again for six months, at the age of eleven, when working as a half-timer in a cotton mill, but at twelve "school attendance automatically and inevitably ceased".[3]

Will Thorne (born 1857), later member of the S.D.F. and founder of the Gasworkers' Union, had a childhood of extreme poverty and hardship. "My first job," he writes, "came when I was only a little over six years of age; it was turning a sheet for a rope and twine spinner" for twelve hours a day. On Saturday he worked from 6 a.m. to 8 p.m. and on Sunday from 8 a.m. to 2 p.m. The eldest of four children of a widowed mother (his father was killed in a brawl when he was seven), his family often had recourse to poor relief and was constantly in hunger. His mother, who rose at 4 a.m. to make his breakfast, finally insisted that he give up this work even though "someone would have to go short". "My mother's rebellion against the way I was being worked," writes Thorne, "is the rebellion of many mothers. It is the rebellion that I feel and will continue to carry on. . . . Here was I, a boy of nine years of age, that should have been in school, getting up in the cold of the early morning, leaving home at about 4.30, walking four miles to work, and then, after a long twelve-hour day, walking back again, a fifteen-hour day by the time I got home, dead tired, barely able to eat my scanty tea and crawl into

1 Snell, op. cit., 12.   2 W. Stewart, J. Keir Hardie (1925 edn.), 3.
3 Robert Smillie, My Life for Labour (1924), 14-15.

bed."[1] Poverty and long hours of work were the common experience of working-class children in the 1850s and '60s.

In spite of these conditions many found the means to self-education, as their forerunners in the Chartist movement had done. Joseph Arch had barely three years' schooling (from six to nine) but he was helped by his mother ("educated as in the true sense of the word") and when a young labourer "bought books and studied hard, and educated myself".[2] The young Harry Snell was first stimulated by the secularist speakers in Nottingham Market Square; in 1881 he heard Bradlaugh: "I remember, as clearly as though it was only yesterday, the immediate and compelling impression made upon me by that extraordinary man." When unemployed he read widely in the advanced literature of the time—"every hour that was not spent in looking for work was devoted to my own education".[3] Robert Smillie was taught to read by his grandmother and by the age of fourteen "knew something of Burns, and had read several of Shakespeare's plays and some of his sonnets". Like others he became enthralled by Shakespeare, and read Dickens, Scott, Morris, Shaw and later collected books. "Before I had been ten years married I had a fair library for a working man. . . . Today the walls of my sitting room are not only lined with books, but hung with portraits of Carlyle, Ruskin, Russell Lowell, Longfellow, Walt Whitman, Burns and Scott."[4] The young Keir Hardie attended night school and grew very fond of reading. His parents owned, besides the Bible, *Pilgrim's Progress*, Paine's *Age of Reason*, Burns' poems. Circumstances made him a labour agitator as early as the age of twenty; but his study now became more systematic, comprising Carlyle, Ruskin and Emerson whose writings now began to form his outlook.[5]

It was their actual conditions of work that turned many of these men towards socialism in the 1880s. Will Thorne, for instance, gives a horrifying description of the munitions factory in which he worked as a boy. Why was he always in the forefront of industrial struggles? "The only reason I am able to give . . . is that the system we lived under at that time, the poverty and hardships the workers had to endure—the hard work and long hours, and the tender age at which we were thrown into the industrial battlefield—made us rebels." When challenged by the resident engineer of the gasworks at which he was employed in 1885 as to why he was a socialist, Thorne answered:

[1] Will Thorne, *My Life's Battles* (n.d.), 15, 19-20.   [2] Arch, *op. cit.*, 24, 27
[3] Snell, *op. cit.*, 31, 47.   [4] Smillie, *op. cit.*, 15, 53.   [5] Stewart, *op. cit.*, 6, 20.

"I told him that I had learnt from books and pamphlets that I bought with the few shillings I had to spare; that I had learnt it in the works where I had been employed; that I had learned it from bitter experience."[1] So also John Burns, who had "from my earliest infancy been in contact with poverty of the worst possible description", read hungrily and actively sought education; when he joined the S.D.F. in 1884 he had already for three years been speaking at Radical Clubs and Secular Societies, urging the need for working-class combination not only for economic but also for "civic and political" purposes.[2]

There were others who profited from the gains won through organised struggle by the skilled workers, but this pointed the need for more effective organisation. Tom Mann, who, as apprentice in a Birmingham engineering factory in 1871, gained immeasurably from the great victory of the Tyneside engineers which assured the nine hour day, later became the leader of the Eight Hour movement. He himself made good use of the time released by shorter working hours. For three nights a week he attended classes studying machine construction and design and learning arithmetic and English. Once a week he went to a Bible class run by a Quaker who taught him the use of language and clear speech. On Saturday night he went to a temperance society meeting, on Sunday twice to Sunday school (as scholar and later teacher) and to church or chapel; the seventh evening was usually spent learning the violin or at the public library, the theatre, or political meetings. At the Sunday school a gifted teacher awoke what was to become a "lifelong passion for poetry". "More intense and imaginative than many," writes his biographer, "his life was not very different from that of hundreds of the best skilled workers in days when education could only be won by strenuous effort and when only craftsmen whose unions had gained them the shorter working-day could hope for more than the barest elements of culture." When he moved to London in 1877 Tom Mann's horizons widened. By chance he was given the job of cutting through a meteorite for the British Museum, and this developed an interest in science, leading to the purchase of a telescope; astronomy became his favourite hobby for the rest of his life. In London also he discovered Shakespeare. His interest in economics and politics developed through reading Henry George, followed up by Thorold Rogers, J. S. Mill, Carlyle and Ruskin. In 1885 Tom Mann heard John Burns speaking in the open air at Battersea Park,

1 Thorne, *op. cit.*, 46, 63.   2 Quoted in Torr, *op. cit.*, 185-6.

and joined the S.D.F.[1] So workers from the ranks of the skilled and the unskilled, from agriculture and industry, sought opportunities for education and in one way or another acquired the rudiments of a socialist outlook; in the S.D.F. they learned more systematically and began in their turn to propagate the idea of socialism.

The S.D.F. grew out of the Democratic Federation, started in 1880 by H. M. Hyndman with a Radical programme. In 1881 Hyndman's *England for All* popularised the scientific socialism of Karl Marx, if without acknowledgment. The book was widely read and when the Democratic Federation adopted a socialist programme in 1884 this reflected the Marxist outlook. It was at first preponderantly intellectuals who came together in this organisation, in groups as small as their ideas were large.

"They were stirring times, those days of the early eighties," wrote Harry Quelch, one of the working-class members, some twenty years later, "when, fired by enthusiasm for democratic ideals, burning with indignation at oppression at home and piratical financial enterprises abroad, and disgust at the broken faith of the newly-formed Liberal Government, a few earnest men gathered together to form a new political party." They stood alone, a mere handful, "but we were enthusiasts, fanatics, what you will, imbued with the faith that moves mountains; and it was wonderful the amount of work done and the effect created by this little knot of fanatics".[2] There was an early split which led to the formation of the Socialist League alongside the S.D.F., but this did not lead to any reduction of the work—on the contrary, both groups seem to have gone ahead with redoubled energy.

The early motto of the Democratic Federation recalls that of the Owenite Socialists of the 1840s: "EDUCATE—we shall need all our Intelligence, AGITATE—we shall need all our enthusiasm, ORGANISE—we shall need all our force." If William Morris and the Socialist League tended from the first to put the main emphasis on education Hyndman was not far behind in practical work to this end. "It begins at all events," Morris wrote of the Socialist League to his daughter May, "with the distinct aim of making Socialists by educating them, and of organising them to deal with politics in the end."[3] Socialism can only be won, he had written earlier, by "First, educating the people into desiring it, next organising them into claiming it effectually."[4] This

[1] Torr, *op. cit.*, 40-1, 57, 66-7, 80, 85-6.
[2] *Social Democrat*, Vol. 7, No. 1, January 1901, 7.
[3] Quoted in E. P. Thompson, *William Morris, Romantic to Revolutionary* (1955), 415.
[4] *Ibid.*, 378.

made it necessary to foster an active discontent among the workers, discontent, not for its own sake, but to provide the force and the means to the regeneration of mankind. "I am sure it is right," Morris wrote to his friend Burne Jones, "whatever the apparent consequences may be, to stir up the lower classes (damn the word) to demand a higher standard of life for themselves, not merely for themselves or for the sake of the material comfort it will bring, but for the good of the whole world and the regeneration of the conscience of man: and this stirring up is part of the necessary education which must in good truth go before the reconstruction of society."[1] The workers, he said, echoing Thomas Hodgskin of an earlier generation, must learn "what the due social claims of labour are".[2] Nor was it only a question of discontent, of an understanding that another world, another existence, was possible and desirable. This would motivate men for social change—a change which William Morris thought must be revolutionary; but such a revolution must be a conscious one, intelligently led; not only must the workers generally be educated but, he said in 1885, there should be among them "a body of able, high-minded, competent men, who should act as instructors of the masses and as their leaders during critical periods of the movement. It goes without saying," he added, "that a great proportion of these instructors and

MEMBERSHIP CARD OF THE DEMOCRATIC FEDERATION
DESIGNED BY WILLIAM MORRIS

[1] *Ibid.*, 377. [2] *Ibid.*, 415.

organisers should be working men. . . . I should like to see 2,000 men of that stamp engaged in explaining the principles of rational, scientific Socialism all over the kingdom."[1]

"You see, my dear, I cannot help it," wrote Morris to a friend. "The ideas which have taken hold of me will not let me rest: nor can I see anything else worth thinking of."[2] The same was true of many others in the small grouping of 1884-5, not only Hyndman himself, but the ex-Eton schoolmaster J. L. Joynes, H. H. Champion, Belfort Bax, Hunter Watts—and such working-class members as James Macdonald, J. E. Williams and Harry Quelch. A new dawn had broken, a new light flooded across the world, and there was business to do. The spreading of this outlook is well illustrated in the appeal of Andreas Scheu, "Educate! Educate! Educate!", in the fifth number of *Commonweal* (1885), organ of the Socialist League. "*Educate,*" he enjoins, "reform and train, enlighten and invigorate yourself and fellow workers in mind and soul and body; for the battling to be done needs men and women of clear intellect, of sympathetic social impulse, of strong determination and enduring frame."[3]

This is not the place to chronicle in detail the educational and propaganda activities of the early socialists, but the main direction of activity may be indicated. In the first place they took their message out to the open and initiated a pattern of week-end open air meetings. Thus on Sunday, 26 April 1885, outdoor lectures were given at eleven places in London alone, Hyndman speaking at Islington Green, Quelch at Salmon's Lane, and J. Macdonald at Stamford Hill.[4] It was at such a meeting that Tom Mann first heard the socialist standpoint expounded by John Burns. The energy of leading members in those early years was extraordinary. At the time of the breakaway of the Socialist League in 1884, Hyndman had spoken at open air meetings held on sixty-six consecutive Sundays; as for Morris, besides carrying on his own work as well as writing, organising and attending innumerable committee meetings, he gave, in 1884, some forty lectures in London, Bradford, Leeds, Edinburgh, Sheffield, Newcastle and elsewhere. He delivered forty lectures again in the following year, about sixty in 1886 and as many in 1887.[5]

---

[1] Thompson, *op. cit.*, 447.
[2] J. W. Mackail, *The Life of William Morris*, Vol. II (1911 imp.), 150.
[3] *Commonweal*, June 1885.
[4] *Justice*, 25 April 1885. James Macdonald, later secretary of the London Trades Council, is not to be confused with J. R. Macdonald.
[5] Torr, *op. cit.*, 341n.; H. W. Lee and E. Archbold, *Social Democracy in Britain* (1935), 77.

A most important field for serious lectures and discussions on socialism was offered by the local Secular Societies up and down the country. Here many middle and working-class people of a generally progressive character, interested in ideas, were gathered together, and it was not long before there was a radical change in the character of meetings under the impact of socialist speakers. In Leicester, for instance, there was a flourishing Secular Society (still in existence) with its own building erected in 1881. The first number of *Justice*, the journal of the S.D.F., reports a lecture on socialism given there by Hyndman: "The audience was good and among the numbers were many old Socialists of the time of Robert Owen."[1] A fortnight later William Morris delivered for the first time his well-known lecture on "Art and Socialism"—in the following year, Edward Aveling was speaking at Leicester to a crammed hall, endeavouring to win his audience to attack capitalism rather than Christianity.[2]

This infiltration did not take place without opposition, leading to a major controversy. Bradlaugh was, of course, a strong, indeed violent opponent of socialism, and early in 1884 delivered a series of lectures expressing his views at the Hall of Science in London—these led to a public debate between Hyndman and Bradlaugh which marks a turning point in the history of ideas in that, before a large audience, the basic principles of socialism versus individualism were argued out point by point by the chief protagonist of each view.[3] It is generally conceded that Hyndman came off the better of the two—so much so that, shortly after, Annie Besant, another leading member of the secular movement (Bradlaugh's main partner for over two decades), and Edward Aveling, joined the S.D.F.

The Bradlaugh-Hyndman debate sparked off the great "Radicalism or Socialism" controversy among secularists which was sharply fought out over the next twenty or thirty years. The pages of *The National Reformer* (journal of the National Secular Society) at this period report discussions on socialism in local secular societies all over the country. Annie Besant, who had the entry as one of the leaders of the movement, was particularly active in these societies. A fine speaker with great powers of persuasion, she frequently lectured on socialism. Among the first of many working men who moved from secularism to socialism at this time was John Burns.

1 *Justice*, 19 January 1884.
2 *Ibid.*, 2 February 1884; *Commonweal*, October 1885.
3 The debate is fully reported in *Justice*, 19 April 1884.

THE LEICESTER SECULAR HALL

Another fertile ground for educational activity was provided by the Radical Clubs and similar organisations. The lecture lists in *Justice* and *The National Reformer* show the extent of this further infiltration in 1884-6. Lectures are given by H. M. Hyndman and others to the Central Radical Club, Sheffield; the Woolwich Invicta Working Men's Club; to the four Radical Clubs in Chelsea (Sir Charles Dilke's constituency), to the Leicester Radical Association, the Preston Radical Association, the Hackney Radical Club (by Sidney Webb), the Manhood Suffrage League (on *England for All* by Hyndman), the Deptford Liberal Club, the Manchester Radical Association—the list could be extended indefinitely. On New Year's Day, 1887, the *South London Press* could report that "for a considerable time past not a week has elapsed that four or five lectures have not been delivered or debates held, principally in the Radical Clubs or other working men's organisations". These were held under the auspices of the Liberty and Property Defence League, an anti-socialist organisation, as well as the Social Democratic Federation. "One of the most remarkable features in the campaign," the report continues, "is the eagerness evinced by the working classes to hear the question of Individualism versus Socialism discussed.... Most of the numerous Radical Clubs south of the Thames are arranging for a continuance of these debates ... in which working men eagerly join."[1] Lectures were also given by the "Labour Emancipation League", affiliated at this time to the S.D.F., and another body, the "Social and Political Education League".

The early socialist pioneers did not confine their attention to London. Already in 1884 two leading working-class members of the S.D.F. were successfully popularising the doctrines of socialism among the Lancashire cotton workers, then engaged in a two months' strike. William Morris, J. L. Joynes and H. M. Hyndman spoke at a mass meeting at Blackburn and branches of the S.D.F. were formed at Blackburn, Rochdale, Salford, Bolton, and elsewhere in the cotton area. This marks the beginning of organised socialism in Lancashire.[2] Three years later there was a further break-through in the industrial north—among the miners of Northumberland and Durham. It was here that the fight to extend the franchise had reached a high level before 1884 and the workers of the north-east had since suffered greatly from a long-drawn and bitter strike in 1887. Here Tom Mann, on behalf of the S.D.F., and J. L. Mahon, for the Socialist League, worked

[1] Quoted in Torr, *op. cit.*, 220.
[2] *Justice*, 23 February 1884; *Social Democrat*, Vol. 7, No. 1, January 1903, 17.

as full-time socialist organisers in 1887; the former established branches of the S.D.F. in Newcastle and the mining villages around, while Mahon organised the North of England Socialist Federation with over twenty branches in the area. In the pit villages, meeting after meeting supported the basic tenets of socialism, and at the great miners' demonstration held at Horton that year, 10,000 were present to hear Hyndman and Morris and to carry a resolution on socialism.[1]

Again it was in March 1887 that the first organised work began in Wales, *Justice* reporting that "a vigorous propaganda would most certainly result in the formation of powerful branches in all the principal towns".[2] In the same year Mahon was active in Scotland; branches of the Scottish Land and Labour League, affiliated to the Socialist League, were set up in Forfarshire, Fife, Aberdeen, Dundee and elsewhere. "In the mining villages of West Fife, Mahon was on virgin territory: and yet found the miners willing to enrol in tens and twenties at the first or second open-air meeting. It was only necessary for him to put round handbills advertising his meetings, to get a large and eager audience."[3]

Thus from 1884 onwards small groups of socialists began to come together in many parts of the country to launch educational and propaganda activities, often in the face of great hostility and difficulties. In Leeds a young Catholic worker, Tom Maguire, moved towards socialism and already in 1885 was conducting an open-air campaign; the small branch of the Socialist League formed here acted as "a centre of propaganda" extending throughout the West Riding—the members "tramping through the South Yorkshire coalfield or through the Dales, holding meetings and selling literature on the way".[4] In Norwich a pioneer grouping, besides going out to the countryside, was closely involved in working-class struggles in the city, drawing audiences of 1,000 to its open-air meetings in 1886, and on one occasion of 5,000.[5] In Sheffield a Socialist Club was opened in February 1887; Edward Carpenter had settled nearby and made many converts. At Nottingham a small group which included Harry Snell ran John Burns as S.D.F. candidate in 1886, gaining 598 votes, and thereafter conducted continuous activities. In Bristol, a Socialist Society was formed in 1884, and although a broadly based Labour League came into being in 1889 "practically all the work of open-air meetings and education of the people in the economics and ideals of socialist and

---

[1] *Justice*, 16 April 1887; see also Torr, *op. cit.*, 242ff. [2] *Justice*, 26 March 1887.
[3] Thompson, *op. cit.*, 558. [4] *Ibid.*, 491-2. [5] *Ibid.*, 492, 595n.

labour doctrines was confined to the socialist bodies themselves".[1] Small though the membership of the S.D.F., the Socialist League, and the independent socialist societies such as that at Bristol might be, their influence in this early phase was out of all proportion to their numbers. "The compelling power of the socialist appeal at that time was extraordinary," writes Snell, "it held captive, and placed its yoke upon young and old alike . . . it was this creative enthusiasm which gave to the early socialist movement . . . a freshness and driving power such as Liberalism did not possess and Toryism could not buy." The main impact was made especially by the young socialists—"the fervour of their appeal was arresting and highly infectious; its hopefulness passed from soul to soul, awakening, energising, and transforming."[2]

It was in these organised socialist groupings that serious and systematic study of economics and politics began—a revival of the tradition of independent working-class education which can be traced back through the Chartist and Owenite Socialists to the Corresponding Societies in the 1790s. The Norwich branch of the Socialist League itself developed from a class, "The Norwich Pioneer Class for the Discussion of Socialism", formed in 1885.[3] The Bristol Socialist Society was preceded by a "Pioneer Class" organised to discuss "democratic and social reform schemes and the mutual improvement of all its members"; at the first meeting a paper was read on socialism.[4] But possibly the first working-class study groups based on Marxism were those organised by the S.D.F. and the Socialist League together in Edinburgh in 1887, and by Tom Mann at Bolton in 1888. The latter was an economics class using as textbooks Marx's *Wage Labour and Capital*, translated by J. L. Joynes—the first work of Marx's available in English (1886)—and *The Socialist Catechism*, a systematic exposition of Marxist economics in the form of question and answer, written by Joynes.[5] In Edinburgh the class, tutored by the Rev. W. Glasse, studied Marx's *Capital*, first in German (the tutor translating) but very soon from the English translation by Moore and Aveling (1887). These classes were probably attended by James Connolly who, in the early 1890s developed Marxist discussion classes through the Scottish Socialist Federation.[6]

From such small beginnings widespread educational activity was later developed, sometimes extremely rapidly. Thus in 1889 the Bristol

1 S. Bryher, *The Labour and Socialist Movement in Bristol* (1929), Pt. II, 14.
2 Snell, *op. cit.*, 99. 3 Thompson, *op. cit.*, 492. 4 Bryher, *op. cit.*, Pt. I, 18.
5 Torr, *op. cit.*, 252-3; Tom Mann, *Memoirs* (1923), 69.
6 C Desmond Greaves, *The Life and Times of James Connolly* (1961), 30-1, 37.

MAY DAY CARTOON FROM *Justice*, 1896

ANNIE BESANT IN 1885

CHARLES BRADLAUGH

TOM MANN

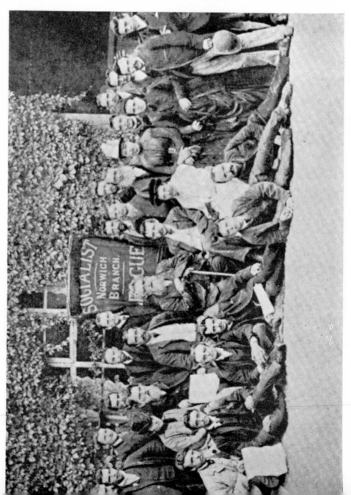

NORWICH BRANCH OF THE SOCIALIST LEAGUE (WILLIAM MORRIS IN THE CENTRE)

Sunday Society, which began as a small group of socialists meeting regularly on Sunday evenings, was organising open meetings beginning with a musical programme and followed by a socialist speaker and discussion. Topics ranged over the sciences, history, and the arts and these lectures, which have been described as "the greatest socialist educational force the city has at any time possessed",[1] were continued for many winters, at first drawing an attendance of 300 to 500 but later many more: by 1898-9 the society was renting a theatre to accommodate an average attendance of 1,700. Activities of this kind, paralleled in other provincial cities, linked organised educational efforts with more general political activity.

No assessment of the educational and propaganda activities of the early socialists would be complete without reference to the Fabians. Developing from an earlier ethical Owenite grouping, the Fabian Society, like the S.D.F. and the Socialist League, came into being in 1884. Its members were chiefly middle-class intellectuals and from an early date it stood opposed to the revolutionary outlook of the other socialist organisations. But the Fabians of the late 1880s and early '90s nevertheless concentrated on educating the public in socialist principles. In 1891, for instance, 1,400 lectures were given by some ninety Fabian lecturers, while the society issued numerous cheap booklets and tracts, packed with information on municipal and other social issues.

Though leaders of the Fabian Society were already at this time espousing the cause of "municipal socialism" as against the revolutionary ideas of Marxism, it is important to stress that divisions between socialist organisations were not yet hard and fast; whether a socialist joined one or the other organisation was often a matter of chance and local organisation, and many belonged to more than one body. As late as 1895 the Fabian Society could count as members men as various as Keir Hardie, Tom Mann and Sidney Webb. In the 1890s, with their "Book Box" scheme and corresponding classes as well as lectures and publications, the Fabians, though small in membership (739 in 1895-6), played an important part in promoting education.

2. THE NEW UNIONISM AND THE DEVELOPMENT OF INDEPENDENT POLITICS

The early socialist pioneers began their organised work in a period of mounting industrial struggles, when the revolt against poverty

---

[1] Bryher, *op. cit.*, Pt. II, 31.

and hideous industrial and social conditions was bringing new sections of the working class into action in support of demands for higher wages, shorter hours, and improved working conditions. The severe depression which began in 1886 lay behind these developments. It was during the unemployed agitation of the following year that John Burns was arrested, delivered his famous "impassioned and defiant speech" from the dock, and received a prison sentence which "aroused popular feeling to a degree which was quite unexpected".[1] The growing militancy of the Labour movement found expression in two main directions: first, in a new insistence on the need for independent labour representation in Parliament, and second, in the organisation and struggle of the unskilled workers. In both these spheres, socialists played a leading part.

Milestones in the political field during these years were the return of eleven working-class M.P.s at the 1885 election on the new franchise (all of them, however, followers of the Liberal party), the formation of Labour Electoral Associations up and down the country, Keir Hardie's participation as an independent Labour candidate at the famous Mid-Lanark by-election of 1888, his subsequent formation of the Scottish Labour Party to "educate the people politically" and return independent Labour M.P.s, and the first attempts to win the liberal dominated T.U.C. for this same objective.[2] This political movement received a new impetus from the great wave of organisation among the unskilled workers, beginning in London with the match-girls' strike of 1888, which reached a high point in 1889 with the successful struggle of the London gasworkers led by Will Thorne to win the eight hour day and organise the gasworkers' union, and the great London dock strike, led by Tom Mann, Ben Tillett, John Burns and other socialists, as a result of which the Dockers' Union was formed. As the mass of the workers were drawn into the fight for the Legal Eight Hour Day there took place in 1890, with this as the main slogan, the first working-class May Day celebration in this country. "On May 4th 1890," wrote Engels, who watched this massive demonstration of hundreds of thousands of workers, "the English working class joined up in the great international army. . . . The grandchildren of the old Chartists are entering the line of battle."[3]

The "New Unionism" of the 1890s initiated a wider conception of the role of the trade union, which owed much to socialist leadership.

[1] Snell, op. cit., 106.   [2] Henry Pelling, The Origins of the Labour Party (1954), 73-5.
[3] Marx-Engels Selected Correspondence (1936 edn.), 469.

It was symptomatic that Annie Besant and Herbert Burrows, both members of the S.D.F., who participated wholeheartedly in the match-girls' struggle, should assist them not only to form a trade union but also to establish a club "as an educational and socialist centre for the girls", as Ben Tillett put it;[1] and that Tillett and Tom Mann, leading figures in the dockers' struggle, should envisage a new role for trade unions. "Poverty, in our opinion, can be abolished," they wrote in 1890, declaring that this was the job of the unions. "We want to see the necessary economic knowledge imparted in our labour organisations, so that labour in the future shall not be made the shuttlecock of political parties. Our Trade Unions shall be centres of enlightenment and not merely the meeting place for paying contributions and receiving donations . . . our ideal is a co-operative commonwealth."[2] Mann and Tillett were as good as their word, organising meetings to provide explanation and enlightenment for the Dockers' Union on Sunday mornings and at other times. In 1893 and again in 1894 socialists in the T.U.C. (James Macdonald and Tom Mann) won the annual Congress to support socialist resolutions.

The time was ripe for new political developments. In December, 1891, Robert Blatchford had founded *Clarion*, a weekly with a wide popular appeal. In the north of England in particular, socialism was now beginning to become a mass movement involving thousands of ordinary rank and file workers. In 1893 the Independent Labour Party was born and, during the subsequent year some 400 I.L.P. branches came into being which, alongside the S.D.F., acted as centres of education and propaganda. In the general election of 1895 there was, for the first time, a genuine socialist challenge, the I.L.P., led at this time by Hardie and Mann, putting up twenty-eight candidates and gaining 44,322 votes, the S.D.F. contesting four seats, and winning 3,730 votes. But the Tory party won the election with a majority of 152, a victory ushering in a period of reaction at home which, coupled with an aggressive imperialism, had far-reaching repercussions on the Labour movement. Thus it was largely in response to an offensive by the employers which threatened the legal basis of the unions that the Labour Representation Committee was at last set up in 1900; the strength of the emerging Labour Party, firmly grounded in the trade unions, was to become manifest in the election of 1906.

During the closing decade of the nineteenth century, education and

---

[1] Ben Tillett, *Memories and Reflections* (1931), 108.
[2] Tom Mann and Ben Tillett, *The "New" Trade Unionism* (1890), 14.

THE
Independent Labour Party.

THE FIRST CONFERENCE OF THE
INDEPENDENT LABOUR PARTY.
BRADFORD. 14TH JANY 1893

❧ REPORT ❧
OF THE
FIRST GENERAL CONFERENCE.

GLASGOW:
PRINTED BY LABOUR LITERATURE SOCIETY, LTD., 105 LONDON STREET,
1893.

propaganda for socialism reached entirely new levels. At Bradford, for instance, a remarkable number of societies and local clubs had become established by 1892, including not only a Fabian society, a Labour Church, a Trades Council and trade union branches, but also twenty-three local Labour clubs all "concentrating on the instruction rather than the entertainment of their members" numbering some 3,000.[1] One of these, "not the largest, ran three lectures, an orchestral perform-ance, a shorthand class, in a typical week". It was this kind of club, with lectures and educational classes, that developed throughout York-shire. The Lockwood Labour Club in Huddersfield, for instance, held a weekly *Merrie England* class, a chapter being read each week "and then carefully examined and discussed by the workers".[2] The enor-mous success of Blatchford's *Merrie England*, published in 1894, and selling 750,000 copies within a year, both reflected and contributed to the growth of a socialist outlook among the masses.

Everywhere the workers were on the move, and the socialist group-ings made the most of their opportunity. Two examples must suffice. In the early 1890s, Harry Snell had moved to Woolwich where he was associated with the earliest attempts to conduct labour propaganda "of a distinctly socialist character". Open air meetings in one of the main squares were arranged every Sunday at which all the leading socialist speakers appeared: Burns, Mann, Tillett, Thorne, Andreas Scheu, Herbert Burrows, Aveling, Eleanor Marx, Quelch, Hyndman. "Together with a handful of local stalwarts," writes Snell, "we laid the foundations on which the Woolwich Labour Party was afterwards built."[3] In Scotland also the work went on apace. In Edinburgh in the autumn of 1895, for instance, the Operetta House was engaged for a series of lectures by Eleanor Marx, Edward Aveling, Dan Irving and Harry Quelch. The theatre held 1,500. "There was never such days," said one of the socialists, comparing these mass meetings to their beginnings ten years earlier "in a shack in a back street".[4]

It was particularly under the leadership of Blatchford and the *Clarion* that the socialist movement broadened out in new ways, reaching to

[1] Pelling, *op. cit.*, 120.
[2] *Ibid.*, 164-5. M. Ostrogorski, in his classic *Democracy and the Organisation of Political Parties* (1902) pays particular tribute to the educational activities of the socialists. "In the orthodox parties political education is talked about a great deal but . . . little or nothing is done for it. The I.L.P. and the other socialists are the only parties which systematically cultivate men's minds by classes and lectures, by discussion, by readings in common. The activity which they display in this respect has given an intellectual impulse even to their opponents." Vol. I, 576.
[3] Snell, *op. cit.*, 80.   [4] Greaves, *op. cit.*, 55-6.

wider sections with varying interests. The paper itself was profession-
ally written and lively, including, besides articles on socialism, the
I.L.P. and political matters generally, poetry, dramatic criticism and
other features. But for Blatchford, the idea of socialism was concomitant with that of fellowship, and the paper actively promoted an
enormous variety of social and cultural activities linked to the socialist
movement. A typical number of *Clarion* in 1900 would include two
long columns reporting activities of "Fellowship Clubs"—socialist
choirs, co-operative holiday clubs, field clubs, supper clubs, Cinderella
Clubs (of which more later), dramatic societies, Clarion Clubs and
Cycle Clubs. In most of the towns in the north of England Clarion
choirs (known as "Vocal Unions") were active, holding combined
concerts, singing at meetings and lectures, and generally working for
socialism.[1] In June 1896, the first Clarion Women's Van set out on a
fifteen weeks' campaign in Cheshire, Shropshire, Staffordshire, Yorkshire, Durham and Northumberland. "Everywhere . . . the people
simply flocked to welcome them," runs one report, "showing themselves actually hungry for socialism. Literature was seized greedily.
The pamphlets and papers might have been prizes. *Merrie England*,
Looking Backwards, *Clarions*, Fabian, *Clarion* and Land Nationalisation
leaflets were given away by the thousand."[2] Several of these vans
were fitted up, the "vanners" visiting otherwise inaccessible places,
lecturing on socialism, selling and giving away immense quantities of
literature. I.L.P. branches were inaugurated and socialist ideas brought
to the countryside.

The Clarion movement was one of the few socialist organisations to
pay specific attention to young people. The Clarion Scouts, started by
Blatchford in 1894 as groupings of young socialist pioneers, claimed
by 1896 to have 120 clubs with 7,000 members. These set up the
Clarion Youth Houses—forerunners of the Youth Hostels—and carried
the socialist message through the countryside and to neighbouring
towns on cycles.[3] The Bristol Clarion Scouts, for instance, were the
first to bring socialism to Bath and then systematically covered Somer-
set and Gloucestershire establishing socialist groups.[4] Tom Bell pays
tribute to the pioneering work of the Glasgow Clarion Scouts at the
turn of the century as a powerful force for socialism; during the week-
ends groups of young people would cycle out to the mining villages

[1] In the first decade of this century Rutland Boughton, Ethel Smythe and Edgar
Baignton worked with Clarion choirs in Birmingham and elsewhere.
[2] *The Labour Annual*, 1897, 185.   [3] Pelling, *op. cit.*, 171.
[4] Bryher, *op. cit.*, Pt. II, 69-74.

in Lanarkshire with papers, leaflets and parcels, holding public meetings and stimulating lively discussions. So the ground was prepared for the I.L.P. and the future Labour Party in Lanarkshire.[1]

Nor were the Clarions alone in work of this kind. The English Land Restoration League, which stood for the abolition of landlordism, launched their Red Vans which toured the countryside—580 meetings were held in 1895 and 500,000 leaflets distributed—encountering considerable hostility from the landlords and police. "Education is the great leveller," reported the secretary of the Land Nationalisation Society, which also toured the countryside with its Yellow Vans, "and the . . . Society has done its utmost during the past year to open the eyes of the people to the stupid and unfair system which makes private property of the land which should be a public trust. . . . It is the *ignorance* of the landless masses themselves" upon which rests this "gigantic injustice."[2]

In the 1890s a new form of activity, the Labour Church movement, developed especially in the north of England. Based to some extent on the traditions of nonconformism and methodism, this recalls the Christian Chartist movement half a century earlier. The pulpits were open to such Labour leaders as Tillett, Mann, and Blatchford, and both hymns and sermons had a socialist content. These churches also ran adult classes "for the study of ethics, economic history, social history and religion".[3] This was the time when the Socialist Sunday School movement also came into being—sometimes connected with the Labour Churches, but also with the local branches of the I.L.P. or S.D.F.—which we will return to later.

Such were the various educational implications of the growth of the Labour movement from 1870 to 1900. During this period a considerable section of the working class broke free from the domination of Liberal ideas and from their actual allegiance to the Liberal Party. Increasingly well organised on the industrial front, the workers formed independent political organisations and the movement as a whole began to be infused with socialist ideas—with the belief that education and action must be directed to winning economic and political emancipation. The whole process by which this took place had an essentially educational significance, insofar as it involved a complete change of outlook—a new direction of activity. This activity was itself partly

---

[1] Tom Bell, *Pioneering Days*, (1941), 39.   [2] *The Labour Annual*, 1896, 48.
[3] Pelling, *op. cit.*, 144; for the Labour Church movement see K. S. Inglis, *Churches and the Working Classes in Victorian England* (1963), 215-49.

YELLOW VAN OF THE LAND NATIONALISATION SOCIETY

directed to winning the necessary conditions in which this educational work could be carried on. Such were the long drawn out struggles for a reduction in the hours of labour, for freedom of speech and of the press, both as steps towards emancipation generally and as prerequisites for the extension of education.

3. THE STRUGGLE FOR THE CONDITIONS OF EDUCATION

(i) *"Leisure to Live"*

Socialist leaders of the New Unionism played a leading part in the fight for the eight hour day. "The demand we, as workmen, now make," wrote Tom Mann in 1891, "is for *leisure, not idleness*. Leisure to think, to learn, to acquire knowledge, to enjoy, to develop; in short, *leisure to live*."[1] It will be recalled that, as a young worker, Tom Mann himself made the fullest use of his newly won leisure hours—his avid curiosity, wide interests, desire for knowledge, epitomise the best of the skilled workers of his time—and he quickly came to recognise to whom he owed these opportunities. "It was the trade unions that did this," he wrote, "these trade union men were the cause of the little bit of leisure and education that came to me and all those who suffered as I did."[2] In the mid-1880s, he determined to bring the fight for the eight hour day into the centre of the industrial struggle.

[1] Quoted in Torr, *op. cit.*, 38, from *The Eight Hour Day: How to get it by Trade and Local Option*, one of two pamphlets by Tom Mann; in 1899 he wrote *The Eight Hours Movement*.
[2] *Ibid.*, 39.

This was to carry on in a new context a struggle for what had long been a major objective rallying mass support. In the 1830s a great movement had swept Yorkshire and Lancashire led by Oastler and Stephens, directed at winning the ten hour day in the textile mills. In the 1840s agitation again rose to a climax and, in 1847, despite strong opposition from the employers, the Ten Hour Bill passed into law. During the next twenty years this struggle was carried further, the building workers and the engineers, in particular, winning certain successes.

This pressure to reduce working hours is of key significance in the history of education; on its success hinged all prospects of genuine educational advance, whether for children or adults. If the children were to be educated—as Robert Owen was among the first to see— they must be withdrawn from the factory; as will appear later, this issue came to the forefront after 1880. By the same token, adult workers engaged in arduous manual labour, sometimes up to sixteen hours a day, had no opportunity for education. From the first the workers linked shorter hours with opportunities for self-development.

Although the eight hour day was one of the demands in the S.D.F. programme, in fact it was regarded by many—including at first John Burns—as a diversion from the real struggle for socialism. It was Tom Mann's main contribution to see the more limited objective as an essential step towards wider aims and, as his biographer says, through this and similar demands to make "socialism the inspiration of revolutionary trade unionism". In establishing this view Mann casti- gated workers who held the view propagated by some S.D.F. members that the eight hour day would only rivet capitalist chains more firmly on the workers. "I can understand," he writes, "some workmen re- flecting the opinions of these theory-loving, poverty-accentuating blockheads merely because they are middle-class. But I cannot under- stand a workman who through youth and early manhood has been battling against long hours in order that he might attend the institute, listen to lectures, and read the works of able men, and by these means has succeeded in having a mind worth owning . . . hindering rather than helping in a shorter hours' movement. He practically says by such conduct that the leisure he uses so well as to become a man thereby, others will use so ill that they will continue fools."[1] In Tom Mann's view, leisure and education would not only add to the general intelli- gence of the workers, but would enable them to see through current

[1] Torr, *op. cit.*, 217.

theories which denied the possibility of socialism and of working-class advance—in particular contemporary neo-Malthusianism and current theories concerning the iron law of wages.

By the time Mann threw himself into the struggle in 1885-6, the demand for legislation to introduce the eight hour day had already been raised at the Trades Union Congress. The first sign of the new spirit in the T.U.C. (as the Webbs call it) was when Adam Weiler, a close friend of Marx and member of the First International, advocated this policy at the 1878 Congress, calling for the legislative reduction of hours in order to give workers "time and opportunity for rest and amusement, and the cultivation of their minds".[1] Another resolution a few years later, although carried, had no result.

In the late 1880s, the movement towards the legal eight hour day began to move towards its climax—bound up, as it was, with the struggle within the Trades Union Congress between the old unionism and the new. In 1887, when Keir Hardie, delegate of the new miners' union in Ayrshire, moved the demand for an eight hour day he was subjected to ridicule and abuse from Broadhurst, secretary of the T.U.C. In 1887 and again in 1888 the T.U.C. arranged for plebiscites among affiliated unions on this question, a delaying move but one which served to show that the old unions were swinging round. In 1889, after an extremely hard fought debate, the old guard won again—but for the last time. New developments were decisively changing the balance of forces. The unskilled workers were to force the issue.

It was the victory won under the leadership of Will Thorne at the Beckton Gas Works and the accompanying organisation of the gas workers that marked a turning point. At this works new machinery was introduced, production speeded up, and the workers, on a twelve hour shift, driven to the point of exhaustion, sometimes working up to 18 hours a day. The men were desperate, writes Thorne, "I saw the time was ripe; the day that I had waited for so long had at last dawned."[2] With the help of other socialists, he took the first steps towards forming a union—one which, incidentally, was to be in the forefront of the struggle for education for the next twenty years. Within a few weeks 3,000 joined. "Never before," writes Thorne, "had men responded like they did." "I knew what I was going to do," he adds. "I kept in mind all the time my pledge to the men at the first meeting. To work and fight for the eight-hour day—that

[1] S. and B. Webb, *History of Trade Unionism* (1892), 375.
[2] Thorne, *op. cit.*, 66.

was my first objective." The objective was gained. "The formation of our union," writes Thorne, "and its first victory, put heart into thousands of unskilled, badly paid and unorganised workers. . . . It was a milestone in trade union history. . . . I wish my readers could have seen the joy in the smiling faces of the men and the delegates when I reported our victory."[1]

The struggle for the legal eight hour day, therefore, became the platform of the New Unionists, that is, of the socialists, who held that the limitation of the working day required legislative interference—that it could never be assured by private settlements, easily abrogated by the employers, but only by general political action on the part of the trade union movement. It was this point that the leaders of the older craft unions could not concede and on this issue, therefore, that battle was joined. In 1889, as we have seen, the old leaders had won decisively. In 1890 they were as decisively defeated. At the T.U.C. that year, the socialist "New Unionist" leaders, and especially Tom Mann and John Burns, carried the key resolution by 193 votes to 155. An attempt by the old guard to get the resolution reversed failed in 1891 and in 1892 the socialist victory was sealed when the cotton unions at last moved over to the support of the new policy.[2] It was another matter actually to achieve the eight hour day—this was not in fact gained, except in the mining industry, until after the 1914-18 war—but henceforth the limitation of working hours, which lay at the heart of the new unionism, was the accepted policy of the T.U.C.

"We claim now material necessities to lift us above worrying for food and shelter;" Tom Mann told the second conference of the Dockers' Union, "but we claim more—we yearn for culture, we demand opportunities for physical and mental development, and we openly and fearlessly declare war against all that tends to keep us riveted to earth."[3] This approach at a time when tens of thousands of workers were being drawn into organised industrial struggle for the first time, spread widely a new understanding of the potentialities of life, a new conception of the dignity of man and the rights of the workers as human beings. That they would make full use of increased opportunities for education and self-development appeared self-evident to the pioneers of this movement; that to open this perspective would

---

[1] *Ibid.*, 72-3. For an analysis of this "trade union explosion", its origins and significance, E. J. Hobsbawm, "The British Gas-workers, 1873-1914" in *Labouring Men* (1964), 158-78.
[2] Allen Hutt, "The Hours of Labour", *Marxist Quarterly*, January 1955.
[3] From Minutes of the second annual conference of the Dockers' Union, 1891. I owe this reference to Mr. E. P. Thompson.

also lead to a more active discontent with the conditions of life—in William Morris's sense—and so serve the cause of socialism, they had no doubt at all.

(ii) *Freedom of Speech and Assembly*

There were, of course, other aspects of the struggle for the conditions of education—in its widest sense. The first objective of the small group of early socialists was to take their message out to the people; in Morris's words, to "make socialists". This involved open air speaking—in the parks and at the traditional meeting places in the cities—and, as already described, both the S.D.F. and the Socialist League immediately set about this work with considerable energy. "The right of free speech for the workers," commented *Justice* in July 1885, "practically depends upon the right to address their fellows in open spaces. They cannot afford to pay for halls and lecture rooms; they are shut out from the Board Schools which they keep out of their labour; they are deprived of the churches and cathedrals which really belong to them. The open air alone remains to them: the chair at the street corner is their sole political platform."[1] But, from the start, there was active intervention to suppress socialist open air meetings.

An early climax was the banning of demonstrations in Trafalgar Square and the events of Bloody Sunday in November, 1887. With the development of the New Unionism in the early 1890s and the wider propagation of socialism at that time, there were renewed attempts to suppress meetings—the famous struggle at Boggart Hole Clough in Manchester took place as late as 1896.

These battles for free speech were carried through with considerable pertinacity. They were, in the end, victorious, because the socialists won the support of the mass of the advanced workers organised in the Radical Clubs. It was such an alliance that won the first great test case at Dod Street in Limehouse, where the S.D.F. established an open air pitch in 1885. While speaker after speaker was arrested and some were imprisoned, huge crowds began to turn up for the meetings and massive gatherings followed to protest against arrests. It was the Radical Clubs that "initiated the great combined procession which . . . marched in with bands and banners and took possession of Dod Street".[2] With a crowd of 30,000 asserting the right to freedom of speech, the police gave way. When the victory was finally won, a great demonstration was organised at the West India Dock gates at which, according to

---

[1] *Justice*, 25 July 1885.   [2] Torr, *op. cit.*, 197.

Will Thorne who took the chair at one of the platforms, over 50,000 were present.[1]

Seven years later, another classic test took place at World's End, Chelsea, described by the secretary of the S.D.F. as "the longest, bitterest and most expensive that the S.D.F. [had] ever been called on to undertake". "For nearly six months the struggle went on," he adds. "Sunday after Sunday, during the whole of that period, members of the S.D.F. were arrested for championing the right of public meeting, in places where no actual obstruction was caused, against unwarrantable police interference."[2] Twenty-four members, and some non-members, were arrested in the course of the campaign which was finally successful. In Manchester, in 1896, it was the I.L.P. that took the lead; among those deliberately courting conviction by insisting on the right to speak were J. Bruce Glasier, Keir Hardie and Mrs. Pankhurst. Two speakers (Leonard Hall and Fred Brocklehurst) were imprisoned for a month. But all the time the audiences grew and finally the authorities gave in.[3]

The right to free speech had become a broad popular issue. From the banning of meetings organised by the S.D.F. on behalf of the unemployed in Trafalgar Square in 1887—which led to the battles of Bloody Sunday when tens of thousands attempted to challenge the ban—to countless engagements in provincial towns and even country villages, this matter was fought out. There is in fact no legal "right" of free speech in this country—nor was there then. On the other hand there is a very real tradition of freedom of speech and assembly, and this tradition was maintained and extended by the socialist pioneers. This was to gain the first essential condition for the spread of ideas among the people at large.

A closely allied problem was the provision of facilities for serious discussion and indoor meetings—a perennial problem for the Labour movement. Forty years earlier Chartists and early socialists had established Chartist Halls and Halls of Science in the main cities.[4] A few of these evidently survived (for instance in London and Oldham) but by the 1880s most had fallen by the way. In the 1860s and '70s organisations such as the Working Men's Club and Institute Union had their own buildings, but these were often linked to the Church and gentry and can hardly be regarded as independent.

In the 1880s there was a new impetus to provide adequate meeting

---

[1] Thorne, *op. cit.*, 57.   [2] *Justice*, 6 August 1892.   [3] Stewart, *op. cit.*, 131ff.
[4] B. Simon, *Studies in the History of Education, 1780–1870* (1960), 235ff.

places. The Radical Clubs and debating societies often possessed their own premises, with facilities for lectures and discussions. Secular Societies began to build their own halls, as, for instance, at Leicester. More important was the proliferation of Trades Halls up and down the country, especially in the areas where trade unionism was strong. These varied from buildings belonging to particular unions (for instance, Miners' Institutes, the Moulders' Hall at Edinburgh, the Spinners' Committee lecture rooms in the north of England) to Trades Halls built by local trades councils which became a feature of most provincial cities. In the 1890s these were supplemented by the club-rooms of local Labour clubs, which were usually open every evening as well as at week-ends for lectures and discussions. Sometimes the local Labour movement was strong enough to maintain a central building—it was in the newly acquired Bradford Labour Institute that the I.L.P. held its inaugural conference in 1893.

Perhaps the most energetic organisation in this regard was the Co-operative movement. Since the days of the Rochdale pioneers this had maintained the Owenite ideal of linking co-operation and education, though it now survived in a somewhat attenuated form. Nevertheless local co-operative societies and the newly formed women's guilds sponsored a variety of educational activities. Classes, discussions and lectures were organised on a wide scale and by 1899 almost £60,000 was spent annually to these ends. Regional groupings of local societies—such as the Midlands Section Educational Association—were set up to foster this work, run conferences and so on. The extent of facilities can be judged from the fact that, by 1900, 260 reading rooms were open in the North-Western Section alone, where in the preceding year, over 450 lectures and 420 concerts had been held.[1]

One of the greatest services rendered by the Co-operative movement at this time was the provision of co-operative halls in major cities and industrial areas. Many of these spacious buildings put up in the 1880s and '90s are still in use, and though they may no longer be considered beautiful, remain the chief meeting places for all types of working-class and socialist organisations. The appearance of these halls in the main industrial centres helped to solve what had been a perennial problem—the finding of meeting places, other than the public house, where political and social issues of every kind could be discussed, and where all working-class and socialist organisations were welcome.

[1] *32nd Co-operative Congress Report*, 1900, 26-7.

(iii) *The Labour and Socialist Press*

Besides the spoken word there was also a new diffusion of the written word, as has been suggested by reference to the great influence of *Clarion*. There were a few working-class papers and journals in existence in the 1870s and early '80s, notably the *Bee-Hive*, managed by George Potter. After 1884, however, the situation was radically changed—the revival of socialism was marked by a "flood of socialist periodicals and pamphlets".[1] The S.D.F. launched its journal, *Justice*, the Socialist League *Commonweal*, but there were also journals run by individuals such as Annie Besant's *Our Corner*, *Today* edited by Belfort Bax and J. L. Joynes, Thomas Bolas's *Practical Socialist*, the *Christian Socialist* (organ of the land reformers), the *Link* (organ of the Law and Liberty League set up after Bloody Sunday), Champion's *Labour Elector*. In 1891 *Clarion* appeared, to attain a readership of 80,000 a week, followed by the *Labour Prophet* (1892) and the *Labour Leader* (1894). By the 1890s there were also various weekly newspapers, for instance, the *Cotton Factory Times* and the *Bradford Labour Echo*; in 1892 the *Workman's Times* was started. Such new papers attained a considerable circulation among the working class, "building up a network of working-men's political clubs, which in turn had little broadsheets of their own for local purposes".[2]

By 1897 the *Labour Annual* was printing an immense list of reform magazines, newspapers and periodicals. What has been described as "a unique range of propaganda literature" was becoming available. This included popular pamphlets and cheap books on social and economic or political questions. A selection may be taken from the first number of *Justice* (19 January 1884). There are advertisements of *A Summary of the Principles of Socialism* by Hyndman and Morris, and Hyndman's *The Historical Basis of Socialism in England* which popularised the views of Marx and Engels; a publisher of "Socialist literature", W. Reeves, brought to attention works by Henry George, William Morris, A. R. Wallace, H. M. Hyndman, and others at prices varying from 1*d.* to 8*d.* H. H. Champion, who ran the Modern Press, and printed the early numbers of *Justice* himself, also brought out many penny pamphlets. From 1893 *Clarion* issued large numbers of cheap pamphlets, mostly at 1*d.*; the first, *The Pope's Socialism*, was written by Blatchford (Nunquam) in reply to the *Catechism of the Rights and Duties of the Working Classes* issued to popularise the papal encyclical

---

[1] Pelling, *op. cit.*, 48.   [2] *Ibid.*, 103.

attacking socialism entitled *Rerum Novarum* (1891). Later the Clarion Press issued the famous "Pass On Pamphlets" which, appearing every Friday fortnight, were intended "to explain the need for Socialism, to explain what Socialism is, to answer objections to Socialism, and to suggest methods for the attainment of Socialism".

More ambitious undertakings date from 1892 with the formation of the Twentieth Century Press—originally set up as a means of off-setting the losses on *Justice*; this was established despite extreme difficulty in raising the necessary money, and published many socialist and Marxist works. A similar venture was the Labour Press. Started in a small back room in Manchester in 1892 this press published many books and pamphlets with the object of spreading "a knowledge of the principles and objects of every movement calculated to improve the conditions of the labouring classes"; by 1896 the press employed thirty and claimed to have sold 1,500,000 pamphlets, half a million being its own publications.[1] More weighty socialist literature appeared in the famous Socialist Library sponsored by Swan Sonnenschein— publishers of the English edition of Marx's *Capital* in 1887. Thus, although beset by financial difficulties, the Labour and socialist move- ment established an effective press in a very short time, one which played a major part in providing the materials for education—an achievement resting on the classic struggles carried through by Richard Carlile, Henry Hetherington and other working-class leaders half a century earlier.

4. TEACHING THE YOUNG

As the movement gathered way, attention was increasingly turned to educating the children. The main course taken was to transform the Sunday School movement, which, for historical reasons, had deep roots among the working class. If the traditional Sunday Schools taught Christian ethics and inculcated a Christian outlook, with all its social overtones, why should not the socialist movement teach socialist ethics and a socialist outlook to the young?

Here again an earlier tradition was being revived, although whether this was realised at the time is doubtful. Both Chartist and Owenite socialists had established Sunday Schools and sometimes even day schools for their children; to provide schools in which rational know- ledge would be taught in a rational way, had, indeed, been a major

[1] *The Labour Annual*, 1897, 12, 246.

WILLIAM MORRIS

BRIGHOUSE SOCIALIST SUNDAY SCHOOL, 1908

LABOUR CHURCH SUNDAY SCHOOL BIRTHDAY CARD, I

aim of the early Co-operative movement in the period 1828-32.[1] While these schools went out of existence in the late 1840s and '50s there is some evidence that the secular movement carried on the tradition, if on a small scale. Certainly by 1886 a number of Secular Sunday Schools were in existence, with the aim of teaching a secular rather than a Christian morality.[2]

The Socialist Sunday School movement, however, commenced in 1892, when the first school was started in London by Mary Gray, wife of a stonemason and member of the S.D.F. But it was in Glasgow that the movement really got under way four years later when four or five schools were operating as a result of the initiative of Caroline Martyn. From here the movement spread once more to London and the provinces, particularly Yorkshire and Lancashire, some schools being organised in connection with Labour Churches, others by the local S.D.F. or I.L.P. branch, or by an independent socialist society as at Bristol.

These Sunday Schools brought together socialists of many faiths; that at Bristol, for instance, started in 1898, was sponsored by Christians, Jews, Secularists, Marxists, Theists, Theosophists. Previous discussions had led to the conclusion that "the moral truths of all faiths found their highest expression in Socialism". The ethical basis of the school was found in the belief that "Socialism is a religion teaching morality and brotherhood of man as taught by Christ and others. The central principle (its God) is Love and Love of Humanity. It strives to abolish unjust laws and customs which enable the idle rich to rob the industrious poor. It demands honesty, truthfulness, frankness of character, and purity of life." The school soon enrolled between 80 and 100 scholars.[3] In general the schools organised directly by S.D.F. members tended towards concrete socialist teaching and a materialist outlook, while the I.L.P. schools leant more towards ethical teaching on the lines adopted at Bristol.

[1] Simon, *op. cit.*, 235ff.

[2] Ben Turner refers in his autobiography (*About Myself* (1930), 47-8) to "the noted Secular Sunday School" at Huddersfield, and gives a good description of it, and of its value to him: "we were taught reading, writing, arithmetic, geography, history, elocution, singing, etc. . . . It was there I heard Annie Besant, George Jacob Holyoake, Harriet Law, Charles Watts, Dr. Aveling", as well as Bradlaugh ("what a giant he was! He was the working man's orator"). Turner became its secretary at the age of eighteen, in 1881. Secular Sunday schools were being run by the Portsmouth, Battersea and Glasgow branches of the National Secular Society as well as at Huddersfield in 1885-6; *National Reformer*, 4 January 1885, 10 January 1886, 21 November 1886. Probably several more were in existence.

[3] Bryher, *op. cit.*, Pt. II, 54.

D

The Socialist Sunday Schools originally adopted the form and methods of the traditional schools, but transformed the content. Instead of hymns there were songs carrying a socialist or ethical message, a song book being later specially compiled. The place of the ten commandments was taken by ten precepts preceded by a Declaration, embodying the ethics of socialism based on "Justice and Love".[1] The aim was to bring children to an understanding of the meaning of socialism, as well as of the structure and nature of existing society. Special attention was given to teaching the elements of a secular, socialist morality. The school opened with a song, followed by a short address by the "superintendent"; classes were then held for different age groups on some aspect of socialism, followed by more songs, readings and recitations. Attempts were made to provide libraries, to run excursions for the children, and so on.

This movement was only getting under way at the close of the century. Articles in *Justice*, the *Labour Prophet* and other journals in 1895 and 1896 were stressing the need for Sunday Schools and giving advice on how to run them.[2] In 1896 the Glasgow Union of Schools was formed. By 1900 local groups of Sunday Schools were meeting together—*Justice* reports a Yorkshire conference where Halifax claimed 159 scholars, Bradford 112 and Huddersfield 50.[3] In 1901 there appeared the first number of *The Young Socialist*, journal of the Sunday School movement, which has been in continuous existence ever since.

The schools movement expanded considerably in the first decade of the twentieth century, surviving the decline of the Labour Churches. By 1910 when a national union had been formed, about 100 schools were in existence attended by nearly 5,000 children and over 1,000 adults. Apart from their weekly activities these now took part annually in the great demonstrations on May Day. "Our children carried hundreds of red flags," runs one report of a London May Day (1909), "and to add to this were the school banners high above the brakes floating in the air"—the children's demonstration "reached nearly half a mile in length".[4] A year later 2,000 London children participated

---

[1] "We desire to be just and loving to all our fellow men and women," runs the Declaration, "to work together as brothers and sisters, to be kind to every living creature and so help to form a New Society with Justice as its foundation and Love its law."

[2] *Justice*, 2 November 1895, 28 March 1896; *Labour Prophet*, July 1895. The *Labour Annual* for 1897 advertises (p. 62) a journal *The Young Socialist*, which "desires to consolidate the children's movement by education and organisation: helps in the formation of Socialist Sunday Schools wherever needed". Published in Ashton-under-Lyne, this must have been a forerunner of the journal mentioned later in the text.

[3] *Justice*, 15 September 1900.

[4] *The Young Socialist*, Vol. IX (1909), 479.

in 103 brakes,[1] 1,000 children took part in the Glasgow May Day celebrations, while at Leeds the Socialist Sunday Schools again "headed a monster procession through the Leeds streets".[2] In 1912 the Leeds schools filled the Great Coliseum with nearly 600 performers and an audience of 3,500. As has been seen, although the teaching varied with the outlook of the organisers, the schools came together in a united movement which grew rapidly.

Many notable future socialists attended Sunday Schools, others sent their own children. Though never very large, the Socialist Sunday Schools—some of which still exist today—provided a focus for young socialists in many cities. Among the organisers and teachers were men and women who devoted their lives to this task. Perhaps the most venerated name in the history of the movement is that of Alex Gossip, leading trade unionist, who became the first President of the National Union in 1909, and devoted enormous energy to building up the schools in London, teaching, organising, and forming new schools.[3] Other leading socialists also gave their time and energy, especially Margaret McMillan, Caroline Martyn, and Lizzie Glasier. But all over the country rank and file socialists, men as much as women, made work for the schools their main contribution to the socialist movement.

The Sunday Schools were not the only form in which children and young people were brought into the socialist movement; one of the outstanding features of the Clarion movement was the attention given to the young. The Cinderella Clubs can, perhaps, hardly be described as socialist organisations, although their aim was to bring some warmth and joy into the lives of working-class children. These clubs not only fed poor children, they were the means of providing excursions, concerts and social activities of all kinds. More directly concerned with the propagation of socialism were the Clarion cycling clubs already referred to, perhaps the first effectively organised grouping of young people for socialist purposes. At a time when a variety of youth organisations were being sponsored chiefly by the Churches with philanthropic support, the Clarion youth groups stand out as one of the few independent working-class youth organisations. But effective local co-operative societies also ran large youth sections—mainly for social and recreative purposes but to some extent imbued with co-operative social ideals. In these ways the adult movement endeavoured to ensure that a new generation would be imbued with the

[1] *Ibid.*, Vol. X (1910), 721.   [2] *Ibid.*, Vol. XI (1911), 970, 972.
[3] See S. Harrison, *Alex Gossip* (1962), 13-16.

ideal of fellowship and prepared to enter the active movement to win
socialism.

5. WILLIAM MORRIS AND THE "VISION" OF THE EDUCATIVE SOCIETY

In their arduous struggles for social betterment socialists were
motivated by the concept of a new society. It was, above all, William
Morris who provided a vision of what socialism could mean, not least
in terms of human development—of education—while he also insisted
on the way to attain it. In lectures couched in simple and direct
language, some of which achieved a wide circulation as pamphlets,
he contrasted existing "civilisation" with a new state of "practical
equality" which he called "real society". Following Marx he affirmed
that social transformation could be brought about by successful
prosecution of the class struggle, so directly linking the workers'
struggles on immediate issues with the socialist ideal. Essentially a
humanist, Morris expressed an overriding sense of human potentiality,
human dignity, and the potentialities of "real society" to liberate men
from their present degradation. His simple, rational morality tore
through the hypocrisies of contemporary society. Presented with
confidence and directness, with a very real sense of urgency, this and
the personal example he set ensured that his influence was both profound and extensive.

Morris started from one basic position: labour is a necessity of
human existence. Just as nature makes other such necessities pleasurable, so "it is of the nature of man . . . to take pleasure in his work".[1]
Labour brings man's "slumbering energies into action", but to derive
pleasure from it he must exercise "mind and soul" as well as body.
The capacity to create is inherent in all human beings if only it can be
found and nurtured; true art, "all-pervading art", is "the expression
of pleasure in the labour of production".[2] "If we work thus," says
Morris, "we shall be men, and our days will be happy and eventful."[3]

To see labour as the central and formative human activity was to
take up a position very close to that elaborated by Marx when he
first began to reach towards a communist outlook.[4] The concept of

[1] "Useful Work versus Useless Toil", On Art and Socialism, ed. Holbrook Jackson
(1947), 175.
[2] "The Socialist Ideal", ibid., 318.
[3] "Useful Work versus Useless Toil", ibid., 177.
[4] In Economic and Philosophical Manuscripts of 1844 (1959), The German Ideology (1942),
and elsewhere.

labour as the primary human activity underlay the thinking of earlier socialists such as Robert Owen and Fourier; Fourier's doctrine that labour could and should be made attractive is one, wrote Morris, "which socialism can by no means do without".[1] But it was from Marx, particularly from his analysis of the division of labour and its effect on human development, that Morris derived much of his critique of existing society, just as he owed to Marx his revolutionary politics and hope for the future.[2]

To achieve a true humanity man must take pleasure in labour, but conditions of work in the factories made this impossible for the vast majority. The individual craftsman had once performed all the varied operations involved in making a product, but the unit of labour was now a group, and machinery was so used in the service of profit that each labourer was tied to a single detailed operation. The worker thus became "but part of a machine" having "but one unvarying set of tasks to do; and when he has learned these, the more regularly and with the less thought he does them, the more valuable he is".[3] The product of such work bears the marks of its manufacture. Above all, writes Morris, "it is of necessity utterly unintelligent, and has no sign of humanity on it". It is also ugly "for the labour which went to the making of it was thankless and unpleasurable, little more than a mere oppression on the workmen".[4] Work of this kind fails to exercise "the intellectual part of a man", turns him into "the perfect machine which it is his ultimate duty to become", so leading to the "complete destruction of individuality".[5] Machines should minimise repulsive labour and so give "added life", but they have only "driven all men into mere frantic haste and hurry". Instead of lightening they have intensified labour. Work has become a burden.[6]

The cause of this misuse of resources Morris sees in the search for profits and prestige, the division of society into classes and the resulting oppression which vitiate the quality of living for all men. The people have lost access to enjoyment, to art, and in losing this have lost "the natural solace of their labour . . . the opportunity of expressing their own thoughts to their fellows" by means of labour.[7] The capitalist may grow wealthy by paying the worker less than the value of his

---

1 "The Hopes of Civilisation", *ibid.*, 291.
2 "Here then was at last a hope of a different kind to any that had gone before it", wrote Morris of Marx's analysis; *ibid.*, 292.
3 "Art, Wealth and Riches", *ibid.*, 121.   4 *Ibid.*, 122.
5 "The Hopes of Civilisation", *ibid.*, 286.
6 "Art and Socialism", *ibid.*, 97; "The Hopes of Civilisation", *ibid.*, 287.
7 "Art and Socialism", *ibid.*, 97.

product but he does not find fulfilment either. Morris castigates "the unhappy rich" for "the futility of their amusements and the degradation of their art and literature";[1] isolated from their fellow men, cut off from the traditions of the past as well as the life of the present, their art is "the art of a clique and not of the people".[2]

More generally the search for profit degrades all England—producing "the black horror and reckless squalor of our manufacturing districts", ensuring that trashy wares are forced on people, transforming society itself into a system of individualist anarchy and competition, a "sordid, aimless, ugly confusion".[3] All true values become inverted. Those who do the work are regarded as an inferior species with whom the middle and upper classes can have no true association: "those who consume most produce least, and those who produce most consume least".[4] This was the "civilisation" Morris held up to obloquy, insisting on its ugliness and hypocrisy, the lack of art and pleasure and community, the "organised selfishness". It was impossible to live at peace while these conditions obtained. "To condemn a vast population to live in South Lancashire," he wrote, "while art and education are being furthered in decent places, is like feasting within earshot of a patient on a rack."[5]

Hence Morris's sense of urgency, of the crying need to work towards the new society of "practical equality", which led him to become an active member of the socialist movement. The new society could only be brought into being by the action of the workers, "the only possible elements of true society",[6] through the elimination of class divisions. It was the oppression of one class of men by another that caused the degradation of humanity, of art. "True society" must, then, be an association of equals in which men stand in a direct relation to each other; a society based on co-operation instead of competition, allowing each individual the opportunity of engaging in creative labour and so of developing his own particular capacities. "Let us be 'fellows'," enjoined Morris, "working in the harmony of association for the common good, that is, for the greatest happiness and completest development of every human being in the community."[7] In a society giving free scope for expression of individuality through work art would flourish as the indigenous product of labour. This would be, in the deepest sense, an educative society.

---

[1] "True and False Society", *On Art and Socialism*, 309.
[2] "The Socialist Ideal", *ibid.*, 321.
[3] "Art and Socialism", *ibid.*, 109; "How I became a Socialist", *ibid.*, 277.
[4] "True and False Society", *ibid.*, 306.   [5] "The Socialist Ideal", *ibid.*, 323.
[6] "Communism", *ibid.*, 329.   [7] *Ibid.*, 177.

How could this end be attained? Only by substituting a new ethic for the profit motive which set each man's hand against the other and determined that man exists to serve industry rather than industry to serve men. This implied eliminating private property which lay at the root of the division of society into classes. The new society must be one whose wealth, resources, means of production, were owned by the community for the benefit of the whole, in which each would do "his due share of labour" and receive "his due share of wealth resulting from that labour".[1] Under such conditions all would be in a position to satisfy their material needs but none could become very rich. This would be the first, socialist, stage of the new society with "the means of production communised but the resulting wealth still private property", but the changes brought about would so transform men's consciousness that there would inevitably be a movement on to the higher stage of communism. Once men live comfortably, once society is grounded on co-operation, the urge to accumulate private possessions will die away, Morris affirms, and pride in communal possessions will take its place. "When public institutions satisfied your craving for splendour and completeness and when no-one was allowed to injure the public by defiling the natural beauty of the earth, or by forbidding men's cravings for making it more beautiful to have full sway, what advantage would there be in having more nominal wealth than your neighbour?" Thus communisation of the product of industry would naturally follow communisation of the means of production establishing "complete equality of condition amongst all men". Every man "whatever work he did, would have the opportunity of satisfying all his reasonable needs". Society would take the form of a federation of self-governing communities.[2]

Socialism was for Morris not only a way of organising society to provide for the greatest good of the greatest number but a philosophy defining the purpose of living. "I assert first," he said in his lecture on "The Socialist Ideal", "that socialism is an all-embracing theory of life, and that as it has an ethic and religion of its own, so also it has an aesthetic."[3] It is this new standard of values regulating men's behaviour to each other that, first arising within the old society, directly motivates men to seek social change, to bring to birth "that true society which means well-being and well-doing for one and all . . . the society of well-wishers, of reasonable people conscious of

[1] "True and False Society", *ibid.*, 299.   [2] "Communism", *ibid.*, 333-4.
[3] *Ibid.*, 317.

the aspirations of humanity and of the duties we owe to it through one another".[1] This implies a new religion or ethical outlook, a new purpose for society, that of raising men to the highest level of which humanity is capable through full development of all their creative powers. It implies a new aesthetic; art naturally becomes the property and the creation of the whole people, the end of all work, since "the pleasurable exercise of our energies is at once the source of all art and the cause of all happiness: that is to say, it is the end of life".[2] Art, declares Morris, "is a necessity of human life" and the source of progress; it is by infusing life and the environment with the products of his activity that man creates the conditions for his own higher development.

To ensure that all men have access to art and enjoyment, the means to development, the process of labour must be made attractive. Labour must contain "hope of rest, hope of product, hope of pleasure in the work itself".[3] It must, above all, involve mind as well as body, intellectual capacities as well as physical powers. Under socialism machines, "these miracles of ingenuity", could for the first time be used not to intensify work but to minimise the time spent in unattractive labour; mere machine minding should be shared by all, so that it becomes a light burden on each. Otherwise there should be short hours of work combined with opportunity for leisure, to allow rest of mind and body, to enable thought, imagination, dreaming. "It is right and necessary," wrote Morris, "that all men should have work to do which shall be worth doing, and be of itself pleasant to do; and which should be done under such conditions as would make it neither over-wearisome nor over-anxious."[4]

Summarising the three essential conditions that make labour attractive Morris stressed that it must always be directed to useful ends, it should be varied and it must be undertaken in pleasant surroundings. Work will have "conscious usefulness" when it is directed towards social needs, when its nature is determined by a social morality, a sense of responsibility towards human life. Variety of work is a basic need; men need to engage in different kinds of activity, sedentary and outdoor, to command different forms of expertise. It was variety of talent that enabled the craftsman of old to produce work in which the ornament was part of the product itself, arising from and integrally

1 "True and False Society", *On Art and Socialism*, 316.
2 "The Socialist Ideal", *ibid.*, 321.
3 "Useful Work versus Useless Toil", *ibid.*, 176.
4 "Art and Socialism", *ibid.*, 98.

linked with its function and expressing human pleasure. All education should, therefore, aim to develop individual capacities in such a way that pleasure and fulfilment may be found in a variety of activities. Finally, places of work should have space, order and beauty. Factories should extend their function to offer "a full and eager social life surrounded by many pleasures", to provide not only variety of work but also of intellectual interests.[1]

As he saw in labour the primary source of human activity, enjoyment, self-development, so Morris saw the factory as a primary educational centre of socialist society. This idea he developed in an article "A Factory as it Might Be", that is, in a society "when we shall work for livelihood and *pleasure* and not for profit".[2] This, again, was to develop the ideas of socialist forerunners. It was Robert Owen, as Marx pointed out, who was the first to combine learning with labour in his factory at New Lanark.[3] Marx himself saw in this link the key to the education of the future. Morris took up the idea in the context of his conception of communism as a free society of artists and scientists. There would be a school, as well as a library and other facilities for study, in the factory of the future; a factory surrounded by gardens, whose buildings would be "beautiful with their own beauty of simplicity as workshops", whose workers would be engaged in labour that was useful and so "honourable and honoured". "Any child who seemed likely to develop gifts towards its special industry would gradually and without pain, amidst their booklearning, be drawn into technical instruction which would bring them at last into a thorough apprenticeship for their craft", manual dexterity and mental abilities being developed side by side. An education of this kind, closely integrating school and workshop, theory and practice, would lead the young worker to produce "for his own pleasure and honour as a good artist". The adult worker would also have opportunities to study deeply the scientific basis of crafts as well as carrying on more general scientific and literary studies.

1 "Useful Work versus Useless Toil", *ibid.*, 189.
2 First published in *Justice* (Vol. I, No. 18) in 1884 this was produced as a pamphlet by the Twentieth Century Press in 1907 (from which the quotations in the text are taken). This article is reprinted in William Morris, *Selected Writings* (1934), ed. G. D. H. Cole. It is not included in Morris's *Collected Works* (ed. May Morris) or in Holbrook Jackson's collection *On Art and Socialism*.
3 "From the factory system budded, as Robert Owen has shown us in detail, the germ of the education of the future, an education that will, in the case of every child over a given age, combine productive labour with instruction and gymnastics, not only as one of the methods of adding to the efficiency of production, but as the only method of producing fully developed human beings." *Capital*, ed. D. Torr (1946), 489.

Not only would the factory of the future educate its own workers in the more formal sense but also provide for recreation and leisure, for musical and dramatic activities. More than this, it would become a centre for the fine arts; pictures, sculptures, products of any and every kind of artistic activity would be displayed. People living under socialist conditions, says Morris, "having manual skill, technical and general education, and leisure . . . are quite sure to develop a love of art . . . a sense of beauty and an interest in life, which in the long run must stimulate in them the desire for artistic creation, the satisfaction of which is of all pleasures the greatest". So, he concludes, the socialist factory will provide "work light in duration and not oppressive in kind, education in childhood and youth. Serious occupation, amusing relaxation, and more rest for the leisure of the workers"; it will also have "that beauty of surroundings, and the power of producing beauty which are sure to be claimed by those who have leisure, education, and serious occupation". All this is a particular expression of Morris's outlook, that the creative labour of men in a society of equals can give rise to new human characteristics and lead to further social and individual progress. It is an essentially educational approach to depicting the educative society.

The socialist movement, wrote Edward Carpenter, has done a great and necessary work: "It has defined a dream and an ideal, that of the common life conjoined to the free individuality, which somewhere and somewhen must be realised, because it springs from and is the expression of the very root-nature of man." The Sheffield socialists, he adds, "though common working men and women, understood well enough the broad outlines of this ideal. They hailed William Morris and his work with the most sincere appreciation."[1] There is evidence enough that both Morris's critique of contemporary society and his "vision" of what life could be for all men under socialism penetrated deeply the thinking of the most advanced workers of his time. On his death in 1896, a member of the S.D.F. wrote that not one socialist would believe him dead, "for he lives in the heart of all true men and women still and will do so to the end of time".[2] But Morris was not only thinker and prophet; he was also a practical politician; in the words of Harry Snell, "a Socialist agitator" who saw the socialist revolution as a moral imperative and used his immense energies to persuade others that social change could and must be

[1] Edward Carpenter, *My Days and Dreams* (1916), 130.
[2] Mackail, *op. cit.*, Vol. II, 347.

brought about. "Intelligence enough to conceive, courage enough to will, power enough to compel," he affirmed in his lecture on communism; "if our ideas of a new society are anything more than a dream, these three qualities must animate the due effective majority of the working people; and then, I say, the thing will be done." All this is possible, he added, "for I do declare that any other state of society but Communism is grievous and disgraceful to all belonging to it".[1]

1 "Communism", Holbrook Jackson, *op. cit.*, 326, 334.

CHAPTER II

EDUCATION AND SOCIAL HARMONY

SOCIALISM, like Chartism before it, was seen by contemporary observers not merely as a set of political opinions but a threat "to the stability of society, fed by ignorance and atheism", in the words of the historian of the boys' club movement. It was a natural reaction to provide clubs and centres in which the workers and their children could be brought under religious influences. The Victorian middle class naturally "identified infidelity with seditious discontent and knowledge of the Scriptures with the social as well as personal virtues". Awareness that discontent was, in the 1880s, increasingly finding a political outlet—this was the time when a tiny group of men in the S.D.F. could bring out demonstrations of up to 50,000 in protest against unemployment—hastened action. "The local government franchise was already wider than the parliamentary, and agitation for placing decisive national power in the hands of artisans was gaining strength . . . the importance of qualifying the masses for the vote and, if possible, winning them over to sensible views became the more apparent."[1]

The Congregational Union, undertaking an investigation in the East End of London with a view to establishing a mission, found that parishes with populations of from 12,000 to 40,000 served by only one incumbent were not unusual. As an outcome a Congregational minister, Andrew Mearns, published his famous pamphlet, *The Bitter Cry of Outcast London* (1883), which awoke many to what was euphemistically called "the social problem". One of the first to see the need for practical action in the East End was Samuel Barnett, founder of Toynbee Hall, himself vicar of a Whitechapel parish and a Christian Socialist. "He rode to the top of the wave of anxiety lest Socialism, brought to life by Henry George's *Progress and Poverty*, and Hyndman's Democratic Federation, should sweep popular discontent, which was seen to be well-founded, into revolutionary channels."[2] From this beginning there developed a whole movement to establish settlements or missions, one in which the ancient universities and public schools

[1] W. McG. Eager, *Making Men* (1953), 32. [2] *Ibid.*, 183.

played a key role. If this was directed towards adults another movement aimed to draw in youth. The Y.M.C.A., Y.W.C.A., Boys' Brigade, Church Lads' Brigade, Girls' Friendly Society, are among the best known of many youth organisations, lay as well as religious, which had their inception or developed on a mass scale at this time.

If the initiative was often taken by Christian Socialists and Tractarians, whose consciences were challenged by the conditions of the masses, the movement as a whole drew on many others motivated not only by religion and a sense of justice but also self-interest and expediency. Though such supporters may have been conscious only of humanitarian motives, they nonetheless acted as supporters of church and state, enemies of secularism and socialism; their actions, often involving great personal sacrifice, can only be objectively assessed if this aspect of their work is taken into account. All were concerned, as Eager puts it, with a "para-political" movement of thought. Their predominant aim, as in the case of all such efforts in the past, was "to preserve the established order in Church and State by educating the masses in manners and morals, and up to political responsibility, which meant, of course, acquiescence".[1] Their various activities received full support from the established authorities.

1. INITIATION OF THE YOUTH MOVEMENT

It was not until the younger children had been provided for at school that attention turned seriously to the fourteen to twenty age-group. "The discipline and order secured by the elementary schools was almost miraculous," writes Eager, "but within two or three years the well-trained schoolboy degenerated to the larrikin of the streets, ignorant, foul-mouthed and predatory."[2] Much the same point is made by Russell, who played a leading part in the Boys' Club movement in Manchester in the 1880s and '90s. "It is at this age," he writes, "when the organised control of the school has ceased, and parental authority, slight as it often is, has lost most of its cogency, that the boy ... is most susceptible to influences good and bad, that his character may be formed and his career determined."[3] Once recognition was accorded to the "Youth Movement", adds Eager, there was a general awakening to the importance of " 'getting hold of the young', and of holding on to them until manhood was achieved".[4]

[1] Ibid., 149.　　[2] Ibid., 365.　　[3] C. E. B. Russell, Lads' Clubs (1932 ed.), 3.
[4] Eager, op. cit., 169.

The doyen of all youth organisations—the first in point of time—
was the Young Men's Christian Association, and it is significant that
it is precisely in the 1880s that the Y.M.C.A., initiated in 1844, begins
to make a mass impact. Primarily intended to meet the needs of the
lower middle class, shop assistants, clerks, and the like, it had by this
time acquired sufficient backing to buy the great Exeter Hall in London
for its headquarters. At a celebration on this occasion Lord Shaftesbury
shared the platform with the Archbishop of Canterbury, "members of
the noblest families in the land", the Lord Mayor of London, "the
most prominent ministers of all denominations", as well as city mer-
chants and employers such as Samuel Morley who had provided the
necessary funds. George Williams, founder of the Y.M.C.A., was an
acute businessman as well as an evangelical Christian. "He knew the
value, the attraction, of a big name," writes his biographer. "He knew
that the best way . . . to impress the great public . . . was to place at
its head men whom the world, from worldly motives, was bound to
have in respect."[1]

Williams, who had himself come to London without backing and
amassed a fortune, was a man of enormous energy and pertinacity.
As an employee in a drapery establishment in the City of London he
showed much evangelical fervour in winning young men to a Christian
outlook and participation in missionary activities of various kinds,
while at the same time he began to promote social, recreative and
educational activities. By upbringing a "Tory of the old school", conservative in outlook and temperament, he did not consciously work
with political ends in view.[2] In its early days the Y.M.C.A. encouraged
members to work in Sunday Schools and Ragged Schools, to organise
banking and clothing clubs, teach evening classes, run mothers' meetings, work in temperance societies, take Sunday and weekday services
and speak at open air meetings in Hyde Park, on the beaches and elsewhere. Later, recreative and social activities were developed, club-
rooms, libraries and news rooms opened. But the movement owed its
subsequent success to the pressures of the times. The Y.M.C.A. was
set up, as it has been said, to meet the need for "spiritual strength and
refreshment". It attracted influential support because, in the latter
years of the nineteenth century, "ministers of religion of all denominations awoke . . . to a more sensitive appreciation of their
responsibilities", in particular, "the need to consolidate those essential

[1] J. E. Hodder Williams, *The Life of Sir George Williams* (1906), 151, 225-7, 240.
[2] *Ibid.*, 179.

institutions which the new forces in society were in danger of pulling apart"—the family and the home. More particularly, from the late '70s and the '80s, the desire to consolidate religious organisation was becoming widespread: "in the various denominations, the need to bring up the young in the traditional beliefs was impressed on the leaders by the rise of secularism . . . the founding of various Associations and fellowships followed the appreciation of this need."[1] As Williams put it in a speech to an annual conference of the Y.M.C.A. in the early 1880s: "We ought to comprehend in our regard and prayerful sympathies every young man in the kingdom, from the Prince of Wales down to the lowest beggar, every young man from fourteen to forty. In England at the present time, great power is being given to the working classes. How is it to be turned to the best account? Is Bradlaugh to be allowed to have his say to the working classes, and are there to be no young men amongst us able to meet his attacks on revealed religion?"[2]

One of the features of the Y.M.C.A. was the support it received from employers. The original group had successfully won over their own employer, George Hitchcock, who contributed generously to the funds in the early days and became treasurer. "The fact that, from the very commencement, a large employer of labour identified himself so closely with the work was of supreme moment," writes Williams' biographer, it put an end to the suggestion that "this association of young employees was aimed against those in authority, and . . . did much to secure . . . the serious consideration of other employers".[3] Williams, who married Hitchcock's daughter and eventually took over the firm, made a great business coup during the Franco-Prussian war when continental fabrics were not available. As one of the leading London employers in this line for a large part of his active life, he became himself the best possible guarantee of the respectability of the movement.

The jubilee of the Y.M.C.A. fell in 1894. After half a century the movement had become world-wide, while in England the last ten years in particular had seen a rapid growth: from 316 to 893 Associations with a total of 87,500 members.[4] The Jubilee Conference was

---

[1] Alicia C. Percival, *Youth will be Led*, (1951), 42-3.
[2] J. E. Hodder Williams, *op. cit.*, 218. "Only on one occasion was he tempted to take any active part in the struggle of politics," when he seriously considered standing as a Christian candidate against Bradlaugh. He was dissuaded, since "defeat at the hands of Mr. Bradlaugh—and against such an antagonist victory was out of the question—would have been of more than political significance, would have been advertised by the opponents of Christianity as a triumph of secularism." *Ibid.*, 179-80.
[3] *Ibid.*, 185.   [4] *Ibid.*, 281.

attended by delegates from all parts of the world, a special service was held in Westminster Abbey, and the delegates welcomed "by the City of London, by 'the nobles and great people', by the Prime Minister and by Her Majesty the Queen".[1] Williams himself was knighted and received the Freedom of the City of London at "a brilliant function at the Guildhall". "The Christian principles of fortitude, true temperance, chastity, and obedience inculcated by the Young Men's Christian Association," said the Chamberlain making the presentation on behalf of the City of London, "have had a far-reaching influence upon society at large, and been productive of many blessings."[2]

The Y.M.C.A. did not at this stage cater specifically for the working class.[3] It was a Scotsman, William Smith, who first tackled this problem in 1883 by establishing the Boys' Brigade; its object, "The Advancement of Christ's Kingdom among Boys, the promotion of habits of Obedience, Reverence, Discipline, Self-respect and all that tends towards a true Christian manliness."[4]

Smith, born in 1854, "came from soldier stock, and his boyhood was nourished in tales of military glory".[5] In 1874, after attending a Moody and Sankey revivalist meeting, he joined the Free Church (the local Minister was the present Lord Reith's father), and a year later the Lanarkshire Volunteers. He also joined the Y.M.C.A., participating in Sunday School teaching. Here, in the Glasgow Sunday Schools and on the streets, he came to recognise the disorder and lack of purpose of work with boys, the failure of the Sunday Schools to hold their interest and rouse enthusiasm; his response was to launch the first company of what became the Brigade.[6] Realising that

---

[1] J. E. Hodder Williams, *The Life of Sir George Williams*, 277.

[2] *Ibid.*, 282-3. The Y.WC.A. was established about 1877 as the result of the coming together of a number of societies for prayer and the care of young women—its main efforts were directed at evangelism, establishment of registries, provision of libraries, and the encouragement of thrift and total abstinence. Cf. Percival, *op. cit.*, 53ff.

[3] The Y.M.C.A. was not exclusive in character, but it did not attract working-class youth. At the turn of the century efforts were made in this direction. "The great artisan section is calling for the Y.M.C.A.," wrote J. E. Hodder Williams. "The working man will have his own Christian Association or none at all. Only those who have made a careful study of the subject have any adequate idea of the evil being wrought among the working men of Great Britain by so-called social and political clubs." *Ibid.*, 344.

[4] Roger S. Peacock, *Pioneer of Boyhood*, (1954), 28-9. The word "obedience" did not figure in the first statement of aims—it was added later. See also Percival, *op. cit.*, 70.

[5] *Ibid.*, 13. "The battlenames of Sebastopol, Alma, Balaklava, and Inkerman were afterwards emblazoned on many a regimental colour, and such episodes as the charge of the Light Brigade, immortalised by Tennyson, doubtless stirred the martial blood of young William Smith and his comrades in the days of their early boyhood." *Ibid.*, 2.

[6] "Those were the days when the Sunday School movement was at its zenith, but in less prosperous districts was sadly lacking in the very qualities it desired to foster. Many schools became hotbeds of disorder, mischief and monkeying." *Ibid.*, 20.

something other than Bible classes was required, he found the answer in organised weekday as well as Sunday activities.

The Boys' Brigade sought, from the start, to weld together martial forms with religious purposes. Smith found that drill with dummy rifles and the suggestion of a uniform was an effective means of dealing with otherwise unruly boys, and of winning their adhesion and loyalty. The point was underlined by Professor Drummond, an ardent supporter, in the well-known remark: "Amazing and preposterous illusion! Call these boys 'boys', which they are, and ask them to sit up in a Sunday class and no power on earth will make them do it; but put a fivepenny cap on them and call them soldiers, which they are not, and you can order them about till midnight."[1] It was through such activities, as well as the camps he pioneered, that Smith aimed to engender "that *esprit de corps* which public school boys acquire as a matter of course, but which was almost entirely lacking in elementary school boys".[2]

The movement grew rapidly, expanding from companies to battalions, spreading from Scotland to England. It was a condition that to ensure a Christian basis every company must have a definite connection with a church. But the movement met with a good deal of opposition from churchmen who disliked the dissemination of religion by military methods, and also evoked hostility from young people themselves.[3]

Like the Y.M.C.A. the Boys' Brigade received encouragement and support from the highest quarters. Lord Aberdeen acted as Honorary President from the earliest days; the Duke of York, later George V, acted as Patron for forty years; Dr. Benson, one time headmaster of Wellington College and Archbishop of Canterbury, became Vice Patron, "thus early stamping the Brigade with the hall-mark of the Church".[4] Field-Marshal Lord Roberts also played an important part. The links with church and state were, therefore, very evident. With some 20,000 members in 1890, 50,000 in 1900, the climax of the

---

[1] Eager, *op. cit.*, 325.   [2] Percival, *op. cit.*, 69.
[3] "Many are the tales of strife and battle which veterans, whose memories reach back to Victorian days, can recall. Those were the days when what is now a historic ditty . . . first issued from the lips of the more junior ranks of the opposition:

> Here comes the Boys' Brigade
> All smovered in marmalade,
> A Tup'ny-'apenny pill-box
> And 'arf a yard of braid."
> Peacock, *op. cit.*, 56-7.

[4] *Ibid.*, 71-2.

E

Brigade's early days was the Royal Coronation Review in 1901, arranged "with the encouragement and aid of the highest authorities".[1] William Smith also received a knighthood in due course.

Both the Boys' Brigade and the Y.M.C.A. were undenominational; others, including denominational organisations, followed in their wake. In 1889 the Boys' Life Brigade was established by churchmen who opposed militarism; though drill was used its activities were focused around life-saving. In 1891 Anglican churchmen including Dr. Winnington Ingram, later Bishop of London, set up the Church Lads' Brigade, as also the London Diocesan Church Lads' Brigade which eventually amalgamated with the former. The aim, as in the case of the Boys' Brigade, was to unite in the boy's mind "the Bible Class or Sunday School with some weekday recreation, thus integrating his loyalty to his Church and his Club". The organisation was to provide "a training ground for instructed and faithful Church membership". As an official document put it: "The 'Brigade' boy has only one loyalty and one motive; religion is the primary duty and discipline of this 'Christian soldier' and his personal loyalty is to a leader who is an elder brother in Christ; his secondary duty and discipline is in the physical fitness and social well-being of himself and his comrades expressed by the drill and gymnastic work of his 'parades'."[2] In 1900 the Girls' Guildry was founded as the sister organisation of the Boys' Brigade.

> "Like a mighty army
> Moves the Church of God"

had its appeal, as one commentator puts it. The Brigade movement sought to harness this sentiment behind the established order in church and state.[3]

The Y.M.C.A., Boys' Brigade and their imitators were youth organisations on a national scale, but of at least equal importance, if less centrally organised, was the Club movement which also developed rapidly in the 1880s with, in general, a similar motivation. "Without overdoing the parallelism," concludes Eager in his study of this movement, "it should be observed that each phase of voluntary effort

[1] Roger S. Peacock, *Pioneer of Boyhood*, 95.

[2] Percival, *op. cit.*, 78. Other imitations of the Boys' Brigade were also founded at the turn of the century: The Jewish Lads' Brigade, Catholic Lads' Brigade, and the Girls' Life Brigade (1901). *Ibid.*, 80.

[3] Baden Powell's Scout movement, which adopted a much more flexible approach, and in consequence had a greater success, was not started until 1908. At first Baden Powell hoped that the Boys' Brigade would merge into the new organisation, but nothing came of this. E. E. Reynolds, *Baden Powell* (1942), 150-1.

for working boys coincided with agitations which widened the parliamentary franchise. Boys' Clubs began to take positive form before the second Reform Bill, 1867. Public School and University Missions weighed in powerfully when the third Reform Bill, 1884, was in gestation, and at that time also William Smith launched the Boys' Brigade. It was after the fourth Reform Bill, 1918, that Boys' Clubs drew together in a national organisation."[1] Percival suggests that it was "the growing realisation of social responsibility" that led to the "Club" movement in the big cities, but goes on to remark that motives varied "from something not much better than the payment of guilty conscience money in the desire to divert revolutionary tendencies, to the burning spirit of . . . Christianity".[2] So far as the churches were concerned the overriding aim was to supplement Sunday School work with weekday social activities having a religious basis— and so to provide something to interest and hold the child throughout the week. The Church Clubs in particular had "the very definite aim of making young people aware of, and ardent in, their allegiance to a Church".[3]

Whatever the motives, certainly a great deal of effort was put into the Club movement—in the East End of London in the 1880s and '90s particularly by public school men; indeed the whole movement closely tied in with the public school and university missions which were concerned mainly with adults. The Club movement also had a primarily religious basis and was remarkably active for a time. In 1889 the Hon. T. W. H. Pelham, an old Etonian who took the lead in setting up a London Federation of Working Boys' Clubs in 1888, could write that there had been a remarkable expansion during the last few years. A club "is now considered the necessary part of parochial machinery in every populous district. There are now about 300 parochial institutions for young men and boys in the Diocese of London and about fifty others not connected with any church. Twenty years ago there were probably not a score."[4]

Boys' clubs varied widely in character, from those specifically for "rough boys, and girls", to highly organised affairs such as the Webbe Institute in Bethnal Green, opened in 1889 by Prince Albert Victor of Wales.[5] In general, however, they had a threefold aim: recreative, educative and religious. The London clubs, particularly those under

[1] Eager, *op. cit.*, 431.   [2] Percival, *op. cit.*, 43-4.   [3] *Ibid.*, 97.
[4] Eager, *op. cit.*, 240. Pelham was a son of the Earl of Chichester.
[5] *Ibid.*, 195-6.

the aegis of public school missions, often concentrated on games with the aim of developing standards of sportsmanship among the working class—teams from the Eton and Harrow missions once being permitted to play each other at Lords—and as a result a wide range of athletic activities developed. Educational activities in the form of lectures and classes met with varying success. As for religious affiliation, while in some clubs "a fervent system of evangelical teaching was pursued, and prayer meetings were held almost every night",[1] most adopted a less aggressive approach. The muscular Christianity of Kingsley and Hughes was, of course, well adapted to club life and many of the men who ran them—the Eton Mission Club, we learn, "had an all-round programme with a virile religious purpose". But most clubs, whether church or lay, held Sunday services and for the rest relied rather on personal example, individual talks, and simple and unobtrusive teaching. Some clubs, which had their own premises, also had chapels. Summing up their experience, Russell writes that "under wise management, clubs may do more than any other existing organisation to arrest among the youths of our crowded cities and towns the advanced decay of interest in all that is usually implied by the word religion".[2]

A more definite religious purpose inspired the federation of village girls' clubs known as the Girls' Friendly Society. Its original purpose was to save girls who often went out into "service" as young as twelve or thirteen from "falling". At a preliminary meeting at Lambeth Palace, it was decided that only girls with a good moral character were to be accepted and the aim was defined as "to unite girls and women in a fellowship of prayer, service and purity of life, for the glory of God". By 1885 clubs of the Girls' Friendly Society were organised throughout the country "organically connected with the Anglican Church, being in each diocese 'under the patronage and sanction of the Bishop, and having Diocesan Councils which the Bishop had the right to attend'", the parish priest serving on the local committee.[3] Other religious groupings also welded local clubs into national organisations. For instance the "Wesley Guild" for Methodist youth was defined as "A Young People's Society, closely linked with the Church, holding weekly or periodical meetings for devotional, literary or social purposes and centring round itself various branches of young people's work".[4]

The public school mission movement which rapidly developed in

---

[1] Russell, op. cit., 163.   [2] Ibid., 157.
[3] Percival, op. cit., 83-5.   [4] Ibid., 95.

the 1880s is a social phenomenon of considerable interest. Just at the time when the public school system was becoming firmly established partly as a result of the complete exclusion of the poor or "lower classes" (as analysed in the next chapter), these schools discovered the East End and its problems, established "missions", supported boys' clubs and religious teaching, and sought by these means to transcend class differences. In 1883, Montague Butler, who as headmaster of Harrow had finally succeeded in eliminating local tradesmen's sons and others from the school,[1] "preached a terrific sermon in the University Church at Oxford, holding a copy of *The Bitter Cry* in his hand. 'God grant', he said 'that *here* in this great home of eager thought and enlightened action and generous friendship the bitter cry of outcast London may never seem unintrusive or uninteresting but that year by year her choicest sons may be arrested by it'."[2] The Harrow mission was established in that year in a very depressed part of Notting Dale where a fine church was built, and boys' clubs, girls' clubs and an adult men's club organised.

Characteristically it was Thring, who had served as a priest in a working-class area in Gloucester before being appointed headmaster of Uppingham, who first conceived the idea of a public school mission. Starting with the principle that "the rich boys must learn to help the poor boys", he got his school to contribute, from 1864 onwards, to the support of a Boys' Home and some years later, to adopt a parish and contribute to the clergyman's stipend, first in Victoria Docks, North Woolwich, and later in Poplar.[3] One of the earliest to follow this example was Dr. Percival, the first headmaster of Clifton College—a new proprietary school at Bristol. An admirer of Thring, he followed his example "in interesting the senior boys and staff in the struggle of the Church to cope with the ignorance and infidelity of the new industrial masses", and established a mission in Bristol which, under T. W. Harvey, included a workmen's club, a young men's club, a lads' club and a girls' club.[4]

It was in East London, however, that the public school mission

---

[1] See B. Simon, *Studies in the History of Education*, 314-17.

[2] Eager, *op. cit.*, 211.

[3] Eager, *op. cit.*, 77-8; Percival, *op. cit.*, 99-100.

[4] Eager, *op. cit.*, 293ff. Harvey was a most unusual Missioner. Not a public school man and a militant Christian Socialist "he fought the unsocial Christians and found that the Socialists were not unchristian". "Of all the Public School and College Missioners", adds Eager, " he may be judged to have made the greatest mark on the history of his time; he demonstrated that the Church was not necessarily on the side of the possessors of wealth and power; he kept the Labour Movement sweet in a city whose mob had often been particularly destructive and vengeful." *Ibid.*, 296-7.

movement developed most rapidly. The primary aim, as the "Jubilee Memorial" account of one such mission puts it, was specifically religious: "to bring the benefits of the Church to a part of London which had previously had little opportunity to enjoy them". Starting often with the founding of the mission church, "the clubs and other organisations which were so soon to spring up . . . were to be purely ancillary to this main purpose". "The reason why in many areas, clubs—and particularly boys' clubs—had to be started soon if the spiritual side of the mission was to achieve any wide success, is not hard to see," writes one commentator, "briefly, it was necessary to approach young people's minds and souls through their bodies."[1]

In 1876 Winchester established a new East End Mission parish (All Hallows', London Docks), contributing to its upkeep for six years before transferring its attention to Portsmouth.[2] Four years later, Eton undertook both to finance and man a mission district in East London and there started the first public school boys' club: "the long-limbed Etonians strode along the mean streets of East London . . . teaching a good deal, learning a lot, taking the sting out of class-consciousness."[3] It was from this mission that the Federation of London Boys' Clubs originated. In the same year the Marlborough mission was established in Tottenham, there followed later in the '80s initiatives by Charterhouse, Wellington, Tonbridge, Felsted and Rugby, in the '90s by Clifton, Haileybury and Shrewsbury. Most of these established boys' clubs.

"No branch of charitable work is more productive of good results than the Boys' Clubs," wrote Pelham in 1890. "They can, if efficiently managed, be in some degree to the poor what the public schools and universities have been to the rich. They develop, as no other agency can, that *esprit de corps* in which the poor are, for the most part, so lamentably deficient. They afford unequalled opportunities for those who have received a good education to bring their influence to bear on their poorer brethren at an age when they are most in want of training and direction; they enable hundreds of boys to steer clear of many of the temptations by which the poor of our large towns are constantly surrounded; they offer wholesome recreation to those who otherwise would have few pleasures, or only such pleasures as are

[1] Percival, *op. cit.*, 99-100.
[2] Eager, *op. cit.*, 214; see *Ten Years in a Portsmouth Slum* (1897), by R. R. Dolling, who had to resign one post for allowing Stewart Headlam, the socialist Church of England parson, to talk politics from the pulpit.
[3] *Ibid.*, 206-7; see *An Eton Playing Field* (1896), by E. M. S. Pilkington.

vicious and degrading. Indeed, it is not too much to say that on the Elementary Schools, Polytechnics and the Boys' Clubs the future of the working-classes in England largely depends."[1]

Certainly there were many who responded to this appeal in the 1880s and '90s. When Alexander Devine founded the first boys' club in Manchester in 1886—the Hulme and Chorlton-on-Medlock Lads' Club—he persuaded Lord Aberdeen to accept the Presidency and perform an opening ceremony at which Lord Derby, the Bishop of Manchester, Lord Egerton, C. P. Scott, and the headmasters of Uppingham and Rossall were present.[2] The second club he founded two years later was opened by the Prince of Wales, while a third was financed by Sir William Crossley, head of one of the leading engineering firms in the district. By the 1890s there were over fifty clubs in Manchester and many in other provincial cities.

It is not easy to assess the influence of the public school clubs and missions in London. Some concentrated chiefly on establishing some contact between the boys of different classes, others on providing financial support from afar for a parish. Eager concludes that as parochial missions they have been an ineffectual social force, while the majority of the public schools failed to keep up boy to boy contact in any consistent way. Those that made it their aim "to create friendship between boys of different classes, with a sense of social obligation on the one hand and of sharing tradition on the other, have accomplished something of value . . . it bred the spirit of unity, the true bond of social peace, in the hearts of many young men who ventured and understood." But "very few schools . . . have kept continuously and consistently to the line of bringing home to their boys the fact that boys of their own age who happen to be born in poverty are made of the same clay as themselves and that, however different their accents and conventions may be, they are 'decent fellows', good sportsmen and members of the same nation".[3] This assessment serves to underline that the movement was a reaction to the problems of a particular period, to a particular, and a menacing, social crisis; it was from this that its early momentum derived.

2. Working Men's Clubs and Adult Schools

Just as the last two decades of the century saw the development of an organised youth movement, so a variety of social and educational

[1] Quoted in Eager, *op. cit.*, 253.   [2] *Ibid.*, 269.   [3] Eager, *op. cit.*, 224-5.

organisations designed specifically for adults—the Settlement movement, University Extension, Working Men's Clubs and, if perhaps of
lesser significance, the Adult Schools—have their origin at this time.
While these differed considerably in character, each formed part of a
complex web of institutions whose purpose was to bridge the gulf
between the classes—in particular, to reach out to the working class.
The fortunes of each of these movements varied considerably.

The Working Men's Club and Institute Union, launched in 1862,
had as President the eighty-four-year-old Lord Brougham, who had
played a leading part in the establishment of Mechanics' Institutes
forty years earlier. Brougham's presence was symbolic. The early
Mechanics' Institutes had the clear political aim of meeting the growing
demand of the working class for education and knowledge while under
the control of industrialists who provided the resources. This design
had failed since the working class, resenting patronage and rejecting
the type of knowledge provided, voted with their feet and left the
Institutes to the lower middle class, establishing instead their own
independent educational institutions. In the 1860s a more careful
approach was adopted; patronage was to be avoided and the stress
placed on social intercourse. The new institutions were to some extent
influenced by the experience of the Working Men's College founded
in London in 1854 by the Christian Socialists. Here workers, organisers
and lecturers met on a basis of equality and mutual respect.

The leading figure in the movement for adult clubs was Henry
Solly, an extremely energetic Unitarian minister, who had worked in
the temperance movement, and who became secretary, for a time,
of the new Union.[1] The aim of the Union was to encourage the
formation of clubs allowing for "unrestrained social intercourse",
where the gentry could be brought into touch with, and influence,
the working class. "Notwithstanding all the efforts made to improve
the character and condition of the working classes in this country,"
announced the first prospectus, "intemperance, ignorance, improvid-
ence and religious indifference still abound among them to a deplorable
extent." The efforts so far made had been too narrow; the Mechanics'
Institutes, it was suggested, had failed because they did not provide for
recreative activities. "Recreation must go hand in hand with Education
and Temperance . . . while efforts should be specially made to awaken
and cherish a brotherly spirit of mutual helpfulness among working
men themselves, as well as between them and the classes socially above

[1] See his *Working Men's Social Clubs and Educational Institutes* (1867).

them." The aim should be to encourage the establishment of clubs where working men "can meet for conversation, business and mental improvement, with the means of recreation and refreshment, free from intoxicating drinks".[1] Classes, libraries, newspapers were to be encouraged—working-class activities should be removed from the public house.

Solly was another who was extraordinarily successful in winning support from aristocrats as well as prominent members of the middle class; Vice-Presidents included many peers and churchmen, as well as such men as Matthew Davenport Hill, who, with Brougham, had played a leading part in launching and sustaining the Society for the Diffusion of Useful Knowledge in the late 1820s. During the period preceding the Reform Bill of 1867 he obtained subscriptions from half the twenty-two Dukes then extant as well as from the Prince of Wales, who contributed quite frequently. Later, subscriptions were forthcoming from such bankers and industrialists as Lord Rothschild and Sir Thomas Brassey. "Certain it is," writes the historian of this movement, "that so comprehensive a list of distinguished men and women of the Victorian era, led by Lord Chancellors and Archbishops, was never before or since attached to any scheme."[2] The Earls of Shrewsbury and Lichfield, and the Dukes of Argyll and Devonshire gave active support in the mid-1860s, presiding over "social meetings" which brought the gentry into touch with the workers. Leading trade unionists were also courted but found on the whole to be "shy and suspicious".[3] At this stage the clubs acted chiefly as social-recreative institutions, though definite efforts were made to organise educational classes or lectures and to develop libraries; but "entertainments" in which the local gentry sometimes participated, were the most popular item.

By the mid-1880s, however, the movement had extended and clubs were being set up by the workers themselves, a move that was to have important repercussions. The annual report for 1883, pointing out that the Union had been in being for twenty-one years, could claim that a new type of institution had come into being popular with the working class. The underlying purpose was outlined, again in terms of the extension of the franchise: "These clubs must exercise a large influence in shaping the habits, tastes and ideas of their members and

---

[1] B. T. Hall, *Our Fifty Years* (1912), 14, 16.   [2] *Ibid.*, 21.

[3] "Robert Applegarth is, as usual, hearty and downright in support. But W. R. Cremer is coy; and Coulson, Allan, and other members of the Junta are at best negatively neutral. George Howell is a worker inside the Union." *Ibid.*, 30-1.

of the people generally. . . . The social and political problems with which the growing democracy will have to deal are serious. To prepare for their solution we must not depend upon the 'chapter of accidents', but upon enlightened and systematic efforts. *These clubs may become in time schools where half a million adults learn how best to take part in the great evolution which the next generation or two will witness.*"[1]

During these years the direction of the Union remained firmly in the hands of a largely self-elected council. On Brougham's death in 1867 Lord Lyttleton became President and was actively concerned with the organisation—he was later succeeded by Lord Rosebery and Dean Stanley ("Lady Augusta Stanley and the Dean frequently invited large parties to Westminster Abbey and to tea at the Deanery"), while Solly's place was taken by a trio including Auberon Herbert, an aristocratic Radical, Hodgson Pratt, a retired Indian civil servant, and Thomas Paterson, a working cabinet-maker well known for his attacks on secularism at public meetings. In 1873, as a direct result of the demand for affiliation fees from local clubs, the large Council, which until that time had no workmen on it, provided places for five "elected or selected" members of clubs; a year later Benjamin Lucraft, London trade unionist, was added.[2] Aristocrats and industrialists continued to make donations to the funds while one of the latter, Sir Thomas Brassey, presented the Union with 500 copies of his book *Work and Wages*.

It was at this stage that a remarkable upheaval took place in the government and character of the Union which, in 1884, had 557 clubs in membership, Brassey as President, and an "imposing and remarkable" list of Vice-Presidents. The revolution in government, according to Hall, reflected "the seething tumult of violent political and religious differences which in those years bubbled into every phase of social life". The club movement, for all the talk, had signally failed to avoid the aura of patronage and, in the sharp political atmosphere of the mid-'80s this was driven home. "There was much talk of 'patronage' as hateful", writes Hall.[3] The membership insisted on a directly elected Council, representative of the clubs in the country, although subscribers were permitted to elect their own members. The list of Council members for 1884 indicates how profound was the change; it includes, for instance, representatives of the Towers Hamlet Radical Association, one of the most advanced of working men's clubs. Matters were brought to a head when the name of

[1] Hall, *op. cit.*, 76–7.   [2] *Ibid.*, 45.   [3] *Ibid.*, 84.

Bradlaugh, hero of the radical and secular movement, was added to the list of Vice-Presidents by a majority of one. Lord Lyttleton, the Duke of Devonshire and others immediately resigned, taking with them the clubs under their influence. Bradlaugh withdrew his name while continuing to assist the clubs by lecturing for them, but a fundamental rift had come to light. This incident "offered an illustration of the difference of attitude of the workmen members and that of others, and there can be no doubt that the treatment accorded to a man, whom many thousands of workmen believed to be . . . the greatest and best, did colour and embitter subsequent proceedings".[1] In 1886 the Union, now under democratic control, drew up a new constitution which made no provision for the office of Vice-President, and, at a meeting in Westminster Hall, "bade a long farewell to all its great ones". With "Princes and potentates" departed, a new chapter opened in the history of the Union.[2] A complete overturn of the old order had taken place.

If the direct control of the movement now passed into the hands of the workers themselves, the clubs still offered a rich field for endeavour. As we shall see, those engaged in the Settlement movement in the 1880s and '90s fully recognised their importance and devoted a good deal of attention to working within them, setting up a federation of Working Men's Social Clubs in London. The approach of the Settlement movement was, however, specific to its ethos and character. Before turning to this, we may briefly consider another educational effort affecting adults at this stage—the extension of Adult Schools.

Sunday Adult Schools had first been established in the decades 1810-30—also a period of upheaval. Their aim at that time was strictly limited—to teach the "labouring poor" to read the scriptures. A great controversy had taken place as to whether these schools should also teach writing, but in general this was discountenanced. Subsequently the number of such schools had sharply declined; their revival in the late 1850s and '60s was due specifically to the Quakers and in the first place to Joseph Sturge of Birmingham. It was from this time that the Rowntrees, Cadburys and other leading Quaker families as well as their friends (Joseph Chamberlain was an Adult School teacher as a young man) began to found and to teach in Adult Schools.

The Adult School movement, like the Y.M.C.A., was at this time evangelical and primarily "redemptive". The "new" workers in this field had "a different vision" from that of their forerunners in the

<hr/>

[1] *Ibid.*, 91.   [2] *Ibid.*, 88.

1820s. "All their work was religious, and all its aim was to make men and women the disciples of Jesus."[1] The Adult Schools, wrote Rowntree and Binns in 1903, "must be a true order of St. Francis, fervent in spirit, serving the Lord. And theirs must be the evangelical gospel of freedom and hope, not narrowly or doctrinally interpreted, but in the broadest charity and in the deepest faith."[2] In the 1880s the movement began to move ahead rapidly, under the aegis particularly of William White, Lord Mayor of Birmingham in 1882 at a time when Liberal-Radical influence was at its height. By 1884, a total of sixty-nine Adult Schools had been started by the Society of Friends; by the time White died in 1900, the number had largely increased while membership totalled 28,000. Many of the later schools were started by non-Friends.

Adult Schools normally met early on Sunday morning for study of the Bible and for teaching reading and writing. The latter opportunity exercised the most appeal in the 1860s and '70s; as White was fond of saying, "they will come if you advertise the school for reading and writing. Being crafty, we catch them with guile."[3] But to this basic fare were added social functions such as tea meetings and entertainments, lectures, athletic activities—sometimes a savings bank (to encourage thrift), a fund for the sick, libraries, temperance activities and so on. In the 1880s and '90s discussions, debates and lectures on secular subjects were developed as, with the rise in literacy, demand for the teaching of reading and writing declined.

The revival of the Adult School movement from the 1850s epitomises a new interest in social problems on the part of Quakers; the transformation of what had been "the most exclusive religious denomination—a peculiar people—into a body as deeply concerned as any in the world for the reformation and reconstruction of the social and economic conditions".[4] William White himself had been closely concerned with measures for civic improvement, and it was through

---

[1] G. Currie Martin, *The Adult School Movement* (1924), 85.

[2] *Ibid.*, 85-6, quoting J. W. Rowntree and H. B. Binns, *A History of the Adult School Movement* (1903), 76.

[3] Currie Martin, *op. cit.*, 115.

[4] *Ibid.*, 151. Thus J. W. Rowntree wrote, "The Adult Schools have been to us not merely a new and successful form of Christian endeavour, but have been of critical importance to us in our development as a Church. They have liberated our pent-up energies in a sphere of fruitful service." In the Adult School Movement the Quaker Church had "come upon a vein of gold; but if we are fully to work the vein, we shall need a large increase in power, for the quartz is obstinate, our miners few, and our machinery inadequate". From *Essays and Addresses* (1905), quoted by J. F. C. Harrison. *Learning and Living, 1760-1960* (1961), 304.

NOTICE.

School for Working Men.

A School is held at the FRIENDS' MEETING HOUSE, East Stockwell Street, to which Working Men above 18 years of age are invited, who desire instruction in

READING AND WRITING

The School is open every SUNDAY MORNING from 9 o'clock to a quarter-past 10, and a SCHOOL is held in connection with it on TUESDAY EVENINGS from 8 o'clock to half-past 9.

HANDBILL ANNOUNCING THE OPENING OF AN ADULT SCHOOL

the Adult Schools that the Rowntree and Cadbury families—becoming large employers of labour—first came closely into contact with the workers and their problems; subsequently they sought to overcome the antagonism between capital and labour by building model factories and villages such as Bournville, and educational institutes such as that at Selly Oak.

At the turn of the century the Adult School movement entered a new phase of development to which we may return later, but this was on somewhat different lines. In its late nineteenth century form it represented a particular, predominantly Quaker, reaction to the growing secularism, antagonism and poverty of the masses. "Sectarian bitterness dead," wrote a leader of the Bradford Adult School dreaming of what his city might become a century later, "the aloofness of classes gone, Capital and Labour shaking hands with something of the love which thinketh no evil, places of worship crowded with intelligent and appreciative audiences fresh from the Adult Schools."[1] This, if somewhat naïvely expressed, was the perspective.

[1] Currie Martin, *op. cit.*, 110.

3. MISSIONS AND SETTLEMENTS—THE "NEW FEUDALISM"

The Settlement movement, which began and indeed reached a climax in the mid-1880s, was also primarily concerned with the relations between rich and poor, with establishing social peace and with society as an organic unity. Again it was a direct response on the part of members of the privileged, or "educated", classes to the social crisis of the 1880s, in which the initiative was taken largely by members of the Church of England. The actual settlement of men of this kind in the heart of the East End of London followed from a recognition that activity with a solely missionary purpose, directed and financed from outside, had been a failure. The idea of a Settlement whereby the privileged lived among (if not with) the poor, derived from what may be called a neo-feudal outlook.

Acquaintance with the conditions of life in the East End, particularly after the irruption of East Enders in the West End of London during the unemployed agitations in the 1880s, had an immediate and a profound effect. "It is difficult after thirty years," wrote Alfred Spender later, "to realise the shock of novelty with which revelations of the conditions of the poor came to comfortable people in the '70s and '80s, or the sensation which such a pamphlet as *The Bitter Cry of Outcast London* made when it was first produced. The separateness of the poor life and the rich life had hardened to a point at which mutual ignorance and repudiation of responsibilities threatened to become fixed in English thought. Social legislation was declared to be outside the sphere of Parliament, and most philanthropic schemes were denounced as pauperising the poor."[1] It was to the end of overcoming these divisions and providing some immediate remedy that the Settlements worked.

The key figure in this movement is Canon Barnett, vicar of St. Judes, Whitechapel, since 1873, a broad churchman, deeply concerned with social questions, who had links with Christian Socialism and was influenced by Carlyle and Ruskin. It was Barnett's eloquence and energy that fostered the movement as a whole, as well as the establishment of Toynbee Hall in 1884; it was he who won many leading undergraduates, at Oxford in particular, to turn their energies towards the East End and to settle there.[2] What was above all needed, he

---

[1] *The Westminster Gazette*, 19 June, 1913, quoted in Mrs. S. A. Barnett, *Canon Barnett, His Life, Work and Friends* (1921 edn.), 309-10.

[2] It has been argued that the Settlement movement did not originate with Barnett, but with Edward Dennison and J. R. Green who were both active in Stepney in the late 1860s. "Other laymen, following in Dennison's footsteps, made their homes in the East End." Eager, *op. cit.*, 182-3.

claimed, was what until now had been shunned, personal contact. "Such poverty of life," he said in one of his talks to undergraduates, "can best be removed by contact with those who possess the means of higher life. Friendship is the channel by which the knowledge—the joys—the faith—the hope which belong to one class may pass to all classes. It is distance that makes friendship between classes almost impossible, and, therefore, residence among the poor is suggested as a simple way in which Oxford men may serve their generation"; in this way "they will do something to weld Classes into Society".[1] "Let University men become the neighbours of the working poor, sharing their life, thinking out their problems, learning from them the lessons of patience, fellowship, self-sacrifice, and offering in response the help of their own education and friendship," wrote Cosmo Lang later, recalling one of Barnett's Oxford talks. "This," he added, "will alleviate the sorrow and misery born of class division and indifference. It will bring classes into relation; it will lead them to know and learn of one another, and those to whom it is given will give."[2]

Close personal contact—interpenetration of rich and poor, educated and ignorant, the strong and the weak—this was the direction in which Barnett saw a solution of the social problem. "The two nations, that of the rich and that of the poor, are very evident," he wrote in 1895. "Each grows strong, and the danger of collision is the great danger of our time. The question of questions is how to make peace and goodwill."[3] The same point was put with much greater emphasis by Sir John Gorst, Tory M.P. and close friend of Barnett, in his Rectorial Address at Glasgow University in 1894. Modern civilisation has crowded "the destitute classes" together in the cities "making their existence thereby more conspicuous and more dangerous"; these "already form a substantial part of the population, and possess even now, though they are still ignorant of their full power, great political importance". While the destitute are left to battle for mere existence, the leisured enjoy their culture and refinement "only by going away, shutting their eyes and ears to facts, and wrapping themselves up in class egotism. But," he added, "the evil may be on the increase. Almost every winter in London there is a panic lest the condition of the poor should become intolerable. The richer classes awake for a moment

[1] Barnett, *op. cit.*, 307-8.
[2] Cosmo Lang was Archbishop of York when he wrote this on Barnett's death in 1913; *ibid.*, 310.
[3] Rev. Canon Barnett "Hospitalities", in *The Universities and the Social Problem*, ed. John M. Knapp (1895), 55.

from their apathy, and salve their consciences by a subscription of money. . . .[1] The annual alarm may some day prove a reality, and the destitute classes may swell to such proportion as to render continuance of our existent social system impossible." This the working class could already achieve "by their lawful power at the polls"; they might even, stirred up by "designing persons" and promises of "social salvation", attempt it by "revolutionary outbreaks".[2] It was one of Gorst's conclusions that the people need "wise counsellors" whom they trust; "such a position University men and women settled amongst the poor have every prospect of attaining. They are not generally wealthy; they do not incur the suspicion of looking upon questions from the capitalist side; they have no object of their own to serve." They have, therefore, a key role to play in overcoming a state of things both "discreditable to our Christianity and civilisation, and . . . dangerous to the stability of our present social system".[3]

Barnett contrasted modern with feudal society to the disadvantage of the former. The cash nexus has taken the place of the personal nexus, the rich separate themselves from the poor, living secluded, and building up every year new barriers of luxury. "They give, but they will not share; they send their money, but keep themselves and their homes behind servants, conventionalities, and high walls." The feudal lord, on the other hand, "entertained his followers and welcomed strangers", they met, and learned to know each other. Could not a similar relationship now be established? "Entertainment societies, employers' feasts, the parsons' parties are the appliances by which our generation has tried to supply the place of the hospitality of old days." But entertainment is not hospitality, these functions do not rise to the level of sharing, "do not provoke a sense of common possession by interest in one another's possessions" and so increase goodwill between poor and rich. This is the first object of the Settlement, "to bring people together, to promote the contact by which virtue passes from human being to human being, to allow of the personal touch which breaks down the barriers made strong by fear and suspicion". If the

---

[1] The distress in the winter of 1885-6 led to the opening of a Mansion House Fund. In twenty days it collected £19,000. Then the Trafalgar Square demonstration took place resulting in the smashing of windows in St. James's Street, and in two days the fund rose to £72,000; Barnett, *op. cit.*, 627. "The alarm of the rich at the indication that the poor were becoming restive from suffering was shown in the outpourings of their money, and their demands that relief should be given instantly and discontent assuaged." *Ibid.*, 624.

[2] Sir John Gorst, " 'Settlement' in England and America", in Knapp, *op. cit.*, 5-6, 16.

[3] *Ibid.*, 16-17, 28.

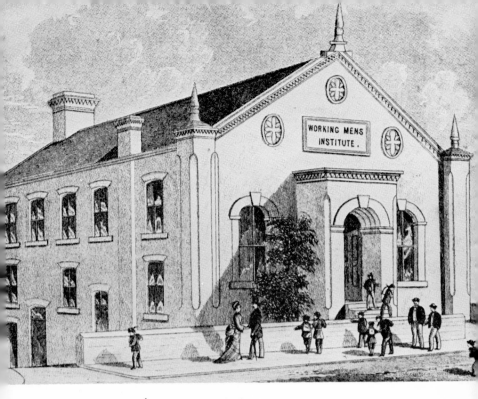

WORTLEY WORKING MEN'S INSTITUTE, 1876

CANON AND MRS. BARNETT

UPPINGHAM: THE ORIGINAL GRAMMAR SCHOOL, 1584

UPPINGHAM: THE MAIN ENTRANCE TODAY

"horizontal cleavage in society" is to be overcome, many of the rich and educated must live among the poor: "if settlements became so frequent as to cease to seem settlements, if they kept clear of all appearance of a mission, then rich and poor would so know one another that legislation and government would be armed to do the greatest good in the best way."[1]

This was the appeal that made so strong an impact on Oxford in the 1880s. With his many years' experience in Whitechapel, Barnett could speak with authority, and he won the ear and support not only of undergraduates, but of some of the most influential and far-sighted of Oxford personalities—T. H. Green, A. L. Smith, and in particular the Master of Balliol, Benjamin Jowett.[2] "Barnett came down and preached in our College Halls," wrote Canon Scott Holland later, "and the whole university laid hold of his idea and understood. He came as a prophet just when it was wanted, and men saw in his Settlement proposal exactly the opportunity which their gathering interest in the problem of poverty demanded for its exercise and fulfilment."[3] A whole organisation was set up at Oxford, with secretaries in many colleges to arrange meetings, collect funds, interest other students, and generally keep Oxford in touch with the East End.

At Cambridge, there was similar enthusiasm and support; a committee for the study of social questions was set up and in 1884 a meeting held at the Guildhall in support of Barnett and the Settlement movement. Here the main resolution was moved by Professor Westcott, later Bishop of Durham, and supported by H.R.H. Prince Albert Victor of Wales (who was in his first term at the university) and Austen Chamberlain, then a leading light of the Union.

Toynbee Hall, the first actual settlement of university people in the East End, opened its doors on Christmas Eve, 1884,[4] the official opening

[1] Canon Barnett, "Hospitalities", in Knapp, op. cit., 53-60, 65-6.
[2] Although Jowett was at first concerned about the effect of the appeal on his best students: "I used to be afraid of sending my men to you," he once told Mrs. Barnett, "not knowing what you would do with them; but now I safely send them, for you are ambitious for them. A man's career should be his first concern." Barnett, op. cit., 415. The remark is characteristic of Jowett who had transformed Balliol into a nursery of statesmen and proconsuls. He need not have worried—"scores of Toynbee Hall residents achieved later fame" in Parliament, in the Indian and Home civil service, in Commerce and Industry. Eager, op. cit., 185.
[3] Barnett, op. cit., 309.
[4] The Hall was named after Arnold Toynbee, one of the Oxford students who stayed with the Barnetts frequently in Whitechapel in the late '70s and early '80s, and who " turned men's thoughts and faces towards the East End and its problems" at Oxford. His health was poor and he died young in 1883, "succumbing to the results of his efforts to give lectures in opposition to Henry George's Poverty and Progress to unsympathetic audiences"; Barnett, op. cit., 307. See the memoir Arnold Toynbee by Lord Milner (1895).

taking place the following March, with Barnett as Warden and fourteen graduates of Oxford and Cambridge in residence. Thereafter the movement spread rapidly. In the same year Anglo-Catholics at Oxford, holding that Toynbee Hall was insufficiently religious, decided to start a Church settlement and established Oxford House in Bethnal Green.[1] In subsequent years Cambridge colleges set up a number of missions and settlements, one of which, the Trinity Mission, was taken over by the university; this was established in 1896 as Cambridge House in South London, being launched at "a notable meeting at the Cambridge Guildhall with the Vice-Chancellor in the chair", and speeches by three bishops, Arthur Balfour, Alfred Lyttleton and others.[2] In 1897 Oxford Evangelicals established the Oxford Medical Mission in Bermondsey. Before this, Nonconformists had entered the field with Mansfield House in Canning Town (1890), the Bermondsey Settlement (1891) and the Robert Browning Settlement in Walworth (1895). Women's colleges at Oxford and Cambridge established the first Women's University Settlement in Southwark in 1887. The Maurice Hostel in Hoxton (1899) was organised by Christian Socialists while the Passmore Edwards Settlement (1896) was specifically non-religious.[3] Outside London, Glasgow University established a settlement in 1889, Manchester one at Ancoats in 1895, and others followed later.

The methods used varied with the outlook and character of the settlement—from street preaching and religious processions, the building of churches and substantial club rooms, to the widespread educational activity for which Toynbee Hall in particular is famous.

The Keble Anglicans who set up Oxford House had a dual aim, "not only to construct a passage-way from Oxford to the East End, but also to reinvigorate and reinspire the Church in Bethnal Green". "Colonisation by the well-to-do seems indeed the true solution to the East End question," wrote the Hon. J. G. Adderley, head of this Mission, in the first Annual Report, "for the problem is, how to make the masses realise their spiritual and social solidarity with the rest of the capital and the kingdom: how to revive their sense of citizenship, with its privileges which they have lost, and its responsibilities which they have forgotten." The people could only be taught "thrift and prudence" by men who will associate with them "and thus induce them to face the elementary laws of economy"; hence the importance

---

[1] Barnett, op. cit., 421.   [2] Eager, op. cit., 191-2.
[3] Ibid., 192-3. The Passmore Edwards Settlement was instigated by Mrs. Humphrey Ward and is now known by her name.

of a living contribution of energy, pluck and enthusiasm from "the imperishable youth of Oxford".[1] Adderley's successor, Hensley Henson, "was essentially a fighting man who gloried in meeting secularists in open-air skirmishes or in pitched battles in the Oxford Hall", a tradition that was carried on by Winnington Ingram who took over in 1889.[2]

One way the residents made contact with the workers was by joining existing working men's clubs or establishing new ones; of the fifteen Toynbee Hall residents in 1888, nine did so.[3] "The club I managed to be made a member of," wrote one resident later, "was one of the oldest of its kind, radical to the back-bone and with no inconsiderable influence in local politics"; here a class was started on political economy. "For many clubs," writes Mrs. Barnett, "lecturers were found who told in informal talks of the scientific harvest of our age, or discussed politics from a standpoint other than that of class interests."[4] A federation of Working Men's Social Clubs was set up from Oxford House—clubs which excluded politics, as well as alcohol and gambling. As one resident freely admitted, the approach was neo-feudal. A successful club "needs constant attention, tact and resource; it needs implicit confidence and friendliness between the organiser and his members; it needs the knack of mingling on terms of perfect equality with the men, while yet, by some *je ne sais quoi* in himself, he shall preserve their freely accorded social homage". This leader is, in fact, "the *Kyning* of the new feudalism which is springing up in this present time, raised on the shields of his kin, for that in their hearts and consciences they acknowledge his superiority".[5] Consequently the Federation can be "a very real engine of social regeneration", more "it may become *par excellence, the* crucible in which the 'two nations' may be fused into one".[6]

The leaders of the Federation (Oxford House for the East End Clubs, Trinity Court for the Surrey side) placed a great deal of importance on games as a means of inculcating "the true sportsman spirit", that spirit "which impels sixteen youths of the dark and light blue to toil

[1] Eager, *op. cit.*, 194-5.
[2] *Ibid.*, 196. Both Henson and Ingram later became bishops.
[3] Barnett, *op. cit.*, 484-5.   [4] *Ibid.*, 461-2.
[5] Gerard Fiennes, "The Federation of Working Men's Social Clubs", in Knapp, *op. cit.*, 218. He adds: "In democratic London a *kyning* is all-essential. It is a strange feature to those who understand club life, how utterly inept the working man is for running the concern on his own." Working men cannot put confidence "in any of their own kind" to guide things. " 'We want one of you Oxford House gentlemen to work it for us' that is the reply of almost every club to an enquiry as to what their requirements are."
[6] *Ibid.*, 220.

and moil at the oar for weeks for the glory of their Varsity"; so
self-restraint, good temper in adversity, the interest of the community
before self, were emphasised. Outings were organised to bring the
two nations together, friends with country places within easy reach of
London being asked to invite members. As the appeal ran, "it will not
mean much—permission to roam over their grounds and disport
themselves in such ways as they please; a little tea and light refreshments".[1]

Toynbee Hall, however, provided a very wide variety of social and
educational activities—an actual "bill of fare" for a single week
"taken haphazard" is given in Booth's famous survey of London; it
runs to nearly two pages and includes ten lectures, nine reading parties,
two literary society meetings, thirty-five classes of various kinds, a
concert, two "parties" and other activities. Barnett developed the
settlement as a centre of social and cultural activities of all kinds,
including university extension lectures (the Duke of Devonshire took
the chair at the inaugural meeting one year), and an enormous variety
of societies. Among the openers of debates were such working-class
leaders as Ben Tillett, Tom Mann, Herbert Burrows and George
Lansbury—Barnett was sympathetic to organised labour, often lending
rooms for trade union meetings, and personally supporting the dockers
in their great struggle of 1889.[2] Industrialists, aristocrats, politicians
and philanthropists were also frequently invited to open debates, to
discussions and services,[3] while some, for instance Sir John Gorst,
stayed as guests. Toynbee Hall also developed as a centre for the
study of social problems; it was here that William Beveridge among
others had his apprenticeship. Public libraries, the Whitechapel Art
Gallery, children's homes and in general a more systematic approach
to charity—these and many other projects originated at Toynbee.[4]

It is doubtful whether the Settlement movement ever affected the

---

[1] Fiennes, in Knapp, *op. cit.*, 224, 227. Toynbee Hall also arranged such outings.
[2] The Central Strike Committee, including Burns, Tillett and Tom Mann, and sixty
others were entertained to supper after their victory. Barnett, *op. cit.*, 458.
[3] West Enders were specially invited to the annual service at Advent Sunday: "There
were the wonderful gatherings in Church on Advent Sunday," writes Mrs. Barnett,
"when the Aristocracy, Plutocracy, Democracy all met in that little East End Church to
pray to *Our* Father. On these occasions the Canon never failed to take the wind out of
the sails of the *whole* congregation by pointing to duties left undone and waiting."
Ibid., 114.
[4] Barnett had a vision of Toynbee as a centre of an East London University. In 1887
and 1890 Wadham House and Balliol House were opened as residential hostels for
students and part of the Toynbee foundation (cf. Barnett, *op. cit.*, 405-6). R. L. Morant,
later much concerned with the 1902 Education Act, was for a short time resident at
Toynbee Hall, acting as "Censor" for one of these houses.

mass of the working class, even in the areas surrounding the settlement, though its impact is difficult to assess. Many of the activities evidently appealed more to the lower middle class than the workers,[1] and it is this point that is emphasised in Arthur Morrison's satire of the movement in A Child of the Jago: "and there were classes, and clubs, and newspapers . . . whereby the life of the Hopeless Poor might be coloured, and the Misery of the Submerged alleviated. The wretches who crowded to these benefits were tradesmen's sons, small shopkeepers, and their families, and neat clerks, with here and there a smart young artisan of one of the especially respectable trades. . . . Other young men, more fortunately circumstanced, with the educational varnish fresh and raw upon them, came from afar, equipped with a foreign mode of thought and a proper ignorance of the world and the proportions of things, as Missionaries."[2]

Barnett himself, in touch with many leading politicians, both Liberal and Tory ("On Wednesday we dined with the Courtneys. Balfour, Morley, Asquith, the next Duke of Devonshire, and Hobhouse there"), became a popular figure, although he had his enemies among reactionaries, including the Lord's Day Observance Society. Sympathetic to Labour, outspoken, exceptionally energetic, often extremely perceptive, he tirelessly propagated the concept of an organic society as a mixture of classes—a social hierarchy. Despite his radicalism he was overwhelmed by the Jubilee celebrations of 1887, by the sight of an excited and happy population, like children waving their flags. "Really the week has been an education," he wrote to his brother. "It has shown the value of a big idea and the need for a big expression to convey the idea. People have lived down to the mean side of profit and loss and have been mean; they can live up to the big idea of a nation and be good-tempered and generous. Then big shows are wanted to express the big idea. The week, too, has shown that content is more than discontent, the force for order stronger than the force for disorder."[3] Perhaps the scene that Barnett witnessed and the attitudes that lay behind it best expresses the social ideal of the Settlement movement.

1 "A reproach sometimes levelled at Toynbee Hall, that it caters rather for the 'middle than for the 'working' class, does not apply, at least, to the Debates" (Toynbee Hall Report for 1898, quoted in Barnett, op. cit., 368).

2 A. Morrison, A Child of the Jago (1896), 19-20; Toynbee Hall is here referred to as "the East End Elevation Mission and Pansophical Institute".

3 Ibid., 467-8.

4. UNIVERSITY EXTENSION

One further movement concerned primarily with the education of the working class may be examined—the University Extension movement which, first taking organised form in 1873, reached its climax in the late 1880s and early '90s when up to 60,000 students were attending lectures and classes.[1] A large proportion of these were organised by Oxford and Cambridge, this development of extra-mural work being a response not only to working-class needs but also to the demand for higher education on the part of women and of the lower middle class—both effectively excluded from the ancient universities. Here, however, only the working-class aspect of the movement will be examined.[2]

In the 1860s there was a new demand for education in some industrial areas, recalling Chartist and socialist educational activities in the 1830s and '40s. Most striking was the case of the Lancashire cotton operatives during the cotton famine occasioned by the American civil war. Here, thousands of unemployed workers crowded the lectures on science and other subjects arranged by Henry Roscoe, an initiative intended in part to divert the men from serious outbreaks. In 1866-7 and again in 1870-9 Roscoe organised Penny Science lectures for working men, filling the Free Trade Hall in Manchester with audiences of nearly 4,000 for lecturers like Tyndall and Huxley and following some of the lectures with classes for more intensive study.[3] In London, T. H. Huxley lectured widely to working-class audiences, audiences which, as he later said, he preferred to any other addressed during his whole career. Well before the University Extension movement got under way, therefore, a desire for education on this level had found expression among sections of the workers.

This was highlighted by the fact that two of the four memorials presented to Cambridge University in 1871, asking for an organised system of university extension, came from the Crewe Mechanics'

[1] The estimate was made by the Bryce Commission. T. Kelly, *A History of Adult Education in Great Britain* (1962), 223.

[2] For the movement as a whole, see Kelly, *op. cit.*, 216-42, and J. F. C. Harrison, *Learning and Living, 1790-1960*, 219-45. There is a good deal of contemporary literature on the early Extension movement, but no recent history of it has yet been written. Reference may be made to R. D. Roberts, *Eighteen Years of University Extension* (1891), and W. H. Draper, *University Extension, 1873-1923* (1923).

[3] H. E. Roscoe, *The Life and Experience of Sir H. E. Roscoe* (1906), 124-31; Kelly states that "under the auspices of the Council of the Cotton Relief Fund, adult elementary schools were established throughout the district in disused mills and other converted premises . . . during the winter of 1862-3 there were at one time 48,000 men and youths in attendance", *op. cit.*, 218n.

Institute and the Rochdale Equitable Pioneers' Society.[1] James Stuart, Cambridge don and later Professor of Mechanics, who took the lead in organising extension work, had already been invited to lecture on science to these organisations, as also to women's groups in the north of England. At Crewe he lectured to railway workers and at Rochdale attracted audiences of nearly 1,000. "It was my experience at Rochdale," he writes, "that not only greatly encouraged me, but that determined me to go on—that opened my eyes, in fact, to what was needed, and that gave me confidence, never since shaken, that the demand existed if the supply was only forthcoming."[2]

What of the supply of teachers ready and willing to lecture to working-class students? The Royal Commissions of the 1850s and early 1870s and subsequent legislation had done a good deal to transform Oxford and Cambridge, but it was still to all intents and purposes impossible for the lower middle class or working class to gain entry as students; despite changes the ancient universities remained essentially seminaries for the ruling class, buttresses of church and state. But both universities were concerned to maintain their supremacy in the educational field generally and here, it seemed, was an opportunity to meet criticisms of exclusiveness without risking any fundamental transformation. Some such system had, therefore, been suggested earlier when in 1850 William Sewell of Oxford proposed the establishment of professorships at Manchester, Birmingham and elsewhere: "by originating such a comprehensive scheme," he wrote, "the universities would become, as they ought to be, the great centres and springs of education throughout the country, and would command the sympathy and affection of the nation at large, without sacrificing or compromising any principle which they are bound to maintain". The proposal was supported by Dr. Pusey, leader of the High Church party, while Mark Pattison, leading university reformer, argued that a national university "should be co-extensive with the nation; it should be the common source of the whole of the higher (or secondary) instruction for the country".[3]

It was with this sentiment in mind that Stuart framed his appeal to Cambridge University for an organised system of extension lectures in 1871. There was a definite demand for such teaching: "I believe it is incumbent on us to supply it," he wrote, ". . . and I believe that

---

[1] The other two were from the North of England Council for Promoting the Higher Education of Women and the Mayor and other inhabitants of Leeds.
[2] Quoted in Harrison, *op. cit.*, 222-3.   [3] *Ibid.*, 220-1.

some such system which will carry the benefits of the university through the country is necessary in order to retain the university in that position with respect to the education of the country that it has hitherto held, and to continue in its hands that permeating influence which it is desirable that it should possess."[1]

The university responded by organising experimental courses in Nottingham, Leicester and Derby in 1873; two years later a permanent organisation was established at Cambridge. In 1876 the London Society for the extension of university teaching was formed while Oxford, spurred on by Benjamin Jowett, made "a tentative beginning" in 1878; here A. H. D. Acland was the first secretary but the work expanded rapidly after 1885 when Michael Sadler took his place. In 1886 the Victoria University, comprising colleges at Manchester, Liverpool and Leeds followed suit, as also Durham. The University Extension movement was well under way. It should be noted, however, that neither Oxford nor Cambridge devoted much resources to it—the lectures had to be self-supporting, i.e. paid for by the fees of the students who attended; Oxford and Cambridge paid no salaries to lecturers, confining financial support almost entirely to the salary and expenses of the organiser.[2]

University extension began its operations, as Peers puts it, "just when the golden age of Victorian prosperity was approaching its decline", and some years before the socialist revival of the mid-1880s. Its context was that of the formation of the great Liberal party led by Gladstone, combining employers and workers under the leadership of the former. "By the end of the age of Victorian prosperity," continues Peers, "there had been a temporary reconciliation of opposing class interests. *Laissez-faire* was apparently justified in its results and the teachings of orthodox political economy were widely accepted." He quotes a leading member of the Executive Committee of the Northumberland Miners' Union: "Trade organisations have secured the

---

[1] Quoted in Kelly, *op. cit.*, 221. "He was also apprehensive of impending criticism of the universities from various outside quarters and felt that 'their position would be greatly strengthened if they ministered to the needs of a wider area than they did' "; Harrison, *op. cit.*, 222.

[2] With one exception, Hudson Shaw—an extension lecturer—was guaranteed a minimum income and made a fellow of Balliol (Kelly, *op. cit.*, 235). The failure of Oxford radically to support this movement was severely criticised by Barnett in the early twentieth century. *The Oxford Magazine*, in reply, wrote: "Canon Barnett ought to know something about Oxford, but his statement about University Extension work is reckless to a degree beyond even what we are accustomed to in our critics. He says that Oxford gives hardly any direction and practically no financial support to it. . . . The university gives a grant of £550 a year and privileges which are worth at least £150 more." Barnett, *op. cit.*, 501.

settlement of trade disputes by conciliatory methods. The energy that used to be spent on industrial quarrels is now free to be spent on educational work."[1] It was among the miners of Northumberland and Durham that University Extension had its greatest success—and also, significantly, its greatest failure.

The agreement between workers and employers in the north-eastern coalfields, reached by "conciliatory methods", introduced a sliding scale of wages, so guaranteeing a profit without ensuring a living wage. But when the price of coal was high wages were good, and it was in this situation that the most striking chapter in the history of university extension opened. Courses in political economy were started as early as 1879, but in 1880 the movement really got under way with over 1,300 working miners attending lectures in political economy in five centres. On the Tyneside, colliery owners subsidised the scheme, so keeping the cost of the courses down, and these shortly covered a wide range of subjects including science, literature and mining technology. At this time, writes Welbourne in his history of the Northumberland and Durham miners, "there was an unprecedented and perhaps un-equalled awakening of interest in education. . . . In 1883 the University Extension lectures were given the official support of the Durham Miners' Association. At union meetings, in the union circulars, the advantages of study were urged upon the miners. Over a thousand men attended the lectures given that winter, losing wages, and paying fines for shifts missed to learn elementary science, history, and political economy. The local secretary of the movement paid a high tribute to the intelligence of his new pupils, to their straightforwardness of speech, and their appreciative attention. . . . The local newspapers devoted whole pages to articles on mining science, law and history, even to subjects more abstruse such as economics and philosophy." He adds that secular education of this kind, combined with political interest "dealt heavy blows to the old enthusiasm for Methodist religion. Economic law was quoted where once the Sermon on the Mount had sufficed. On the union banners party cries replaced the Bible texts."[2]

The often extraordinary efforts made by the miners to attend and develop these classes, whatever the difficulties, have been vividly

---

[1] Robert Peers, *Adult Education, a Comparative Study* (1958), 49, 56-7.

[2] E. Welbourne, *The Miners' Unions of Northumberland and Durham* (1923), 204-5. "All at once," wrote a Northumberland miner, "Cambridge and everything pertaining to it becomes interesting, and the class to which the lecturer belongs is regarded with generous feelings." R. D. Roberts, *Eighteen Years of University Extension*, 37.

described by R. D. Roberts, at one time the local secretary.[1] But, after this brief and sudden upsurge, indicating great potentialities and enthusiasm among the working class, the movement died rapidly away. "Everyone has heard," wrote Margaret McMillan in 1911, "how, in the North Country, the miners and colliers made up an audience that delighted the heart of the greatest teachers, such, for example, as Huxley . . . the history of University Extension has no more thrilling chapter than that which tells how, after grim labour, colliers walked miles to hear the lectures, and how, later, some actually became class leaders themselves and began to teach what they had learned to others. . . . But the candle, lighted in the North, went out suddenly. It was quenched by a great miners' strike. After the struggle there was no money for the paying of fees or the buying of books."[2]

Certainly the great four months' strike of 1887, consequent on a wage reduction of $12\frac{1}{2}$ per cent, reduced the miners to penury—but it may be questioned whether it was only economic factors which quenched the movement. During the bitter struggles of subsequent years the nature of the sliding scale was exposed and with it the concept of class reconciliation, so that the workers increasingly moved to politics. This was the period when socialism first began to win a hearing in the north-east, when the workers, moving towards political action, elected their own representatives to Parliament. The political economy taught in extension classes had begun to lose its flavour and it was no longer to Oxford and Cambridge that the workers looked for intellectual leadership so much as to Tom Mann, J. L. Mahon, H. M. Hyndman and William Morris. In 1887, for the first time, socialist speakers, including Hyndman and Morris, were invited to the miners' annual demonstration on Easter Monday.

Elsewhere University Extension made definite contact with the working class in parts of Lancashire and Yorkshire, where many local co-operatives supported the movement financially, and in London, where the work was to some extent subsidised by City Companies and an educational trust.[3] Between 1888 and 1896 Hudson Shaw, a very popular lecturer, held working-class audiences at the Oldham Co-operative Society which averaged 650 and rose to over 1,000 in his last year.[4] When Michael Sadler took over at Oxford, he made special

[1] R. D. Roberts, *Eighteen Years of University Extension*.
[2] M. McMillan, *The Child and the State* (1911), 148-9.
[3] Kelly, *op. cit.*, 225; Roberts, *op. cit.*, 59-60.
[4] Harrison, *op. cit.*, 236. "In Hebden Bridge, a town with a population of some 5,000, 600 working people attended his lectures in 1888-9." *Ibid.*

efforts among the co-operative societies in the two counties, but the working-class centres established tended to have a short life; of twenty-nine Oxford Extension centres in Yorkshire during the period 1885-1902 only six had an actual majority of working-class students. In the country as a whole working-class students did not amount to more than 20-25 per cent of those attending.[1] On the whole, therefore, University Extension developed very much as a middle-class affair. Ladies of leisure, schoolgirls and boys, pupil-teachers and others from the lower middle class, sometimes professional men and their families, tradesmen—these predominated.[2] In these circumstances it was inevitable that the local committees organising the courses should also be dominated by the middle class. At Leeds, for instance, Sir Edward Baines was President, "and prominent clergymen, lawyers, and their womenfolk" comprised the majority of the committee. "It was not to be wondered at," comments Harrison, "that such working-class representatives as there were from the Working Men's Hall and the Co-operative Society scarcely felt that it was their organisation," the result was "a predominantly middle-class audience".[3] As has been suggested, even at Toynbee Hall in the centre of the East End, where concerted efforts were made, the experience was the same—"many of the students were lower middle-class rather than working-class, and nearly half of them came from other parts of the city";[4] the Extension lectures Barnett later wrote in some disillusionment, "are suited to the needs of the middle classes, and are generally supported and controlled by middle-class committees".[5]

This was also the experience of Edward Carpenter who in 1873 resigned his fellowship at a Cambridge college having "come to feel that the so-called intellectual life of the university was (to me, at any rate) a fraud and a weariness". Anxious to throw in his lot with

[1] *Ibid.*, 237.
[2] "The presence of so many young middle-class women as students . . . stamped the movement indelibly from the very beginning. Sadler estimated that in 1888-9 two-thirds of the students in the Oxford Extension courses were women." *Ibid.*, 231. This assessment is confirmed by R. D. Roberts writing in 1891: "The audiences proved to be thoroughly mixed. Not only did a large number of ladies attend, but persons drawn from various ranks of society, and of all ages above school age, while young men between the age of eighteen and twenty-five were, as a rule, present only in small numbers. Business and professional men, sometimes well over middle age, have constantly been regular attendants." *Op. cit.*, 13-14, see also 55.
[3] Harrison, *op. cit.*, 239. "The same was true," he adds, "of the Extension Committees at York, Halifax, Bradford and Sheffield."
[4] Kelly, *op. cit.*, 241 (from J. A. R. Pimlott, *Toynbee Hall* (1935), 60).
[5] Barnett, *op. cit.*, 500. For the Toynbee Hall experience of the Extension movement, about which Barnett was originally enthusiastic, cf. *ibid.*, 332-9.

the working class he took up Extension lecturing "because it seemed to promise this result. As a matter of fact it merely brought me into the life of the commercial classes." During the eight years that he worked in the movement "the bulk of the pupils . . . were of the 'young lady' class".[1] In 1881 he gave it up.

By the turn of the century it was clear that the Extension movement had failed to win the interest and enthusiasm of even a small proportion of the working class. This experience, as Harrison notes, was "similar to that of other middle-class organisations which sought to provide workers' education in the nineteenth century", one which resulted from a like cause, "namely, a totally inadequate realisation of the extent and depth of the sense of alienation among the working class".[2] In other directions university extension was successful; some of the centres, for instance, Reading and Exeter, developed as University Colleges, while the movement certainly played an important part in the fight for higher education for women. But for the attempt to reach the working class "the inescapable conclusion" is that, "despite limited success in a few localities", it failed.[3]

5. The Mass Political Party

Working Men's Clubs and Institutes, Adult Schools, Missions and Settlements, University Extension, all these were means whereby members of the upper and middle classes sought to make contact with and influence sections of the working class, not least in the light of a recognition of the new powers gained by the masses by extension of the franchise. A more direct means, however, was the formation of political parties with many auxiliary organisations on new lines.

This is not the place to trace the fortunes of the National Union of Conservative and Constitutional Associations formed, significantly, in 1868, nor of the National Liberal Federation (1877); nor to follow the attempts of Randolph Churchill and Joseph Chamberlain respectively to use these partially democratic mass organisations against the leaders of the Tory and Liberal parties. But if all this belongs to political rather than educational history what is of interest here is the relative success of efforts to involve large numbers of workers in political-

---

[1] Edward Carpenter, *My Days and Dreams* (1916), 72, 79.

[2] Harrison, *op. cit.*, 240.

[3] *Ibid.*, 243. Its deathknell in this respect was sounded by the foundation of the Workers' Educational Association in 1903; *ibid.*, 238.

educational activities; this helped to provide the mass support that had now become essential to the main political parties.

Local party organisation dates from the 1832 Reform Act, which required voters to take the initiative in registering. In the 1840s and '50s, the Conservatives were especially active in forming registration societies, often on class lines, all over the country. "Register! Register! Register!" was Peel's cry in his famous Tamworth speech of 1841. "The battle of the constituencies will be fought in the registration courts." Lancashire in particular proved fertile ground, societies of mill operatives being formed as early as the 1830s, often providing reading rooms (with Conservative papers) and other facilities, with honorary members recruited from the local gentry.[1]

Several of the North of England Working Men's Associations had large and active memberships; the Liverpool Working Men's Association, for instance, claimed in 1868-9 that it had over 1,500 paying members, and had canvassed over 1,000 Tory voters at the election.[2] But it was the Radical-Liberals in Birmingham who first showed the way to mass organisation of the rank and file electorate with the establishment of "the Birmingham Six Hundred"—or the "caucus" as it came to be called.[3] Electorally this was highly successful, as well as promising participation of the rank and file in policy making and Parliamentary affairs. Similar organisations were developed elsewhere and it was these that formed the National Liberal Federation in 1877.

In the past, of course, the entire control of political parties had been from the centre outwards, since the 1830s from the Carlton Club and the Reform Club. The need for mobilising working-class support, however, necessitated mass organisation—even if control was still to be retained at the centre—and here the Tories were particularly active among the working class in the 1870s, the man most directly responsible being John Gorst, an "anti-capitalist" Tory, and therefore

---

1 Janet H. Robb, *The Primrose League, 1883-1906* (1942), 13, 145.
2 *Ibid.*, 146.
3 The Birmingham caucus arose directly out of the 1868 election. Birmingham had been allotted three seats under the 1867 Reform Act, on the basis that, since about one-third of the voters were expected to vote Tory, this would allow the minority to be represented by one M.P. It was, therefore, a three-member constituency. The Liberals realised that if they organised and allocated all their votes correctly, they could win all three seats, which they proceeded to do. To win rank and file support for this line, and to organise it, a very democratic organisation was set up for the city. Each ward, in a public meeting, elected delegates to an Executive Committee; they also elected delegates, in private meetings, to a general Committee which included the Executive Committee. The General Committee had about 600 members—hence the title. *Ibid.*, 17-18. The fullest discussion of the development of the caucus is to be found in M. Ostrogorski, *Democracy and the Organisation of Political Parties* (1902), Vol. I, 161ff.

particularly suitable for the task. Gorst formed some clubs consisting only of working-class members, others of mixed membership. His campaign probably had some influence—as he certainly claimed himself —on the Tory victory of 1874.

If the general run of Tories and the "Whig" element in the Liberal party hated and feared the caucus, this was not the case with the meteoric Lord Randolph Churchill, who, with the cry of "Tory Democracy", bent all his efforts in the early 1880s to winning mass working-class support for Toryism. The caucus, he said revealingly, is "the only form of political organisation which can collect, guide and control for common objects large masses of electors".[1] It was Churchill who, with Gorst, A. J. Balfour and one other, formed the small group, the Fourth Party, which violently attacked Liberal and Tory leadership alike in the Parliament of 1880-4. This group, having initially come together as leaders of a wholly reactionary fight against Bradlaugh's admission to the House of Commons, went on to work in wider fields; conscious of the need for an auxiliary social and educational organisation to support Toryism, they launched on a sceptical party in December 1883 the Primrose League—an organisation which in less than twenty years claimed that it included in its membership nearly one and a half million workers and agricultural labourers.[2]

From the first the League had a ritual of its own—based on study of Masonic practices as well as those of working-class Friendly Societies— and degrees of membership: knights, dames, associates, etc., designed to retain the interest and allegiance of members. The declaration, drawn up by Gorst to be signed by every member ran as follows: "I declare, on my honour and faith, that I will devote my best ability to the *Maintenance of Religion*, of the *Estates of the Realm* and of the *Imperial Ascendancy of the British Empire*, and that, consistently with my allegiance to the Sovereign of these Realms, I will promote with fidelity and discretion the above objects, being those of the Primrose League."[3] As the founders wrote later, "Having in view the failure of Conservative and Constitutional Associations to suit the popular taste or to succeed in joining all classes together for political objects, it was desirable to form a new political society which should embrace all classes and all creeds except atheists and enemies of the British Empire."[4]

[1] Robb, *op. cit.*, 20.   [2] *Ibid.*, 148.
[3] W. S. Churchill, *Lord Randolph Churchill*, (1906), Vol. I, 258.
[4] Robb, *op. cit.*, 148. A contemporary (and amusing) analysis of the role and character of the Primrose League is given in Ostrogorski, *op. cit.*, Vol. I, 534-52.

As will be clear, the Primrose League, like some Settlements, had an essentially feudal flavour. In theory all members, whether Knights, Dames or Associates (the working-class rank), had equal rights in government of the local "habitations", but in practice control rested with the gentry and upper classes. The League proved more successful than the Conservative Working Men's Clubs partly because women and children were able to attend the social functions and because it did allow for some social mixing. Occasionally, however, the classes were separated at social functions, while it was apparently unusual for working men to receive the highest honours: "Amongst those who were summoned to receive promotion," wrote the *Primrose League Gazette* describing one such function, "was a working man, the sub-warden of Benson, who had the good fortune to be decorated with the Hon. Knight's Badge and Diploma."[1]

The League was particularly successful in the rural areas, of special significance to the Conservatives electorally. The techniques, ritual, and feudal overtones chimed in with traditional practices and attitudes among sections of the rural population and provided an alternative social and political centre to chapel life in the villages that was sharply anti-Tory—for Liberalism had made considerable inroads among the country population.[2] Community singing, entertainments, concerts, "a half hour of political oratory", social contact with the gentry—all this was capitalised through the League in the Tory interest; its "most conspicuous achievement was its success in penetrating and taking root in the rural areas." In 1888 over half the membership was said to be in agricultural areas and small towns.[3]

The League's main function was, of course, to carry on Conservative propaganda and education. League speakers and lecturers toured the "habitations", speaking on a great variety of subjects, particularly "the more picturesque aspects of foreign or overseas policy", and especially imperialist topics.[4] At all such meetings, "the Grand Council directed . . . there should be free discussion from the floor and that the meeting should be open", but the League representative should introduce the

---

[1] Robb, *op. cit.*, 149. The *Gazette* also described a social function at Bournemouth where Lady Shelley "provided tea in the Manor House for the Knights and Dames and refreshments in a large tent for the Associates". *Ibid.*

[2] *Ibid.*, 161ff.

[3] *Ibid.*, 173. "It is, in short," wrote the *Illustrated London News*, after describing a typical habitation meeting, "a return to Merrie England's traditions for the village folks. But mark! It is politics all the same: Every woman, as well as every man there, will feel a degraded and contemptible traitor if, when the election comes, they fail to work for 'the Primrose Cause'." *Ibid.*, 166.

[4] *Ibid.*, 150.

topic and summarise the discussion at the end. Both before and after the Dock Strike of 1889, the League frequently attacked trade unionism as a monopoly, and "persistently warned trade unionists to keep away from any tie-up with socialists". "Working men must be taught to think for themselves," wrote the *Gazette* with reference to a trade dispute, "and the Primrose League can supply them with the information upon which to base their mental processes."[1] It was, perhaps, a contradiction in terms, but this adequately sums up the main aim of the organisation.

By the late 1880s, therefore, there were new and apparently more democratic political machines at the disposal of the leaders of both main political parties which engaged in educational activities on a considerable scale. It was also at this period that daily newspapers began to achieve a mass circulation, newspapers which, while taking popular interests into account, propagated basically similar political views. This was a time when the Churches began to patch up quarrels and close their ranks, to turn towards the task of revitalising the religious life of the people. These were the general trends in the decades following the Reform Act of 1867, the background to more specifically educational initiatives which nevertheless were also framed to meet the new situation brought about by extension of the franchise, to ensure that democracy in this sense would not mean equality in others —above all would not open the doors to secularism and socialism. All this helps to explain why, despite the fears felt and expressed at the time, and despite the strong appeal of socialist propaganda, nearly forty years passed before the working class established an independent political party capable of gaining representatives in any number in Parliament.

Where there was not a frankly neo-feudal approach, the emphasis was on mitigating harsh conditions, forgetting grievances and antagonisms, on achieving not social justice but "social harmony". It was the conflict between two essentially opposed aims, between efforts to maintain the established order and working-class aspirations towards social justice that determined later educational developments.

[1] Robb, *op. cit.*, 159-61.

CHAPTER III

CLASS DIVISIONS IN EDUCATION—PUBLIC SCHOOLS AND ELEMENTARY SCHOOLS

THE initiatives described in the preceding chapter were in large part designed to bridge a gulf between two nations, a gulf which was simultaneously being widened and deepened by the consolidation of two quite separate systems of schooling. The educational policies of the decades 1850-70 had been consciously designed to establish different types of school for different social classes; schools for the upper and upper middle class, the professional middle class, the lower middle class. The seal was set on the process by the Education Act of 1870 which laid the foundations of a system of elementary schooling, bringing together hitherto scattered church schools and allowing for the development of board schools.

During the closing decades of the nineteenth century further steps were taken to develop a system of "public" schools; this was, as Kitson Clark has put it, "the final stage of the consolidation of the caste . . . of a new type of aristocracy".[1] At the other end of the scale a different kind of school system took shape. "The Education Act of 1870," wrote H. G. Wells, in his autobiography, "was not an Act for a common universal education, it was an Act to educate the lower classes for employment on lower class lines."[2] Notwithstanding recognition in some quarters of the dangers, and concerted efforts to mitigate them, there was a progressive consolidation of the two separate nations in terms of schooling. We may briefly look at the forms this took before returning to the more specifically educational demands of the working-class movement which arose from the rigours and injustice of the educational situation as immediately as did other demands from intolerable social and industrial conditions.

1. "Consolidation of the Caste"

By 1900 there had come into being a recognisable "system" of public schools, comprising some hundred schools with approximately 30,000

[1] G. Kitson Clark, *The Making of Victorian England* (1962), 273-4.
[2] *Experiment in Autobiography* (1934), I, 93.

pupils.[1] When the Clarendon Commission was appointed in 1861 to enquire into leading schools its attentions were confined to only nine institutions most of which had fallen on evil days, not least because of competition from new proprietary boarding schools such as Marlborough, Cheltenham, Radley and Rossall, founded from the 1840s onwards. This group comprised the ancient collegiate foundations of Eton and Winchester, as urgently in need of reform as the ancient universities, four schools in London—St. Paul's, Westminster, Merchant Taylors', Charterhouse—and three others which had at one time or another achieved national standing, Shrewsbury, Harrow and Rugby.[2]

As a consequence of the recommendations efforts were made to raise standards and to develop those which had local affiliations as national institutions. Harrow and Rugby provide classic examples of the techniques adopted and the success achieved in transforming schools into boarding schools, the latter acting as a model for the new public school system. But already from the 1850s other grammar schools had been shaking off local obligations and the process was hastened by the Endowed Schools Act of 1869 which legalised the use of endowments for purposes other than that for which they were originally made—the furtherance of local education. As the number of private boarders taken by headmasters and their assistants increased, governing bodies and parents were drawn in to support measures to exclude from the foundation sons of tradesmen, farmers and working men who lowered the social tone. Some schools naturally aspired to link up with independent boarding schools rather than remaining within the orbit of the developing system of grammar schools, and as the policy of exclusion came to fruition steps were taken to provide some form of organisation free from all external—or democratic—control; moves in this direction naturally both hastened and guaranteed the development of a specific public school ethos.

(i) The Alienation of Grammar Schools

The process whereby old-established grammar schools were alienated from their locality can be traced at various stages from the 1850s onwards. When Thring became headmaster of Uppingham in 1853 he found twenty-eight boarders on roll; fifteen years later he had

[1] There were 102 schools in membership of the Headmasters' Conference in the summer of 1903 (information from H.M.C.). The figure of 30,000 may be an over-estimate.

[2] Though later reference was usually made to the "seven" great public schools, Merchant Taylors' and Charterhouse (London day schools) being omitted.

raised the number to 268 and was claiming public school status. There
were only fifty pupils, mostly day boys, at Repton when Pears became
headmaster in 1854; when he retired twenty years later there were 260
boys nearly all of whom were boarders.[1] Pears was one of those who
gave evidence to the Schools Inquiry Commission, the outcome of
which was the Endowed Schools Act; in his evidence he emphasised
the social pressure to exclude local boys from the school[2] and in 1874,
under the Act, a scheme was drawn up whereby these were provided
for in a separate elementary school.[3] This also introduced other changes,
including reform of the governing body, and its inauguration made
Repton, in the words of the school's historian, "*de jure* as well as *de
facto* a public school" marking "the beginning of a new epoch in the
history of the school".[4]

The method of using part of the endowment to establish a local
school of lower status for tradesmen's sons named after the founder,
so formally meeting local claims and freeing the grammar school to
develop as a boarding school, was that adopted successfully at Harrow
and Rugby. The "Lower School of John Lyon" was established at
Harrow in 1876 and in 1878 Rugby followed suit with the "Lower
School of Lawrence Sherriff". Others took the same course. At
Oundle, a school under the control of the Grocers' Company, the
"Laxton Modern School" was set up in 1876; this, according to the
headmaster's prospectus, was "a separate Second-grade department . . .
for the education of sons of tradesmen and farmers".[5] The results of
this step were commended in a report by a representative of the
Grocers' Company, the Rev. T. W. Burbidge; he warmly "approved
of the elimination from the Upper School of a lower-class element,
composed chiefly of day-boys from the neighbourhood, now provided

---

1 Alec Macdonald, *A Short History of Repton* (1929), 166.

2 Wealthy people, applying for places for their sons, invariably asked "What is the
character, station and position of the home boarders?" When Pears answered that they
were "of all classes down to the sons of blacksmiths and washerwomen" applications were
immediately withdrawn. Village children ("home boarders") had to be separated from
the others out of school or " he (Pears) should have a constant fear of their being ill-
treated". "It is not the fault of the boys," he added, "it is the fault of society. I think. . . .
I never saw a man yet who would send his boy to a school in order to associate with
those lower than himself." *Report of Schools Inquiry Commission* (1868), Vol. IV, 443-9.

3 At first such of these boys "as were eligible" were allowed to go on to Repton, but
an amended scheme in 1906 provided for them to receive grammar school education at
schools in Derby and Burton. Macdonald, *op. cit.*, 194.

4 *Ibid.*, 194, 197. Most of the buildings in use at this time were erected by the headmaster mainly at his own expense (*ibid.*, 199); much the same thing happened at Uppingham and elsewhere.

5 William George Walker, *A History of the Oundle Schools* (1956), 390. The school was
later called the "Sir William Laxton Grammar School" (1883).

for in an entirely separate school. 'The Upper School, which is a first grade Public School, is now composed exclusively of sons of gentlemen, almost all being boarders' ". It was his conclusion that "judicious separation of classes by the present headmaster has proved a decided success"; though the townspeople, who fought this development, saw matters differently, in terms of an "invidious social distinction between the two Schools".[1] In 1881 there were 172 boys at the Oundle school proper (as against 26 in 1851), while 38 local boys attended the Laxton school.[2]

Sherborne, a school founded in the reign of Edward VI, provides another example. Here, as in the case of Uppingham, there had already been a fundamental change in the character of the school before the Schools Inquiry Commission was appointed and their commissioner, visiting the school in 1865, had been very favourably impressed. "Whatever may have been the class of boy for whom the founder intended to provide education," he reported, "there can be no doubt as to the class who now actually use it, and what might have been a mere provincial grammar school at present bids fair to rank among our great public schools. . . . If intended as a mere local school," he added, "it has completely outstepped the circle of such intention and outgrown the limits of its early constitution."[3] The presence of foundationers, however, still remained something of a problem until this and other matters were cleared up by the new statutes of 1871 which followed the Endowed Schools Act. Only in one quarter was there "sustained and organised opposition to the new state of things"—in the town of Sherborne. The headmaster (Harper) had long tried to establish a "middle school" for local boys, and had incurred criticism. "Now, with the changes of 1871, he was accused of finally sloughing off responsibility for the higher education of local boys and a good deal of indignation was voiced in consequence." In the end a local school was established (Foster's school) by amalgamating local charities, "with the right to have scholarships to the King's School (Sherborne, B. S.), and the promise of a subsidy if necessary". So the division was made, the events of the years 1865-71 constituting "an outstanding landmark

---

[1] Walker, op. cit., 412, 426. T. H. Green, who had visited the school on behalf of the Schools Inquiry Commission in 1866, would have approved: "The manners of the boys struck me as rough," he had then written, ". . . It can scarcely be said, indeed, that the problem of combining the education of the classes, roughly distinguished as professional and commercial, has been solved here, for a parent of the former class, if at all fastidious, would not find the school quite what he wanted." Ibid., 732.

[2] Ibid., 417, 332.

[3] A. B. Gourlay, A History of Sherborne School (1951), 117.

in the history of the school".[1] The headmaster had come in 1850 to "a small school fallen on evil days"; he left it in 1877 as a flourishing public school of 300.

Giggleswick was another school to be transformed along these lines, in this case under the aegis of Sir James Kay Shuttleworth who, as Chairman of the Governors, fought hard and successfully for the adoption of a new scheme drawn up under the Endowed Schools Act (1869). The Endowed Schools Assistant Commissioner, D. R. Fearon, had first proposed an additional "Third grade school" "to provide for the satisfaction of local requirements" and, of course, the charging of fees for the main school, proposals in fact incorporated in the scheme of 1872.[2] "Giggleswick had been founded as a free school," writes its historian, "and the fundamental alteration in its character had been vigorously opposed by the inhabitants of the neighbourhood for close on ten years. They were fighting a losing battle."[3] In the outcome the local boys were directed to an elementary school. In 1868 there had been 66 boys in the school, 22 of whom were under twelve, and 41 between twelve and sixteen. By 1886 "the whole character of the school was transformed", it had a complete set of new buildings, boarding accommodation for 150 boys, and classrooms for 240.[4] The school had arrived as a full public school, one which concentrated on a "modern" education including science.

It is clear from these examples, which could be multiplied, that the most important condition for the transformation of an endowed grammar school into a public school was the exclusion of local foundationers—the sons of tradesmen, farmers or workers. This process was hastened all over the country as the upper middle class increasingly sought a public school education for their sons. "It is the fixed idea with every Englishman, in the lump," wrote Thring (headmaster of Uppingham) to a friend in the early 1870s, "that it is the thing to send

---

[1] Ibid., 120. The reorganisation under the 1871 statutes included a new governing body drawn from a wider radius, abolition of free places for local foundationers, the fixing of a fee, entrance by examination, "institution of entrance scholarships for boys living anywhere, based entirely on merit without reference to any residential qualification", institution of leaving exhibitions, and the vesting of visitorial rights in the Charity Commissioners instead of the Bishop of Bristol. According to the school's historian the new public school provided a "carrière ouverte aux talents" on a much wider basis than before.

[2] E. A. Bell, A History of Giggleswick School, 1499-1912 (1912), 175-6.

[3] "It is always an odious task to change the character of a benefaction, and to deprive people of long-standing privileges," he adds, "but on the other hand it is essential to look at the matter from a different standpoint." Ibid., 177-8.

[4] Ibid., 184.

a boy to a public school, and the ordinary English gentleman would think he lost caste by not doing so." "As regards class feeling," he added, "the thing wisely managed settles itself. As soon as it is possible to make a good boarding school work over a wide area, only those who have time to stay five, six, seven years or more at it have a chance. This at once silently decides that none but the monied classes can form the bulk of the school."[1]

It was by these means, then, that a number of local grammar schools broke through to public school status aided by the operation of the Endowed Schools Act and the ready assistance of the Commissioners appointed under it in revising statutes.[2] New governing bodies were appointed including national figures, representatives of church and state.[3] Fees were imposed, the curriculum to some extent brought up to date, obsolete restrictions swept away, laboratories and libraries provided as also the all-important chapel, and the whole paraphernalia of "houses" and playing-fields. So grammar schools which had originated as common schools serving their locality were alienated and transformed into residential schools, serving a single class.

Many proprietary boarding schools, founded since the 1840s on the joint-stock principle, also achieved public school status in the latter half of the century. Here there was no problem of removing foundationers. Such schools as Marlborough, Cheltenham, Rossall, the Woodard schools (Ardingley, Hurstpierpoint and Lancing) were expressly designed for members of the middle class, if sometimes for different sections of it; to these may be added schools like Mill Hill and The Leys founded somewhat earlier to cater for particular religious groupings. The only one of these schools which can be said to have had a struggle to reach public school status was Wellington, for the terms of the original scheme implied a somewhat limited education for the orphaned sons of Army officers; but Benson, the first headmaster and later Archbishop of Canterbury, was determined to create

---

[1] G. R. Parkyn, *Life and Letters of Edward Thring* (1900 edn.), 426.

[2] One of the last of the local grammar schools to develop in this way was Gresham's School, Holt.

[3] For instance, Uppingham had been governed by the original co-optative body laid down by Archdeacon Johnson in 1625, and consisting mostly of local men. On reorganisation this group was reduced to five out of twenty, the new governors including the Bishop and Dean of Peterborough, the Lord Lieutenant of Rutland, the Chairman of the Quarter Sessions, and two appointed by M.P.'s of neighbouring constituencies, as well as representatives of Oxford and Cambridge and of the headmaster and staff. *The Public Schools and the General Educational System* (hereafter referred to as *The Fleming Report*) 1944, 27.

a public school and succeeded in doing so.[1] The proprietary schools, with neither ancient statutes nor traditions to fetter them, were free to adapt their curriculum to middle-class needs, and tended to expand rapidly. By the late 1860s Marlborough and Cheltenham were already sending more boys on to Oxford and Cambridge than several of the nine "public" schools, and this was, perhaps, the most striking sign of their success.[2]

It was by no means only the better known proprietary schools that attained public school status, new schools were also being founded and the process was cumulative. "Kent was typical," writes the historian of King's School, Canterbury, an ancient Cathedral foundation, outlining this school's struggle for survival in the nineteenth century. "The headmastership of James Ind Welldon at Tonbridge, 1843-75, revitalised that rival to the King's School, while in East Kent Dover College was founded in 1871 and St. Lawrence College, Ramsgate, in 1879. In Canterbury itself was St. Edmund's School, moved in 1855 from London where it had been founded as the Clergy Orphans' School in 1749. If the King's School under Dr. Mitchinson had not responded to the demand of the Victorian middle classes for a public school education both economical and efficient, it would not have persisted among such competition."[3] So a growing number of exclusive and expensive boarding schools came into being in the closing decades of the nineteenth century to form a system of schooling framed to the needs of the upper class. That this system developed as an organised and cohesive one was largely because of the establishment of a body bringing those key men, the headmasters, together; a body that first came into being to ensure that developing public schools were not classified in the category of grammar schools, from which they had been at such pains to dissociate themselves—that indeed they should be free from any form of external guidance and control.

(ii) The Independence of Public Schools

It is significant that it was Thring, head of a school which had

---

[1] See David Newsome, *A History of Wellington College* (1959), 84-176.

[2] The Schools Inquiry Commission (1868) found that the nine "public" schools accounted for 557 undergraduates at Oxford and Cambridge, but of these the bulk came from Eton (161), Rugby (109), Harrow (107), and Winchester (74). Marlborough accounted for 76, Cheltenham for 41, and Rossall for 33. Of the endowed grammar schools Repton sent 36 and Uppingham 35. Of the 782 schools (grammar, proprietary and private) considered by the Commission 550 sent no pupils to Oxford and Cambridge, 89 sent one, and 43 two. *Fleming Report*, 27-8.

[3] D. L. Edwards, *A History of King's School, Canterbury* (1957), 134.

evolved from a local grammar school, who took the lead in setting up the Headmasters' Conference in 1869. This move resulted immediately from the need to organise opposition to the Endowed Schools Bill introduced in that year. But more generally there was a determination to keep public schools free from outside control in an era of democracy, a fear not only of popular control but also of secularising tendencies which might even lead to disestablishment of the church. Who could tell what the future might bring? Thring clearly expresses his fears in the course of arguing that Uppingham must be recognised as essentially a church institution, a position which he felt to be endangered. "I myself fully think that at no distant period a complete upheaval and readjustment of all English polity is at hand, and I wish in that hour of change and violence to have the generation know distinctly what Uppingham belonged to; after that let them do what they like."[1] He developed the point to Lord Lyttleton, the chief Endowed Schools Commissioner, when discussing the new scheme proposed for Uppingham. This, said Thring, would be satisfactory if the Church of England were not disestablished, but if it were, any school which had its connection with the Church now broken off would be regarded as state property and "seized". Lyttleton commented that this was speculative and "a great jump". "Perhaps," replied Thring testily, "but these are days of jumping; we are getting familiar with great jumps, and it is necessary to provide for jumps in these jumping days."[2]

A number of causes combined to unite the developing public schools against the very radical proposals of the Schools Inquiry Commission (which Thring regarded as "disastrous") and the subsequent first draft of the Endowed Schools Bill. The old-established public schools had already been legislated for in 1868 and their independence from direct state control was fully assured. The Endowed Schools Bill, however, brought in by the erstwhile Radical, W. E. Forster, was a very different matter, threatening these schools with considerable external control, and even proposing that the schools concerned cover the outlay. The Bill, intended to apply to all endowed schools, has been described as "a bold attempt to put the more pressing of the recommendations of the Commissioners into effect". The Commissioners appointed under it were to be empowered to alter school statutes in any way deemed "conducive to the advancement of education", to enquire into religious education, and above all, "to require the pupils to be examined centrally under the supervision of a special Educational Council" the

1 Parkyn, *op. cit.*, 151.   2 *Ibid.*, 164.

expenses of which were to be defrayed by a tax amounting to five per cent of the educational outlay of each school.[1]

Benson of Wellington played a leading role in organising resistance and it was at this stage that Mitchinson, headmaster of King's School, Canterbury, called a meeting of headmasters. "The Endowed Schools Bill was before Parliament," he wrote later; "it contained important provisions of a somewhat drastic character, largely concerning the future of grammar schools, and the fortunes of their masters; no common action was being taken." From this first meeting a deputation went to Forster.[2] Benson, who saw the Bill as a threat to his whole attempt to develop Wellington as a public school on a par with the greatest, who thoroughly objected to being placed "wholly and entirely at the mercy of the new council" and who was in a strong position since his governing body comprised many leading figures in church and state, wrote sharply protesting to such influential men as the Earl of Clarendon, Spencer Walpole, the Archbishop of Canterbury, Gladstone, as well as Forster himself. "Severance from the category of public schools," he wrote to Temple, head of Rugby, who disagreed with him, "and union with decayed grammar schools, consolidated doles of Parish Bread, and hitherto scholarless school houses" was what he objected to. "Half our boys are brothers of Eton, Harrow, Winchester, Rugby boys. . . . The change will shock them." Wellington College had "grander auspices, finer buildings, a finer race of boys, a more devoted and capable staff, than any of the others ('endowed' so called) and than several of the 'seven' . . . and there is no justice in calling us their labelled inferiors."[3]

Harper of Sherborne was another who stood out strongly against the threat of organised government control. He also felt that a school which was in all essentials a public school was being unfairly discriminated against. "It seemed cramping to its rising prospects if Sherborne . . . was merely to be classed with the great mass of smaller grammar schools, many of them far less successful."[4] He also "spared no pains to let his views be known in the highest quarters", and became deeply involved, with Thring, in the organisation of the Headmasters' Conference. But it was probably Benson's influence

[1] Newsome, op. cit., 136-7.   [2] Parkyn, op. cit., 169-71.

[3] Newsome, op. cit., 137, 140-1. The governing body of Wellington in 1898 included: The Prince of Wales (Edward VII), the royal Dukes of Connaught and Cambridge, Prince Christian, the Archbishop of Canterbury, the Duke of Wellington, the Earls Rosebery, Derby and Northbrook, several bishops and generals, and one field-marshal. Ibid., 276.

[4] Gourlay, op. cit., 118.

that was decisive. The governors of Wellington, among them royal princes, dukes and earls, "were able to exercise powerful influence against Mr. Forster's far-sighted Bill", and it was withdrawn. The new draft, introduced later in the year, was by comparison innocuous. Benson at least had won hands down; Wellington College was altogether exempt in so far as endowments less than fifty years old were ruled out.[1]

This Bill was enacted and, as we have seen, the Endowed Schools Act gave a great impetus to the development of grammar schools into full public schools; even Harper of Sherborne recognised that the changes were entirely beneficial. For Thring, however, a further battle lay ahead. His "real anxieties" began with the passage of the Act in 1869, which resulted in the appointment of Commissioners to re-constitute ancient trusts and foundations. Even the modified Act constituted, in his view, a threat, in particular to the religious character of his school, in general of external control.

In 1872 the draft scheme for Uppingham was sent down. "Thring found his worst fears confirmed" and was contemplating resignation if he could not get his way on a number of issues. He mobilised support particularly among influential parents and, at an interview with the Commissioners (Lord Lyttleton, H. J. Roby and Canon Robinson) fought strongly for his point of view. "The up-shot was the doctrine of non-interference and supervision was admitted," he wrote later, "and they declared themselves ready to modify all the obnoxious clauses."[2]

Thring regarded his struggle for the independence of these schools as having an unqualified success; "it cheered him to feel that the strong stand which he had taken for Uppingham would make the future safer for other schools," writes his biographer. In a letter to a friend Thring decried other schools as "limp", concerned in "a mere scramble for a little more money", patronage, etc. "If we had given way . . . all would have been lost . . . the fact of Uppingham standing firm for principle has been a turning point. . . . On the most important points of school management all the great schools had already given way and quietly accepted the dead hand of ignorant, external power . . . to prevent this is a cause worth fighting for, and now I can breathe again."[3]

[1] Newsome, *op. cit.*, 142. Wellington College was established in 1859.
[2] Parkyn, *op. cit.*, 166.
[3] Parkyn, *op. cit.*, 167. For a more detailed discussion of this struggle, see Peter Stansky "Lyttleton and Thring: a study in nineteenth century education", *Victorian Studies*, Vol. V, No. 3, March 1962.

This was the man who constituted the main force behind the Head-masters' Conference. "If they won't combine they won't," he wrote in October 1869. "If they will, my position as the leading school under this Bill makes me the fittest person to send out the summons." So, after the initial meeting called by Mitchinson, he sent a letter to sixty heads, stating that the government had already taken action, other measures were contemplated but that "nothing has been more remarkable than the absence of any decided voice from the great body, whose work is being handled by external power". Twelve heads attended a meeting in the middle of winter, most of them from grammar schools threatened by the Bill.[1] But a year later Thring was able to record in his diary: "The seven school delusion broken up. Winchester and Shrewsbury there; Eton has joined since. A committee formed to look after school interests. In fact a great power is certainly started." In 1879 the Confer-ence met at Eton; this, wrote Thring, "was a great success in putting the finishing stroke to its power and importance", it was "sumptuously received", the meeting at Eton was a "striking fact . . . and marks a remarkable epoch".[2]

The outcome of all this activity was to establish the public schools as independent schools, to free them from control by any elected body whatsoever; this clearly remains, as the official committee on "The Public Schools and the General Educational System" pointed out in 1944, "the most striking difference" between these and other secondary schools.[3] That this special status should have been sought and achieved at a particular moment, when political democracy was being extended, underlines the position attained by the public school system as a cornerstone of class society, a system both reflecting and perpetuating deep social divisions but beyond the reach of the normal democratic process. This system developed in the closing decades of the nineteenth century as a united and cohesive one. Then, as now, public schools, whatever their origin, could be ranked according to social prestige but the ranks were closed and in the Headmasters' Conference there was a leading body commanding extensive connections

[1] Those attending the first meeting came from Uppingham, Repton, Sherborne, Ton-bridge, Liverpool College, Bury St. Edmunds, Richmond (Yorks), Bromsgrove, Oakham, King's School (Canterbury), Felsted, Lancing and Norwich.

[2] Parkyn, op. cit., 177, 181.

[3] Fleming Report (1944), 43. The committee go on to say that many of these schools are constituted by, and in some respects subject to, schemes approved by the Board of Educa-tion as successor to the Charity Commissioners, and therefore the Board has certain rights in connection with surveillance of the endowments; "but, within these limitations, the schools are almost entirely independent corporations".

which could gain the ear of any government; a body formed at a
critical moment, geared to defend the public schools, as Thring put
it, in "the hour of danger".[1] It is significant that the Headmasters'
Conference should in 1894-5 refuse to give evidence to a new Royal
Commission on Secondary Education, in so doing following the
precedent of the unreformed Oxford and Cambridge colleges fifty
years earlier: a new privileged sector had become established that
would increasingly act as a brake on educational progress.

(iii) *The Public School Ethos*

What attitudes, interests and modes of behaviour, what kind of
general outlook did the public schools seek to inculcate? No other
country in the world paid such close attention at this time to the
education of its governing class. Certainly no other country could
boast so highly organised and segregated a system of schools in which
pupils could be submitted to consistent social and moral, as well as
intellectual guidance. In the boarding school the total environment
could be controlled to produce the desired result.

This aspect of boarding school education, the emphasis placed on
"the formation of character", was itself a product of the first stage in
the rise of the public schools. It was in the 1830s, with such men as
Thomas Arnold of Rugby, that efforts originated to civilise the
aristocratic, amoral and even anarchical boy republics which had come
into being in old-established schools, and turn these into institutions
primarily concerned with inculcating a particular moral outlook and
mode of behaviour. As Arnold's example was followed, both old and
new public schools became desirable educational institutions, increasingly well filled with sons of the affluent and respectable; as has often
been said, they played a key part in bringing about that fusion between
new industrialists and old aristocracy that gave birth to the Victorian
upper middle class.

This had been the first stage, but the era of reforming zeal had
passed when the public schools solidified into a system. The middle
class which, up to the 1850s, acted almost as a revolutionary force in
developing new institutions and transforming old ones to meet their
needs, had by the 1880s themselves become a governing class at a
time when new forces were beginning to make themselves felt. This
was no time for transformation but rather for consolidation. During
the closing decades of the century the public schools, in the words of

[1] Parkyn, *op. cit.*, 178.

their historian, entered "a period of fulfilment and stability". All of them, Eton included, were subject to the prevailing influence of the Victorian upper middle class.

Criticism, which had flared up again and again during the preceding century up to and including the 1860s, now died down. The new *status quo* was instead defended by "the ruling classes who patronised the public schools and the masters who taught in them, and the motives for their defence were a combination of direct self-interest, class snobbery, and that satisfaction of their social and economic needs which they believed the public schools gave".[1] The upper middle class "having won most of the moral and intellectual reforms which they had demanded, and having become part of the ruling class, deserted the banner of liberalism". They equally deserted the cause of educational reform. "By 1875 no one except a few spokesmen of the lower middle classes and of the relatively powerless working classes and a handful of intellectuals advocated any considerable change in the public schools."[2] Otherwise criticism gave place to admiration. Indeed, a mystique of public school life was cultivated which reached its climax in the poems of Henry Newbolt in the first decade of the twentieth century. "Public school alumni poured forth their joyous recollections of schooldays and their sentimental worship of their alma maters" in memoirs and novels; all were variations on the same theme.[3] All this went to make up "a wave of adulation unequalled in previous public school history".[4]

The general tendency in those schools was now towards a more rigid conformity, the production of a more stereotyped product than had been the case in the past, while the Arnoldian insistence on scholar-ship—or rather on learning—was giving place to athleticism and the Kingsley-Maurice ideal of "manliness".[5] For one thing the differences between the schools themselves were disappearing—"the public schools were developing into an almost completely standardised system of education"—partly as a result of common external pressures.[6] Consolidation of the house system, control by masters and prefects,

---

[1] E. C. Mack, *Public Schools and British Opinion since 1860* (1941), 106.

[2] *Ibid.*, 107.

[3] *Ibid.*, 136. "They are less novels than lyric poems, glorifying the greatness of public school ideals and of the boys who transmit them," writes Mack of Newbolt's and other novels. The school is seen as "the embodiment of heroic traditions". *Ibid.*, 205.

[4] *Ibid.*, 117.

[5] The transition in the public school ethos from the Arnoldian ideal to that of a philistine athleticism and conformity is brilliantly analysed in David Newsome, *Godliness and Good Learning* (1961).

[6] Mack, *op. cit.*, 120.

compulsory games, a strictly ordered day—every day, especially Sunday —all these led to a growing regimentation of school life where the ordinary boy was under perpetual supervision.[1] Social pressures in the form of an accepted way of wearing clothes, particular forms of speech and slang, played their part in inducing this conformity. "All the forces in public school life in the '80s and '90s," writes Mack, "worked against the creation of originality of thought or character." Most of those who passed through Eton or Harrow "learned at school to have their thoughts governed by what was good form and had their personalities moulded to the dominant type".[2]

In 1885 Henry Salt resigned from his post as a master at Eton and joined the Social Democratic Federation. "Little *is* taught," he wrote of the school, "and little *can* be taught" either of classics or modern subjects; the boys are "irretrievably unintellectual." Eton and the other public schools, he added, "have long been regarded as one of the chief bulwarks against socialism", a phenomenon they made no attempt to understand.[3] According to another contemporary, the then headmaster, Warre, represented the new type of public school master: "The Head cannot understand being on the side of any except one's own class, country and school." The interest in classical scholarship and a cultivated leisure which had characterised Eton in the past died away. "No one who now guided the destinies of Eton cared any longer for leisure, culture, or freedom of thought." Warre's ideal was neither intellectual nor aesthetic: "His great desire was for boys to acquire moral health, which meant chiefly honesty, loyalty and courage; they would then become the best baronets ever seen, loyal and true and kind, the salt of the earth; . . . honest secretaries of state, open-handed village squires, broad-minded bishops. They would serve their country unquestioningly, honourably and effectively."[4]

Much the same outlook prevailed in the early twentieth century. Norwood, a later headmaster of Harrow and by no means a hostile critic, described public school boys in 1909 as "ignorant of life,

---

[1] "Routine, drab even in restrospect, dictated the course of each day. Morning-school at seven began the day, followed by the long hours of ordered activity which were so arranged . . . to give to the authorities the satisfaction of knowing not only what any given boy should be doing at any particular moment, but 'exactly what the said boy would be doing at 3.30 p.m., six weeks hence'. Life was painfully parochial. The dormitory was the unit, and beyond that there was no opportunity for seeking congenial companionship. Even the Corps was arranged in sections by dormitories. 'We had thus,' writes Harold Nicolson, 'no privacy and no leisure, there was never open to us the choice between two possible alternatives. I entered Wellington as a puzzled baby and left it as a puzzled child.' " Newsome, *Wellington College*, 264.
[2] Mack, *op. cit.*, 124.   [3] Mack, *op. cit.*, 168-9.   [4] *Ibid.*, 129-30.

contemptuous of all outside the pale of their own caste, uninterested in work, neither desiring nor revering knowledge".[1] Freedom, individuality, intellectual excitement and curiosity, these qualities found little scope in schools which served purely class ends; instead such qualities were fostered as would favour an unquestioning acceptance and defence of the *status quo*. This also is the conclusion reached by the Fleming Committee, the only official enquiry into the public schools undertaken in nearly a century; from 1870 to 1914, the public schools became "more conventional, stereotyped and complacent" tending to produce a recognised type "loyal, honest and self-confident" but undervaluing qualities of imagination, sensibility and critical ability.[2]

This trend was intensified as imperialist sentiments were actively fostered, particularly under the impact of the Boer War. Schools such as Wellington, Cheltenham, Haileybury, Marlborough and Clifton now, through their old boys, played a direct part in Britain's expansion not only, of course, in South Africa, but throughout the African continent, on the Indian frontiers and elsewhere.[3] The death of the public schoolboy in some remote part of the world, surrounded by alien tribes, but dreaming of his school, is the subject of some of the best known of Newbolt's poems, which did much to spread a conception of public school education as a preparation not merely for leadership and combat, but for a hero's death. "To die young, clean, ardent; to die swiftly, in perfect health, . . . to die scaling heights . . . is that not a cause for joy rather than sorrow?"—so runs a sermon in a popular public school novel written immediately after the Boer War.[4] The system which had justified itself in terms of consolidating a caste now justified itself anew in the consolidation of an empire.

As the public schools expanded, connections with Oxford and Cambridge colleges were strengthened; in the half-century 1850-99 over four-fifths of students came from these schools, a higher proportion than ever before or after. Only seven per cent came from local grammar schools.[5] The colleges of the two ancient universities took up where the schools left off, performing much the same social function

---

[1] *Ibid.*, 282, quoted from C. Norwood and A. H. Hope, *The Higher Education of Boys in England* (1909).
[2] *Fleming Report* (1944), 29.
[3] A. H. H. Maclean, *The Public Schools and the War in South Africa* (1903), contains a great deal of material on the public schools' contribution to the Boer War. For its effect on a particular school see Newsome, *Wellington College*, 249-51.
[4] H. A. Vachell, *The Hill* (1905).
[5] These figures are derived from a sample investigation by Hester Jenkins and D. Caradog Jones in "Social Class of Cambridge Alumni", *British Journal of Sociology*, Vol. I, No. 2, June 1950. A further 12 per cent were educated in private schools.

if on a different level. Tightly integrated institutions, the public schools and ancient universities now constituted a more or less closed system of education which played a vital part in formulating and disseminating the values and upholding the status of the upper class in a deeply divided society.

2. The Organisation and Direction of Elementary Schooling

While the public school system developed in response to the demands and needs of the wealthy, elementary schools were being established in large numbers to provide instruction for that other nation, the poor. The Education Act of 1870 defined the elementary school as one in which fees did not exceed 9d. a week. The code of regulations under which such schools operated further defined their function; it was to provide strictly circumscribed teaching up to the school leaving age which, under local by-laws, could be as early as ten. This Act did not, as is often thought, introduce compulsory education, just as it did not make education free. It was not until 1880 that attendance finally became compulsory throughout the country, though even then "school pence" were still due—not until 1891 was an Act passed to make education free and even this did not cover all elementary schools. What the 1870 Act did, however, was to lay essential foundations on which could be built a highly organised and strictly segregated system of schooling designed specifically for the working class.

There had, of course, been elementary schools of various kinds long before 1870, primarily those which were directly descended from eighteenth century charity schools and the monitorial schools associated with the names of Bell and Lancaster, sponsored respectively by Churchmen and Dissenters. But when with the extension of the franchise attention became focused on the attitudes and outlook of the working class, educational deficiencies came clearly to light. Surveys of the great cities showed that tens of thousands of young children were not in school at all. Some escaped schooling altogether, the majority had no more than two or three years' teaching usually between the ages of six and nine. It was by no means merely a matter of lack of enthusiasm for education. The various voluntary bodies, each working on its own lines and receiving only minimal grants from the Committee of Council (precursor of the Board of Education), had not between them managed to provide anything like sufficient places to accommodate children of school age. It was a primary aim of the 1870 Act to

THE GOVERNORS OF WELLINGTON COLLEGE: SPEECH DAY, 1898

[Standing] * General   General   The Earl of   The Archbishop of   The Bishop of   Field-Marshal   Sir C.   Sir W.
Sir D. Probyn   Sir G. Higginson   Northbrook   Canterbury   Winchester   Sir L. Simmons   Ryan   Anson

[Seated]   The Duke of   The Earl of   H.R.H. The Duke   H.R.H. The Prince   H.R.H. The Prince   H.R.H. Prince   The Bishop of Oxford   Col. The Hon.
           Wellington   Derby   of Connaught   of Wales   H.R.H. The   Christian   (Dr. Stubbs)   Sir P. Talbot
                     (Dr. Temple)   (H.M. King Edward VII)   Duke of Cambridge

* Sir Arthur Blomfield, the architect (not a Governor)

FREE DINNERS FOR POOR CHILDREN, 1890

A PENNY DINNER FOR BOARD SCHOOL CHILDREN, 1885

"fill the gaps", but if this was hardly a far-sighted policy the organisational structure initiated offered promise for the future; under the Act School Boards were to be elected empowered to spend on education funds raised by local rates.

In 1872 there were some 8,700 children in board schools; eleven years later these schools catered for over a million pupils and by 1896 for just over two millions. The Church of England and, if on a smaller scale, the Roman Catholics, also made an all-out effort during these years—from just over a million children in voluntary schools in 1870 the figure rose to 2,500,000 in 1896.[1] Though there were more pupils in voluntary than in board schools at the close of the century it was the latter, supported by greater financial resources, that made the running. Manchester provides a case in point. In 1875 the School Board was conducting five schools with an average attendance of 1,151 pupils; seven years later it was responsible for 16,849 pupils in 38 schools, 13 of which had been built by the Board, the rest having been purchased or transferred.[2] The average number of pupils present weekly at all elementary schools in the city (both board and voluntary) rose by 20,000 in a decade—from 30,581 in 1871 to 50,855 in 1881.[3] It was chiefly children between the ages of five and eleven, previously often running wild in the streets, who were effectively brought into school and, therefore, under the control of local authorities.

From 1880, when attendance was generally compulsory, great efforts were made by the authorities to ensure that it was regular, that there was a high and constantly rising level of attendance. Parents could be fined if their children stayed away and it was the "Board man's" job to rout the defaulters out, sometimes with the aid of the police;[4] in addition the school's grant was partly dependent on the attendance figures and, as a result, there was insistence on an elaborate system of registration. It was, of course, particularly difficult to improve attendance figures so long as fees were charged, but the proportion gradually rose so that during the '80s and '90s the great majority of children were finally brought under the umbrella of the elementary school.

This vast and growing system of schools was administered, before the creation of the Board of Education in 1899, by the Education

---

1 *Report of the Committee of Council on Education, 1896-97*, p. lxxiii. The figures refer to the number of children in average attendance.

2 Many "British" and other schools run by Dissenters were transferred to School Boards when they were set up.

3 *Report of the Royal Commission on Technical Instruction* (1884), Vol. V, 149.

4 See the illustration opposite page 145.

H

Department, a government office staffed by Oxford and Cambridge graduates with good connections; it was inspected by Her Majesty's Inspectors, also products of the ancient universities who were able to get a "place".[1] What was their attitude to the schools for which they were responsible? According to Kekewich, who became head of the Education Department in the late 1890s, "the staff of distinguished and aristocratic scholars from the Universities"—of whom he gives a vivid description—"treated elementary education and elementary teachers with contempt". They had no use for village Hampdens, no conception that a child from the "lower" classes might possess a modicum of brains. "A ploughman's son was destined to be a ploughman as his father was." The great majority of the higher officials, Kekewich adds, had probably never seen an elementary school; the existence of the National Union of Teachers was not even recognised.[2] The testimony of an inspector, who was later able to look back critically on his activities as a young man, is also on record. It was his job to conduct the annual examination of children in elementary schools in order to assess the grant due, for this was the era of "payment by results" in relation to teaching as well as attendance. "For me," he writes, "they were so many examinees; and as they all belonged to the 'lower orders', and as (according to the belief in which I had been allowed to grow up) the lower orders were congenitally inferior to the 'upper classes', I took little or no interest in my examinees either as individuals or as human beings, and never tried to explore their hidden depths."[3]

The officials were part of a machine controlled from above but some inspectors, in direct contact with the schools, were prepared to draw attention in their reports to the educational conditions of the poor by comparison with those in better schools. One, for instance, contrasts the conditions in two local grammar schools, each with 120 pupils and staffed by six or seven "well educated adult teachers", with those in a typical elementary school where the same number of children of

[1] "It happened by specially good fortune that my father knew two of the Ministry, one of whom was in the Cabinet. The services of both statesmen were invoked," writes E. M. Sneyd-Kynnersley who was appointed in the early 1870s. H.M.I., Passages in the Life of an Inspector of Schools (1908), 76. G. W. Kekewich, later Secretary of the Board of Education, also gives an amusing description of his original appointment, which was also by nomination. His father, an M.P., was a connection by marriage of Sir Stafford Northcote, Chancellor of the Exchequer. His interview (with the Duke of Marlborough and the Secretary of the Department) was "of exceedingly short duration, and included no inquiry whatever into my knowledge of education or of the system then in operation, of which I was of course absolutely ignorant." The Education Department and After (1920), 3-7.

[2] Kekewich, op. cit., 11-12.

[3] Edmond Holmes, In Quest of an Ideal (1920), 64.

the same age are taught by "one adult teacher assisted by two pupil teachers, who very possibly are raw and ignorant children of fourteen or fifteen".[1] In fact the overall staffing ratio in elementary schools was some 35 to 1 (in 1897) even counting pupil teachers as full staff members; many schools had only one adult teacher.

The necessary corollary was a rigid and severe discipline. "To look at a photograph of a class in a school of those days," writes G. A. N. Lowndes, "hands folded on the rail in front, backs straight, eyes on the teacher, is to realise something of the iron code of authority which was in many schools a seemingly inseparable concomitant of the system, particularly where, as was frequently the case, from 70 to 120 children had to be controlled by a single teacher, or even sometimes a pupil teacher, for the allotted 5½ hours. The amount of punishment which was inflicted in the five day week must in many cases have far exceeded that now inflicted in five months or even five years in most modern schools. In boys' schools every sum wrong, every spelling mistake, every blot, every question which could not be answered as the fateful day of examination drew near, was liable to be visited by a stroke of the cane." A mature pupil-teacher, in the years 1889-93, is quoted in corroboration: "I never remember seeing my headmaster in school when he had not a cane hanging by the crook over his left wrist. Every assistant master had a cane and so had the pupil teachers, but we were not allowed to have a crook so that if any questions arose they were only pointers. There were no backs to the desks and backs of boys were straightened by means of a stroke of the cane."[2]

The system of "payment by results" dominated the elementary schools during this period. Its immediate aim was radically to reduce government expenditure on elementary education, and in this it was successful.[3] Its further aim was to concentrate the efforts of the teachers on the 3 Rs (reading, writing and arithmetic), and in this it was partially successful, but only at the cost of forcing entirely mechanical drill methods of teaching on the schools. It was this aspect of the Revised Code, introduced by Robert Lowe in 1862,[4] that was from the start sharply criticised by such men as Kay Shuttleworth, who believed that education should be concerned with the development of the rational

[1] Quoted by Frank Smith, *A History of English Elementary Education, 1760-1902* (1931), 304-5.
[2] G. A. N. Lowndes, *The Silent Social Revolution* (1937), 16-17.
[3] The Treasury grant to elementary schools fell from £813,441 in 1861 to £636,806 in 1865.
[4] Although the Revised Code was promulgated in 1862, for the vast majority of schools it only became operative in 1863.

powers of the mind. But this outlook, a survival from the days of
Bentham and James Mill, was no longer being propagated and carried
little weight, so that a fundamentally restrictive system persisted with
slight modifications for over thirty years.

The system was effectively enforced by an annual examination of all
schools receiving a government grant, conducted by the inspectorate.
The "standards" to be attained in reading, writing and arithmetic
were precisely defined by the Education Department—they ranged
from Standard I to VI.[1] Grants to schools were calculated on the basis
of the number of passes in each subject at each standard, together with
the level of attendance during the year. While the teacher's salary did
not usually directly depend on the grant earned—which went to the
school managers or the School Board—yet according to Edmond
Holmes, a Chief Inspector of Schools, in "far too many cases" the
teacher received a given proportion of the grant, consequently his
value in the market, and therefore prospects of promotion tended to
turn on his effectiveness as a grant earner.[2]

No system could have been better designed to limit and stultify
the educational process. Teachers saw it as their duty, indeed a necessity,
to get as many children through the examination as possible, and the
most effective way of doing this, especially with very large classes, was
by rote learning and drilling. Children learned their reading books off
by heart. According to Holmes, who inspected hundreds of schools
throughout this period, "child after child stands up, reads a minute or
so, and then sits down, remaining idle and inert (except when an
occasional question is addressed to him) for the rest of the time occupied
by the so-called lesson". By the time a child left school at fourteen he
might "have attended some 2,000 or 3,000 reading lessons".[3] Arithmetic, according to the same source, was taught in such a way as to
"make the child an inefficient calculating machine, which, even when
working, is too often inaccurate and clumsy, and which the slightest
change of environment throws at once and completely out of gear".[4]

---

[1] The system was extended in 1882, when a new Standard (VII) was introduced. The
"standard" was a level regarded as appropriate for each year group, but children could
be either advanced or retarded. The content of each standard is given in C. Birchenough,
History of Elementary Education (1914), 279, and in succeeding reports of the Committee
of Council.

[2] Edmond Holmes, *What is and What Might Be* (1911), 103n.

[3] *Ibid.*, 125, 128. "I consider it to be my duty," wrote an inspector, "according to the
letter of the Code, to *pass* every child who can read correctly and with tolerable fluency,
whether he or she understand or not a single sentence or a single word of the lesson."
Smith, *op. cit.*, 268.

[4] Holmes, *What is and What Might Be*, 123.

It was the same with the so-called "class subjects", for instance, history, geography, elementary science, which were later allowed to be taught and to rank for grant.[1]

Already in the late 1860s, Matthew Arnold, an Inspector of Schools, discerned a clear deterioration as a result of the new system. By comparison with an earlier period, he found in the schools "a deadness, a slackness, and a discouragement which are not the signs and accompaniment of progress. If I compare them with the schools of the Continent I find in them a lack of intelligent life much more striking now than it was when I returned from the Continent in 1859."[2] Some years later he was referring to "the unawakened and uninformed minds of the majority of our school children, even of those who can pass the examination in reading, writing and arithmetic, and sometimes in an extra subject or two besides".[3] "Memorising, repeating, passively listening," writes Frank Smith, the historian of elementary education, "were the main requirements of the system; small wonder was it that an inspector could give the verdict that in four years he had never heard a child 'ask a question of its teacher on the subject of the lesson'."[4] What the system meant from the teacher's angle appears succinctly in the entries in a log-book of a typical Leicester school:[5]

1863. June 1	School came under the operation of New Code. Received notice of Examination of school.
June 8	Drilled upper classes on paper.
June 18	Drilled all in slate writing.
July 8	Drilled 6th Class in Alphabet and small words and 1st and 2nd, 4th, 5th in Reading, and 1st and 2nd in Spelling.
August 14	Drilled in Arithmetic.
August 18	Drilled all school in writing on slates.
September 17	All classes drilled in Tables and Bookwork.
October 4	Drilled 1st and 2nd in Arithmetic.

The deadening effect of the Revised Code emerges clearly from the reports of inspectors, writes Smith; these give a picture of "uniform mediocrity in the schools". There were no experiments, no references

[1] Ibid., 133-4. See also Smith, op. cit., 310.
[2] Quoted in Smith, op. cit., 266. Matthew Arnold had reported on school systems abroad for both the Newcastle and the Taunton Commissions.
[3] Ibid., 307. [4] Ibid.
[5] The Leicester County Boys' School. Log-books, incidentally, were one of the few positive products of the Revised Code; from 1862 every school in receipt of grant under the Revised Code had to keep one.

to industrial education, "school gardens had gradually disappeared. . . . There was apparently no more singing, or drawing, or science". As the "mechanical fetters" of the system "gradually extended to all parts of a widening curriculum", so "the Revised Code came near to the point of stupefying children between 1862 and 1890". "The child was literally sacrificed to the system."[1]

That this system was specifically designed to discourage all initiative, to develop habits of obedience, docility and passivity—this is the burden of the impassioned attack launched by Edmond Holmes in his remarkable book. *What is and What Might Be* was first published in 1911, when Holmes had retired from the position of Chief Inspector of Schools, but he contended that the methods and attitudes engendered by the Revised Code lingered on long after its abolition in 1897. It was of the essence of the attitudes engendered in the teachers that they aspired to dominate the child, "to leave nothing to his nature, nothing to his spontaneous life, nothing to his free activity; to repress all his natural impulses; to drill his energies into complete quiescence; to keep his whole being in a state of sustained and painful tension". Then, "when severity and constraint have done their work, when the spirit of the child has been broken, when his vitality has been lowered to its barest minimum, when he has been reduced to a state of mental and moral serfdom, the time has come for the system of education through mechanical obedience to be applied to him in all its rigour".[2] The teacher's professional welfare "depends on the examiner's verdict", so the teacher holds himself responsible "for every stroke and dot that his pupil makes". Consequently "the child is not allowed to do anything which the teacher can possibly do for him. He has to think what his teacher tells him to think, to feel what his teacher tells him to feel, to see what his teacher tells him to see, to say what his teacher tells him to say, to do what his teacher tells him to do." In sum, "as an ingenious instrument for arresting the mental growth of the child, and deadening all his higher faculties", the system of payment by results "has never had, and I hope will never have, an equal".[3]

This was an Inspector of Schools speaking, a man who for years had been, as he came to see, "the victim of a vicious administrative system, perhaps the most vicious that has ever been devised". So long as the

[1] Smith, *op. cit.*, 269, 274-5. Although the system was not finally abolished until 1897, it was to some extent modified in 1890. For a vivid description of actual lessons in an infant school observed under this system see F. Storr, *Life and Remains of Quick* (1899), 129-37, and several other passages.

[2] E. Holmes, *What is and What Might Be*, 48-9, 117.   [3] *Ibid.*, 66-7, 110.

system operated "the grooves into which I had been drawn held me fast". But once it was abolished he was able to *inspect* schools in a more real sense of the term. Paying unexpected visits, "I saw," he writes, "how the 'results' I had asked for had been provided; and to that extent my eyes were opened. I saw that many things were as wrong as they could be, that mechanical methods were being blindly followed; that the children were being forcibly dieted on semi-digested food; that they were being relieved, as far as possible, of the necessity of doing anything for themselves—of seeing, thinking, reasoning, planning, purposing, executing; that they had no initiative, no spontaneous activity, no natural outlook on life, that they could do nothing but sit still and wait for the word of command; in fine, that the teachers had drilled themselves into automatism and their pupils into passivity and helplessness."[1]

There can be little doubt that the picture evoked by this passionate condemnation is a true one. It does not tell the whole story if only because, during the late '80s and '90s there were beginnings in introducing more effective teaching in the higher standards, a reaching upwards into the realms of secondary education which was to become of great significance. There were teachers at this period who did their best, under extraordinarily difficult circumstances, to introduce some humanity into the schools, to develop the intellectual capacities and widen the general outlook of their pupils. But, as R. H. Tawney put it later, "the elementary schools of 1870 were intended in the main to produce an orderly, civil, obedient population, with sufficient education to understand a command". With their vast classes, drill methods, their severe and even brutal discipline, they achieved the required end with "astonishing efficiency".[2] These attitudes were regarded as appropriate to the children of the working class. They could be reinforced later through the new social agencies developed in parallel with the schools.

In sum, while sustained efforts were being made in some quarters to bridge the gulf between the two nations, to further understanding between the "educated" class and the working class, the main developments in the educational field aggravated still further the strictly segregated pattern of schooling initiated in the decades 1850-70. It had once been the aim of radical thinkers such as James Mill and Bentham, at a time when they were actively campaigning for the

[1] E. Holmes, *In Quest of an Ideal*, 62, 67-8.
[2] R. H. Tawney, *Education, the Socialist Policy* (1924), 22.

reform of ancient foundations and the improvement of middle-class education, to introduce also universal education for the working class. Supremely confident in their own philosophy, convinced of the correctness of their political and economic analyses, themselves rational and secular in outlook, they had conceived of an enlightened education for all classes—if at different levels. That vision had faded and the schools that came into being at opposite social poles during the period 1870-1900 were of a very different nature, dedicated to the production not so much of rational individuals as of recruits to different castes. This was one thing that public and elementary schools had in common, but there could hardly have been wider differences between the conditions in which they operated and the methods adopted.

In 1858 Sir Charles Adderley, Vice-President of the Committee of Council, had declared that "any attempt to keep the children of the labouring classes under intellectual culture after the very earliest stage at which they could earn their living, would be as arbitrary and improper as it would be to keep the boys at Eton and Harrow at spade labour".[1] No one spoke directly in these terms after 1870, but in practice it could hardly be said that the intellect of the workers' children was effectively cultivated during the brief period they remained in elementary schooling.

[1] Quoted by Graham Wallas in *The Speaker*, 16 March 1901.

CHAPTER IV

POPULAR EDUCATION AND THE WORKING CLASS

THE very conditions and limitations of elementary education were such as to arouse protest from those who saw their children subjected to it, taught by rote methods in huge classes, controlled often by a harsh discipline, and sent out into the world of work at the age of ten, eleven or twelve. Trade unionists who were active in the struggle to improve working conditions naturally turned attention also to the conditions under which their children were educated, the more so when inspired by ideas of the dignity of man and the human benefits that education could bring. It was no accident that it was the Gasworkers' Union, led by Will Thorne, that initiated the movement for a new conception of popular education within the T.U.C. during the closing years of the nineteenth century.

Earlier, trade union leaders had actively participated with the radical bourgeoisie in the National Education League, campaigning for a universal, secular and compulsory system of education.[1] Not all these objectives had been achieved, but the passing of the Education Act in 1870 led to a slackening of pressure. The unions became preoccupied with industrial matters and so far as education was concerned were mainly interested in promoting technical education for their members. As a result the T.U.C., which in 1869 and 1870 had devoted considerable attention to education, later scarcely discussed it and no new perspectives were advanced on behalf of the working class. There was to be a notable change in the 1880s with the revival of the conception which had informed the earlier socialist and Chartist struggles of the 1830s and '40s—that the extension of organised education is an essential aspect of political and economic emancipation.

The socialist groups of this period, as has been seen, promoted education among the workers as their forerunners had done. But there were naturally new preoccupations at a time when a national system

---

[1] Robert Applegarth, Secretary of the Amalgamated Society of Carpenters and Joiners, had been the leading trade unionist concerned; his pamphlet arguing the case for compulsory education sold half a million copies.

of schools was coming into being, notably a concern to ensure the development of this system along positive lines. The very fact that a whole generation of children were being collected together in the schools brought poverty and its consequences to light in a new way. Socialists, therefore, were soon to be found drawing attention to the plight of children who were too ailing or too hungry to profit from the teaching offered. They also conducted an active campaign for the abolition of child labour. But though such immediate issues claimed much attention, the need to improve and extend the education given was also clearly seen. Whereas there had earlier been a generalised claim of the right to education, when this was almost entirely denied, there were now more particular demands: that the barriers set up within the educational system be removed and that the workers' children be educated in the true sense of the word. Again, these were no longer presented in general terms—as William Lovett had earlier outlined a desirable system of education—but rather in terms of remedying the deficiencies of the existing system of schooling. In order to influence developments in this sense it was necessary to gain places on School Boards. We may look here at some of the activities in these directions during the decades after 1870.

1. WORKING-CLASS CRITICISMS AND PROPOSALS FOR REFORM

The wide range of educational issues with which the organised working-class movement was concerned is well illustrated by the evidence given in 1887 to a new commission of enquiry by a representative of the London Trades Council. The Cross Commission was appointed to enquire into the working of the Elementary Education Acts of England and Wales, and Thomas Smyth, described as "a representative of the working class", was a witness in command of much relevant information. A plasterer by trade, he had been elected by the London Trades Council to present evidence "on behalf of the various trades connected with that body". Not only did he claim that the views he put represented those of the London Trades Council, which had discussed educational issues over many years and "had the advantage of consulting with pretty nearly all the leading teachers in London", but also that they were generally held by the workers with whom he had associated in his trade. Smyth was thoroughly familiar with educational problems; a manager of evening classes acquainted with many school managers in the district where he lived, he had seen his own three children pass through the local board schools.[1]

While severely critical of board schools, Smyth clearly expresses the view that these, by comparison with the voluntary schools, had the makings of a genuine system of people's schools. "We are called upon, through the taxes and rates, to help to maintain and pay for them, and we feel that they are our own, more or less; that they are really practically in the highest sense of the thing the beginning of a national system of schools." They "are more the people's schools" than the voluntary schools, he adds: "We feel that we have some control over them whereby we can direct their efforts and make them better than they are." There is no doubt that this expresses the outlook of a wide section of the working class which was already winning representation on the School Boards.

Perhaps the central feature of Smyth's evidence is his demand, strongly argued against such Commissioners as Earl Beauchamp and Cardinal Manning, that all education should be free, from the elementary school to the university. Again and again the Commissioners came back to this question and Smyth made his outright response. "We find that it is necessary to have all the roads to education open, free, and unfettered to the people. We believe that the children of the poor ought to be able to rise from the elementary to the secondary schools, and on to the universities." Arguing first the need for free elementary education, Smyth went on to oppose all class differentiation in education. The grammar schools should not be regarded as middle-class schools, they should be open to all and therefore free. In answer to a question about the universities he affirmed: "There is no poor man who can go to Oxford or Cambridge, or to any of the big colleges, and maintain himself." When challenged he underlined the point: "it would be next to expecting a boy out of a London School Board school to take wings as to expect him to advance by his own efforts to the university."

How was free education to be financed? By the National Exchequer and also by the use of endowments filched from the poor. In Smyth's view grammar schools, originally endowed in order to provide a free education, now charged fees for the express purpose of excluding "the children of poor men". Their endowments were used exclusively for the education of the middle and upper classes. These endowments

[1] Smyth's evidence appears in the *Third Report of the Royal Commission Appointed to Enquire into the Working of the Elementary Education Acts (England and Wales)* (1887), 379-97.

should be taken over by the state and used to finance an effective system of national education, open to all.

This radical proposition, which challenged the whole trend of educational legislation over the past thirty years, shocked the Commissioners. Did not "free education", asked the Rev. Dr. Morse, imply a system of "pure communism"? Did not the wealthier classes, through taxation, subsidise the poor by providing education? On the contrary, answered Smyth, now openly putting socialist arguments, "all property is the result of labour . . . any man who has property has it at the expense of the poor man, at the expense of labour". "We feel," he added, "it is only the rich who get the endowments"; these could be used with added assistance from the Exchequer since the rating system was inequitable. The claims Smyth advanced—that the state should "grant facilities for all the requirements of the human intellect", that it should be responsible for seeing the child is educated, whether the parent agrees with it or not, were challenged as having been a "plank in the International". "You agree to those principles which [are] held to be communism?"—"I do."

True to the traditional outlook of the working class, Smyth also made the case for secular education and for the teaching of a secular morality in school. He approved the practice of the Birmingham School Board (under Chamberlain) which allowed ministers of the various religious groups to take purely voluntary lessons after school hours. But religious instruction should not form part of the regular education in state schools. It "is liable to become the reflex of the teacher's own dogmatism, however guarded against, and there is a widespread feeling against religious teaching being given in schools supported by the rates and taxes, on the part of Catholics, Protestants, Methodists, Baptists, and many other religious bodies, besides a large number of people who are as well disposed as any, and as good citizens, but who do not profess any form of religion." On the other hand a secular morality should be taught in school hours by the regular teachers. In response to hostile questioning by the Commissioners, Smyth maintained that such teaching was both possible and desirable. There was a great deal of feeling about religious instruction, a great many people were opposed to it, an attitude they expressed "very loudly and bitterly". Challenged on the "safeguard" of the conscience clause, Smyth claimed that this was entirely unsatisfactory, a boy withdrawn from religious instruction became a "marked boy". Smyth had withdrawn his own son from religious instruction—he was "put at one end of the room by himself in front of all the school" while the instruction proceeded. The only just solution was a fully secular education.

As for the actual conditions of education in the schools, Smyth sharply criticised the over-large classes, overwork of teachers, and the vicious system of payment by results. In terms which Edmond Holmes was to use over two decades later he complained that the children were driven and taught by "cram" without any attempt to develop their understanding; they retained very little of what they had memorised and did not come out as fully educated people. The system was un-necessary and the teachers would work better without it. Classes were far too large, up to eighty, so that attention to individual pupils was impossible; they should not contain more than thirty-five to forty children. Smyth also came to the defence of the teachers, of whom he had a very high opinion indeed, but who were overwhelmed by every kind of extraneous duty on top of the sheer number of children under their care. "Most of the teachers are employed during a great deal of the school time in writing out notes, and books, and keeping ledgers, and keeping logs, and one thing and another . . . there is so much real work beyond the teaching to do that it is utterly impossible for them to attend to so many." Teachers deserved the kind of conditions in which they could educate.

Finally Smyth expressed very strong objections to any directly vocational education in the elementary school, a matter with which the Commission was particularly concerned. The working class "do not desire it at all; and I might tell you that it is one of the questions that has been discussed and thought out largely and laboriously by all the men that I have become acquainted with upon this matter. They feel that it is utterly absurd and utterly useless raising any such cry as technical education in the primary schools. They feel that it is a waste of time, and that it will interfere largely and prejudicially with the general school work if it is introduced." Certainly the children should be taught elementary science and mechanics, "the use of the lever, the screw jack, inclined planes, pulleys, blocks and falls" illustrated by practical use, but there should be no industrial training. What is required, Smyth maintained, putting the educational view, is "a primary knowledge of applied mechanics and scientific training generally". Even hand work in iron and wood would be "in a manner robbing the children of the necessary time which is now employed in schools". It was not the purpose of the school to provide a specific vocational education for future workers, but to give a general education. This, Smyth went on to affirm, again reiterating a traditional demand of the Labour movement, should be given in a common school. Instead of separate schools for different social classes, there should be one school "common to all". This would be the best way of raising the whole level of schooling.

This evidence admirably summarises the ends to which the more advanced sections of the working class were working in an effort to transform the elementary schools. In effect consistent campaigns were being undertaken on all the main issues Smyth argued and on others as well. Perhaps the most important campaign, at this stage, was that directed to making education free and we may first turn to this.

2. FREE EDUCATION

The Labour movement had long stood for free, compulsory education. This policy had been strongly urged by Ernest Jones at the 1851 Chartist convention and by Applegarth and other trade union leaders on the eve of the 1870 Act. In the event, the Act allowed for the charging of fees (up to a maximum of 9d. a week) while it was left to local School Boards to decide whether or not they made attendance compulsory.[1] The Boards only had the power to remit fees for periods of up to six months if parents pleaded poverty, but they could provide, if the consent of the Education Department was forthcoming, free schools in poor districts. School Boards could also pay the fees of children in voluntary schools whose parents pleaded poverty. This was provided for by the notorious Section 25 of the Act, very strongly fought by the National Education League on the grounds that it allowed rate subsidisation of church schools by the back door. It operated up to 1876 when, under an Act of that year, the duty passed to the Poor Law Guardians.[2]

In practice fees varied between about 2d. and 8d. a week in different schools. School Boards often fixed higher fees for schools in relatively well-to-do areas, so introducing an element of class distinction, and,

[1] The term "elementary school" was only defined negatively in the Act, i.e., the term did *not* include any school or department at which the ordinary payment (for instruction) exceeded 9d. a week (Section 3). Section 17 of the Act stated "Every child attending a school provided by any school board shall pay such weekly fee as may be prescribed by the school board" subject to remittance in the case of poverty on the lines given in the text.

[2] The 1876 Act also provided free education for three years to pupils who had passed standard four at ten years of age and held a Certificate of regular attendance for five years. This provision lasted for five years.

according to Smyth, forcing poor parents in the former areas to send their children far afield in search of a cheaper school.

School fees bore hardly on poor parents with large families, especially in periods of universal distress as in the mid-1880s. It was this aspect that was stressed, for instance, by the President of the T.U.C., Councillor Threllfall, in his opening address to the annual Congress in 1885. Citing the case of a family with an income of 15s. to 18s. a week and four children at school, he pointed out that to find the school-pence meant a drastic limiting of expenditure on food and clothing. "Under proper conditions," he went on, "education would be hailed with joy, but School Board experience will show that the Elementary Education Acts are regarded with hatred, and are constantly evaded by thousands of families."[1] True, fees were remitted by Boards of Guardians in cases of extreme need, but the harsh treatment involved was often distasteful. Harry Quelch of the S.D.F., arguing for the abolition of fees, linked the problem with that of attendance. In London "at least 26 per cent of the children on the school register are always absent from school". This absenteeism, he added, was "mainly attributable to the imposition of fees".[2]

The Labour movement had always stressed that, if the right to education was to be made a reality, schooling must be freely available. In December 1871 a sub-committee of the Birmingham Trades Council, set up to consider "the present state of the Education question", came out strongly for free and compulsory education. "The labouring population of this country," it reported, "would not consider the adoption of a totally free system of education any degradation, but would, on the other hand, view it as a wise distribution of a small proportion of the heavy taxation their toil is producing."[3] The demand for free, compulsory, secular education was one of the main points in the original programme of the S.D.F. and with it was linked another relevant demand—for one free meal a day. A series of articles by John Taylor under the title "Free Schools" appeared in the first volume of Justice, strongly arguing the case for total abolition of school fees, a question, according to the author, "of the utmost importance to the great mass of the working classes of this country". The cost, Taylor argued, would be small, in London $\frac{7}{8}$ths of 1d. in the pound.[4]

---

[1] 18th T.U.C. Report, 1885, 19.   [2] Justice, 16 October 1886.
[3] W. P. McCann, "Trade Unionist, Co-operative and Socialist Organisations in relation to Popular Education, 1870–1902", unpublished Ph.D. thesis, University of Manchester (1960), 493.
[4] Justice, 1 March 1884; 8 March 1884.

By the late 1880s this had become a burning issue. "We hold that all education should be free for all and that everyone should be fully educated at the cost of the community so as to become useful citizens," wrote *Justice* in 1887. The middle class opposed free elementary education and yet increasingly demanded state aid for secondary and higher education, despite the diversion of educational endowments to subsidise middle-class schools—and this at a time when the poor "are being fined and imprisoned for being unable to pay school fees".[1] In 1888 the Central Democratic Committee, set up to run progressive candidates for the London School Board elections (consisting of the Metropolitan Radical Federation, London Secular Federation, Fabian Society and S.D.F.) put the matter in their Appeal as follows:[2]

"You will also find the necessity of free education. More than three-fourths of the cost of our public schools is already defrayed out of rates and taxes, so that the *principle* of free education is no novelty. The 'pauperism', as the reactionists call it, is simply a question of degree. Shall the State pay the balance of the cost, abolishing fees, and throw open the school which it compels children to attend; or shall the worrying of poor parents, the heartburning, the expense of prosecutions and collecting, and the shocking waste of teachers' time be continued?"

If the demand for free education was vocal it met with strong opposition, particularly from the Church of England and the supporters of voluntary schools generally; the school pence constituted an important part of their revenue which could not lightly be foregone. But the main arguments against abolishing fees were moral ones, that to provide free education would be "degrading" for the working class, that it would lead to a decline in parental responsibility. The Bishop of Manchester, for instance, argued at a Diocesan Conference in 1886 that it would mean not only the destruction of the voluntary schools, but also that the cost of education would rise so that working men would have to pay more. But he went further than this. "I oppose this sham free education," he said, "for yet another reason—because free education means secular education, means the exclusion of the word of God, and even all reference to God from the schools in which we train our young." This meant practical agnosticism. "Now, I ask you," he went on, "whether it is fair that Christian men should be taxed to teach their children this alien, chilling, soul-paralysing no faith? Are we to be taxed for the maintenance of the Agnostic sect?

[1] *Justice*, 9 July 1887.   [2] McCann, *op. cit.*, 499.

Are we to sacrifice not merely our money, but the souls and bodies of our children to this modern Moloch?"[1]

Clearly passions were being roused, and they were rising also on a related issue—that of educational endowments. For the demand for a free education naturally raised the question as to where the money was to come from to replace the fees. This point had been effectively ventilated several years before when George Potter, first elected on the London School Board in 1873, who fought strongly for free education, had succeeded in getting a committee appointed (with Benjamin Lucraft as Chairman) to enquire into the endowments available in the London School Board area which might (or should) be applied to education. These included charities administered by the 106 parishes in the City of London (an area of about one square mile) as well as those controlled by the extremely wealthy London Livery Companies. The committee reported in 1879 that the income of the city parochial charities amounted to nearly £105,000, approximately half of which should be devoted to education. Two years later a further report found that, of the total income of the City Livery Companies, approximately £186,000 should be devoted to the same purpose. In the meantime two Royal Commissions had been set up—one on the parochial charities of the City of London, the other on the Livery Companies; these reported in 1880 and 1884 respectively and reached roughly similar conclusions.[2]

Here, then, were substantial funds diverted from their proper use, as Labour and socialist spokesmen were quick to see. When addressing the T.U.C. in 1885, Councillor Threllfall raised this issue, as Smyth was to later before the Cross Commission. "What has become of the vast sums of money which have been left in bygone times for education, for help to the poor?" he asked. "The records of the City Companies are a sample of the uses to which this money has been put. . . . It would never have been bequeathed if the ancient donors could have foreseen its uses for costly banquets, middle-class education, and other

---

[1] *National Reformer*, 21 November 1886. This standpoint is attacked with great force by Annie Besant, *ibid.*

[2] The misuse of the City Parochial charities had been sharply raised in letters to *The Times* by Sir Charles Trevelyan in 1869; cf. *Correspondence, etc., Relating to the Parochial System and Parochial Charities of the Ancient City of London* (1870), where the correspondence is reprinted. See also the London School Board's reports *City Parochial Charities* (1879), *City Companies Charities* (1881), and *Report of the Royal City Parochial Charities Commission*, Vol. I (1880), *Report of the Royal Commission on City of London Livery Companies*, Vol. I (1884). For Bryce's Act of 1883 and the later use of these funds see Sir Philip Magnus, *Educational Aims and Efforts, 1880-1910* (1910), 84ff., and C. T. Millis, *Technical Education, its Development and Aims* (1925), 73ff.

foreign purposes."[1] Threllfall's point received strong support from H. H. Champion, the socialist leader, who in an article in *Justice* seconded Helen Taylor's demand in the School Board Committee's report that the funds of the parochial charities in the City of London be used to abolish school fees. Pointing out that there were now no poor in the City of London he gave several examples of prodigal expenditure on banquets. This bounty had been "appropriated" by those for whom it was not designed. Endowments left for the poor "should be applied to them".[2]

By the mid-1880s, then, new weight was thrown behind the demand for free elementary education. In 1885 the T.U.C. unanimously resolved that "the time has arrived for the government to establish a thorough system of national education, and that in order to accomplish this object the public elementary schools must necessarily be made free".[3] It was in the same year that the Radical, Joseph Chamberlain, in his bid for the leadership of the Liberal party, made the call for free education one of the major planks in his "unauthorised programme"; "We shall sweep the country with free education and allotments", he wrote to Mundella, "and the Tories will be smashed and the Whigs extinguished".[4] Things did not work out quite as Chamberlain foresaw, and the Gladstone government, in its short period of office, took no steps in the matter.

The T.U.C., however, did not let things rest. In 1886 and again in 1887 the Annual Congress returned to the topic, passing unanimously (in 1887) a resolution which stated that "a truly national system of education is not only desirable, but necessary, and seeing that the present system of compulsory and partially free education is not and cannot possibly be worked without causing undesirable friction and anomalies in its administration, we, therefore, instruct the Parliamentary Committee to use their best efforts to expedite the passing of such an Act".[5] Pressure from the working class was maintained. With a Tory administration under Lord Salisbury again in power, the Gladstonian Liberals, seeking popular support, came out for free education and popular management of the voluntary schools. Unless the Tories passed a measure for free education, wrote Chamberlain

[1] *18th T.U.C. Report*, 1885, 19.   [2] *Justice*, 24 October 1885.
[3] *18th T.U.C. Report*, 1885, 44.
[4] Quoted in W. H. G. Armytage, *A. J. Mundella, 1825-1897* (1951), 229. It is noteworthy that John Burns made free education the first point in his election address at Nottingham in 1886.
[5] *20th T.U.C. Report*, 1887, 47.

to Hartington in November 1890, "there will be a tremendous defection of working-class votes both in towns and in the counties".[1] The government, which had earlier denounced free education, now changed its mind; anxious to steal the thunder of the Liberals it carried the Free Education Act in 1891.[2]

The cause was won, though the Act did not bring the voluntary schools under popular control, nor did it, as is often supposed, introduce universal free education in the elementary schools. It did, however, empower School Boards to admit children freely to their schools, without entering into the question of poverty. Further, one year after the commencement of the Act, the Education department could *demand* in every *school area* "sufficient" school accommodation without fees for children over three and under fifteen. To make up for the loss of fees a "fee grant" was made from the Exchequer calculated at 10s. per head of the average attendance of children over three and under fifteen; this was paid to all public elementary schools including voluntary schools (so increasing their subsidy from public funds)[3] if certain conditions regarding the limitation of fees were accepted. The grant was roughly the equivalent of a school fee of 3d. per child.

Meanwhile, fees, if somewhat reduced, continued to be levied in many public elementary and voluntary schools; in 1894 there were still 800,000 fee-paying scholars in elementary schools.[4] Local campaigns therefore continued. In Manchester in the late 1890s the I.L.P. branches were active on this issue, sending deputations to the School Board asking for free places at specific board schools. The Trades Council took up the question and in 1900 held a special extended meeting to support the campaign for free education when addresses were given by Councillor Fred Brocklehurst and Joseph Nuttall, socialist members respectively of the Manchester and Salford School

---

[1] C. H. D. Howard (ed.), *Joseph Chamberlain: a Political Memoir, 1880–1892* (1953). 291–2.

[2] The Act was denounced by the *Economist* which charged both parties with "competing for popularity" on this issue and yielding to the temptation "to pose as benefactors of the working class". Armytage, *op. cit.*, 284.

[3] A point noted by the contemporary biographer of Cardinal Manning, the Roman Catholic leader. "The Free Education Act of 1891, with its new grant of 10s. per child in average attendance to replace fees, was, beyond all, a boon to the Catholic schools", which now received grants for many children who had been able to pay no, or very low, fees. The Act was "a triumph for the Cardinal's cause". The arrangement, he adds, "although it is altogether inconsistent with the principle that education supported out of public funds should be under public control, is not unlikely to be a permanent one". A. W. Hutton, *Cardinal Manning* (1892), 175–6. This was written a few months after Manning's death.

[4] *Report of the Committee of Council on Education*, 1896–7, ii.

Boards. Brocklehurst reported that resolutions to the effect that all fees should be abolished in board schools (except in certain departments of higher grade schools) had been defeated in 1892, 1895 and 1898; "agitations, however, organised by local committees, had been productive of great good, especially in the northern district of the city". Finally, he reported, a scheme was adopted with the aim of providing a free school in every part of the city within a radius of half a mile. "This resulted in ten schools being added to the free list, which meant no fewer than 3,229 additional free places."[1] Clearly a campaign to abolish fees was still very necessary nearly a decade after the passage of the "Free Education" Act.[2]

While the Labour movement welcomed this Act, the Parliamentary Committee of the T.U.C. and the socialist bodies were already looking further ahead. The approval of the T.U.C. was qualified by regret that evening schools were not included and that public control of elementary schools had not been conceded, that is, control over the voluntary schools now increasingly subsidised by public funds.[3] Socialist bodies were more outspoken. A Fabian Tract of 1891 stated bluntly: "We want a national system of education, secular, compulsory and technical, at the public cost, for all classes alike."[4] For the S.D.F. also, the provision of free elementary schooling was only a beginning. What about the grammar schools, the public schools, the universities, were these to remain the privilege of the few? "Are our universities to be closed for ever to those who cannot afford to pay for them?"[5]

Socialists, then, saw the winning of this concession as a springboard for further advance. The I.L.P., in one of its first pamphlets, demanded an extension of the Education Acts to provide free boarding schools in the country: "the respectable working classes will send their children to these schools for the benefit of the children, as the middle classes and the upper classes send theirs to the great public schools of Eton, Harrow, Winchester and others."[6] "Now that we have free

---

[1] *Manchester*, monthly journal of the Manchester and Salford I.L.P., No. 14, June 1900. The fee grant made it possible to abolish fees below 3*d.* a week; in Manchester in 1894, 33 per cent of the children attending Board schools paid a fee of 1*d.* a week or more. The abolition of fees, however, "caused a rush of children into the schools, particularly in poor districts". S. D. Simon, *A Century of City Government* (1938), 242, 252.

[2] Fees could still be charged in higher elementary schools under the 1902 Education Act; they were finally abolished by the Education Act of 1918.

[3] *24th T.U.C. Report*, 1891, 30.

[4] *The Workers' Political Programme* (Fabian Tract no. 11), 9.

[5] *Justice*, 7 August 1886.

[6] H. Russell Smart, *The Independent Labour Party, its Programme and Policy* (1893).

education," wrote J. Hunter Watts in a main leader in *Justice*, "we must get free maintenance, and not only one free meal a day, but much more."[1] This was to raise a matter which the S.D.F. programme had from the outset linked with the abolition of school fees.

3. SCHOOL MEALS AND STATE MAINTENANCE

At its inception in 1884 the S.D.F. had adopted a programme one clause of which advocated "free, compulsory education for all classes, together with the provision of at least one wholesome meal a day in each school".[2] It was an indisputable fact, finally brought to public notice by the reports of official enquiries, that large numbers of children were attending school in a state of near starvation. These children were in no condition to benefit from teaching. Having achieved a measure of state education after 1870, therefore, attention was necessarily turned to the physical condition of the children.

This question was brought to attention time and again by the journals of the Labour and socialist movement. "Is it possible with empty stomachs to pay attention to the multiplication table?" wrote a contributor to *Justice* in 1884. "Can it be reasonable to expect that children whose whole thought through school hours is concentrated upon the (to them) most important question whether there will be a piece of bread for them when they get home to be enthusiastic about geography?"[3] The children, wrote a board school mistress, had "immense capabilities for mental development" but their brutalising and stupefying environment frustrated these possibilities. Free meals were an essential condition for development.[4]

Evidence accumulated in subsequent years. A report prepared for A. J. Mundella when he was in charge of education—which, according to *Justice*, he attempted to suppress—illustrated the problem in London. At one board school 36 per cent of the parents were found to be unemployed, as many as 40 per cent of the children sometimes came to school without any breakfast. Of 475 children examined at another school, 125 were pointed out to the Inspector as being half-starved. Bread and tea was apparently the only food many of these children had for prolonged periods.[5] In 1894 a committee of enquiry

---

[1] *Justice*, 28 May 1892; see also 2 May 1891.   [2] *Justice*, 9 August 1884.
[3] *Ibid.*, 29 March 1884.   [4] *Ibid.*, 17 May 1884.
[5] *Justice*, 27 September 1884. This was Dr. Crichton-Browne's *Report to the Education Department upon the alleged over-pressure of work in public elementary schools* (1884); it contained a very sharp indictment of the school system and of the physical condition of the children, written in an unusual style for a blue book: "To look at these

set up by the London School Board, under the chairmanship of Graham Wallas, revealed that over 50,000 children attended their schools hungry enough to require a free meal.[1] In a speech at the T.U.C. in 1896, Ben Tillett claimed that as many as 80,000 children attended London schools every morning without breakfast—hundreds of thousands of children in the country as a whole lacked sufficient food to enable them to profit from their education.[2] In 1899 an article in *Justice* claimed that nearly 500,000 children attended school hungry.[3] This may well have been an underestimate.

Time and again, leaders and articles in *Justice*, especially by Harry Quelch, returned to this question of the physical condition of the children, their environment, and the degeneration of physical standards. In default of any effective public provision, the only way of helping the children was through charity, and various efforts were made. In the winter of 1895-6, for instance, "The Poor Children of Southwark Committee" supplied free 150,355 dinners and 26,780 breakfasts; in 1895, the "Destitute Children's Dinners Society" provided 250,000 dinners for underfed children.[4] The S.D.F. was itself to the fore in this work. Although arguing strongly that private charity was quite incapable of solving the problem, the actual condition of the children, in a period of mounting unemployment, impelled those in touch with the people to action. Early in 1887 the Clerkenwell Branch was providing free breakfasts for a large number of destitute children every Sunday morning and *Justice* also reported that the Battersea Branch had given a good meal to "some hundreds of poor little half-starved waifs", the Deptford Branch was planning to feed 200, and that the Paddington and Bayswater Branches had "gone so far as to feed 600 in one day".[5] Will Thorne gives a vivid description of the East End at this time: "Great suffering was being felt as a result of the large number of unemployed," he writes. "Women and children were starving, especially in Old Canning Town, Tidal Basin and Custom House areas of Dockland. There were no local authorities that could feed these necessitous people. The work of men like George Lansbury and Will Crooks for the starving poor of the East End of London had not yet

---

half-starved children in London schools is to be 'full of sorrow'. Very touching is it to think of the quiet heroism with which, when hunger is gnawing within and the dull misery of want overflows them, they sit uncomplaining at their little desks. . . . These children want blood and we offer them brain-polish; they ask for bread, and receive a problem; for milk, and the tonic-sol-fa system is introduced to them." *Ibid.*, 9.

[1] *Justice*, 7 April 1894.   [2] *29th T.U.C. Report*, 1896, 48.
[3] *Justice*, 25 November 1899.   [4] McCann, *op. cit.*, 503.
[5] *Justice*, 19 February 1887.

started. So I, with a few comrades, decided to make an effort to feed the children at least." Meat and vegetables were collected from local shopkeepers to make soup and a notice put up that children would be fed at 9.30 on Sunday morning. "A more pitiable, heartbreaking sight than those poor ill-clothed children, coming along in the cold and biting winds, cannot be imagined. Sweet, tender young things, they were like ravenous wolves. So hungry were they, it was difficult to keep them in order while they were being served." "This sort of thing," he adds, "was breeding rebels and opponents to a system that permitted the poor to starve in the East End while in the West End others satisfied their appetites with luxurious meals amidst the greatest comfort."[1]

Among those active in such work was Mrs. H. M. Hyndman. *The Times* recalled, when she died in 1913, that "she organised free meals for children, for several winters in succession, in the East End and on the south side of the river, and was also active in the provision of free holidays for children, long before either of those things received any general recognition". According to the *Evening News*, "She was the first to organise a system of free meals for school children, establishing a centre at Battersea, and she carried on the work until it was taken over by the L.C.C." Hyndman wrote that his wife distributed over 30,000 free meals each winter.[2] Robert Blatchford also took up this question with great energy in *Clarion* after 1891, consistently giving publicity to appalling cases of death from starvation. The Cinderella Clubs, which spread particularly in the North of England, were specifically concerned to feed children and also provide them with some form of amusement. The paper reports in 1892 on efforts made by the Socialist Club in Salford to provide meals and that, during the past weeks, more than 2,400 hungry children had been fed in Ardwick.[3] In 1893, Blatchford claimed that the Cinderella Clubs in the North, in the second year of their existence, had fed and amused more than 15,000 children, and the numbers rose in subsequent years.[4]

After the passing of the "Free Education" Act of 1891, the S.D.F., while energetically continuing the campaign for free meals, broadened

---

[1] W. Thorne, *My Life's Battles*, 59-60.
[2] *The Times*, 30 June 1913; *Evening News*, 28 June 1913; H. M. Hyndman, *The Record of an Adventurous Life* (1911), 297.
[3] *The Clarion*, 5 March 1892.
[4] *The Labour Prophet*, Vol. II, No. 18, June 1893, contains an article by Nunquam (Robert Blatchford) describing why he started the Cinderella clubs. The first club was in Manchester; its success led to new clubs in Hull, Bradford, Ashton, Stalybridge, Birmingham, Salford, Halifax and elsewhere.

its approach to advocate "complete publicly organised maintenance for all children". This was seen as the socialist answer to starvation and deprivation, indeed as a stage on the way towards socialism. Just as Smyth in his evidence to the Cross Commission argued that the state was responsible for the education of children, so the S.D.F. was now claiming that the necessary facilities should be provided for full mental and physical development of the children. It was at this point that the socialist perspective, opened up by William Morris and others, began to colour the practical day to day demands of the early socialists. When socialists advocated "state maintenance" this implied a wide variety of aids to welfare and education. It covered not only the necessities of life such as food and clothing, but also swimming baths, gymnasia, playing-fields, school workshops, holidays for children in the countryside, and, last but not least, boarding school education.[1] Some of these proposals derived from the experience of socialist controlled local authorities in France, which were taking children to the countryside for two or three months each year already in the 1890s.[2] This was to work in practical terms towards the broad, humanist conception of education now being advanced not only by Morris but by such men as Herbert Burrows.[3] These proposals were consistently returned to and elaborated in leader after leader in *Justice* towards the end of the century.[4]

Other working-class organisations joined in the consistent public campaign for school feeding and other welfare services. "Free Maintenance Committees" were set up, that at Chelsea, for instance, comprising representatives of socialist and working-class bodies and attempting, by deputation and meetings, to rouse the public conscience.[5] Public marches and demonstrations were carried through—pamphlets were published. In 1893 a deputation consisting of Hyndman, S. D. Shallard, and Will Thorne, saw Acland—the Minister—on the question of free meals and clothing and was sympathetically

---

[1] *Justice*, 28 May 1892; 11 August 1894.

[2] Communes under working-class control in France, such as Lille and Roubaix, fed and clothed thousands of children—hundreds were taken to the country in the summer at public expense. *Justice*, 18 January 1902.

[3] Herbert Burrows, a leading member of the S.D.F., argued his views on education in a series of articles in *Justice*, 29 September 1888; 13 and 20 October 1888.

[4] One of the best statements of the S.D.F. attitude to state maintenance at this period is the article by Dan Irving, *Social Democrat*, Vol. IV (1900), 180-4, which elaborates the case for swimming baths, gymnasia, playing-fields, school workshops, and the feeding and housing of school children.

[5] *Justice*, 9 May 1896.

received.[1] In March, 1896, a "well attended" meeting was held in Trafalgar Square "for the purpose of awakening the people of London to a sense of their duty to the coming generation".[2] This was followed up by a deputation to the London School Board, led by Edith Lanchester, which urged that it petition Parliament for powers to provide maintenance for school children out of public funds.[3]

When the demand for state maintenance was extended—as for instance, in John Richardson's *How it can be done* (1894)—to cover a completely socialist plan for education, it had a utopian aspect. But for the most part the issue was doggedly fought in terms of immediate and practical action. The I.L.P. also took up the question from 1895, and Margaret McMillan at Bradford, as an I.L.P. member of the School Board, saw that practical action was taken. There was no great readiness to do likewise in government circles until a new factor entered the situation. In the words of G. A. N. Lowndes: "The Boer War was probably the turning point. Members of Parliament might be ready to accept with a certain resignation the inevitability of a great mass of physical impairment in other people's children. . . . But when they found that 4,400 potential recruits had to be rejected every year on the ground of defective teeth alone, they bestirred themselves", if only in the first instance to appoint commissions of enquiry.[4] This marked the beginnings of a process which in time led to the establishment of a school medical service and other welfare services.

There had, of course, been other charitable bodies concerned with the plight of poor children during the 1880s and '90s, but socialist groupings pioneered the way in demanding the establishment of regular services, so bringing into the realm of practical politics a wider vision of what education should mean.

4. The Problem of Child Labour

It was Dan Irving, full-time S.D.F. organiser in Burnley, the heart of the cotton district, who first related the demand for state maintenance to the continued exploitation of children in the factories. Irving, a member of the Burnley School Board in the late 1890s,

---

[1] *Justice*, 11 February 1893. Acland was described in *Justice* as "the most competent man who has yet filled the post of Education Minister". *Ibid.*, 5 August 1893.

[2] *Ibid.*, 7 March 1896; 14 March 1896.

[3] *Ibid.*, 21 March 1896. For the case presented to the London School Board see McCann, *op. cit.*, 502ff.

[4] G. A. N. Lowndes, *The Silent Social Revolution* (1937), 227.

knew at first hand the real meaning of the half-time system in the Lancashire cotton mills, but also made clear its economic basis in an article in *Justice* in 1897.[1] The fact was that not only the employers but also the organised textile workers favoured the half-time system. Weavers, for instance, employed one child in the morning, another in the afternoon; this enabled them to operate six looms rather than four, and so increase earnings. Full state maintenance for the weavers' own children would solve this problem. It would remove the economic incentive "from the very worst form of capitalist exploitation".[2]

The half-time system had its origin in the Factory Acts dating back to 1802; even after the passage of the 1870 Education Act the laws governing school attendance continued to derive from a variety of Factory and Education Acts, engendering a confusion which led to many lawsuits. As a result the half-time system remained embedded, to bedevil the whole matter of fixing and raising a leaving age, until it was finally abolished by the Education Act of 1918. Up to 1893 children in the areas of certain School Boards could leave school altogether or for half-time employment at the age of ten (which was fixed as the minimum age of employment in the Act of 1876) provided they had reached a certain standard of education, or had put in a given number of attendances at school over the previous five years (this was known as the dunce's clause, since it obviated attaining any standard). In 1893 the age of employment was raised to eleven. On the other hand, School Boards had powers to insist on compulsory attendance between the ages of five and thirteen, though these were not necessarily operated.[3]

The half-time system flourished chiefly in the textile areas of Lancashire and Yorkshire. In 1891, in Lancashire, nearly half the child population of over ten—50,000 children—worked half-time in this way. "The day I was ten years of age, I went into the mill as a half-timer," writes Ben Turner. "We had to go to school one half-day and the mill the other half-day. One week we started work at 6 a.m. and went on to 12.30 p.m. with a half-hour for breakfast. We then had to go to school from 2 to 4.30 p.m. The opposite week we went to school at 9 a.m. until 12 noon, and to work from 1.30 p.m. until 6 p.m. It was

---

[1] "The Textile Operatives and Child Labour", *Justice*, 20 November 1897.

[2] The economic basis of the textile workers' support for the half-time system is also clearly analysed in J. R. Widdup, "The Abolition of Child Labour in Factories", *The Social Democrat*, Vol. I, No. 11, November 1897.

[3] See Frederick Keeling, *Child Labour in the United Kingdom* (1914), vii-xxxii, for a full summary of the position.

a bit cruel at times", he adds, "when on the morning turn at the mill—for it meant being up at 5 a.m., getting a drop of something warm, and trudging off to the mill a mile away to begin work. In winter it was fearful."[1] His work was for the most part trivial and repetitive.

Supporters of the system still claimed that it was educationally desirable; the Benthamite Edwin Chadwick, for instance, launched a paean of praise in its favour at the Social Science Congress of 1880.[2] On the other hand, opposition was growing. The Royal Commission on Labour of 1892 found that 6,000 half-timers in Lancashire were working in the mornings in temperatures of 80-110 degrees Fahrenheit; when at school in the afternoon "they could no longer be stopped from dozing off". "I see bright rosy children in my school," said one teacher, "who go to work half-time, I meet them afterwards in the streets, grown into sallow young women of sixteen or seventeen."[3] In Halifax, the local School Board permitted children to become half-timers if they passed Standard 2 as late as 1897.[4] On any human grounds the system was indefensible.

The direct exploitation of child labour through the half-time system was from the first opposed by the S.D.F.—and it is to its credit that it took this issue up at a time when such a stand did not make for popularity among textile workers or in other quarters. In the second number of *Justice*, J. L. Joynes launched a sharp attack on Essex farmers who, to ensure cheap child labour at ten, had abolished the necessity of the child's passing any standard at all before going to work.[5] "Anxious as we are for industrial education for the children of all classes" wrote *Justice* in the following year, "we are bitterly opposed to the hideous industrial exploitation which goes on at the expense of their physical, mental and moral development".[6] In the *Historical Basis of Socialism* (1884) Hyndman had already clearly illustrated the stunting and demoralising effect of the half-time system on young children.

In the 1890s the I.L.P. added its voice to demand a clear raising of the school leaving age—to a level that was not in fact to be attained until 1947. "Child labour should be entirely forbidden, a limit of

---

[1] Ben Turner, *About Myself* (1930), 36.
[2] Edwin Chadwick, "On the Rise and Progress of the Half School-Time System of Mixed Physical and Mental Training". *Transactions of the National Association for the Promotion of Social Science, 1880* (1881), 500-3.
[3] D. Torr, *Tom Mann and his Times* (1956), 163.
[4] *Justice*, 31 July 1897.
[5] "School Boards in Arcady", *Justice*, 26 January 1884.
[6] *Justice*, 19 December 1885; see also the article passionately denouncing the half-time system in the previous number.

fifteen years being fixed, and the children should be kept at school till that age", stated the first I.L.P. pamphlet to be published.[1] "The child is now the most pitiful victim of our social conditions . . . our educational system is little better than a farce and will remain so until the school age of children is raised, and until children are protected against premature wage earning."[2] In 1895 the annual conference of the I.L.P. unanimously demanded that the minimum age of child labour be raised from eleven to twelve "as a concession to social decency and industrial justice",[3] but a year later it called for a raising of the minimum age for employment to sixteen with free state maintenance and compulsory technical education provided between the ages of leaving elementary school and entering work. The "only possible excuse" for child labour was that it was educative, but since technological developments had broken down the apprenticeship system this was not so; rather it was injurious to the physical, intellectual and moral welfare of the children.[4]

At this time the S.D.F. also strengthened its agitation, the conference of 1897 deciding, on a motion put by Edward Aveling, to launch a campaign for the abolition of child labour and the institution of free maintenance for school children.[5] Among other activities a leaflet was produced on the subject which was widely distributed in Lancashire and Yorkshire with the aim of educating the textile workers to understand the real issues at stake.[6] By this time the matter had been taken on to the floor of the Trades Union Congress for the first time. Once again it was the Gasworkers' Union, led by the socialists, who fought on this question year in and year out against the textile workers, in an attempt to win the unity that was essential if the trade union movement was to bring its full force to bear in ending child labour.

In 1895, a very strong resolution was moved at Congress by J. R. Clynes (of the Gasworkers' Union), who significantly came from Oldham, the heart of the cotton district. Characterising the exploitation of child labour as "a crime against the human race" he called for the raising of the age of entry to work to fifteen (in discussion he reduced this to fourteen) and for the abolition of all night labour until eighteen.[7] In 1897 the same resolution, moved by Pete Curran also of

[1] The I.L.P., its Programme and Policy (1893).
[2] The Independent Labour Party, What it is and Where it stands, 14 (I.L.P. tract, City of London branch).
[3] 3rd I.L.P. Conference Report, 1895, 9.   [4] 4th I.L.P. Conference Report, 1896, 20.
[5] 17th S.D.F. Conference Report, 1897.   [6] 18th S.D.F. Conference Report, 1898.
[7] 28th T.U.C. Report, 1895, 56.

the Gasworkers' Union, was passed by a vote of 595,000 to 274,000. In the following year the President, James O'Grady of Bristol, made it the first point of his address to demand that something be done "to free our industrial conditions from the blinding shame and disgrace that is attached to it in the half-time system and child labour generally". Of the estimated potential school population aged eleven to fourteen, 500,000 had left school, while another 120,000 were half-timers, three-quarters of them in Lancashire and Cheshire. Much of the responsibility for this "abominable traffic", he said, lay with the textile leaders.[1]

In 1899 the government at last took action, raising the age for total or partial exemption from eleven to twelve.[2] A year later School Boards were given powers to compel part or full time attendance at school up to the age of fourteen instead of thirteen (although by-laws permitting exemption below fourteen had to be established). This was as far as any government was prepared to go for another twenty years. Moving the now annual resolution at the T.U.C. in 1899, Pete Curran welcomed the Act but once again demanded the abolition of all child labour below fourteen, winning the resolution by an increased majority.[3] Despite continued opposition from the textile leaders, the T.U.C. continued to fight on an issue which clearly bore closely on other measures for educational and social advance. "The Congress had in many resolutions declared its desire in favour of increased educational facilities for the children of the working classes," runs the report of a speech by the representative of the Gasworkers in 1900. "But how were these facilities to be obtained if they had to go to work at twelve or thirteen years of age? The real difference between their class and that which governed them was educational. He desired that the children of the working class should have a chance of obtaining knowledge that had been denied to their fathers and grandfathers because he did not think it right that they should for ever continue to be hewers of wood and drawers of water, ignorant of their position and of their social and political status."[4] This was to put the case against the continued exploitation of child labour in the context of the wider demand for education as essential to the political and economic emancipation of the working class.

Children must eat before they can learn; equally opportunities for

---

[1] *30th T.U.C. Report*, 1897, 41; *31st T.U.C. Report*, 1898, 29-30.
[2] Except in agriculture, where a leaving age of eleven was still permitted.
[3] *32nd T.U.C. Report*, 1899, 71.
[4] *33rd T.U.C. Report*, 1900, 88. The mover of the resolution was T. Hurley, a gasworker from Oldham, socialist member of the Blackburn School Board.

physical and mental development depended on freeing them from the obligation to work. In pursuing these points, and advocating adequate maintenance and welfare services to make up for loss of earnings and poverty, the Labour movement was advocating the only policies that could make universal education a reality.

5. AN ENLIGHTENED EDUCATION IN THE SCHOOLS

Free education, free maintenance, the abolition of child labour—these conditions had to be won, as the early socialists saw it, before the children were in a position to benefit from education. It was around these issues, therefore, that they concentrated their main efforts. But what of the character of the education available to children? What was the distinctive attitude of the socialists to the content and methods of education?

The broad vision of social and educational change that inspired men like William Morris has already been described. Here was a perspective towards which socialists might aim; but to realise this vision in practice involved a total social change, and was, therefore, primarily a political issue. In the day to day struggle on education, however, it is apparent that the early socialists now began to see a connection between educational and social change—to see their attempts to bring about an enlightened education as part of the movement for socialism.

Smyth's strong insistence on the need for a secular education before the Cross Commission in 1887 has already been quoted. So far as the content, character, and general aims of education were concerned, this was a crucial issue for the working class and had been recognised as such for nearly 100 years. For the whole of this time the most advanced sections of the working class had fought consciously against the domination of education by the churches and by the sects. Their struggle can be traced from the days of the Corresponding Societies, through the agitation of the Hampden Clubs, the early co-operative movement of 1828-32, rising to a climax at the time of the Chartist movement when, in spite of differences in policy, men like G. J. Harney, William Lovett and later Ernest Jones stood together in the fight for secular education.

For socialists particularly—utopian or scientific—"secular education" was no mere catchword; it was fundamental. The workers who sought education throughout the nineteenth century did so because they came to desire knowledge both for its own sake and as a means to political and economic emancipation. In their view education stood for the pursuit of truth, the discovery of real relationships between things. It was necessary that men should learn the secrets, not only of nature, but also of society. If they were to do so their rational powers must be developed—the child must learn to reason, to find things out for himself. It was in the light of these views that the influence of the churches and the prevalence of religious teaching was condemned. All teaching which inculcated irrational beliefs was to be deplored and the kind of teaching given was particularly open to criticism in that it fostered the values of an inequitable society. The only way to eliminate this and ensure a true education was by freeing the schools from clerical control.

It was in this tradition that the socialists of the 1880s advanced the demand for secular education at a time when the Church of England was making new efforts not only to consolidate voluntary schools but also to dominate the School Boards. "We stand for a purely secular education, just as we insist on the purely materialist basis of socialism," wrote Harry Quelch in 1894, referring to a recent attempt by the clerical majority on the London School Board to strengthen its position. "We can have nothing to do with creeds, for or against. The duty of the community as regards the education of the children is to see that every field of knowledge is opened out to them to the fullest extent, and that their characters shall be trained to the fullest development of the social instinct, and to the fulfilment of their duty to society."[1] "The object of the clerical party in securing representation on the School Board," *Justice* had stated in a main leader six weeks earlier, "has not been to assist the work of education or even primarily to maintain religious instruction, but to stifle, perhaps, and injure in every possible way a system of popular elementary education which was not completely under clerical domination."[2]

The S.D.F. was not, of course, alone in its fight for secular education. As has been noted earlier, secularism had spread widely among the working class; moreover nonconformist Labour leaders and trade unionists for the most part agreed that religion should be separated from education, which should be purely secular. In 1888 the S.D.F. and the Fabian Society collaborated with the Metropolitan Radical Federation and the London Secular Federation in a Central Democratic Committee, to fight the London School Board elections. The traditional outlook of the Labour movement found full expression in

[1] *Justice*, 26 May 1894.   [2] *Justice*, 14 April 1894.

the Committee's Appeal to the electors, rendered the more urgent by the challenge of the Church party:

"The reactionists are making a desperate effort to put public education under clerical control, and this is the first danger you have to confront. If the school is made subordinate to the Church, the schoolmaster to the priest, education to theology—the life of the State Church will be prolonged, secular interests will be sacrificed, the whole tone of popular instruction will be degraded below even its present standard, and the mental and moral development of the people will be indefinitely delayed."[1] Religion, therefore, should be excluded from the public schools. A militant campaign ended in success. Both Annie Besant and Stewart Headlam were elected to the London School Board—the former at the head of the poll in her district. A Christian Socialist and Anglican parson, Headlam remained a consistent supporter of secular education throughout the battles that lay ahead.

The foundation of the I.L.P. brought into the organised socialist movement many nonconformists, and, at its inaugural conference in 1893, this body adopted as part of its programme "free, unsectarian, primary, secondary and university education"; an amendment for secular education apparently receiving no support.[2] Four years later, however, the I.L.P. came out for secular education, insisting on the need to develop positive instruction in moral values in the school. That same year a "Moral Instruction League" was established to press for the teaching of a secular morality in the schools in place of religious instruction.[3] The need for moral education had been advanced by Smyth in his evidence to the Cross Commission. From the days of the late eighteenth century advanced educationists had always held that secular moral teaching was an imperatively necessary part of an all-round education.[4]

To achieve a secular education, or to defend the considerable degree of secularism in the board schools that had been won through the 1870 Act, this, then, was a major objective of socialist educators. But there was much in the kind of education given in these schools which was

[1] Quoted in McCann, op. cit., 500.
[2] H. Pelling, Origin of the Labour Party (1954), 125.
[3] See F. H. Hilliard, "The Moral Instruction League, 1897-1919", in The Durham Research Review, Vol. III, No. 12, September 1961.
[4] Thomas Day, the Edgeworths, and others gathered around the Lunar Society and the Manchester Literary and Philosophical Society in the late eighteenth century regarded the teaching of a secular morality as the mainspring of education. It was this outlook that was taken up by such men as Richard Carlile, Robert Owen, William Thompson, and later by Lovett and others who saw such teaching as the essential basis of a rational education.

THE LONDON SCHOOL BOARD IN 1882

A LONDON SCHOOL BOARD CAPTURE IN 1871

A LONDON BOARD SCHOOL ERECTED IN THE EARLY 1870'S

open to attack. What was the attitude of the socialists to wider questions of the content and methods of education?

A sharp critique of the content of education in these schools was made by H. W. Hobart in a series of articles in *Justice* in 1894. A print-worker, Hobart was one of the socialists most concerned with education, and stood more than once as an S.D.F. candidate for the London School Board.

His first article, on elementary education, ranged widely over the curriculum and analysed the kind of outlook fostered by the schools. The history textbook used in board schools covering the period 1485–1880 contained 160 references to war and bloodshed and only 60 to peaceful social reform. Geography was mainly confined to the areas where British arms had been successful. The content of these subjects, together with the teaching of writing and arithmetic, was extremely limited. But Hobart reserved his main polemic for the total effect of board school education which, he claimed, aimed to develop submissiveness and acceptance of a capitalist morality. "Honour the Queen, obey your superiors, and run away from every policeman", such was the attitude inculcated by the schools:

"Every item which receives attention is so prepared for administration to a submissive and patient race of children that it is nothing short of marvellous that any of them, when they become adults, break away from the old rut of submissive obedience. The commercial spirit of greed and gain is fostered in every possible way. A successful man is picked out and held up as an example worth imitating. If they are taught proportion the sums are put in this way: if I purchase an article for three farthings and sell it for a penny what per cent profit should I make on an invested capital of £100? . . . The elementary education given today in our Board Schools does no more than prepare the minds of the children for their patient obedience to the domination of a proud and haughty middle and upper class. The spirit of competition . . . is encouraged; the grab-all, grasping idea of 'profit' is held up as an ideal to be striven for; the individual, personal, selfish doctrine of 'get on, honestly if possible, but get on', is rammed and jammed down the children's throats, but not a single word or hint of the advantage of co-operative association for the welfare of all is ever breathed."[1]

Hobart, advocating a fundamental revision of the content of education, advanced several proposals particularly in relation to technical

[1] *Justice*, 30 June 1894.

K

education. Similar ideas were voiced by Annie Besant in an article on "Socialism and Education", which argued for a rational education; she advocated the training of reason, memory and observation, the revision of history teaching, and the development of a secondary education covering science, technology and the humanities.[1] To put forward ideas of this kind was implicitly to criticise the prevailing methods of teaching, forced on the schools by Robert Lowe's system of payment by results.

It was this system of drilling which roused the greatest anger among socialist educators—as among progressive educationists and teachers generally. "Week by week, month by month," wrote Hobart, "in the most barren and sterile ground, the teacher has to hammer and drive the course of education laid down by law. The children are urged, persuaded, and coaxed into trying to become efficient for the so-called examination."[2] "The whole system of teaching in Board Schools is radically wrong", H. H. Sparling had written in *Commonweal* several years earlier. "Children are turned into animated small hoppers; the names and dry bones of ever so many sciences and arts are crammed into them by means of cumbersome, expensive and wasteful machinery. A multitude of bare facts and figures are forced into them willy-nilly. . . . There are but few faculties brought into play in a worker's daily task; fewer still of the things he has learned in school have any bearing thereupon; it is no wonder, therefore, that most of his faculties become atrophied from disease, and that his brain rejects the unrelated 'learning got by rote'."[3] It was because monitorial schools had relied on cramming and rote learning, making no effort to develop intellectual initiative, that Owen, William Thompson and others criticised these at the beginning of the century. It was for the same reason that the system of payment by results was rejected by Thomas Smyth, Hobart, Annie Besant and others half a century later.

This humanist outlook also found expression in the attempt to ameliorate harsh methods of punishment, widely used in the board schools. If children were to be treated as rational beings, with respect and love, and this was the socialist tradition in education, then the use of physical violence must be brought to an end. It appears that working-men's Radical Clubs, in particular, protested against the use of the cane in board schools.[4] S.D.F. members of School Boards were to the fore

[1] McCann, *op. cit.*, 228-31.   [2] *Justice*, 7 July 1894.
[3] "Does Education diminish Industry?", *Commonweal*, 9 April 1887.
[4] "The teachers [lost] a good deal of progressive and working-class sympathy by their insistence on full freedom to inflict corporal punishment"; Asher Tropp, *The School*

in the attempt to stamp out this evil; in the late 1890s socialist members of the Reading School Board conducted a long-drawn campaign against corporal punishment which was given considerable publicity in *Justice*.[1] The I.L.P. was also concerned with the matter, many of its School Board members playing a leading part in the activities of the "Society for the Reform of School Discipline" formed at the turn of the century to oppose corporal punishment in schools.[2]

Socialists, therefore, consistently advocated a new outlook in the schools, not only teaching on enlightened lines but also a human attitude to discipline, and respect for children as individuals; in this they stood in the classical tradition of the humanist educators of the past.

6. WORK ON THE SCHOOL BOARDS

The most direct way of influencing developments in the schools was to ensure that socialists gained a place on the School Boards. These were directly elected *ad hoc* bodies which, from 1870 to 1903, controlled all local schools except the church schools. Since candidates were elected on a cumulative voting system under which each ratepayer had as many votes as there were places on the Board, and these votes could either be distributed or "plumped" on one candidate, it was possible for minorities to gain representation. It was under this system that those working towards independent politics and the election of working-class representatives were able to gain their first, isolated successes, so asserting the right to serve on public bodies.

Immediately after the passing of the 1870 Act, when the backwash of the united movement in support of universal education was still being felt, a number of working men stood for election, sometimes on the lists of the various denominations, but occasionally as independent candidates of a Liberal-Radical persuasion. As many as thirteen went to the poll in London at the first elections; one was successful, Benjamin

Teachers (1957), 134n. The Finsbury Clubs Radical Association and the Hackney Radical Club were among those that protested in the early 1880s against the London School Board's proposal to place the cane in the hands of assistant teachers; M. E. Highfield and A. Pinsent, *A Survey of Rewards and Punishments in Schools* (1952), 47. Benjamin Lucraft, of the London School Board, introduced a working men's deputation to the Board on the same issue; Thomas Gautrey, *School Board Memories* (n.d., c. 1937), 59.

[1] Cf. *Justice*, 28 January 1899.

[2] McCann, *op. cit.*, 293-4, cf. *I.L.P. News*, July 1901. Of the sixty-three members of the committee of this organisation, eleven were I.L.P. School Board members.

Lucraft.[1] The struggle for independent Labour representation that these candidatures implied aroused strong resistance from sections of the Liberal Party. In Birmingham, for instance, home of the National Education League, the Radicals, who had made much of the support of the working class in their campaign of 1869-70, refused to accept a single working-class candidate on their list. When W. J. Davis, a national trade union secretary of Liberal persuasion, stood at a by-election in 1875 as an independent working-class candidate, the reaction of the Liberals was violent. They feared above all the presentation of class issues that such a candidature implied.[2]

By the mid-1880s trades councils or trade union branches were beginning to make a wider challenge. At Bristol, for example, a Labour League was set up with the aim of winning Labour representation in Parliament and on all local bodies, not only the School Boards, but the City Council and the body of Guardians of the poor. The League first fought the School Board elections in 1886, putting up John Fox, secretary of the Bristol Trade and Provident Society, who stood on a programme of free, compulsory and secular education. When an approach was made by "a prominent member of the School Board" to gain withdrawal of the candidate, the secretary of the Labour League replied in terms which reflected the rising militancy of the period:

> "No Sir, there is not the ghost of a chance of our withdrawing our man. He is going in, and let me tell you as emphatically as I can that from this day forward the working men of Bristol will have to be consulted in these matters. . . .We are determined that a principle shall be planted on that Board which will strongly protest against the domination of the so-called upper classes over the working class—a protest against that which has brought the workers to the fearful state in which we today find them."[3]

It was this spirit of determination that gained some seats on the

---

[1] McCann, op. cit., 71. Elsewhere, trade union and working men's candidates won isolated successes, for instance at Plymouth, Nottingham, Hanley, Longton, Liverpool, Walsall. Ibid., 72-3.

[2] McCann, op. cit., 84-8.

[3] S. Bryher, The Labour and Socialist Movement in Bristol (1929), Pt. I, 35. The enthusiasm that a challenge of this kind aroused was reflected in the success of the two candidates put up by the Gasworkers' Union immediately after its formation for the Barking School Board. With an election committee of 1,600 (the gasworkers in the area, mostly employed at the Beckton gas works) both were successful, their victory being celebrated by a torch-light procession of 10,000. Justice, 5 October, 19 October, 1889.

School Boards for working men, representing the outlook of the class for whom the schools were designed.

At this time, also, the first challenge was made by the organised socialist movement. In 1885 the S.D.F. ran four candidates in London, including H. H. Champion, Harry Quelch and Herbert Burrows. None was successful, but Burrows gained 4,232 votes in Tower Hamlets.[1] At the next contest, three years later, a socialist (H. H. Gore) was elected at Bristol, Stewart Headlam and Annie Besant in London, while at Newcastle, Tom Mann, S.D.F. organiser, successfully organised the return of three socialist members to the School Board.[2]

It was in London that the socialists made their major challenge during the early years. Here lay the headquarters and the main strength of the S.D.F. and the Fabians, while linked with these were many secular societies and Radical clubs. From the days of Lucraft's election a tradition of working-class representation existed—in 1873 George Potter, well-known trade unionist and manager of the *Bee-Hive*, had gained a seat and conducted a consistent struggle for free education; it was he who was successful in getting the committee of enquiry set up into endowments under the control of the London School Board and the City Companies. In 1876 John Stuart Mill's step-daughter, Helen Taylor, was returned at the top of the poll for Southwark as an Independent Radical Democratic candidate. She played a very important part on the Board for nearly ten years, as she moved towards socialism, demanding return for the use of the working class of the many endowments originally given to the poor, as well as in many other matters. "Miss Taylor," wrote *Justice* in 1885, referring to a series of addresses she was giving to her constituents, "by her entire devotion to the cause of the poor, and her bitter hostility to the jobbery and robbery which finds so much favour with the majority of the

---

[1] The first members of the S.D.F. to be elected on to School Boards may well have been Jonathon Taylor of Sheffield and George Smart of Salford, whose victories were announced in *Justice* in 1885 (14 November 1885). Taylor had first been elected in 1879: "There was a bright spark called Taylor who seemed to run a party entirely on his own, with considerable success", writes J. H. Bingham in *The Sheffield School Board, 1870-1903* (1949), 16. He joined the Democratic Federation early in the 1880s and became, "like Helen Taylor . . . a great advocate of free education". H. W. Lee and E Archbold, *Social Democracy in Britain* (1935), 89-90.

[2] Lee and Archbold, *op. cit.*, 123; their names were Hill, Laidler and Stewart. According to Beatrice Webb, this victory upset the Liberal politician, John Morley, M.P. for Newcastle. "He is anxious about the socialists at Newcastle," she wrote in her diary, "up till now he has treated them with indifference, not to say contempt; but they mustered two thousand votes at the last School Board election, and Morley began to take them seriously." *My Apprenticeship* (1926), 306.

members, has made herself the most popular person among the workers of Southwark."[1] Another advanced member of the early London School Board was Edward Aveling who was elected with the help of London secular and radical clubs in 1882, and served until 1885.[2]

This was the year in which the S.D.F. first contested the elections, and from now on socialist and democratic organisations consistently fought each campaign on a progressive educational policy, both *Justice* and *Fabian News* devoting considerable attention to London educational problems. In 1888 the Central Democratic Committee issued the programme and manifesto already referred to, launching the campaign which gained seats for Annie Besant and Stewart Headlam who were joined by a third socialist, A. G. Cook. Annie Besant, member of both the Fabian Society and the S.D.F. but by this time far closer to the outlook of the latter, ran a very effective campaign for the Tower Hamlets constituency on a programme of free secular education, free meals for poor schoolchildren and "fair wages" not only for School Board employees but for all those employed by firms carrying out School Board contracts. "There were outdoor meetings and indoor meetings, daylight meetings and torchlight meetings", and Annie Besant, who had Herbert Burrows as her agent and Bernard Shaw as one of her speakers, was returned at the head of the poll. She made a tremendous impact on the School Board during the next three years, taking up a whole number of progressive issues with Headlam's support, often successfully. She did not, however, contest the next election, having by this time found her way to theosophy.[3]

In 1891, again in 1894 and 1897 the S.D.F. and the Fabians fought the triennial elections. In the first of these years the "Moderates", headed by the hated J. R. Diggle and in fact a reactionary grouping, again gained a majority, Stewart Headlam being the only socialist returned. In subsequent years the Fabian Tracts "Questions for School Board Candidates" and "The Workers' School Board Programme" were issued to strengthen the fight, and in 1894 the Progressives, supported by the Fabians, nearly achieved victory; the S.D.F. with nine candidates (one of whom was H. W. Hobart) and an independent

---

[1] *Justice*, 2 May 1885. Helen Taylor was working closely with the socialists at this time. For a brief description of her work among her electors and on the School Board, see F. W. Soutter, *Recollections of a Labour Pioneer* (2nd ed. 1924), 84-8. She withdrew her candidature during the contest of 1885 (*Justice*, 7 November 1885).

[2] *Justice*, 7 February 1885, includes a letter from Aveling on his conduct on the Board.

[3] Annie Besant's campaign and actions on the London School Board are graphically described in Arthur H. Nethercot, *The First Five Lives of Annie Besant* (1961), 276-86.

campaign run by George Lansbury, increased its vote to over 44,000, but without gaining a success.[1] Of the Fabians, Headlam was again successful and he was joined by Graham Wallas. There was a further swing in 1897 when the Moderates were finally defeated and Graham Wallas and Headlam achieved positions of considerable influence as Chairman of the School Management Committee and Evening Classes Committee respectively. For the S.D.F., W. G. Pearson nearly won the Tower Hamlets constituency, and though the I.L.P., whose strength lay in the provinces, ran no candidates, Mrs. Bridges Adams was elected for Greenwich as an "Independent and Labour candidate" on a clear policy of equal educational opportunity.[2]

In the provinces also the campaign received an impetus with the foundation of the I.L.P. in 1893. Earlier successes in Bristol and at Newcastle have already been mentioned and, in the late 1880s, such men as Keir Hardie, Robert Smillie and Ben Turner were finding their way on to School Boards—Keir Hardie at Auchinleck, Bob Smillie at Larkhall where the miners ran him as a Labour candidate and Ben Turner at Batley.[3] In the elections of 1894 a number of successes were achieved, partly as a result of more highly organised campaigning; in Birmingham, for instance, an I.L.P. candidate, David Millar, standing for the first time with the backing of the Trades Council and the support of the local branch of the S.D.F., came third in the poll, taking votes from the famous "Liberal Eight" who had dominated the School Board for many years.[4] In Manchester a United Labour Party was brought into being by the Trades Council and I.L.P. and put up three candidates for Manchester and Salford—all I.L.P. members, including Mrs. Emmeline Pankhurst—who fought the campaign on a broad, progressive programme. Although these were unsuccessful, another I.L.P. member, Joseph Nuttall, was elected for the first time at the neighbouring city of Salford; the Labour movement had begun to show its potential force and, at the next election in 1897, Fred Brocklehurst of the I.L.P. was elected to the Manchester School Board while Nuttall retained his seat.[5] Other

[1] *Justice*, 1 December 1894. To strengthen their case at this election the Progressives published *The Case against Diggleism*, subtitled "plain facts concerning the reactionary policy of the present majority on the London School Board, 1891-4".

[2] McCann, *op. cit.*, 262.

[3] W. Stewart, *Keir Hardie* (1925 edn.), 33; Ben Turner, *About Myself* (1930), 170-1; R. Smillie, *My Life for Labour* (1924), 94-5. "It is rather remarkable that I, to whom anything but self-education was denied by inexorable circumstances, should make membership of the Larkhall School Board one of my first objectives," wrote Smillie.

[4] McCann, *op. cit.*, 257-9.   [5] *Ibid.*, 245-56, 261.

important successes at this time included that of Charles Hobson, President of the Trades Council at Sheffield, who headed the poll, of Tom Hurley, socialist candidate at Blackburn who also topped the poll, and, of particular significance, that of Margaret McMillan at Bradford. Recently arrived as a socialist agitator in the city, Margaret McMillan found herself immediately concerned about the position of the children; she was elected to the School Board as an I.L.P. candidate in 1894.[1]

In subsequent years there were other noteworthy contests fought to a successful conclusion. In Burnley, an S.D.F. stronghold, Dan Irving, S.D.F. organiser and later M.P., was elected top of the poll in 1897 with over 14,000 votes.[2] In Reading, another S.D.F. centre, G. H. Wilson and J. F. Hodgson began in 1895 a militant struggle on the School Board, while in 1899, *Justice* particularly welcomed the success of the S.D.F. candidate in Norwich, whose programme "was as definitely and outspokenly socialist as any of us could wish".[3] There were other S.D.F. victories at Barry, Darwen, Ilkeston, Nottingham, Blackburn and elsewhere. The Chairman of the Annual Conference of the S.D.F. held in Manchester in 1899, T. M. Purves, devoted most of his opening speech to education, congratulating *Justice* on its "Educational Notes", now a regular feature, and stressed the important functions of the School Boards in the struggle for national secular education.[4]

The *Labour Annual* of 1897 prints a list of fifty-seven socialist members of School Boards, the great majority being I.L.P. members; in 1899 the I.L.P. officially claimed seventy-one, among them Ben Riley of Huddersfield, whose job was to co-ordinate the work of I.L.P. School Board members, Philip Snowden, R. Smillie, E. R. Hartley, Margaret McMillan, Mrs. Bridges Adams (in London), Fred Brocklehurst and Joseph Nuttall. Speaking in the House of Commons in 1896 John Burns claimed a total of 500-600 working men on School Boards, but this was no more than a guess.[5] But whatever the overall figure, there is no doubt that members of the I.L.P. and the lesser

---

[1] Fenner Brockway, *Socialism over Sixty Years* (1946), 60-1.
[2] *Justice*, 19 May 1900, carries an article on Dan Irving's work on the Burnley School Board.
[3] *Justice*, 2 December 1899. His five-point programme included: (1) Raising of the school leaving age to sixteen, (2) total abolition of the half-time system, (3) free maintenance, (4) a purely secular education, (5) limitation of pupils in a class to thirty.
[4] *14th S.D.F. Conference Report*, 1899.
[5] McCann, *op. cit.*, 262-3. There are no reliable figures and considerable research would be necessary to establish the position.

Leicester School Board Election,

MONDAY NEXT, December 6th, 1897.

To the Burgesses of the Borough of Leicester.

IES AND GENTLEMEN,

Having been adopted by the Independent Labour Party as a candidate for the School Board, I respectfully to solicit your Vote and Interest on their behalf. I am not new to Educational Work, having ed a term of nine months on the Leicester School Board. I regard the principal of Labour representation ll public bodies as a just and legitimate right, therefore I take this opportunity of making the influence of ur felt and respected on our local School Board; our hope as a nation lies in the correct education of the lren of the workers, and it is of vital importance that we should, individually and collectively, do our utmost ecure the best possible education for them. I am a Trade Unionist of eleven years' standing; my whole life been spent in the building trade, and as a practical man I should be of great service on the Building amittee.

I am in favour of abolishing theological teaching and substituting for it systematic moral instruction.

Having come in personal contact with the sufferings of our poor, I should urge the Board to endeavour btain the power to give at least one free meal per day to needy children.

I should advocate the appointment, by the Board, of Medical Gentlemen in various districts to examine lren, as required by the Board, and grant Certificates free of expense.

I am in favour of Higher Grade Schools being provided for the advanced scholars, so that the children of poor may have equal opportunities with those who are better off.

I think that facilities should be given for Lessons in Swimming for both sexes, and that the physical lopment of the children should receive attention as well as the intellectual.

I should advocate the Board doing its own work direct without the intervention of a contractor, and thus the extortionate sums of money which flow into the pockets of contractors, and that only practical men be inted as Clerks of Works.

I am in favour of the enforcement of a penalty for any evasion of the Board's terms of contract.

I am in favour of all employees under the Board retaining their citizenship and being free to organise or ke any public position, providing such does not interfere with their duties.

I am also in favour of Evening Sittings of the Board, in order to give greater facilities to working men to as representatives.

Should you honour me with your support, I trust my devotion to my duties as a representative during the t three years will justify the confidence you repose in me.

I remain, yours faithfully,

St. Saviour's Road.   **HENRY PAYNE.**

PLUMP FOR PAYNE!

15 VOTES.   NO CROSSES.

Printed and Published by the Leicester Co-operative Printing Society Limited, East Bond Street.

ELECTION ADDRESS OF AN I.L.P. SCHOOL BOARD CANDIDATE, 1897

numbers for the S.D.F. were beginning to make their mark, bringing into the deliberations of the School Boards a distinctive working-class and often a socialist policy on education.

Working-class representatives were, of course, always in a minority. Indeed they were sometimes completely isolated on Boards whose members for the most part either represented or supported one or other religious body—Anglican, Nonconformist or Roman Catholic.[1] As a result their powers were often limited and indeed to achieve any-thing worth while involved winning other members to their point of view—a step sometimes involving public campaigning on a mass scale as, for instance, in the case of Mrs. Besant. Nonetheless the record of work of some of these members is impressive, ranging as it did from broad demands for free secular education and for the provision of meals and medical facilities, to proposals to purchase pianos for schools out of the rates. It is only possible here to outline some of these activities.

One matter taken up with great energy was not strictly an educa-tional issue at all, but of considerable significance for the trade union movement—that School Board contracts be given only to firms that paid "fair wages". For years the trade union movement had worked for official recognition of a standard minimum wage, urging, in particular, that the government and local authorities should insist on this clause in all their contracts. This was one of the issues on which Mrs. Besant campaigned in the elections of 1888; it was also the main point in the platform of A. G. Cook, a London printer who was also successful. "By their eloquence and technical skill," write the Webbs, the socialist members persuaded the London School Board to accept this condition early in 1889.[2] This break-through had important reper-cussions throughout the country. Other socialists took up the issue in their localities—Joseph Shufflebotham at Bolton, Joseph Nuttall at Salford, Ben Turner at Batley.

One of the main educational issues was the abolition of school fees. The part played by Fred Brocklehurst and Joseph Nuttall in this agitation has already been mentioned. Nuttall, who opened his cam-paign in 1898, at one time ran a series of weekly meetings to put the facts of the situation before the working class.[3] In Bolton, partly as a

---

[1] "The Board was divided into four parts," writes Ben Turner, "the Liberals, or Non-conformists, the Churchmen, or Conservatives, the Catholic Priest—a real trojan for his folks—and myself." *Op. cit.,* 170.

[2] S. and B. Webb, *History of Trade Unionism,* 385.

[3] McCann, *op. cit.,* 278.

result of the activities of an S.D.F. member of the School Board, all elementary schools (other than the higher grade schools) were made free by 1893.[1] London socialists, backed by the S.D.F. and other organisations, ran a consistent campaign on this issue from the time of their election in 1888. But the abolition of school fees was only one aspect of the matter. In many areas there were other costs, particularly charges for books, which bore hardly on an impoverished working class. Robert Smillie conducted a classic battle on this issue on the Larkhall School Board for over six years. He found no support whatsoever when he first raised the question. Nor, he claims, would he have gained any at the end but for a threat at the final meeting before the election. "I told the members of the Board that I was going to make that election a fight on free books," he records in his autobiography. As a result a majority pledged themselves to vote for free books if returned. Larkhall was the second town in Scotland to adopt this reform. "I am prouder of nothing in my life than of this triumph," Smillie writes, "which was accomplished after a very hard, uphill fight."[2]

Socialists also carried into the Boards the long-standing working-class demand for secular education. The election of Annie Besant, in particular, was a demonstration of support for secular principles, as member of the London School Board she advocated the teaching of science, criticised religious teaching, and questioned the position of the Church schools and training colleges.[3] After 1891 Headlam was equally active. In a lecture on the work of the socialist members he gave a vivid picture of the London School Board after the Church and Tory victory of 1891. In spite of the deficiency of accommodation, he said, whenever the Board proposed to build a school, the majority took care to hear all possible objections. "So a dismal procession of clergy and local aristocracy come before them; the clergy beg for time to enable them to collect funds to enlarge or rebuild their often insanitary sectarian schools; and the landlords come to complain that the proposed site is shockingly close to the mansion of the Dowager Duchess of Pimlico, or to the residences of the aristocracy of Dalston and Tower Hamlets. To such complaints the Board lent a willing ear."[4]

Similar tactics were used in the provinces, and it was perhaps not

---

[1] Ibid., 270.   [2] R. Smillie, My Life for Labour, 95.
[3] Nethercot, op. cit., 283.
[4] Fabian News, Vol. IV, No. 4, June 1894.

unusual for working-class members of School Boards to find themselves in the position of Joseph Nuttall of Salford defending the whole Board School system against attacks by the Churchmen. "On a resolution opposing the purchase of a plot of land in Seedley on which to build a school," he states, in the course of a very competent report on his work to the Trades Council, "the Rev. J. E. Gull went out of his way to make a severe and unjustifiable attack on the School Board system, stating that it was responsible for the present immoral condition of the people. In contradiction of this groundless and base statement I defended the Board Schools, their teachers, and the people, pointing to facts which were admitted by subsequent speakers which went to prove the high moral tone of the present education given in Board Schools."[1]

Free education, free books, these severely practical measures were seen as necessary, but far more than this was required if every working-class child was to be in a position to gain something from his education; in particular the children needed to be properly nourished and cared for. School Boards were not permitted to spend money on the feeding of school children, but members of the S.D.F. were not deterred from advancing the demand for one free meal a day. In London in 1888, of all the School Board candidates only Annie Besant and Stewart Headlam made the provision of school meals a main point in election addresses. On the School Board itself, Annie Besant took up this question with her customary energy, assisting in setting on foot an official enquiry which found that an average of 43,000 children were underfed in London schools alone. She also helped to set up the non-party "London Schools Dinner Association" to provide meals for hungry children,[2] and in 1889 claimed to have raised herself sufficient money to provide some 36,000 lunches for poor children. According to George Lansbury, her exposure of "the absurdity of the idea of trying to educate half-starving children" was one of her greatest contributions to social reform at this time.[3]

It was, perhaps, in connection with the health and welfare of school children that the most remarkable work was done by socialists before the turn of the century. In Bradford, Margaret McMillan became a pioneer of school feeding in the course of her long battle for the

---

[1] McCann, op. cit., 516. Joseph Shufflebotham of Bolton reprinted as a pamphlet (*A Plea for Secular Education in our Board Schools*) a speech made on the Board which the press failed adequately to report. *Ibid.*, 272; the pamphlet was reviewed in *Justice*, 18 June 1898.

[2] *Ibid.*, 267.   [3] Nethercot, op. cit., 283.

medical care and health of deprived children; in other areas, socialist
School Board members took what steps they could in the same direction. In London, Annie Besant's work laid the foundation for the
system of medical inspection and treatment that was later to come into
being.[1] In Bolton, Reading, Salford, Bradford and elsewhere socialist
and working-class School Board members began at this time to seek
special provision for defective children, especially those with defective
eyesight. In Burnley, Dan Irving succeeded in getting special classes
organised for mentally and physically defective children. Members of
the S.D.F. on the Reading School Board gained an official enquiry
which found 795 defective children; the result was the appointment
of a Medical Officer in a consultative capacity—an important achievement in itself and perhaps even more important as a precedent.[2]

Margaret McMillan's long-drawn struggle at Bradford towards the
close of the century took on something of an epic quality and became
the model of what an isolated socialist on a School Board could
achieve. In spite of strong opposition at the outset she fought for the
deprived, under-nourished and sickly slum child with such energy
and vitality and with such a single consuming purpose as finally to
rouse the whole country on these issues and become a national figure.

Margaret McMillan began her career on the School Board (as the
youngest member and only woman) by leading an agitation against
the half-time system which was particularly widespread in Bradford.
"The half-timers fell asleep at their desks, exhausted," she wrote,
"still from streets and alleys children attended school in every stage
of physical misery."[3] Speaking at open-air meetings and at mass
rallies at the St. George's Hall on Sunday nights she attracted vast
audiences to whom she conveyed something of her feeling about
education and the potentialities of life. In 1895 she led a deputation to
Asquith, the Home Secretary, on the half-time question and wrote a
Clarion pamphlet, *Child Labour and the Half-Time System*, which played
a part in assuring the raising of the age to twelve.

With Dr. Kerr, the School Medical Officer (the first appointment of
its kind in the country), Margaret McMillan set out to reveal the true
physical state of the children as a first step to ensuring effective measures
for treatment. Investigations were made of children's noses, throats,
ears, of children's heads and clothing (showing the need for fumigating

[1] *Ibid.*, 283.   [2] McCann, *op. cit.*, 275.
[3] Quoted in Miriam Lord, *Margaret McMillan in Bradford* (1957), 9, the fourth Margaret
McMillan lecture, from which this summary of her work in Bradford is taken.

stations for verminous children, over 100 of whom had not had their clothes off for six to eight months) and on similar matters. These reports made clear the need for systematic medical inspection—the first of these, covering 300 children, was reported at a Town's meeting, and led to a campaign for school clinics that was finally successful, and for the appointment of school nurses and the first school dentist. A four-year battle for school baths and showers was finally won and in 1897 the first school baths in the country were opened in Bradford.

To improve physical health was to lay the basis for improving education. Margaret McMillan was also concerned with the lay-out of classrooms, improved ventilation, the provision of small tables for young children instead of desks, and so on. She actively took up questions bearing on the broadening of the curriculum, the development of higher grade schools, the training of teachers. Indeed to review the work of socialist members of School Boards is to find them working on the practical plane to realise, step by step, the aims summarised in their programme as "state maintenance". In addition to the many activities already described they pressed for the free use of swimming baths by school children, the right to take them on educational visits to museums and botanical gardens, the development of school libraries. They spoke up on School Boards for improved salaries for teachers, equal pay for men and women, the raising of the leaving age to fourteen and even sixteen. It was to make the work of the Boards better known to electors that they pressed for the placing of minutes of the Boards' meetings in the city libraries, as also to change the time of meetings to the evening and to allow free use of the schools for public gatherings. In all these ways they sought to extend democratic control over the schools, to broaden education, and so to realise in practice—even under the most difficult and distressing conditions in industrial cities—that broad view of the role and purpose of education which formed so essential an aspect of the socialist outlook.

7. ACHIEVEMENTS AND TRENDS

The system of board schools, administered by locally elected bodies, was always in danger, as has been illustrated by Stewart Headlam's description of the London Board after the election of 1891. The School Board in Manchester, writes the historian of Manchester city government, "had a majority of Churchmen and Roman Catholics for the whole of its existence, and these members were elected primarily to see that the new Board schools which they had to manage did as little damage as possible to their own schools, in which many of them were naturally more interested".[1] From the outset there had been concerted efforts to control and limit this new system, brought into being by the Education Act of 1870, efforts which, as we have seen, the radical and Labour movement worked to counteract. Frederick Engels reviewed the background of these moves in 1892, in the introduction to the English edition of his *Socialism: Utopian and Scientific* which achieved a wide circulation. The English middle class, he wrote, "had shared their power but reluctantly with the working class. They had learnt, during the Chartist years, what that *puer robustus sed malitiosus*, the people, is capable of. And since that time they had been compelled to incorporate the better part of the People's Charter in the Statutes of the United Kingdom. Now, if ever, the people must be kept in order by moral means, and the first and foremost of all moral means of action upon the masses is and remains—religion. Hence the parsons' majorities on the School Boards, hence the increasing self-taxation of the bourgeoisie for the support of all sorts of revivalism, from ritualism to the Salvation Army."[2]

If the School Board system could not be controlled—and there was increasing evidence that the schools were outgrowing limitations— then it must be undermined and destroyed. Throughout the 1880s Anglicans and Roman Catholics, who had consistently opposed popular control of education, attacked the School Board system with increasing confidence and at the same time consistently demanded increased support for voluntary schools from public funds.[3] With the return of a Tory government in 1895—to last for ten years—those opposing the board school system gained the ascendant. A. J. Balfour raised the cry of the "intolerable strain" to which voluntary schools were subjected. One of the first concerns of this government was, then, to extend fresh aid to church schools, threatened by the growing efficiency and numbers of board schools, and to curb the activities of School Boards. In 1896 a government Bill was introduced conceding a

---

[1] S. D. Simon, *A Century of City Government* (1938), 240. "When any question of the provision of extra school accommodation by the Board arose, the proposal was fought by the voluntarists on the ground (1) that there were sufficient places in existing denominational schools, (2) that the new Board schools would undersell existing and poorer Church and Roman Catholic schools and (3) that it was a waste of the ratepayers' money to erect them." *Ibid.*, 241.

[2] K. Marx and F. Engels, *Selected Works*, Vol. II, 104.

[3] Thus Cardinal Manning worked with the Church of England and Wesleyans in the Voluntary Schools Association in the 1880s demanding rate support for voluntary schools. A. W. Hutton, *op. cit.*, 173.

"Special Aid Grant" of 4s. for every child in average attendance in voluntary schools, and limiting the amount of the rate School Boards might levy. In addition the Bill proposed repealing the famous Cowper-Temple clause of the 1870 Act to allow denominational teaching in board schools; it also proposed that the County and County Borough Councils should be the authorities for secondary and technical education, and included a provision which would have resulted in the abolition of School Boards in country districts where the powers of the education authority might be vested in the county councils—by comparison bodies representing parson and squire.[1]

It was the introduction of this Bill that caused the I.L.P. to come out for secular, as opposed to unsectarian education, although within the I.L.P. certain rifts were shown which were to have some importance when the vital battles were joined over the 1902 Act. It has been suggested that the Bill took the Labour movement by surprise—the S.D.F. however, was quite clear in its opposition. "Apart from the proposed raising of the age and the grant to secondary education, the measure may be described as wholly bad," wrote *Justice* in its first comment on 9 May 1896. Many School Boards might be incompetent but "they are not as bad as the committees elected by Town and County Councils are likely to be"; these, entirely free from ratepayer control, "will be practically irresponsible". In effect the Bill would put education under the charge of the Church.

This was the main ground for opposition—the subsidising of clericalism, the handing over of public money to religious bodies without any public control. A fortnight later *Justice* devoted a main leader, "Social Democracy and Education", to castigating clericalism as the enemy and calling for the rallying of all progressive forces against the Bill.[2] The standpoint of the Labour movement was made clear at a meeting called by the London Trades Council—still active in the cause of education—on June 12. This was attended by representatives of thirty-four Trades Councils, many Radical and Liberal Clubs, Fabians, London I.L.P. and S.D.F. branches, the Hammersmith Socialist Society, the Metropolitan Radical Federation and the London Secular Society. The meeting strongly condemned the Bill on a

---

[1] B. M. Allen, *Sir Robert Morant* (1934), 105-10. See also E. Halévy, *Imperialism and Rise of Labour* (1961 edn.), 191-2; Halévy describes the Bill as "a clumsy makeshift". The Bill attempted, in its clauses on the County Councils, to take into account the proposals of the Royal Commission on Secondary Education (the Bryce Commission) which had reported in 1895.

[2] *Justice*, 23 May 1896.

number of counts. It protested against the expenditure of public money on schools not controlled by representative bodies, opposed the setting up of committees of the County Councils to administer education, criticised the failure to bring secondary education within the reach of the workers, and finally demanded three free meals a day for all children.[1] Trades Councils at Sheffield and Birmingham organised or supported meetings protesting against the Bill as an attack on religious liberty and popular education.[2] There was a similar reaction from the T.U.C., its Parliamentary Committee characterising the Bill as "of a retrograde and questionable character".

Liberals, acting in the nonconformist interest, also strongly opposed the Bill—the proposed repeal of the Cowper-Temple clause "threatened to raise the religious question in the House of Commons in its acutest form"; the "bitter hostility of the School Boards" was aroused by the proposals concerning the control of secondary education—in this and other clauses the School Boards saw "a desire to bring about their extinction".[3] Opposition showed itself even among some supporters of the government who feared that the Bill would lead to higher rates for education.[4] In the outcome it was completely abandoned by the government, a collapse which was described in *Justice* as "one of the most remarkable in modern political history". But *Justice* correctly warned that the matter would not be left there, that another Bill would be presented in the following year.[5] This was so, but for the moment the move to curb the School Boards had been defeated; the Act passed in 1897 was confined to meeting the immediate needs of church schools by providing further subsidies. It was in this year that the T.U.C. first adopted a militant policy covering the whole field of education. The forces were beginning to line up for a decisive struggle.

By the turn of the century the political and educational situation was very different from that obtaining in 1870. It is true that the mass of the workers continued to elect members of the middle class to represent them in Parliament, as James Mill and others had affirmed would be the case. Equally an hierarchical system of education, reflecting and

---

[1] McCann, *op. cit.*, 345-6. (From London Trades Council Minutes.)
[2] *Ibid.*, 349.
[3] Allen, *op. cit.*, 108-9. A National Education Emergency Committee was set up in 1896 to counter the growing influence of the denominationalists. Its aims were (1) to preserve the principle of public control, (2) to frustrate any attack on the School Boards, (3) to restrain all proselytising in the elementary schools, etc. In 1896 it published *The Education Crisis, a Defence of Popular Management in Public Education*, and several pamphlets.
[4] *Justice*, 20 June 1896.   [5] *Ibid.*, June 1896. 72

perpetuating social divisions, had been successfully established and there had been fresh efforts to persuade the workers that their interests were best served through co-operation and the promotion of social harmony. But the Labour movement was now much more highly organised and beginning to challenge policies not only on the industrial but also on the political plane. In 1895 the I.L.P. and S.D.F. together put up twenty candidates for Parliament; five years later the Labour Representation Committee had been formed and the first parliamentary seats were gained. This was a clear indication that the organised workers were no longer playing the role assigned to them in the "democratic model".

In the field of education progress had certainly been made with the policies laid down in the years 1850-70—the overall system that had come into being was clearly stratified on class lines, a direction of development underlined by the rise of the public schools at one pole and the limitations imposed on elementary schools at the other. But there had been notable developments in the system of board schools. The fight to abolish fees, to extend welfare services, end child labour, humanise school discipline and further the development of rational and secular forms of education—this symbolised the aspiration of the Labour movement towards education in a real sense of the word for all. In this connection there was warm support for the extension of elementary education into higher grades—a subject to be covered in a subsequent chapter—which led to a new and more specific demand, not merely for universal elementary education but for secondary education for all. This implied rejection of the concept of different forms and levels of education for different classes, the idea which had informed educational developments over the past half-century. Just as the militant Labour movement demanded in the industrial field conditions proper to human beings, so it advanced educational policies that would realise the right to be men. Pressure from below was by no means always effective, objectives were rarely fully gained, but it was this movement that now began to force the pace of educational development.

In the late 1890s, therefore, conflicts were maturing which were to culminate in great disputes both in Parliament and at large over a new and far-reaching Education Bill. This was a response not only to the immediate educational situation that has been outlined but to a whole range of economic and social problems which accompanied the development of Britain as the leading imperialist power.

PART II

A TURNING POINT—
THE EDUCATION ACT
1902

CHAPTER V

IMPERIALISM AND ATTITUDES TO EDUCATION

THE attitude of the Labour movement towards educational advance has hitherto taken the centre of the stage, but in considering the background of the Education Act of 1902 it is necessary to examine briefly deep-seated economic and political trends affecting education at this time. The development of Britain as a leading imperialist power during the closing decades of the nineteenth century was in part a product of the industrial depression of those years. While there was a clear realisation of the need to extend education in some quarters, in others there was an equal determination to resist change or at least to guide it into safe channels. Although public controversies about educational policy were conducted predominantly in political and religious terms, fundamental economic and social issues were at stake.

Already in the 1860s the more farsighted among industrialists had begun to voice considerable concern about the state of education. On the continent new technological advances were being made, industries were established which made use of the latest techniques and there had been parallel educational developments. In Germany particularly, though a unified state had yet to be established, a whole system of scientific and technological education was evolving, epitomised in the great Technical High Schools which were much more closely integrated with industry, more rationally organised and of a higher standard than any similar institution in Britain. It was an awareness that industries on the continent benefited materially from this higher standard of education that led many industrialists to support the Education Act of 1870. Advanced industrialists such as the ironmaster Bernhard Samuelson, scientists of the calibre of Lyon Playfair, T. H. Huxley and H. E. Roscoe co-operated in urging the extension of scientific and technical education. The Great Depression of the 1870s to '90s had the effect of strengthening the determination of this grouping, and various organisations were set up, the most important being the National Association for the Promotion of Technical Education (1887), which conducted widespread propaganda.

Already in 1870 a Royal Commission on Scientific Instruction and the Advancement of Science had been set up (the Devonshire Commission); its report was published five years later. This was followed in 1881 by the Royal Commission on Technical Instruction, which included among its members Samuelson and Roscoe and made many radical suggestions for the improvement of scientific and technological education. This grouping was also responsible for the relatively progressive Minority Report of the Cross Commission (1886-8)—the Royal Commission on elementary education mentioned earlier. The reports following on these enquiries, especially those of the Technical Instruction Commission, provided striking evidence both of the scientific and technological weaknesses of British as compared with Continental industry, and of the deficiencies in the educational system.

It was not, of course, only a matter of producing reports and conducting propaganda. Colleges were set up which began to embody the policies advocated, while old institutions were transformed to meet new needs, more particularly in the great industrial centres. Many of the universities in the great provincial cities have their inception during this period, either developing from Colleges of Science, as at Leeds and Newcastle, or from new endowments by local industrialists as at Manchester and Birmingham; in both cases, however, having a very definite bias towards local industry and local technological needs. Roscoe, Professor of Chemistry at Manchester and member of the Royal Commission on Technical Instruction, was particularly active in efforts to relate university education to the industry of the area.

Once more, therefore, as in the earlier nineteenth century, educational ideas began to be translated into practice which was sharply at variance with the prevailing classicism of the ancient universities and older public schools. The most outright exponent of the view that the study of science must be the central feature of education was Herbert Spencer, but Thomas Huxley was, perhaps, the most influential, underlining that both scientific and literary studies were essential to an all-round education. It was this conception that found expression in the report of the Royal Commission on Secondary Education, set up by the Liberal government in 1894 under the chairmanship of James Bryce.

There were, then, important moves towards extending scientific and technical education, particularly on the part of certain industrialists who appreciated the need to adopt new techniques and were stimulated to modernise processes by continental competition. But there was little or no concern with these matters on the part of established industries which continued to follow traditional practices and nonetheless to find an outlet for their products. Moreover, the Great Depression, which lasted some twenty years, resulted in a more general economic trend which militated as strongly against the re-equipment of Britain's basic industries as it operated to strengthen imperialist influence at large—the flow of capital abroad. Higher returns could be gained from investing in colonial and other under-developed countries than from investment in Britain's traditional industries, especially during a period of acute depression. The industrial consequence was a tendency towards technological stagnation, a failure to re-equip basic industries with modern processes which, beginning at this time, persisted during the first decades of the twentieth century. The dangers were masked by a privileged trading position and the opening of new markets, particularly within the empire; these enabled the nation to maintain a surplus in overseas trading, and home industries to make profits, in spite of an increasingly obsolete technological base. This tendency towards the "freezing" of technique had a clear educational significance. An integrated system of science and technology—of education and industry—on the German or Swiss model no longer seemed so urgent. The pressure on the part of forward-looking industrialists in the 1870s and '80s for a great advance of scientific and technological education could, therefore, no longer be sustained at the same level.[1]

Britain's rapid development as an imperialist power, however, had a second, allied effect, which also had its educational counterpart. This was connected with the development of Britain, and particularly of London, as an international banking, insurance and commercial centre—in short as a world financial centre. The greatest shortage now remarked was not so much of technologists as of clerks, particularly in the capital but also in the great commercial centres of the Midlands and the North. So much was this the case that German clerks were widely recruited in the 1890s owing to the lack of supply in Britain itself. Towards the end of the century it was the need for schools that

---

[1] Halévy gives the following figures for British capital invested abroad: 1842, £144,000,000; 1877, £600,000,000; 1882, £875,000,000; 1893, £1,698,000,000; 1905, £2,025,000,000. *Imperialism and the Rise of Labour*, (1961 edn.), 13-4. An acute analysis of the causes of the relative failure of British industry to utilise new techniques is given in H. J. Habakkuk, *American and British Technology in the Nineteenth Century* (1962), 189-202.

would provide a good educational grounding for clerical workers of all kinds that received most stress.[1]

Important shifts in political alignment also accompanied the rapid growth of imperialism, the most dramatic and significant being the move of the Liberal Unionists, led by Joseph Chamberlain, from a Radical standpoint to alliance with the previously execrated Tory party. So men who had earlier voiced demands for scientific and technical education and for educational advance generally now tended to neglect this cause for imperial politics. Chamberlain's firm profited greatly from developments in South Africa towards the end of the century and he himself was appointed Colonial Secretary in the Tory government of 1895. During the same period, as we shall see, the Radical interest in Birmingham, which had for over a quarter of a century controlled educational developments, suffered a reverse at the hands of the Church.

The development of imperialism, the new opportunities and rivalries engendered, had therefore a dual effect in relation to education. On the one hand there was competition from other nations which, developing their industries at this later stage, threatened to outstrip an older established British industry; this stimulated demands for technological advance and more scientific education which continued to be voiced by the more far-sighted—for instance by Richard Burdon Haldane. On the other hand there was a captive market to support older industries and fresh developments on the financial and commercial planes which operated to dampen interest in science and technology. This produced a demand for more education of the kind provided by the traditional grammar school, and, in relation to the schools (as apart from higher education), it was the latter demand that clearly predominated. Moreover it dovetailed in with the prevailing desire to curb rather than encourage the extension of educational facilities of the kind that appealed to and were made use of by the working class.

If the growth of imperialism influenced the general direction of education, it had a further effect of a political nature which must also be grasped as a clue to the politics of the period. It gave rise to the concept of a united nation, led by men of vigour, and comprising a healthy, energetic people capable of extending and exploiting Britain's

[1] Between 1881 and 1911 the proportion of clerks in the occupied population nearly doubled; city firms often preferred to employ German clerks because of their higher educational level and efficiency. S. F. Cotgrove, *Technical Education and Social Change* (1958), 51-2.

rule. "An Empire such as ours requires as its first condition an imperial race, a race vigorous and industrious and intrepid," said Lord Rosebery, leader of the Liberal Imperialists, "in the rookeries and slums which still survive, an imperial race cannot be reared."[1] This brings to light one of the salient features of the time, the link between imperialist expansion abroad and social reform at home. There was, then, a new interest in promoting health and welfare of the people on the part of those not hitherto concerned with this matter, inspired by an outlook directly opposed to that of the socialists working to the same end.

Closely allied was a new acceptance of the state and its role, a clear recognition of enhanced state powers and the need to use them for clearly defined ends. In the traditional Liberal view, based on individualism and *laissez-faire*, state power was an evil to be kept at arm's length; for imperialists, Liberal and other, it was the main instrument not only for the defence and extension of the empire, but also for the fostering of an imperial race through social betterment. This outlook, the very antithesis of views once held by Cobden and Bright, had spread widely by 1900, in particular under the impact of events in Africa. Men of various political shades—Conservatives, Liberal Unionists and Liberal Imperialists such as Rosebery, Haldane, Asquith and Grey—lined up behind the imperialist banner, to be followed by such Labour leaders as Blatchford, and, discreetly but no less firmly, by the leading Fabians, Bernard Shaw and Sydney Webb.

The movement of thought which linked imperialism with a new veneration for the state found its theoretical justification in the neo-Hegelianism that dominated Oxford philosophy from the 1860s onwards. T. H. Green and his successor Bernard Bosanquet, reacting sharply against the atomistic, highly individualist utilitarianism of J. S. Mill and Herbert Spencer, stressed instead the realisation of individuality through society, and advanced a new concept of the organic nature of the state as embodiment of the people's will. A natural corollary was the desirability of positive state action in matters of social reform. This philosophy also opened the way to an assertion of the primacy of the state *vis-à-vis* the individual. "The Nation-State," declared Bosanquet in 1899, "is the widest organisation which has the common experience necessary to found a common life."[2] Since the criterion of enlightened state action was "efficiency", everything should be done to raise this to the highest possible level. A

[1] Quoted in B. Semmel, *Imperialism and Social Reform* (1960), 62.
[2] Quoted in Semmel, *op. cit.*, 57.

generation of Oxford students were taught by Green, including Asquith and Milner who was later to become a leading protagonist of imperialist politics.[1]

Thinking which embodied revulsion from individualism and which was influenced to some extent by Darwinian concepts concerning the survival of the fittest, eased the way for a development of racial senti- ment which imperialist activities operated to promote.[2] This move- ment of opinion met the increasingly jingoistic sentiments of wide sections of society at the time of the Jameson raid, the relief of Mafeking and finally during the Boer War itself; it was to be clearly evidenced during the Khaki election of 1900 which returned the Tories trium- phantly to power. Britain's historic mission, as it was seen, was idealised and clothed in splendour, not least by the philosopher- politician Haldane, close friend of Sydney Webb and one of the leading politicians to concern himself with education.

"The end which the State and its members have to strive after is the development of the State," Haldane affirmed in an address to the stu- dents of Edinburgh entitled "A Dedicated Life", perhaps the best expression of his outlook.[3] Subordination to the state is necessary for "the realisation of some great purpose". Haldane is here fundamentally concerned with the achievement and maintenance of world supremacy. The nation's great need is to develop the quality of leadership—this depends not so much on brute force as on moral power, as well as on the capacity to submit to authority. In Germany in the nineteenth century the leadership of great men (of Scharnhorst, Clausewitz, Moltke and Bismarck) gave the state "a new significance". "When a leader of genius comes forward," adds Haldane, "the people may bow down before him, and surrender their wills, and eagerly obey"; for in these circumstances "to obey the commanding voice was to rise to a further and wider outlook, and to gain a fresh purpose".[4] He instanced the contemporary Japanese officers, who had recently sub- dued Manchuria; trained to obey, submitting themselves to authority, they lived for the corps and not for self.

It is in the context of this outlook that Haldane counts education as

---

[1] For an analysis of T. H. Green's outlook see Melvin Richter, *The Politics of Con- science; T. H. Green and his Age* (1964).

[2] Epitomised in the work of Benjamin Kidd, Karl Pearson and many others, and academically respectable since the new imperialism was preached in the universities by men like H. J. Mackinder, W. J. Ashley, William Cunningham. *Ibid.*, Chs. 2, 8, 10, 11.

[3] Viscount Haldane, *Universities and National Life* (3rd ed., 1912), 65-6. This Rectorial Address was given in 1907.

[4] *Ibid.*, 78.

IMPERIALISM AND ATTITUDES TO EDUCATION 171

of crucial importance. It is education that gives the moral and intellectual power required for leadership—the power of domination depends on "a deeper insight". Since the state, as the instrument of this development, requires leaders, "it must apply itself to providing the schools where alone leaders can be adequately trained". These are the public schools, Eton, Harrow and the rest, where boys are trained in self-reliance; from public schools derive "Heaven-born" leaders who "come to the front by sheer force of . . . genius".[1] "But," adds Haldane, "in these days of specialised function a nation requires many leaders of a type less rare—subordinates, who obediently accept the higher command and carry it out, but who still are, relatively speaking, leaders." It is the role of the universities to produce these. Their part is a necessary one, and so "the State must provide for their production and nurture". Students should, therefore, see themselves as of a special order; they must live for their work, though the way is steep and hard. "So only can they make themselves accepted leaders; so only can they aspire to form a part of that priesthood of humanity to whose commands the world will yield obedience."[2]

This was to adapt the Platonic pattern to the prevailing situation, assigning the public schools to provide the gold, the universities and grammar schools the silver, elementary schools the brass. This concept, here highly developed, carries forward in a new age the idea of a structured "democracy" advanced by Robert Lowe after 1867. It is not surprising that such views were widely held at a time when imperial expansion abroad was accompanied by the first challenge of a socialist movement at home. Of a similar outlook was the civil servant who leapt from obscurity to fame as the directing hand behind the 1902 Education Act, R. L. Morant. "Bitterly contemptuous of the parliamentary machine", according to Beatrice Webb,[3] he also called for discipline and leadership, decried individualism and expressed contempt for the abilities of ordinary people. Each nation must have its "directive brain centres" to watch developments and plan changes; especially is this important in a democracy where "the impulses of the many ignorant" must be voluntarily submitted "to the guidance and control of the few wise", the special, expert governors or leaders appointed to the task. In default of this a democracy will be overcome "by the centrifugal forces of her own people's unrestrained individualism

[1] *Ibid.*, 69.
[2] *Ibid.*, 69, 107. See also Haldane's addresses in 1899–1901 published in *Education and Empire* (1902).
[3] M. I. Cole (ed.), *Beatrice Webb's Diaries, 1912–1924* (1952), 178.

and disintegrated utterly by the blind impulses of mere numerical majorities".[1]

This determination to bridle democracy, this contempt for the capacity of ordinary men, was shared by the Tory politician chiefly responsible for the 1902 Act. To A. J. Balfour, writes Eaglesham, " 'systems' of thought and belief were for the few; . . . the bulk of men were satisfied with 'a mood or temper of thought, an impulse not fully reasoned out' ". Himself an idealist in philosophy, author of *Foundations of Belief* (1895), Balfour "believed profoundly both that *all* worth while education must be permeated with the religious spirit and that the teaching of popular science, or the teaching of any science, to those who were not of the intellectual *élite* was harmful to the very foundations of society and to the continuance of that 'tender plant'— progress".[2] This, then, was the dominant outlook of men with the power to influence educational developments at the turn of the century.

But there was another group which was to play a particular role at the time of the 1902 Act, which also voiced, indeed developed, the critique of Benthamite *laissez-faire*, and which, at the close of the century, fully accepted Britain's role as an imperialist power. These, perhaps surprisingly, were the Fabians, who had links with other socialist groups but particularly close connections with trade union leaders.

It is at this period that divergent trends in the socialist movement become increasingly apparent in terms of differing attitudes towards educational policy. Up to this time there had been a common approach in the fight for educational advance whatever differences of view on other matters.[3] Nonetheless differences were fundamental, particularly between the Fabians and the S.D.F. The latter, as has been noted, had adopted a Marxist outlook from its inception, if often in the particular and somewhat dogmatic form this was advanced by Hyndman. This involved acceptance of the existence of a class struggle, of a fundamental clash of interests, with the resultant need to build up working-class strength in order to achieve the social revolution. The S.D.F. claimed a membership of 9,000 in 1901, including many of the best known names in the Labour movement. Some had been continuously active since the early 1880s not only on the streets and in the factories,

---

[1] B. M. Allen, *Sir Robert Morant* (1934), 125.

[2] Eric Eaglesham, "Planning the Education Bill of 1902", *British Journal of Educational Studies*, Vol. IX, No. 1, November 1960, 23-4.

[3] Though Sidney Webb had expressed his dissent from the educational policy of the Labour movement several years earlier; cf. *Justice*, 1 August 1896.

but as leaders of trade unions, and latterly, as members of School Boards.

While the S.D.F. was a disciplined nucleus, holding specific views, the socialist movement ranged much more widely to take in men of varying outlook. Many of those who joined the I.L.P. in its early days had a nonconformist background. The strength of its leaders, of men like Blatchford and Keir Hardie, lay in their closeness to the people. They shared the hatred of capitalism, believed the future lay with socialism, and engaged in many an active struggle, but they lacked a clear political theory in the light of which the strategy of the struggle for socialism could be agreed. It was in this context that the I.L.P. developed as an organised party; by 1901 it claimed a membership of 13,000.[1]

By comparison the Fabians remained a select but well-organised group, numbering 861 in 1901, in which intellectuals largely predominated; as a result they could and did act as a powerhouse transmitting ideas to the Labour movement—as the S.D.F. also did in its own way. The Fabians, however, having at this stage lost confidence in the power and ability of the Labour movement to bring about change, and believing that the movement of society must inevitably be towards socialism, turned their attention to influencing politicians of other parties. As this implies, Fabians rejected the idea of class conflict, favouring rather conciliation and agreement to work towards specific reforms, an outlook which spread in the Labour movement to be adopted by such leaders of the I.L.P. as Ramsay Macdonald and Philip Snowden. This was to come close to the position of non-socialists who were increasingly aware of the need for social reform. Strongly favouring state action to this end the Fabians aspired, as informed "collectivists", to permeate both liberal and conservative parties with ideas which would influence the cause of reform. Impatient of all amateurism, they—the Webbs in particular—were strongly attracted by the idea of an inner *élite* of highly intelligent professional men and women who, in the last resort, would control society. The Webbs were untrammelled by theoretical considerations and tended to act as pragmatic opportunists, aiming to win social reform as it were by stealth.

This outlook is evidenced in reactions to the Boer War which caused

[1] Various attempts had been made after 1893 to bring about unity between the S.D.F. and I.L.P. but all proved fruitless. The membership figures of the socialist organisations are taken from the *1st Labour Representation Committee Conference Report*, 1900.

a crisis in the society. The bulk of the organised Labour movement strongly opposed all imperialist developments and took their stand on internationalism. The Fabian society was forced to make its position clear and, in the discussions which followed, the anti-war grouping was defeated, several resigning as a result. "The majority of the society," writes Pease, its historian, "recognised that the British Empire had to win the war".[1] In the manifesto *Fabianism and the Empire*, drafted by Bernard Shaw, the Fabian attitude was outlined: the theme is the "over-riding claim of efficiency, not only in our own government, and in our empire, but throughout the world". The partition of the world between the Great Powers "is now only a question of time". Imperialist interference was justified since "the notion that a nation has a right to do what it pleases with its own territory" is untenable. "The state which obstructs international civilisation will have to go, be it big or little"—China or Monaco. This was to translate Bosanquet's conception of "national efficiency", which leading Fabians had adopted and developed, to the international plane. In short they were concerned with "the effective social organisation of the whole Empire, and its rescue from the strife of classes and private interest".[2]

This led directly to proposals relating to education. If there were to be citizen-soldiers, in a constant state of readiness to defend the empire, then there must be only half-time employment below the age of twenty-one and the hours gained must be spent on "physical exercises, technical education, education in civil citizenship . . . and field training in the use of modern weapons".[3] "It is in the classrooms . . . that the future battles of the Empire for commercial prosperity are being already lost," wrote Sydney Webb at this time in a challenging article. The people know that Rosebery and the Liberal Imperialists meant well by the empire, but the working class now wanted to know "what steps" they would take "to ensure the rearing of an Imperial race".[4]

What was needed was a group of the *élite* to work out in detail "how each department of national life can be raised to the highest possible level of national efficiency". In November 1902 Sydney and Beatrice Webb had called such a group together, men with a "common faith" and "common purpose", to plan "the aims and methods of Imperial policy". The group was intended as the nucleus of a party of "National Efficiency" which would abolish the slums and sweated

[1] Edward R. Pease, *History of the Fabian Society* (1916), 128.
[2] Bernard Shaw, ed., *Fabianism and the Empire* (1900), 3, 6, 44-6.   [3] *Ibid.*, 41.
[4] Quoted in Semmel, *op. cit.*, 73.

trades, improve education, and recapture commercial prosperity; it included such well-known imperialists as Haldane, Grey, Mackinder, Hewins, Amery, and later, Henry Newbolt and Viscount Milner.[1]

Particular attention has been devoted to the Fabians because they were the only grouping connected with the Labour movement, and with a place on the Labour Representation Committee from its inception in 1900, which failed to oppose Tory educational policy at this critical time. Close friends of Haldane, the Webbs were on intimate terms with leaders both of the Liberal Imperialists and of the Conservatives; they worked with Morant and knew Balfour and Chamberlain well. All these accepted Britain's imperialist role and sought to extend it, all held to the conception of a "managed" democracy. All participated in the great struggles around the Education Bill, introduced in the House of Commons the day after British arms were finally victorious in South Africa.

[1] Semmel, op. cit., 72–82.

CHAPTER VI

THE BACKGROUND TO LEGISLATION, 1897-1900

WHEN the Tories returned to power in 1895, after a brief Liberal interregnum of three years, the conditions were maturing for a heightened struggle on education. A matter uppermost in the minds of legislators was the need to increase the aid given by the state to assist the church schools and, similarly, to curb the energetic efforts of the more advanced School Boards. This was the more urgent in that many board schools had developed additional standards which qualified them as "higher grade schools". In face of these developments, and to secure a position that was being progressively undermined, churchmen set out resolutely to capture the School Boards. The government lent support with measures intended decisively to prevent the further development of what had been intended as elementary schools. It was to expose and deflect what was seen as a planned offensive against popular education that the activities of the Labour movement were directed from the summer of 1900, indeed right up to the introduction of what was to become the 1902 Education Act.

1. Success of the Higher Grade Schools

While statesmen and philosophers concerned themselves with long-term plans and theories about the role of education and the structuring of democracy in the era of imperialism, the elementary school system was beginning to push forward—in the more advanced School Board areas, indeed, it was threatening to get out of hand. The children were now in the schools and the level of attendance rising. In spite of the fetters imposed by financial stringency and the system of teaching, new developments were beginning to take place. The massive board schools built in some areas, with their striving for a new form of secular architecture, sharply contrasted with the tiny church or chapel-like buildings that housed the typical voluntary school before and after 1870. Erected sometimes in the midst of the worst kind of slum property, these towering structures represented in an important sense the means of a new life for the mass of the people. By the late 1890s, riding high above the rows of slum houses in the cities, the horizon was now cut not only by church spires and factory chimneys, but also by the patent hot air heating towers of the board schools.

By now there was a general trend towards staying on at school beyond the age of twelve. Figures for the Manchester schools in 1876 show a vast preponderance of children in Standards I and II (seven to nine years) amounting to 70 per cent of those in attendance. But in 1881 only 46 per cent were in the younger age-groups and a gradual increase of numbers in Standards VI and VII was apparent; while pupils aged twelve to fourteen constituted only 0·5 per cent of the total in 1876, the proportion had risen to 5 per cent in 1881.[1]

Taking the country as a whole, 75 per cent of all children aged twelve to thirteen "of the class usually found in public elementary schools" were on the registers by 1893-4 according to the official estimate.[2] The number staying on over thirteen was also rising; children aged thirteen to fourteen on the rolls numbered 146,000 in 1890-1, 198,415 in 1894-5, while the number aged fourteen to fifteen rose from 39,263 to 53,611.[3] This was a very important development, transcending the limitations of what had been designed as a system of elementary education.

Under the Code of Regulations governing elementary schools, it had become permissible—after 1867—slightly to widen the scope of education beyond the original "standard" subjects (reading, writing and arithmetic, and needlework for girls) by the inclusion of one or two so-called "specific" subjects on which grants could also be earned. In 1871 the list of "specific" subjects was greatly extended, including mathematics, branches of science, and languages. As a result, certain schools in which the proportion of children staying on to the higher standards was relatively high began to develop a "top" and provide a more advanced education. This development of higher level work, especially in science, was given considerable impetus by the grants available from the Science and Art Department.[4]

A number of "higher grade schools" were developed by this means

---

[1] *Report of the Royal Commission on Technical Instruction* (1884), Vol. V, 149.

[2] *Report of Committee of Council on Education*, 1893-4, xx.

[3] *Ibid.*, 1896-7, 100. The estimated size of the age-group thirteen to fourteen at this time varied from 525,642 in 1890-1 to 568,700 in 1894-5.

[4] The Science and Art Department was set up in 1853 for the purpose of "supplying scientific and artistic instruction to the industrial classes", as its first Report stated. Although the legal situation was confused, these grants were used by School Boards in the 1880s and '90s to finance higher level work in the higher grade schools. See Eric Eaglesham, *From School Board to Local Authority* (1956), 88-101.

M

in the 1880s and '90s. Some School Boards now began to take the logical step of centralising the higher grades, bringing together in a separate school the older and more advanced pupils from a number of schools whose parents wished them to stay on to thirteen, fourteen or even fifteen and older (no upper age limit was than imposed). Certain higher grade schools of this kind, for instance, those run by the Birmingham School Board, took in their youngest pupils at the age of thirteen, others recruited at twelve or eleven. In some schools, the pupil's education could be taken beyond Standard VII, the top standard of the elementary school; financed under the regulations of the Science and Art Department, these were sometimes known as Organised Science Schools.[1] "The movement," as Morant pointed out in a memorandum written in 1897, "was mainly in the great industrial and manufacturing towns of the north."[2] The first higher grade school of the central type was opened in Sheffield in 1880, but Bradford, Nottingham, Halifax, Manchester, Leeds and Birmingham were not far behind.

In 1882 many of these schools were visited by the very energetic members of the Royal Commission on Technical Instruction (who included Roscoe and Samuelson) and it may be as well to see through their eyes something of the work done in the early days in Manchester. "The first and most remarkable" of the two higher grade schools the Commission gave as examples was the Central School, taken over by the School Board in 1880.[3] This school had an interesting history—founded, apparently, by the Swedenborgians in 1827 it developed, according to its headmaster, Scotson, as one of the best elementary schools in Manchester. From the mid-1850s the number of older pupils increased rapidly, and first the infants, then Standard I, then Standard II were excluded, until by 1884 boys were only admitted if they had passed Standard IV, normally taken at the age of eleven. Equipped for science teaching, the school then had a total of 320 boys and 150 girls. "The results of the science teaching in this school," reported the Commissioners, "are well worthy of notice. Out of a total of 320 boys, 276 have passed Standard VI, and are taught during the day, mathematics, physiology, chemistry (both practical and theoretical), sound, light and heat, magnetism and electricity, physical

---

[1] A "School of Science" was one which adopted the overall scientific curriculum put forward by the Science and Art Department; other schools took individual subjects, receiving a grant for each subject. Eaglesham, *op. cit.*, 187-8.

[2] *Ibid.*, 188.

[3] *Royal Commission on Technical Instruction* (1884), Vol. I, 425.

geography and mechanics. French, too, is taught throughout the school. A girls' higher elementary school forms one half of the buildings, of the scholars of which 93 are above Standard VI." There were twenty scholarships available at the school, and others from the school to the Manchester Grammar School. "The Commissioners," as they record, "were impressed by the high character of the teaching, and the enthusiasm which animated both teachers and scholars." The other Manchester school, Ducie Avenue, was also commended in the main report, the work done in the two schools illustrating "what can be accomplished by the School Board in a large city, even with as low a rate as 2d. in the pound".[1]

Higher grade schools, with official support, developed rapidly and by 1895 there were sixty-seven with nearly 25,000 scholars. Some of these were successfully preparing their pupils for university matriculation and so, by filling the gap between primary and higher education, assuming the role of secondary schools. Such, indeed, was the intention in some cases, as A. P. Laurie, one of the Assistant Commissioners to the Bryce Commission, noted after a visit to the Leeds Higher Grade School (in 1894): "It is impossible to convey," he reported, ". . . the impression which this school makes upon one of efficiency, energy and vitality, and I think no one who has spent some time inside it can fail to realise that we are here in the presence of a new educational force which has already developed to a vigorous and lusty youth and that it is impossible to say what may be the limit of its growth, or how soon, to quote Dr. Forsyth (the headmaster) himself, 'the organisation which was originally devised for the elementary education of the country, passing with great strides across the realms of Secondary Education, may soon be battering at the doors of the ancient universities themselves'." He went on to interpret this phenomenon: "This higher grade school represents a new educational movement from below, and a demand from new classes of the population for Secondary Education which has sprung up in a few years."[2]

Another focus of this movement towards secondary education was

[1] *Ibid.*, Vol. V, 157-64; Vol. I, 425-7. Among other higher grade schools of the central type which impressed the Commissioners was that at Sheffield where, "as in the graded schools of some other towns, the best scholars from the surrounding board schools are gathered for more advanced teaching". *Ibid.*, Vol. I, 467.

[2] *Report of the Royal Commission on Secondary Education* (1895), Vol. VII, 162-3. By 1903, ninety-three of the pupils of the Leeds school had passed the London University Matriculation examination, and approximately as many again the Victoria University Preliminary examination. Sixty-five of its old scholars had gained university degrees. H. B. Philpott, *London at School* (1904), 166. Higher grade schools had a total of 42,069 pupils in 1900-1.

to be found in the arrangements made for the further education of pupil-teachers. These boys and girls, aged between fourteen and nineteen, were apprentice teachers; teaching during the day they were originally given further instruction before or, more usually, after school hours by the headmaster. The pupil-teacher system, initiated in the 1840s, was the main avenue to the teaching profession for the working class, and, with the rapid growth of the elementary school system, the number of such apprentice teachers greatly increased. Again the most efficient course was to bring such pupils together; this was originally done through evening centres, but when half-time teaching was introduced after 1884, instruction was given during mornings or afternoons. The teaching in these centres, covering mathematics and science among other subjects, was clearly not elementary in character, although it was carried on by elementary school teachers under the elementary school code.[1]

It was not long before this growth of higher grade schools began to meet with strenuous opposition—a point of view which already found full expression before the Cross Commission in 1884-7. It was not only that they transcended the rigidly demarcated structure of education planned but also that the new, lively and cheaper structure of near-secondary schooling in the great cities was, in some cases, threatening the existence of the endowed and somewhat stagnant grammar schools. "Many of the grammar schools were beginning to feel the competition of the higher grade schools with their lower fees and more practical education," writes Lowndes, "a competition which was to reduce seriously the numbers in the London endowed secondary schools before 1902."[2] It was precisely this point of view that was put by the Rev. Joseph Nunn, chairman of the Manchester School Board which was responsible for the schools. Remarking that there was considerable abuse of the four higher grade schools in Manchester, he went on:

"The Higher Grade schools undersell the middle-class schools and draw children from such schools and bring in a large number of such children from the outlying districts." This he characterised as "a very great abuse". He cited as example: "The Commercial School, which is a public school under the supervision of the Deans and Canons and

[1] The system of collective instruction of pupil-teachers was pioneered by the Liverpool School Board in 1876. By 1885 the "centre" system had been adopted by London, Birmingham, Bradford, and by some voluntary organisations connected with the Church of England. J. W. Adamson, *English Education, 1789-1902* (1930), 377.
[2] G. A. N. Lowndes, *The Silent Social Revolution* (1937), 55.

other Churchmen has lost a very large proportion of its pupils and is in danger of being closed, the scholars being drawn away very largely to this Central School of which I have spoken." The Manchester Grammar School was also suffering in the same way—"During the last two years they have not had as good a supply of candidates for [their] scholarships as they had before", since "the candidates who should compete for them are detained in the higher grade school, the Central School". There was a reason for this, namely that the Science and Art Scholarships available at the Central School left something over for maintenance, and were therefore more valuable than a free place at the Grammar School. These scholarships, he described as "extravagant".[1]

The Cross Commission devoted a good deal of attention to the question of the higher grade schools and their place in the system of education now developing. This Royal Commission was appointed by the Conservatives after their electoral victory of 1885. Its clear political purpose was to support the voluntarists (Church and Tory interests) in their long drawn struggle against the secularising influence of the School Boards, and the Commission (especially its original members) was weighted on this side, including such leading denominationalists as, for instance, Cardinal Manning and Canon Gregory. On the other hand Samuelson, Lyulph Stanley, R. W. Dale and others made up a Liberal-Radical group of considerable influence on the Commission which consequently split completely along these lines, producing a majority and a minority report.[2] It is not surprising that the question of higher grade schools was one on which differences arose. Reference has already been made to some of the reports on Manchester schools but it is worth examining here the alternative standpoints set out in the majority and minority reports of the Commission.

The majority were deeply disturbed about the tendency to extend the content of education as laid down in successive Codes of Regulations. Their concern was that elementary education was gradually

[1] *Second Report of the Royal Commission on Elementary Education* (1887), 776-7. It was not only in the large cities that the grammar schools were feeling the pinch. The assistant commissioner for the Bryce Commission (F. E. Kitchener) who surveyed the smaller grammar schools in Lancashire, for instance, found "a very unsatisfactory state of affairs in most instances". "Either the existing grammar schools must be provided with proper staff and teaching equipment," he wrote, "or they had better be swept away and replaced by higher grade board schools. Under existing conditions the competition between the two is as unequal as that between Nelson's *Victory* and an ironclad." *Report of the Royal Commission on Secondary Education* (1895), Vol. VI, 189.

[2] Samuelson and Stanley were added to the original list on A. J. Mundella's recommendation. W. H. G. Armytage, *A. J. Mundella, 1827-1897* (1951), 232.

including "a range of subjects proper to schools of higher education". In their view primary (or elementary) and secondary education ought to be strictly defined and delimited, the underlying assumption being that, for the working class, education should be "elementary", but for the wealthier classes, it should be "secondary". If, they concluded, higher grade schools continued to develop "it would offer a temptation so to enlarge the curriculum as practically to convert primary schools into secondary schools, in which a portion of the cost of the education of the children of wealthier persons would be defrayed out of the rates or Imperial funds". This convoluted argument recalls others advanced by the Schools Inquiry Commission some twenty years earlier when arguing against free education for the working class.[1]

The function of such schools, the majority argued, should be strictly controlled. If their curriculum "is restricted within due limits, avoiding all attempts to invade the ground properly belonging to secondary education, and if due precautions are taken to secure that promising children of poor parents are not excluded from the privileges to be enjoyed in them, then we are of opinion that such schools may prove to be a useful addition to our school machinery for primary education". But since other than working-class children attend these schools, "we think it is desirable that the State should recognise the distinction between elementary and secondary education to an extent not yet attempted".[2] In short, if the workers' children were to have anything more than the minimum elementary teaching it was best that they should have it in elementary schools, but the latter should not be allowed to teach the subjects considered proper to "middle class" schools. The request for a clearer distinction between "elementary" and "secondary" education reflects concern to maintain the strictly delimited system of education for different social classes planned in an earlier age. There should be "some system of grading schools", satisfactory "secondary" schools should be provided, with exhibitions for "deserving elementary scholars". But at all costs there must be no more uncontrolled expansion.[3]

The minority report, challenging this outlook, found that the higher grade schools were laying the basis for a widespread system of industrial, technical and commercial education. It was necessary to take a lesson from the Continent where "great efforts are being made to give a more extended elementary education, and to lead up through the

[1] *Final Report of the Royal Commission on Elementary Education* (1888), 145, 217.
[2] *Ibid.*, 169.   [3] *Ibid.*, 145-71, 219.

elementary schools to technical instruction". Higher grade schools
were not only a useful but a necessary addition "to our school machinery for primary education" and should be encouraged "to prepare
scholars for advanced technical and commercial education". These
schools were not encroaching on the secondary sphere. Pointing out
that the pupils left at fourteen or fifteen after completing their school
course, they stressed that they were part of elementary education—such
schools catered for the more intelligent artisans, preparing for the
lower ranks of trade and industry.[1]

Developing this thesis the minority report proposed the introduction
of a system of higher elementary or technical schools which should act
as the "development and completion of the ordinary primary school
course". Thus while some pupils might go on to the grammar schools
at eleven or twelve, "the higher elementary schools would satisfy the
wants of an entirely different class from those who desire really secondary education". Defining secondary education as designed for those
staying at school to sixteen or eighteen, the report assigns to higher
elementary education the role of teaching "more thoroughly those
who must begin to earn their living, or at any rate begin to learn their
trade, at fourteen or fifteen years of age". This would help to introduce a more "practical and scientific spirit" into the top forms of the
elementary schools which, hitherto, "have a tendency . . . to too
literary a character, and lead the children too exclusively to the con-
templation of a clerk's life as the object of their youthful ambition".
In the interest of "national industry" the general level of scientific
and technical education must be improved.[2]

What is the difference between these two standpoints? Basically it
appears to be one of emphasis or degree rather than of principle. Both
are agreed on the main issue, that the higher grade schools should be
preserved as schools for the working class, and that the grammar
schools, as secondary schools for a different section of the population
(with a few exhibitions for working-class children), should be preserved as the main avenue to the universities and professions. Both
are agreed on a limitation of function of the higher grade schools,
although they would differ as to the scope of the curriculum. But while
the majority would *discourage* this development, for fear of the consequences, the minority advanced clear plans for promoting it.

The minority report on the whole reflected the outlook of the larger
School Boards in the midlands and north which were already actively

[1] *Ibid.*, 239, 248, 316.   [2] *Ibid.*, 319.

promoting new developments. For this course they had hitherto found encouragement, for instance, from A. J. Mundella who had been Minister in charge of education in the Gladstone administration of 1882-5.[1] There was now the added support of a considerable section of a Royal Commission and, during the 1890s, more higher grade schools were established, others extended their activities. Official encouragement was still forthcoming from various quarters. Kekewich, permanent secretary of the Education Department, was a strong supporter. Sir William Hart Dyke, a progressive Tory and Vice-President of the Committee of Council before 1892, also gave his full support; in his official capacity he distributed prizes and certificates at schools in Sheffield, Birmingham and elsewhere, "commending their curriculum in all respects, and urging them to increase their efforts in the same direction".[2]

Accordingly in 1895 the Bryce Commission found that these schools were providing a secondary education[3] and, being in favour of extending scientific and technical teaching, suggested they be recognised as secondary schools under the control of the new local authorities proposed. It was by taking up this last point to the extent of advocating the dissolution of all School Boards in rural areas and transfer of their powers to county councils, that the Salisbury government courted defeat for its Education Bill in 1896.

The path of the higher grade schools was not, however, to be a smooth one. The grammar schools, in particular, felt themselves threatened by this thriving development, and it was the grammar school headmasters who led the attack. The Headmasters' Association, as Beatrice Webb later noted, was established in 1890 specifically to insist "that both the local authorities and the central government should maintain and develop a *separate* system of publicly subsidised controlled secondary education—a system of genuinely secondary schools, staffed by secondary school teachers, instead of mere 'tops' to elementary

---

[1] Opening the Manchester Central Higher Grade school in 1884, Mundella said that the "£30,000 spent on these premises is the best investment . . . that the City of Manchester has made for a long time", adding that "as the representative of the Education Department I thank you". He commended the School Board for a "courageous, liberal and enlightened policy". W. H. G. Armytage, *A. J. Mundella* (1951), 224; *The Schoolmaster*, 29 December 1900, 1225.

[2] As he ruefully recalled at a later date, after the schools had come under heavy attack. *The Schoolmaster*, 13 April 1901, 720.

[3] The views expressed approximated to those of the minority of the Cross Commission: "The Higher grade school largely corresponds with a demand for Secondary Education from the lower social strata", such schools were certainly "giving Secondary Education to great numbers who would never have had it". *Report of Royal Commission on Secondary Education*, Vol. I, 67.

schools". This organisation, born to oppose higher grade schools, necessarily came into acute conflict over the next twelve years with "the powerfully organised elementary school teachers, who were supported by the larger and more energetic school boards, by the organised labour movement, and by enthusiasts for a 'democratic' education".[1]

The Bryce Commission had found that there was little overlapping between higher grade and grammar schools. This was not, however, the view of the headmasters of the latter who, through their professional association voiced complaints in a Memorial to the Duke of Devonshire, President of the Committee of Council, in 1896. "Primary schools supported by rates and in most cases free of charge to parents, are overlapping secondary schools, and mischief is arising out of a dual system. In populous districts, such as South Lancashire and the West Riding of Yorkshire, large schools have been built, and are being worked at the public cost, to the detriment of the old foundations, which only require a proper local control and public aid to renew their youth."[2] The higher grade schools, the secondary teachers' associations held, in common with the Cross Commission majority, "should be confined exclusively to higher primary work, and . . . their aims should be 'of a definitely practical character, as intended for handworkers rather than headworkers' ".[3] This outlook was satirised in *The Schoolmaster*, journal of the National Union of Teachers, which represented the elementary teachers: "Give the working-class people just enough of the rudiments of education to make them know and keep their stations in life, reserve all higher training such as is essential for the securing of all professional and higher class mercantile and commercial and government posts for the children of the 'better classes'."[4] A return made in 1897 illustrated the class differentiation as between higher grade and grammar schools: 91·2 per cent of pupils of higher grade schools entered from elementary schools compared with 48·9 per cent of grammar school pupils, while children of skilled and unskilled manual workers formed 34·1 per cent of higher grade school pupils and only 6·8 per cent of grammar school pupils.[5]

The higher grade schools fostered by the more advanced School Boards were, then, a centre of controversy from the late 1880s. Nor was this all, for this movement was paralleled during the 1890s by the extraordinarily rapid development of evening schools, again under

[1] Quoted in Asher Tropp, *The School Teachers* (1957), 175, from an article in the *New Statesman*, 25 September 1915.
[2] Quoted in Olive Banks, *Parity and Prestige in English Secondary Education* (1955), 15.
[3] *Ibid.*, 16.   [4] *Ibid.*, 19.   [5] *Ibid.*, 29.

the control of the School Boards. These, originally intended to give instruction in the three R's and governed by the Elementary Code, came in 1893 under their own Code of Regulations which permitted a wide variety of work for adults as well as youth, much of which was unmistakably secondary in character. "The remarkable increases in numbers of evening school pupils during 1890-1900," writes Eaglesham, "was in many ways the most striking educational phenomenon of the time."[1] Almost any subject could now be taught—French, German, Latin, science, commerce—while under the influence of the Recreative Evening Schools Association, which functioned from 1885 to 1897, such activities as music, dancing and swimming were introduced. Encouraged by the Education Department under Acland during the Liberal interregnum (1892-5), the evening schools went on to provide what was increasingly recognised as a preparation for higher education. Indeed the regulations did not exclude work of university standard and some of the schemes realised by School Boards—especially in London—were "extremely ambitious".[2] This whole development received strong support from the Labour movement, since here was a new avenue to further education under popular control.

This was the position when in 1895 a Tory administration returned to power and began to prepare a counter-attack on the entire system of School Boards. When the first offensive failed, with the Education Bill of 1896, attention was turned to the state of the church schools. But this was only to postpone far-reaching plans to divert educational organisation and development into safer channels.

2. COUNTER-OFFENSIVE BY THE CHURCH

During the decades after the Education Act of 1870 the Church of England became increasingly concerned about the direction developments were taking. When it was first proposed that School Boards be set up, it had been thought the schools they provided would supplement the voluntary system. This, after all, had a long start and the voluntary bodies had also been given a period of grace to build as many schools as they possibly could. Thereafter churchmen were very active, as the attendance figures show—of the 2,500,000 children

---

[1] Eaglesham, *op. cit.*, 55. For a description of this development and of the complex administrative changes which lay behind it see pp. 53-64.

[2] *Ibid.*, 60. The number of scholars in evening schools rose from 298,724 in 1896 to 474,563 in 1899, nearly 50 per cent of whom were over sixteen (68,026 of these were over twenty-one). *Board of Education Report*, 1899-1900, Vol. I, 90.

attending voluntary schools in 1895, almost 2,000,000 were in Church of England schools.[1] Energetic churchmen were raising money, exhorting their parishioners, and building schools as rapidly as possible. James Fraser, once an assistant commissioner to the Newcastle Commission and Bishop of Manchester from 1870, founded the Church Education Society in his diocese, and, according to one of his successors, "covered his diocese with a network of Church schools in response to Forster's Education Act".[2]

The more that was achieved, however, the more there seemed to be done. With the growth of secularism and radicalism, the rise of an organised working-class movement beginning to be infected with socialist ideas, it was increasingly important to strengthen the social role of the church. In the words of Bishop Knox, one of the most energetic champions of church schools at this time, the school would be a "formidable rival to the Church; every child had to go to school, while no one was obliged to go to Church". If the schools became secular—as the National Education League had demanded and as was largely the case at Birmingham where religious instruction was at a minimum—then children could be placed under the "disastrous influence of irreligious or even anti-religious teachers", with possibly catastrophic social consequences.[3]

In this situation, the board schools were clearly making the running —the numbers in attendance were rising more rapidly than in the church schools and in the urban areas especially they dominated the scene; in London, in 1898, there were 513,000 children in board schools to 224,000 in voluntary schools.[4] The "free education" measure of 1891 hit the voluntary schools hard; according to Bishop Knox, the exchequer grant made in lieu of fees, "proved to be inadequate, and increasingly inadequate, as the School Boards raised the scale of

---

[1] E. Halévy, *Imperialism and the Rise of Labour* (1961 ed.), 166.

[2] E. A. Knox, *Reminiscences of an Octogenarian* (n.d. 1935?), 251. In 1870 there were 1,152,389 children in voluntary public elementary schools of all denominations, and none in board schools. In 1896 there were 2,465,919 children in voluntary schools and 1,956,992 in board schools. *Report of Committee of Council*, 1897, lxxiii.

[3] *Ibid.*, 182, 196-7. At Birmingham a short passage of the Bible was read without comment every morning; apart from this, teachers were forbidden to give any religious instruction whatever and hymns or prayers were not permitted. Denominations (as individuals) could rent a school for half an hour twice a week when denominational instruction could be given at the expense of the denomination. This, however, was generally a failure. For a scholarly description of the Birmingham situation and background, see A. F. Taylor, "Birmingham and the Movement for National Education, 1867-77", (unpublished Ph.D. thesis, University of Leicester, 1960). At Huddersfield no religious instruction was given in board schools between 1871 and 1921.

[4] Halévy, *op. cit.*, 166.

teachers' salaries".[1] The acute crisis of the church schools at this time
was attributed to Acland's policy at the Education Department in
1892-5 when, again according to Knox, a not unprejudiced witness,
"all the devices at the disposal of the Board [sic] to depress or ex-
tinguish voluntary schools had been relentlessly used".[2] What he failed
to mention was that the income from voluntary subscriptions—the
sine qua non of the *voluntary* school—was also declining. Taken together
all this spelt financial crisis endangering the very existence of church
schools. On becoming Bishop Suffragan at Birmingham in 1894, Knox
found fourteen with an average attendance of 7,000 "in imminent
danger of being closed. . . . Bank managers had begun to be pressing.
The weary task of begging from parishioners who had not much to
give was consuming the hearts of many of the clergy".[3] Free education, also, had hit the Lancashire church schools very hard: "They lost
heavily by the abolition of school fees in elementary schools, and",
writes Knox, "when I became Bishop of Manchester (in 1903) many
of them were in great danger." Debts amounted to £70,000.[4]

This was the situation which gave rise to bitter complaints about
the "intolerable strain" on churchgoers who not only contributed to
maintaining their own schools but also paid rates to support "their
rivals, the board-schools".[5] As the standards of accommodation required by the Education Department rose, as well as teachers' salaries,
the position became more and more difficult. There was only one long-
term solution to the problem, consonant with the continuance of
church schools: that they be given greatly increased support from
public funds, either direct from the exchequer as heretofore or from
the rates.[6] But any step in the latter direction would undoubtedly
arouse the violent antagonism not only of secularists but also nonconformists. If Anglicans complained about the operation of the 1870
settlement, so did the nonconformists; for the church schools still
provided for the majority of the children and, in particular, had a near
monopoly of schools in the countryside where there was often no
alternative.[7]

---

[1] Knox, *op. cit.*, 184.   [2] *Ibid.*, 185.   [3] *Ibid.*, 200.   [4] *Ibid.*, 240.
[5] *Ibid.*, 184.

[6] Under existing rules there could be no increase in the *per capita* grant from the
exchequer unless there were a corresponding increase in the revenue derived from other
sources. Anglican opinion was divided on the most desirable solution; increased exchequer
support would obviate the danger of local and lay control but there were advantages in
gaining support from the rates. On the tactics used by the Church, see Alan Rogers,
"Churches and Children—A Study in the Controversy over the 1902 Education Act",
British Journal of Educational Studies, Vol. VIII, No. 1, November 1959.

[7] For their attitude at this stage see Halévy, *op. cit.*, 165-6.

When the Tory government was returned in 1895 the time seemed ripe for a new appeal. Many of the members of Lord Salisbury's administration were pledged to take action and four months after it took office a deputation of clergy, headed by the Archbishop of Canterbury, called on the Prime Minister and the Duke of Devonshire to request "relief from the heavy burden imposed on them by the competition of the board schools".[1] The immediate response was the Education Bill of 1896, framed to remove much of this competition, which failed in the face of general opposition. A year later, however, what amounted to a free dole was handed out to the voluntary schools without any arrangement for local control whatever. The voluntary schools were saved, at least temporarily, and, as Halévy remarks, "the Church of England had won a decided success". The Radicals were thrown a sop in the shape of another Act which provided supplementary grants to necessitous School Boards. "The Cabinet estimated that it had made a present of £616,500 to the free (voluntary) schools, and £154,000 to the board schools."[2] For two or three years, the Church of England—as an organisation—was to hold its hand.

These developments took place against a background of increasingly acute conflicts which found expression locally in the School Board elections of 1897 and 1900. The church party's opposition to the School Boards as instruments of secularisation and radicalism was mounting and, if these Boards could not, as yet, be abolished, at least they could be sterilised. It was Lord Salisbury himself, who, in a speech in 1895, launched the campaign, calling upon churchmen to "capture the School Boards". This they had indeed been attempting for a long time, as we have seen in the case of London and Manchester, but efforts were now revived. There seemed no more suitable place to centre them than Birmingham, the home of radicalism, where Joseph Chamberlain had made his name on the education question. Here, since 1873, the "Liberal Eight" had dominated the School Board, pursuing Radical policies, setting up higher grade schools, and, above all, finding their own solution to the problem of religious instruction in board schools.

It was here that Knox, as Bishop Suffragan, was determined to make

[1] *Ibid.*, 191.
[2] *Ibid.*, 193. The Voluntary Schools Act of 1897 abolished the maximum grant figure of 17s. 6d. per pupil; exempted the church schools from payment of rates, and gave 5s. per pupil to associations of voluntary school managers who were grouped together for this purpose (instead of the 4s. proposed in the 1896 Bill). The Elementary Education Act of 1897 gave a supplementary grant *per capita* to necessitous School Boards, with a maximum total grant of 16s. 6d. per pupil.

a challenge. It was here also that the Radicals, concerned at the increasing influence of the Church party, staged the first meeting of the Midland Education League, revived in 1895 after the Tory victory.[1] Anglicans and Catholics then found common ground in setting up a rival organisation, the Voluntary Schools Defence League, packing the Town Hall for their first mass meeting.[2] "But, since the best form of defence is attack, it was not enough to form our Defence League," writes Knox. "We must act on Lord Salisbury's advice and capture the School Board." This was a formidable undertaking, but in the 1897 election the Church put up seven candidates, one the Bishop himself who had been sanctioned by the Archbishop of Canterbury to stand. Though there were other candidates, in effect the "Church Seven" stood opposed to the "Liberal Eight". There was a violent campaign. Four of the "Church Seven" were successful, including Knox. "I had raised the flag of the Church in Birmingham," he writes; heartened by this campaign "we approached the contest of 1900 with some confidence".[3]

When this next contest came round the Liberal forces were in some disarray, partly as a result of the Home Rule controversy. On this occasion the "Liberal Eight" significantly dropped their traditional title, calling themselves the "Education Eight", but they gained only seven seats. The "Church Seven" won six, but they had outside support from a Roman Catholic and one or two independents. So the Church party ousted the Liberal-Radical majority which had reigned for twenty-seven years and Bishop Knox became Chairman of the School Board. He was determined to bring religious instruction into the schools even if only of the non-denominational variety the Church, at this time, deplored, but there was still strong opposition to face. After days of debate a vote was at last taken. "We met on Saturday morning and they succumbed," recorded Knox later. "The struggle was over. Religious instruction was introduced into the

[1] Knox, op. cit., 184. The Midland League was probably a branch of the National Education Association, founded in 1889 by Lyulph Stanley and others "to promote a system of national education which shall be efficient, progressive, unsectarian and under popular control". The Association, with local branches, was very active in 1895-6 and in 1901-3; it included prominent Liberals and nonconformists on its Council. Rogers, op. cit., 40-1.

[2] Knox's speech on this occasion was devoted to showing that in the twenty-five years since 1870 "the Church of England alone had spent £21,000,000 on elementary education, and had opened 6,429 new schools, besides paying their share towards 4,900 board schools. The friends of voluntary schools had endowed the country with millions and millions of money; the board schools had saddled the country with millions of debt." "That was my song," he adds. Knox, op. cit., 187-8.

[3] Ibid., 192.

THE STANLEY ROAD HIGHER GRADE SCHOOL, NOTTINGHAM

DESIGN FOR A PUPIL-TEACHERS' CENTRE AT BRENTWOOD

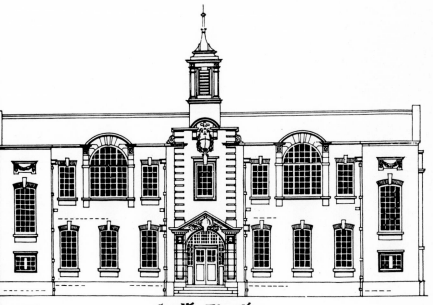

· South Elevation ·

THE DUKE OF DEVONSHIRE IN 1902

A. J. BALFOUR IN 1902

Birmingham Board Schools." As he remarked, this success had repercussions far beyond the city boundaries, and was something of a portent for the future. "The long age of Church despondency in Birmingham was over, and the Church took her place in the very Mecca of Nonconformity. It was an event which was to have some weight in the education policy of the country."[1]

3. THE UNDERMINING OF THE SCHOOL BOARDS

The Tory party, with Liberal Unionist support, held power from July 1895 to December 1905. We have seen that it pursued an active educational policy from the moment of its first election. From 1900 the government's determination on a far-reaching measure became increasingly apparent. The outcome was not foreseen—that success in getting an Education Act on the Statute Book would pave the way to long years in the wilderness.

The steps taken in the late 1890s represented a resort to administrative means designed to prepare the ground for legislation. Several of these measures, which aroused widespread opposition at the time, appear on the surface to be merely technical, but their combined effect made the direction of government policy abundantly clear. Each objectively hurt the School Boards, limiting their sphere of action and that of elementary education generally.

Grants from the Science and Art Department were the main source from which higher grade schools were supported; moneys raised from the rates could not be used for this purpose but only spent on "elementary" education.[2] These grants also aided the now rapidly developing evening schools but these were also supported from the rates though a growing proportion of the work was secondary in character.[3] The whole effort on the part of progressive School Boards to develop popular education, which had met with such success, depended therefore on Science and Art Department grants. Clearly if these were diverted, expansion would be arrested and a major blow struck at this upward movement out of the elementary field.

This was precisely the course taken. After the failure of the 1896

---

[1] *Ibid.*, 194. The fourteen church schools in Birmingham, referred to earlier, were kept in being, and four new schools built.

[2] Although this was something of a legal fiction; money from the rates could be, and was, spent on the lower sections of higher grade schools. The whole matter is discussed by Eaglesham, *From School Board to Local Authority*, 29-45.

[3] The very confused situation here has also been unravelled in *ibid.*, 53-64.

Bill the government set up a committee to examine the method whereby the Science and Art Department allocated its grants, with Sir John Gorst, an inveterate enemy of the School Boards and now the "Minister" in charge of education as chairman. The clear aim was to accomplish by administrative means steps which had been rejected in the legislature, that is, to place the responsibility for administering secondary education with county and county borough councils, so excluding the School Boards. The Tory dominated county councils could also be relied upon to favour the grammar schools.[1]

Adopting the advice of Gorst's committee, the Science and Art Department inserted a new clause into the Directory of 1897 (clause 7), which now for the first time recognised counties and county boroughs as the local authorities for secondary education. This was intended, and regarded, as an invitation to the county councils to take over all higher level teaching, to administer this through their already existing Technical Instruction Committees. True, the rights of School Boards were safeguarded by the terms of clause 7 but they naturally regarded this step as a major threat and protested accordingly. At the same time another important step was taken which was to arouse strong opposition from the Labour movement. Hitherto the proper recipients of Science and Art Department grants had been defined as the "industrial classes" but this term was now omitted, so opening the way to diminishing grants to higher grade schools and diverting them, via the county Technical Instruction Committees, towards aiding grammar schools.[2]

In 1899 an Act was passed embodying one of the recommendations of the Bryce Commission, that the existing Education Department, the Science and Art Department and the Charity Commission be combined in a single department headed by a Board of Education. This Board, made up of members of the government, and presided

[1] B. M. Allen, *Sir Robert Morant*, 113. As Eaglesham puts it: "Gorst's administrative camel, which had, in 1896, been expelled by Parliament with some ridicule from the door of the School Board tent, thus, in 1897, poked its unwelcome head under the flaps at the rear." *Op. cit.*, 108.

[2] Allen, *op. cit.*, 115. Two years later H.M.I.'s reports brought out the importance of these steps. Without the now augmented aid received from the county authorities, runs one report covering ten southern counties, "a very large number of grammar schools would be woefully reduced in efficiency, and some would scarcely survive at all". See also the report on the Leicestershire grammar schools. The work done in the schools of science in the higher grade schools, on the other hand, is positively assessed (e.g. in Lancashire). *Board of Education Report*, 1899-1900, Vol. II, 17, 23, 25, 32. Of the 159 schools of science in England in 1898-9 listed in this report, 64 were in higher grade and board schools, 31 in technical schools and institutes, 20 in other types of institutions, and 44 in grammar schools. These were all doing work of "secondary" level. *Ibid.*, 54-147.

over by the minister in charge of education, was from the first a fiction—it never met.[1] But there was henceforth a considerably larger and more organised department concerned with education. As a result of pressure from the Headmasters' Conference and others concerned with secondary schools a guarantee was given that there would be separate organisational means of dealing with secondary as distinct from elementary and technical education.[2]

A further administrative step in 1899, which operated against the interests of the School Boards, was the decision that classes they organised were not eligible for Science and Art Department grants; these were in future to be available only through county and county borough councils. A year later Education Department grants for the teaching of specific subjects were abolished in favour of a block grant. All these steps seriously undermined the advanced work fostered by School Boards.

There is plenty of evidence to show that the moving spirit behind these measures—all intended to curtail the powers and operations of School Boards—was Sir John Gorst.[3] Holding a key position as the government's spokesman for education in the House of Commons, Gorst had the valuable aid of the civil servant, Robert Morant, and the full support of the Duke of Devonshire and the government. Nor did he confine himself to administrative changes; he also forced the issue by invoking legal action against the School Boards, a decisive step in preparing the way for new legislation.

In June 1899 a case was brought by a School of Art in London which complained of competition from evening classes run by the School Board. But, significantly, this institution was backed by a committee which had been formed "to combat the School Boards" and which included two members of the Cecil family.[4] Moreover both Gorst and Morant were clearly involved in instigating the case, though the

---

[1] The Duke of Devonshire, asked in the House of Lords why a board had been set up rather than introducing a Secretary for education, admitted that he could not remember: "It has the advantage, at all events, of numerous precedents, and it is perfectly well understood that there will be no board at all." P. H. J. H. Gosden, "The Board of Education Act, 1899", *British Journal of Educational Studies*, Vol. XI, No. 1, November 1962, 50.

[2] *Ibid.*, The Education Act of 1899 also contained a clause giving further powers to County and County Borough Councils in the inspection of technical (or secondary) schools.

[3] His objectives, according to Eaglesham, were "to save the voluntary schools at all costs, and to subordinate the school boards to, and eventually replace them by, the county councils, which were . . . expected to be relatively conservative in their administration of education". *Op. cit.*, 179.

[4] Halévy, *op. cit.*, 197.

N

methods used to this end have been the subject of much discussion.[1] However this may be, the judgment given altered the whole complexion of affairs, for the district auditor disallowed expenditure from the rates by the London School Board towards the running of science and art schools or classes. This was the famous Cockerton judgment which necessarily put the whole future of advanced, or secondary, teaching fostered by School Boards in the melting pot.

The London School Board promptly appealed, but the judgment was upheld by the courts in December 1900.[2] A fresh appeal was then prepared which came before the Master of the Rolls in April, 1901. Pending the hearing of this—that is, for a period of nearly two years from the first judgment—the axe was suspended. But the Board of Education was now "the avowed supporter of the County Councils and the open enemy of the School Boards". In the year of its foundation, as Halévy points out, a series of drastic actions had been taken against the latter. Their right "to receive government grants or to employ the rates for the maintenance of schools not in the strictest sense elementary, had been very seriously contested. In February, there had been a departmental decision adverse to the School Boards; in June the government stood entirely aside and left the London School Board to fight its own battle before the auditor Cockerton."[3] Nor was this all. The opponents of the higher grade schools inside the Board (the name by which the department itself came to be known) were quick to follow up their advantage and, in April 1900, issued a minute on "Higher Elementary Schools". This, largely drafted by Morant, was overtly intended both to "prevent any expansion of the higher schools under school boards and take from them some of their most attractive features".[4]

Morant, lieutenant to Gorst, associate of the Webbs, a man of ability who was determined to set the educational system to rights, held unwaveringly to the policy of separating secondary from elementary schooling. Hence the heading to his Minute which implied that if School Boards were to administer teaching beyond the minimum standards it should be no more than "higher elementary" teaching. The main points of the policy laid down have been summarised as follows. First, that an upper age limit of fifteen must be established

[1] Eaglesham denies that Morant acted conspiratorially, as has often been maintained; he clearly thinks, however, that Gorst did so; *op. cit.*, 114-9.
[2] The details of the Cockerton case and the events that flowed from it are fully analysed in Eaglesham, *op. cit.*, 113-42.
[3] Halévy, *op. cit.*, 197.   [4] Eaglesham, *op. cit.*, 51.

and "strictly enforced"; second, that "only a selection of existing higher grade schools would be approved by the Board of Education as entitled to the status of higher elementary school"; third, these "would be confined to a narrow range of pupils, subjects and equipment"; fourth, they should not contain pupils who "ought to have gone" to endowed secondary schools; and fifth, that "the schools were to be 'higher' and therefore must have a very different curriculum and equipment from the ordinary elementary schools",[1] though as they were also "elementary" anything dangerously "secondary" would be barred.

In a memorandum to Balfour, Morant explained the basic purposes quite clearly. "It is necessary to fix a rigid top limit to these Schools," he wrote, "An age limit of fifteen is precise and cannot be evaded"; the pupil might stay on to the end of the school year in which he became fifteen "*but not beyond the year*". This point was of key importance, since the retaining of older pupils was the means of "gradually raising the level of the work done"; as Morant rightly observed it was this practice which had "steadily though imperceptibly brought about the present large number of higher classes" in higher grade schools. He went on to outline measures to "restrict the multiplication of these Schools", including a decisive power of veto by the central authority. The schools should be restricted to a four-year course "mainly Elementary in character". "It is important," he concludes, "that these Schools should be definitely stamped as Elementary Schools", hence the need to assign them the name "Higher Elementary Schools"; "the age limit of fifteen fits in with the plan: and it adds the final 'cachet' of the *Elementary* character of the proposed Schools". So Morant, and the arguments advanced behind the scenes.[2]

This crucial administrative Minute, it should be recalled, was issued after the Cockerton judgment, but before the London School Board appeal had been heard. It is, therefore, as Eaglesham points out, "beyond dispute that the restriction of the age of pupils in higher elementary schools to fifteen . . . was entirely one of government policy", since this issue had not been raised in any way during the Cockerton case, "either by the auditor himself or by the courts".[3] From now on events moved fast. Lord Robert Cecil was briefed by the County Council to counter H. H. Asquith, counsel for the London School Board, and in December 1900 its first appeal failed. The judge "pronounced that the whole of the work that was conducted by the

[1] *Ibid.*, 51–52.   [2] *Ibid.*, 193–6.   [3] *Ibid.*, 51.

London School Board, whether in Day or Evening Schools, under the regulations of the Science and Art Department was illegal and that, further, the School Board had no legal right to give any evening instruction to adults".[1] This judgment was upheld by the Master of the Rolls in April 1901.

Three months later another administrative edict handed the final responsibility for all evening school work over to the county authorities. This Minute included a number of clauses destined severely to restrict the scope of this work. One of these fixed the upper age limit for evening classes run by School Boards at sixteen, others had a very adverse effect on the development of technical classes. The Minute was strongly contested, being "seen to be a deliberate attack, of far-reaching consequence, on the work of School Boards".[2] Again these restrictions in no way derived from the Cockerton judgment though this was always cited as an excuse. "The harm done to education during these critical years was almost entirely of political, not legal origin," writes Eaglesham, summarising his detailed analysis of events. "The Cockerton judgment provided a mere smokescreen."[3] Nonetheless it left a legal vacuum which had to be filled. In 1901 a Bill was introduced enabling county and county borough councils to empower School Boards to carry on higher grade schools for one year and sanctioning other School Board expenditure the legality of which had been challenged. This was bitterly contested, as the administrative Minute had also been, since it clearly subordinated the Boards to the councils and made clear the government's intentions. The Bill passed into law, however, and a similar Act was passed in 1902.[4] These were temporary measures but that a permanent settlement was pending could not be in doubt. The way had been sedulously prepared by legal and administrative steps which cut at the roots of the School Boards and the entire progressive educational movement under their control.

4. Two Trends in the Labour Movement

(i) *The T.U.C. Response to Government Policies*

"The time has come to draw your attention to the conspiracy against the education of your children which has been developing during the last five years." This, the opening paragraph of a Circular

[1] Allen, *op. cit.*, 144; see also Eaglesham, *op. cit.*, 130-2.
[2] Eaglesham, *op. cit.*, 169.   [3] *Ibid.*, 181.   [4] For these Acts, *ibid.*, 134-42.

issued by the Parliamentary Committee of the Trades Union Congress in August 1900 "to the officers of Trade Societies" and "for the careful consideration" of delegates to the T.U.C., expresses vividly the growing concern of the Labour movement as Tory policy unfolded. In choosing as the main target of attack the Higher Elementary School Minute of April 1900, the Committee showed their awareness of the class issues at stake. The T.U.C. had recently received a deputation of those interested in higher grade schools, comprising representatives of the Leeds and London School Boards and the Cardiff Trades Council and was well informed. Since its Circular clearly expresses the attitude of the Labour movement to the developing crisis in educational affairs it deserves detailed attention.[1]

It begins by protesting against the imposition of an age limit of fifteen, pointing out that in Scotland all could be freely educated to eighteen. There have been "many enemies" of elementary education for the people but over the years since 1870 such opposition had been overcome. "Until the present government took office, whatever political party has been in power, progress was made." Now, "the power of the government is turned against the education of the people".

There follows an attack on the government's attempts to prevent the spread of the School Board system—by which the education of the people was under democratic control—and to shore up the voluntary schools which are under no form of popular control whatever. The creation of School Boards, it is claimed, has been successfully resisted in many places for thirty years, in spite of the fact that universal local self-government exists for "every other local matter affecting the welfare of the people". The time has come "to complete the work of 1870 by giving in every district the same democratic control over education". But it is precisely this that the government has thwarted on every possible occasion; it has destroyed the settlement of 1870 by giving "huge doles to the clerical schools until they are now almost entirely supported by public money", and at the same time removed nearly all the safeguards of efficiency. "We do not object," the Circular states, "to clergy and capitalists managing the schools of the people if they are responsible to the people and are elected from time to time by a popular vote, but we object to the education of the people being controlled by irresponsible persons who have other interests to serve and are known to be antagonistic to popular aspirations. The present

1 The Circular is reproduced in the *33rd T.U.C. Report*, 1900, 119-20.

government, while resisting to the utmost the creation of any democratic body, has covered the country with clerical organisations, has
given them power to make the schools more sectarian, and has endowed them for this purpose with a grant of nearly £800,000 per
annum."

After this assessment of the government's overall strategy, the Circular examines the attack on the higher grade schools, affirming that
"it is in regard to the higher education of children of humble birth
that the greatest mischief is being accomplished". Six-sevenths of the
nation's children pass through the elementary schools, does anyone
suppose "that all the highest intelligence is confined to the other one-
seventh"? Many elementary school children capable of advanced
work have their intellects crushed and never surmount the initial
difficulties of life. "This is the problem which the democratic School
Boards in the great towns have, during the last thirty years, attempted
to solve by creating 'Higher Grade' schools and classes . . . mainly
supported by grants for specific subjects and by the grants of the
Science and Art Department, which was established many years ago
to promote instruction in Science and Art *especially among the Industrial
classes*."

But the present government has "struck these words out of the
Directory". It has "withdrawn these grants from many of the scholars
of 'the industrial classes', and diverted them to middle-class schools".
In addition, Education Department grants for "specific" subjects have
just been withdrawn, grants which provided for the instruction of
nearly 350,000 scholars. The government has not only attempted to
declare any expenditure from the rates in support of Science and Art
classes illegal, it has also asked Parliament for power to withdraw all
or part of the subsidy to schools secured by the Free Education Act of
1891.

Accusing the government of setting out to destroy the higher grade
schools, the Circular affirms that this has aroused so much opposition
that the government has been forced to retrace its steps and give a new
grant to a new kind of "Higher Elementary School". But the insin-
cerity of this step has been rapidly shown. The restrictions and regulations concerning these schools make them useless. The London School
Board asked that its seventy-nine higher grade schools should be continued in this form but the government offered to recognise only four.
Other Boards have had a similar experience. The government's intentions were clear; it had already introduced a Bill which would enable

it to divert most of the money now given for the technical education of the working class to the middle-class schools and universities. "Much has been done and much more is threatened." The Circular ends with an appeal and a programme:

> The retrograde steps of the last few years have revealed the weakness of our position, and before the ruin of all the slowly-built edifice of popular education is accomplished we appeal to the workers of England and Wales to speak out.
>
> The education of the nation is a national interest. Equality of opportunity free and ungrudgingly given to every child is of vital concern. The rights of those of humble birth are too precious to be left at the mercy of warring sects or social prejudices. The only safeguard of democratic interest is a democratic franchise and a free, direct, and efficient popular control. We therefore demand that:
>
> (1) The scheme of National Education foreshadowed by the Act of 1870 shall be completed and made secure by the appointment in every district of Education Authorities elected as freely and democratically as other municipal bodies.
>
> (2) That they shall be empowered to provide efficient and suitable education to all who require it.
>
> (3) That the clerical managers and clerical organisations shall not be allowed to control the education of the people to serve sectarian purposes.
>
> (4) That the elementary and higher education of the people shall be at the public expense, free, unsectarian, and under the management of the elected representatives of the people.

This clear expression of working-class aims in education was supported by a strong resolution moved by the delegate of the Shipwrights at the Annual Congress (1900), which was carried unanimously. It demanded the right to educate children in higher grade schools to the age of seventeen or eighteen, withdrawal of the order limiting the age to fifteen, and the immediate restoration of the Science and Arts grants to elementary schools; to secure these ends it called also for the "proper representation of labour and of the people's schools" on the Board of Education, of whose sixteen members "not one . . . represents the working classes of this country". The trade unions were asked to take "strenuous action" to see that the resolution was implemented.[1]

The militant note sounded by the T.U.C. reflected widespread suspicion of the government's intentions among the working class and the teachers. The T.U.C. Circular and Congress had been preceded

[1] *Ibid.*, 90.

by resolutions passed by the Railway Servants and by the Shipwrights at their annual conferences, strongly protesting against government policy on the crucial issues. The government was doing all in its
power against the education of the children of the working class, said
Richard Bell, Secretary of the Railway Servants, who also linked the
Cockerton with the first Taff Vale judgment as blows struck at the
working class.[1] A number of trades councils, recognising the implications of the Cockerton judgment, had quickly organised a public
campaign for a Bill permanently legalising School Board expenditure
on higher education.[2] The Co-operative movement also swung into
action. The Cockerton judgment, it stated in a letter to the Duke of
Devonshire, brought about a situation of the utmost importance to
the working class of the country. It would have a disastrous effect on
the industrial classes, who would be deprived of the means of obtaining
an education which otherwise they could not hope to enjoy.[3]

The T.U.C. Circular and resolution of 1900 expressed clearly the
general line of the organised working class on the most important
contemporary issues in education. In the previous six years the T.U.C.
had begun to devote considerable attention to the formulation of a
general educational policy—a process that took place significantly at
the same time as the New Unionists won the T.U.C. for socialist aims.
These six years were marked by a growing clarity of purpose in this
field, which can be traced in succeeding memoranda and resolutions.

The first statement defining the attitude of the working class to the
question of secondary education took the form of a Memorial presented
to the Bryce Commission (1894-5) "on behalf of Trades and Labour
Councils, Co-operative Societies".[4] Signed by the trade unionists
Henry Broadhurst and George Howell (both M.P.s), by the Presi-
dents and Secretaries of six important trades councils as well as by
officials of various co-operative societies, it set out once again, if in a new
context, the traditional working-class demand for the common school.

Defining secondary education as that "which follows and continues
primary or elementary education", the Memorial attacks the existing
parallel system of elementary and so-called secondary schools, the
latter in fact giving a primary education to the "wealthier section of

---

[1] McCann, op. cit., 387-8.

[2] The Bradford Trades Council circulated a petition to other trades councils calling
for such a Bill. The London and Manchester Trades Councils, as well as the Yorkshire
Federation of Trades Councils, urged this action on the government. The Birmingham
Trades Council put forward a scheme for free education, the higher grade schools forming
an integral part of the system envisaged. Ibid., 395.

[3] Ibid., 396.   [4] Report of Royal Commission on Secondary Education, Vol. V, 494-8.

the community". "The distinction of primary and secondary schools should be . . . strictly and solely *educational*, marking the successive stages of an educational curriculum; and not *social*, marking merely different grades of social rank." All children should be educated in a "common school, and thus realise and enjoy in their youth common interests and pursuits as the children of one country". Parents who wish to contract out of the state's primary school system, should educate their children at their own expense, and "expensive socially-graded schools for the primary education of wealthier people should not be provided by the State under the misleading title of Secondary schools".

In other respects, however, the Memorial reflects the Radical attitude of the "Old Unionists" (of whom Broadhurst was the leading representative) rather than the outlook of the socialist "New Unionists" whose views were shortly to dominate on this issue. This is most noticeable in its acceptance of existing conditions. "After fourteen years of age, at the latest, the children of the wage earning classes must go to work in the daytime", so that, although "they require and deserve" secondary education as much as the wealthier classes, this must be given "in secondary evening schools". A few working-class children "who have shown conspicuous ability" should receive scholarships for full-time study in secondary schools which, they add, should be financed from endowments. This was to accept the scheme originally advocated by the Schools Inquiry Commission (1868) and partially brought into practice by the Charity Commissioners. Fundamentally it involved acceptance of the existing hierarchic structure of the school system. The same somewhat limited approach is evident in the statement that "the secondary education of the working classes must to a large extent be technical and manual. The first necessity for them and for the industries of the country is that they should be skilful and expert workmen and workwomen." This constituted no vital social challenge, rather it echoed the findings of the Cross Commission.

It was in 1895, the year of Salisbury's victory and of the Bryce Commission's report, that Will Thorne introduced the first resolution at the T.U.C. to express the outlook of the New Unionists. It was in no way precise or definite, but it did demand a complete remodelling of the educational system "on such a basis as to secure the democratic principle of equality of opportunity". The existing system was condemned as being based on "commercialism" and out of harmony with the economic forces "working towards collectivism". "The best results of educational science" should be brought into the state schools, so that English children could obtain "such a training—physical, intellectual and moral—as will tend to make them worthy citizens of a co-operative commonwealth".[1] A similar resolution, moved this time by Pete Curran, also of the Gasworkers, was carried in a slightly amended form the following year. In his supporting speech, Curran defined the equalisation of opportunity as involving the opening up of the highest forms of education to the workers. An amendment, reflecting the growing suspicion in the Labour movement of Tory intentions, instructed the Parliamentary Committee "to watch carefully all legislation relating to public education" and to take action where necessary; the Committee was, in fact, censured by one speaker for having given "no expression of opinion or word of guidance" at the time of the crisis over the 1896 Bill.[2]

It was in 1897 that Congress passed for the first time a carefully formulated resolution covering the whole field of education and demanding, in clear terms, a full secondary education for all. This, moved by the Gasworkers and Engineers, opened with the words, "This Congress emphatically condemns the educational policy of the present government", a preamble which prefaced every subsequent educational resolution until the landslide of 1906 brought the Liberals back to power. Taking its stand on the principle of "equality of opportunity" the resolution declared that the workers should not be satisfied "until the highest educational advantages . . . are within the reach of all". School Boards should be empowered to provide food "for the many thousands of starving and underfed children", the half-time system abolished and the school leaving age raised to sixteen, with the provision of maintenance grants so that secondary education becomes "within the reach of every worker's child". The resolution specifically attacks the developing scholarship system in precise terms: "The system of providing secondary education only for the very small proportion of the workers' children who can come to the top after severe competition with their school fellows is to be strongly condemned" both on educational and on social grounds.

At this crucial period, then, the T.U.C. set its face against the whole *élite* conception of education first advanced in the 1860s by the Schools Inquiry Commission in terms of policies which had been gradually translated into practice. Demanding that secondary education be

---

[1] *28th T.U.C. Report*, 1895, 55. The resolution was agreed.
[2] *29th T.U.C. Report*, 1896, 48. Both the 1895 and the 1896 resolutions opposed the grant of public money for education without public control.

available to "every worker's child", the 1897 T.U.C. took the first step towards formulating what was to become the great slogan of "secondary education for all".[1]

This resolution covered other points on which the Labour movement took a specific attitude. The full cost of educational provision should be met from the exchequer and financed by the democratic administration of grants and endowments, a graduated income tax on all incomes above £300 p.a. and graduated death duties. There should be reforms in the training of teachers in order to raise standards. Finally there was the long standing demand for a secular education. Sectarian strife should be dissociated from education; the state should provide only for the teaching of secular subjects "leaving the teaching of creeds and dogmas to the religious denominations". The resolution called for a deputation to the Minister of Education on all these issues.

This resolution, with the substitution of a school leaving age of fourteen instead of sixteen, was moved again in 1898 and 1899 to be carried unanimously. As events moved on towards the conflicts of 1900-2, therefore, by far the most representative organisation of the Labour movement had taken up a clear and unequivocal position on the major questions.

(ii) The Fabian Approach

While the T.U.C. strongly opposed the development of an *élite*, or selective, system of education—one which, by definition, denied the desirability or practicability of secondary education for all—Sidney Webb threw all his weight, and that of the Fabian Society, behind plans to develop precisely such a system. Since 1892, when he became Chairman of the London Technical Education Committee (later Board), Webb had been fully involved in educational administration and had begun to realise his educational outlook in practice.

The Fabian outlook has been briefly outlined. Predominant was the view that all forms of social organisation must contribute to "national efficiency". Here educational institutions at all levels had an essential role to play. But they could only operate effectively if the educational system was totally reorganised on modern, twentieth century lines. Above all it must be unified, all particularist tendencies (especially religious) swept away by administrative action and the chaos of postprimary education sorted out. The immediate need was to establish

[1] *30th T.U.C. Report*, 1897, 50ff. The resolution was carried by a large majority. The textile workers, however, were in opposition; they did not agree to the abolition of the half-time system.

"a really effective national minimum of education", and, with this, energetically to develop secondary schools and universities. To this end "collective" or state action was the pressing issue of the time.[1]

Webb's view of an "efficient" educational system can best be grasped from his writings following the 1902 Act. National efficiency, he wrote in his book *London Education* (1904), depends on our making the most of "the capacities of the whole population, which form, after all, as truly a part of the national resources as our iron and coal". Britain has nothing on which to depend to maintain her pre-eminent industrial position "except the brains of our people". Education was not, therefore, a philanthropic matter, it was one of national concern. In particular it was essential to set up a "capacity-catching" scholarship system in order to give a suitable form of higher education to "all whose brains make it profitable for the community to equip them with more advanced instruction".[2]

As Chairman of the London Technical Education Board Webb had succeeded in introducing the rudiments of a scholarship system. The idea of making local authority grants to schools conditional on acceptance of scholarship winners in fact originated with Webb and Maxwell Garnett in London in 1894. By 1903-4 Webb could characterise the London scholarship system as "one of the most successful developments of the past decade". Every year, he claimed, about 800 of the ablest boys and girls aged eleven to thirteen in public elementary schools "are picked by competitive examination for two to five years' higher education".[3]

The "capacity catching" system—in other words, the selective machinery designed to cement a structured system of education—had been a key question for Webb for many years. The idea that education is valuable for its own sake he clearly regarded as no more than sentimental twaddle. As clearly he pursued the idea that, to ensure maximum efficiency of the state, each child should receive the specific form of education which would maximise his efficiency. It is interesting to note that Webb goes out of his way to attack the idea of the common school which had been a main objective of working-class educational policies throughout the century. This idea, he says, was

[1] S. Webb, *Twentieth Century Politics*, Fabian Tract No. 108 (November 1901), 13-15.
[2] S. Webb, *London Education* (1904), 9-10.
[3] *Ibid.*, 25-6. The scholarship winners were sent to endowed grammar schools, many of these being at that time "in a state of acute depression". These and other subventions helped to revive London's grammar schools. A. V. Judges, "The Educational Influence of the Webbs", *British Journal of Educational Studies*, Vol. X, No. 1, November 1961, 39-40.

BOARD SCHOOL CHILD CLIMBING SIDNEY WEBB'S EDUCATIONAL LADDER:
CARTOON, 1895

advanced by Victorian democratic reformers and may have represented a satisfactory ideal at that stage, but the time was now ripe for a different kind of advance. This should comprise "in all populous centres, the progressive differentiation of the publicly provided school, the 'common school' of our Radical grandfathers—into a number of specialised schools each more accurately fitting the needs of a particular section of children".[1]

Webb entirely accepted the Morant strategy. Secondary schools must be differentiated according to length of schooling—as the Schools Inquiry Commission "ought to have taught us forty years ago".[2] For those leaving school at fourteen or fifteen "the best we can do in the educational way is to provide the most efficient higher grade or 'higher elementary' school". But for those staying on to sixteen or eighteen there should be secondary schools in which work "spread over a longer time, can be taken with a wider outlook" and "there is time for more attention to mental training and cultivation, as distinguished from mere instruction". This implies that "the secondary school is, and must always remain, essentially different from the primary school".[3] Webb softens the picture by arguing that the social distinction between elementary and secondary education "has everywhere been blurred, and sometimes practically obliterated"; certainly the rich can and do pay for education but "the great bulk of the population will, by free places and scholarships, by entrance examinations and judicious selection, have access to just the kind and grade of schooling that their attainments and idiosyncrasies require".[4]

This policy Webb had himself set out to implement in London well before government policies against the School Boards got under way. Inspired by the idea of a unified system of education from elementary school to university he recognised that this must involve a rationalisation of "the educational machinery", and was mainly concerned that steps in this direction should provide "an administratively workable solution". What better policy could there be than that which the government had set about implementing? "Apart from a very few

[1] "The twentieth century recognises that its task is the more complicated one of providing every part of the country with the highly differentiated educational organisation necessary to ensure to every child *the particular kind* of schooling that it needs." S. Webb, "Secondary Education", in H. B. Binns, *A Century of Education* (1908), 287-9.

[2] *Ibid.*, 291.

[3] S. Webb, *London Education*, 108-9. Of the higher elementary school, Webb wrote, in a letter to Wallas in 1900, "It is not their business to lead up to any higher *school*, but to the counting house, the factory, or the kitchen." McCann, *op. cit.*, 538.

[4] Binns, *op. cit.*, 293.

essentially simple ideas," G. D. H. Cole has written of Webb, "he did not trouble himself much about any underlying philosophy. He was fully convinced that the trend of events in the modern world was towards Socialism, and that this trend would continue: so that he saw no need to put himself in revolutionary opposition to the main course of development".[1] In practice, this meant that he could easily agree to projected measures. If church schools which educated half the children in the country were likely to fail from lack of support, then they should be aided from the rates; if School Boards, bar the largest ones, were inefficient and introduced administrative confusion, then they should go. The larger and more efficient county or county borough councils had best administer and control all schools. Anyone who stood out on a question of principle on either issue was an obscurantist—no better than a Victorian Radical.

Webb set out to win the Fabian Society to this standpoint. He was vigorously opposed by Graham Wallas and Stewart Headlam, both members of the London School Board, who argued that to put the voluntary schools on the rates was "too favourable to sectarian education"; Headlam also stood out against the proposal to abolish School Boards. But strong though these opponents were "they were beaten every time"[2] and Webb's victory was signalised by publication of the tract *The Educational Muddle and the Way Out* in January 1901, though Headlam conducted a stout rearguard action to the end. Even before the tract was published, to achieve rapidly a circulation of 20,000, proofs of it were requested from Whitehall where a new Education Bill was in active preparation.[3] Thus, on the eve of what was to be a crucial struggle over educational policy, the Fabian Society, engaged though it was with the Labour Representation Committee, took up a position fully in accord with the policy advocated by Gorst and Morant, the Church of England and the Tory party.

[1] G. D. H. Cole, *The Second International, 1899-1914* (1956), 210.
[2] E. R. Pease, *The History of the Fabian Society*, 143.
[3] The Tract (No. 106) proposed, *inter alia*:
  (i) One central controlling body nationally, responsible for all education up to and including university level.
  (ii) A single local authority also responsible for all levels of education; with the exception of London and some fifty county boroughs this to be the county council acting through a statutory committee consisting of a majority of councillors and of certain co-opted individuals. In the case of London and the large county boroughs the School Boards to continue as before.
  (iii) Voluntary schools to be put under the control of the local education authorities and offered extra grants to improve their efficiency.
  (iv) An exchequer grant system to ensure that every local authority provides a "national minimum" of education.

CHAPTER VII

THE BALFOUR ACT AND ITS AFTERMATH

A T the Khaki Election of October 1900, as we have noted, the Tories were returned after five years of rule with a massive majority (134 over both the Liberals and the Irish). All the conditions were now maturing for a radical educational reorganisation on the lines so long desired by the Church—now more influential than ever[1]— and the Tory leadership. Repeated appeals by the London School Board against the Cockerton judgment had failed so that the entire structure of advanced teaching by School Boards was now stigmatised as illegal. Here was the weak spot in the democratic structure that had been developed over the last thirty years—and it was at this point that the government decided to direct its main assault.

1. THE EVENTS OF 1901

The Education Minister in the House of Commons, Sir John Gorst, who for years had shown his dislike of the School Boards, saw his opportunity and resolved to exploit it "to the utmost" doing "everything in his power to stir up agitation against the School Boards". In a private memorandum to the Duke of Devonshire early in 1901 he had stated clearly that the School Boards intended to give secondary education and that the voluntary schools were threatened with extinction—castigating the "ambition" of the School Boards.[2] Gorst was quick to appreciate the value of Fabian assistance for Tory aims; it was Gorst who distributed proof copies of the Fabian manifesto to his fellow ministers. "One of the most eminent representatives of British socialism, Sidney Webb, had shown them the way," writes Halévy. "At a moment when the Boer War was at its height, they would do

---

[1] "The position of the Catholic Church had improved; within the Anglican Church, the position of the High Church had improved to the detriment of the Low Church; and the position of the Anglican Church had improved to the detriment of the nonconformist sects." E. Halévy, *Imperialism and the Rise of Labour, 1895-1905* (1961 ed.), 188.

[2] E. Eaglesham, "Planning the Education Bill of 1902", *British Journal of Educational Studies*, Vol. IX, No. 1, November 1960, 4.

well to pay attention to the man who in the Socialist camp gave such valuable support to their imperialist policy."[1]

In a speech in March 1900 in the House of Commons Gorst had attacked the School Boards for misleading government departments and breaking the law, going on to announce the government's intention of introducing a Bill creating new authorities for secondary education.[2] Shortly after he stated there should be only one authority for all schools of every grade—implying the end of the School Board system. In May 1901, this Bill, containing two clauses, was introduced: the first was concerned with the setting up of these new authorities, while the second, in order to meet the situation arising from the Cockerton judgment, gave these new authorities the right to empower School Boards to carry on any schools or classes which had been declared illegal—there was no time limit attached to this latter clause.[3] Although this Bill never became law—it was withdrawn in the summer due partly to pressure of business in the House—it gave clear notice of the government's intention. In its place the first Cockerton Act (already referred to), which provided temporary legal authority for the schools and classes declared illegal, was pushed through Parliament in the late summer. This Act itself contained a severe slap at the School Boards, for it specifically placed them under the aegis of the county or county borough councils, and further—and this proposal came from Morant—did so for one year only.

The government's measures of 1901 met with strong opposition, not only from Liberals and nonconformists, but also from the Labour movement and the teachers, who were now drawing closely together in the fight against government policy. The National Union of Teachers, the organisation of elementary school teachers including those in higher grade schools, increasingly disillusioned with the direction of affairs and profoundly suspicious of the government's intentions, took up a position very close to that of the Labour movement. Already in April 1900, strong objection was expressed at the Annual Conference of the N.U.T. to the measures taken by the Board of Education. A year later the conference as a whole reflected a quite new level of militancy. "They had to do with a conspiracy against the advanced instruction of the working classes," declared a London School Board member to "prolonged cheers", "and it was largely the

---

[1] Halévy, op. cit., 200.
[2] B. M. Allen, Sir Robert Morant (1934), 145-6.
[3] Ibid., 147.

o

conspiracy of one family in this country."[1] The Higher Elementary School Minute, which had been "foisted" on the country, involved a "degradation" of the education provided for important sections of the community, declared the mover of the main resolution of protest. At the same time, as a result of other measures, money was being diverted from the industrial classes "to the children of the well-to-do". They had looked to this Minute as the charter of the higher grade schools, said another speaker, and it had simply turned out the line of demarcation between secondary and primary education which they had always been fighting. The Conference should not be misled by Sir John Gorst's assurances that there is no intention to injure the higher grade schools and that a scholarship system was to be established, declared the much respected headmaster of the Manchester Central School, Scotson. "No system of scholarships from elementary to secondary schools could be devised which would at all equal the present system of giving children education in the same kind of school and going on to the Higher Grade school."[2] The N.U.T., another speaker had said a year earlier, stood for a united, co-related, co-ordinated system from the lowest school to the highest university. If the government's attempts to organise secondary education on the one hand, and to delimit primary education on the other, were successful, this ideal was lost for ever.

It is interesting to note that the N.U.T. had originally welcomed the Higher Elementary School Minute, issued a fortnight before the annual conference of 1900, although deploring the age limit of fifteen. But subsequent events had first aroused suspicions and finally brought disillusionment. Of 190 applications for recognition under the Minute, only twelve had been accepted and some of these only conditionally, as the mover of the protest resolution of 1901 pointed out. He also illustrated how, while advanced work was being cut back in elementary schools, middle-class schools were receiving additional aid from public funds, instancing Bradford Grammar school which charged fees of over £10 but now earned a government grant of over £5 a head.[3]

By 1901, then, powerful forces were lining up against the govern-

---

[1] *The Schoolmaster*, 13 April 1901, 719. The reference, of course, is to the Cecils.
[2] *Ibid.*, 684-5. Scotson had been described as "the Prince of Schoolmasters" by A. J. Mundella; in his speech Scotson indignantly protested against Gorst's insinuation (in a recent speech) that the higher grade schools did not endeavour to develop children's minds and give a true education.
[3] *Ibid.*, 21 April 1900, 811-12; 13 April 1901, 684.

ment's policy, which was now widely recognised as involving a genuine threat to democratic aspirations. In that year the report of the Parliamentary Committee of the T.U.C. again gave prominence to education, summarising the standpoint of the Labour movement on Tory educational policy and reiterating the arguments used in the Circular of August 1900. The settlement of 1870, whereby "schools established by the clergy for sectarian purposes were secured from competition, conditionally on the understanding that the schools were efficient, and half the cost of maintenance was provided" was being destroyed. Large doles had been given to clerical schools and nearly all the safeguards for efficiency had been removed. "The greatest mischief" was being done to the higher education for children of the "industrial classes". What was required was the establishment of freely and democratically elected education authorities in every district, having power to provide efficient education for all who require it, and that managers and clerical organisations should "have no control over the education of the people". Such, in essence, was the educational policy of the T.U.C., whose Parliamentary committee reported very strong feeling on these issues in the country.[1]

The T.U.C. had participated actively, both independently and in common with other organisations, in the fight against government policy. It took part in a conference called in February at St. Martin's Town Hall "for the purpose of counteracting the retrograde action of the government", as an outcome of which a large and fully representative deputation from the T.U.C. saw the Duke of Devonshire and Sir John Gorst on 13 May.[2] With the announcement of the government's first Bill (1901), the T.U.C. sent out a petition, addressed to the House of Commons, urging affiliated trade unions to pass resolutions condemning the educational policy of the government and demanding that M.P.s vote against the Bill.[3] Many important trades councils—for instance Nottingham, Manchester, Newcastle, Bradford—followed suit, "the latter inspired the formation of a local committee which was responsible for the despatch of over 1,500 letters to Cabinet Ministers, Members of Parliament and the Education Department, all critical of the Bill", while the London Trades Council "also warned against any interference with the advanced work of the

[1] 34th T.U.C. Report, 1901, 41.
[2] Ibid., 42. A report of this meeting was printed and sent to the trades.
[3] Ibid.

School Boards".[1] In June the T.U.C. as well as local trades councils, trade union branches, co-operative societies, etc., participated in a great conference (1,950 delegates) of "Progressive Educationists" where agreed resolutions were passed covering the main issues: public management of all schools receiving money from public funds, the need for popularly elected authorities, and for the legalisation of advanced work.[2] Leading trade unionists participated in similar meetings in the provinces. According to the Parliamentary Committee of the T.U.C., this agitation was partially effective; referring to the government's first Bill, they add: "finding the opposition of the organised trades and the educationists so very strong, they [the government] felt it to be the wiser course to withdraw the Bill." The Cockerton Act, however, was "the thin end of the wedge of destructive policy". "Every friend of popular education," ends their report, "must be vigilant, otherwise the government will change the whole educational policy of the country to the injury, if not the destruction, of the higher interests of the people."[3]

At the meeting of the Congress itself at Swansea in the autumn the whole question of education was brought to the forefront at the start in the speech of the secretary of the reception committee—a teacher and member of the National Union of Teachers. Saying that he believed that the N.U.T. should be affiliated to the T.U.C. he appealed, in the name of the N.U.T., for "a general uprising of the workers in protest against the attempts made to rob the children of toilers of facilities for higher education". He was followed by the President, Bowerman, who strongly condemned the government for introducing a Bill "directly at variance" with the 1870 Act which had resulted in loud and deep protest "throughout the length and breadth of the country". Legislation of "the most retrograde character" had been attempted—an attempt indirectly to filch from the workers advantages hitherto enjoyed under the School Board system. Instead of narrowing educational opportunities, they should be broadened.[4]

At this Congress the T.U.C. reaffirmed its overall educational policy in a resolution moved by W. A. Appleton of the Amalgamated Lace Makers. This condemned the recent actions both of the government

[1] W. P. McCann, "Trade Unionist, Co-operative and Socialist Organisations in relation to Popular Education, 1870-1902", unpublished Ph.D. thesis, University of Manchester (1960), 406.
[2] Ibid., 408; 34th T.U.C. Report, 1901, 42.
[3] 34th T.U.C. Report, 1901, 42.
[4] Ibid., 27-9.

and of the Board of Education "in imposing hindrances and restrictions on the development of education". It stressed the general policy that all grades of education in districts of suitable size should be under one authority "directly elected, and elected solely for educational purposes" (i.e. School Boards); other clauses asked for the school leaving age to be raised to fifteen, the withdrawal of any maximum age-limit,[1] and the abolition of all fees in elementary, evening continuation, higher grade and technical schools. It also called for adequate non-sectarian training colleges and for representation of Labour on the Board of Education. On this occasion the T.U.C. seems to have retreated from its general line (since 1897) that secondary education should be made freely available for all; it called for free scholarships for working-class children, the "governing principle" of these "being that of intelligence and attainments of the child". The T.U.C. reprinted (for the delegates) the way every M.P. had voted on the Cockerton Act (1901).[2]

Other sections of the Labour movement were also moving at this stage into active opposition to the government. At its Annual Conference in this year (1901) the Co-operative Congress passed a resolution deprecating "any retrograde step" in relation to facilities for higher education in elementary and evening continuation schools, calling for a single, local, specially elected education authority in each district and for an Act of Parliament legalising the advanced work of the School Boards and permitting its extension. Some very effective speeches were made in the debate on this resolution—one by Balmforth of Huddersfield, a School Board member for fifteen years, who said that the School Boards "had brought higher education within the reach of working people, erecting a half-way house to the University", and protested that now "if a school board desired to open higher educational schools they could not do so".[3] In July the Duke of Devonshire refused to see a deputation from the Co-operative movement who saw the Liberal leader, Campbell Bannerman, instead. In various other ways, through letters to M.P.s, resolutions, etc., the

---

[1] James Wignall of Swansea, who seconded the resolution, protested strongly against the imposition of an age-limit in the higher grade schools: "the only hope of the children of the working men was the higher grade school. If by stinting the parents could allow their children to remain in higher grade schools until seventeen or eighteen years of age, it was a scandalous shame that any government should introduce legislation which would debar the children from the benefits of the education within their reach." The Welsh (Intermediate) schools "were out of the reach of the working man's child". The interference with evening schools was also "a great blow to working men". *Ibid.*, 72-3.

[2] *Ibid.*, 96-7.

[3] *33rd Co-operative Congress Report*, 1901, 181-2, 203.

Co-operative movement attempted to drive home their point of view.[1]

At the end of June, as we know, the government withdrew its Bill and substituted the one clause Bill which passed into law on August 1. In July, the Board of Education promulgated the Evening School Minute which dealt a further blow at the School Boards. A vigorous opposition to the government's declared policy in relation to the School Boards was building up in the country—there were many who, rejecting the Fabian-Tory outlook, would agree with Sir Joshua Fitch's standpoint as expressed in an article in the *Nineteenth Century Review* reprinted in the January 1902 number of the S.D.F.'s theoretical journal, the *Social Democrat*: "It is, after all, on the School Boards that the future destiny of English primary education mainly rests . . . it is to them the nation owes all the best educational enterprise of the last few years, the best school buildings and equipment, the most rational and effective experiments in the direction of good organisation and better teaching. In particular it is wholly to their initiative that we owe the higher Board schools, and the continuation and evening schools, which are so popular in our great industrial centres, and which have done so much to invigorate the life and to increase the power and resources of the people. And it is rather to measures which will improve the constitution of the Boards, and invest them with new powers and responsibilities, than to a resolution that would destroy them, that the best friends of education look for the adaptation of our machinery to the changing circumstances and the intellectual and social advancement of the nation in the coming century." But, he continued, there are two classes of people who wish to discredit the School Boards—the Tories "who believe that any further advance in the education of the 'lower classes' will imperil the social order", and those who wish to increase religious teaching in the schools.[2]

In this assessment, Fitch was, of course, correct. In the late autumn

---

[1] McCann, *op. cit.*, 407. The Co-operative movement had a specific interest in the School Boards, as they told Campbell Bannerman; the movement spent nearly £70,000 a year on education, and many of the classes started at the stores had been taken over by School Boards. In 1900, local co-operatives ran seventeen schools with 2,500 scholars, half of these in the adult division. For this they received grant aid which would be stopped if the Bill was passed. *Ibid.*

[2] *Social Democrat*, Vol. VI, No. 1, January 1902. Fitch was, at this stage, one of the Grand Old Men of the state educational system; Principal of the Borough Road Training College, London, as a young man, he was for thirty-six years a leading H.M.I. working for several commissions and enquiries. Unlike most of his colleagues, he was born of poor parents and gained a London external degree; cf. John Leese, *Personalities and Power in English Education* (1950), 165-71.

of that year the government was preparing its draft of what was finally to become the 1902 Education Act.

2. THE EDUCATION BILL IN THE COMMONS

The Cockerton Act of 1901 had been drawn up by a Cabinet Committee consisting of Balfour, Devonshire, Walter Long and Gorst, aided by Morant. Following the passage of the Act, this committee went on to consider the Education Bill to be presented at the next session. The first draft was produced by Sir John Gorst in August.[1]

It was clear to all that radical changes in education were impending, and it may be as well to assess briefly the chief points at issue. The areas of conflict were many, varied and complex, but their general outlines were becoming clear. That which bulked largest in the public eye was the religious conflict which focused on the question of the future of the voluntary (church) schools. Here, to put it simply, the Church of England was fighting for the continued existence of its schools by demanding rate aid with the minimum of local (which was bound to be lay, or secular) control. Some degree of control was, of course, inevitable. The objective was to get the maximum public subsidy while conceding the least possible control, and at the same time, if possible, to reverse the 1870 compromise embodied in the Cowper-Temple clause and obtain entry for Anglican teaching in the board schools. On these issues battle was joined between Anglican (and Roman Catholic) on the one hand, and Nonconformist and Secularist on the other, since both the latter were concerned to reduce the powers of the Anglican church over education. This line-up had very definite political connotations since the Church naturally looked to the Tories for support, nonconformists and radicals to the Liberals.

This particular struggle can in theory be differentiated from the second area of conflict—that over the future of the School Boards, although in fact the two were closely interlinked. The Anglican Church, in essence, opposed the School Boards, and wished to see them brought to an end, since these put secular interests first in education and as a result of their greater financial resources and general enthusiasm for education, threatened the very existence of the voluntary schools.[2] But there were much more formidable opponents of the

---

[1] E. Eaglesham, " Planning the Education Bill of 1902", loc. cit., 4.

[2] Although there were some among the Church of England who did not accept this policy. At a meeting of the Association of School Boards on higher grade schools early in 1901 Dr. Maclure, Dean of Manchester, Chairman of the Manchester School Board and

School Boards, able to take direct action against them in pursuance of a wider policy. This policy—formed by Balfour himself, by Gorst, Morant and the most influential Fabians—was to confine elementary education within clear limits and to build up a unified and co-ordinated system of secondary education parallel to but separate from the elementary schools, with scholarships forming the only link. It could be argued that for this purpose larger units of administration were necessary than the average School Board area could provide and that county and county borough councils were the most obvious and suitable local authorities to become responsible for education.[1]

This latter point did not apply in all cases, since the county boroughs did not cover a larger area than the existing School Boards, in, say, Manchester or Birmingham. For this reason there was hesitation about proposing a change in the larger cities. But other arguments were mobilised against the principle of an *ad hoc* authority, especially that of extravagance. Here was a directly elected authority which was *not* the rating authority, which determined how much to spend on education and then simply passed on a demand for this sum to the local authority which was bound to provide it. The argument of extravagance, if without supporting evidence, was widely used against the School Boards. The conflict on this question also, of course, had a very definite political connotation since the School Boards were for the most part, as Halévy puts it, "citadels of Radicalism". The county councils were almost invariably dominated by parson and squire. The political significance of the changes proposed, therefore, is sufficiently evident.

The development of secondary education also tended to be an issue in itself, though linked to the question of the School Boards. The pressure for the development of a state-supported system of secondary schools had been increasing for two or more decades; it was specifically on this question that the Bryce Commission had reported in 1895.

the last President of the Association of School Boards, made a very forceful speech stressing the value of the higher grade schools and attacking the Minute on higher elementary schools. At the same meeting the Rev. Canon Moore Ede, seconding Lyulph Stanley's motion of protest on this Minute, objected to this work of the School Boards being stopped: "Upon the southern banks of the river Tyne there is a population of 700,000 and amongst these working people there used to be only two small schools which could give education to children above fifteen years of age if the present decision was upheld." *The Schoolmaster*, 23 February 1901, 301-2.

[1] There were 2,544 School Boards in existence, some with only one or two schools to administer.

There were those who regarded the expansion of secondary education, subsidised by the state and local authorities, as an inescapable necessity; but others opposed this view or at least wished to confine developments within narrow limits. This conflict also had a political connotation; while Liberals on the whole wished to see some progress in this field, the Tory attitude varied from lukewarm support to outright opposition to any expenditure of public money whatever on secondary education.[1] In the event the whole question of the future development of secondary education came to be overshadowed by the religious issue. Of the fifty-seven days of debate on the Education Bill, only four were spent on this matter.

The government at first wavered in their proposals for the Bill; due to the complex political situation and to the line-up within the government itself, it was not at first clear to them how far they could go. For one thing, Joseph Chamberlain, who had brought over the Liberal Unionists into the Tory government of 1895, was one of the outstanding figures in the Cabinet, the man who, above all, if thirty years earlier, had conducted the sharpest possible struggle in favour of School Boards and a secular (or at least non-sectarian) approach to education—the man who had threatened the disestablishment of the Church of England and who still in his imperialist phase carried with him much Radical support. The Duke of Devonshire himself was a Liberal Unionist. But, as Eaglesham notes, the church side of the Tory party "was ripe for dramatic action".[2] While Salisbury and Balfour wavered as to the type of Bill to be presented, fearful of the Liberal Unionists' reaction, the Anglican and Roman Catholic churches built up their pressure. Already, the previous July, a joint meeting of Convocations had approved a scheme setting out the essential demands of the Church of England. Now "peers, bishops, rectors, vicars, laymen—all degrees sent numerous letters to Balfour or Morant".[3] "The strain is now at *breaking point*," wrote the Bishop of Rochester to Lord Salisbury; unless something were done immediately the impression would be created that "the game is up". Church schools were already being

---

[1] A point of view epitomised in the debate on the 1902 Act by James Lowther, a Tory M.P., who stated that he had taken part in the 1870 discussions in the House of Commons. "He had divided the House on that occasion against compulsory attendance, and ever since then had strongly opposed any charge being made upon either the rate or the National Exchequer for any education beyond rudimentary and elementary education"; *Hansard*, Vol. 109, col. 1429 (23 June 1902). Lowther was arguing against a clause permitting the raising of a 2d. rate for higher (secondary) education.

[2] Eaglesham, "Planning the Education Bill of 1902," *loc. cit.*, 5.

[3] Eaglesham, *op. cit.*, 17-18.

handed over to School Boards, "enough greatly to weaken the cause".
Others would come down at an accelerating rate.[1]

The key role in formulating the final draft of the Bill presented to
Parliament, and in the preceding negotiations, was played by Robert
Morant.[2] In a memorandum of December 1901, he stated his view
that "the only way to 'get up steam' for passing any Education Bill at
all in the teeth of School Board opposition will be to include in it
some scheme for aiding denominational schools".[3] In other words,
the destruction of the School Boards would only become a political
possibility if all the forces of the churches, Anglican and Roman
Catholic, and associated social and political elements were fully
mobilised. This, in Morant's opinion, could be achieved by proposing
complete rate maintenance of voluntary schools in return for local
(rating) authority representation on the governing bodies, but ensuring
that these representatives would be in a substantial minority (as had,
in fact, been proposed by Convocation).

Such a proposal constituted a head-on challenge and it was, therefore,
modified to give local authorities the option of aiding voluntary schools
out of the rates; by this concession Chamberlain's scruples were
overcome. But Morant saw this as "a serious blot" on the bill, a heavy
price paid for Chamberlain's support. Perhaps it is best to see this as
a purely face-saving affair—the optional clause was removed in discussion in the House of Commons, on an amendment moved by a
Tory (Hobhouse).[4]

In its final form the Bill dealt with both elementary and secondary
education, both School Boards and the proposed new authorities, as
also what was from a contemporary point of view most important of
all, the position of the church schools. Its main proposals, as originally

---

[1] B. M. Allen, *Sir Robert Morant*, 163; cf. Eaglesham, *op. cit.*, 10-11. "It is clear that
some drastic treatment must be found," wrote Morant in a confidential memorandum
in 1902, "unless a large number of voluntary schools are to be extinguished, and board
schools to take their place." Ministry of Education private papers, Public Record Office
(Ed 24/13A/13/10a). I owe this reference to Mrs. A. Shakoor.

[2] This is brought out particularly in Sir Almeric Fitzroy's *Memoirs* (1926), Vol. I, a
book dedicated to "the incorruptible memory of Spencer Compton, 8th Duke of Devonshire". The confusion and conflict in government circles is graphically described; "in
the meantime," noted Fitzroy in February 1902, "the indefatigable Morant flies from
one Cabinet Minister to another and receives the frankest confessions from them all,
the background being a settled feeling of anxiety and disquiet that they have brought such
a hornet's nest about their heads" (p. 74). Fitzroy had been an H.M.I. for seven years;
from 1895 he acted as departmental private secretary to the Duke of Devonshire.

[3] Allen, *op. cit.*, 153.

[4] For Morant's famous talk with Chamberlain, at which he won his support for the
Bill, see Allen, *op. cit.*, 166-9, and Eaglesham, *op. cit.*, 18-19.

laid before the House of Commons and the important modifications introduced, may be summarised as follows:

(1) The abolition of the School Boards, and the substitution of county and county borough councils as local education authorities. In county areas, however, borough councils with a population of over 10,000 and urban district councils with a population of over 20,000 were to be local education authorities with power over elementary schools only. This was, in fact, a concession to local feeling.[1] As originally introduced, the Bill empowered county councils to take over School Board functions at their discretion, a concession to Liberal Unionists and Chamberlain, but in July the latter yielded and this became obligatory. County and county borough councils were required to set up education committees to administer education, with powers of co-option.

(2) The voluntary schools were to be supported from the rates, and to be brought to some extent under the control of the new authorities. Again this was originally to be optional on local authorities but, as we have seen, it became compulsory. Voluntary schools were to be governed by managers in the ratio of four appointed by the body owning the school, to two representing the local authority. The education committee of the local authority was to be responsible for the secular education in these schools (i.e. non-religious teaching), and the authority's *consent* must be obtained for the appointment or dismissal of all teachers (except those giving religious instruction) but the managers would make the actual appointment.

(3) The original Bill dealt somewhat tentatively with secondary (or "higher" as it was usually called) education. Clause 1 defined the authorities capable of administering and organising such education; Clause 2 originally simply stated that "the local education authority *may* supply or aid the supply of education other than elementary", authorities were also given power to levy a rate not exceeding 2d. in the pound for this purpose. In other words the proposed powers were (a) purely permissive and (b) strictly limited. During the passage of the Bill opposition pressure ensured that this clause was strengthened to make it obligatory on local authorities "to consider the educational needs of their area" and then take such steps "as seemed to them desirable" to promote education "other than elementary". It will be seen that, though powers remained permissive, the scope for using them was considerably widened, a point underlined

[1] Halévy, *op. cit.*, 202-4.

by the fact that limitation of the rate to 2d. was lifted in the case of the boroughs.[1]

These are the most important aspects of the Bill. It is important to grasp its character *as originally introduced*, because it is only in the light of this that contemporary attitudes can be assessed. It is also important to recognise that the Bill did not appear, and was not intended to appear, as a great charter for secondary education—though it has since often been so described; if anything, the contrary was the case.

The Bill was introduced into the Commons on 24 March 1902, when the first reading was carried by 176 to 23. The second reading took place on 8 May and the three following days, when it was carried by 402 to 165. The House went into Committee on the Bill on 2 June, the day peace was concluded with the Boers, and the debates begun in earnest. On 7 August, when the House was adjourned, twenty-two days had been spent on the first seven clauses. An autumn session, not usual at this period, was clearly necessary and discussion continued when the House reassembled on 16 October. During this session the new procedure known as the "guillotine", introduced by the government earlier in the year, was ruthlessly used to secure progress, and by this means the Bill finally passed the Committee stage on 20 November. Four days were then spent on the Report stage, and two more on general debate, before the third reading was finally carried by a majority of 123. The Bill, then, had been discussed for fifty-seven days, by comparison with twenty-two spent on the 1870 Act. The Royal Assent was accorded on 18 December.[2] A feature of the Parliamentary handling of this measure was that it was piloted through the House by A. J. Balfour, initially as First Lord of the Treasury, but subsequently, after attaining the office in the summer, as Premier.[3]

---

[1] The permissive nature of the clause was debated on 23 June 1902. It was strongly attacked by the Liberals (Bryce, Asquith, Macnamara, Lloyd George and others) who gained some Tory support (Hart Dyke, Hobhouse). It was, however, equally strongly supported by Tories representing the agricultural interest (Lowther, Chaplin, Rasch). In spite of Gorst's arguments for the original wording, Balfour finally accepted a compromise formulation along the lines given in the text. *Hansard*, Vol. 109, cols. 1401ff. In its final form the Act allowed county councils also to exceed the 2d. limit "with the consent of the Local Government Board". For a brief summary of the Bill as originally presented see Halévy, *op. cit.*, 202–4.

[2] J. F. W. Drury, *Manual of Education* (1903), 162–3.

[3] Salisbury retired in July; in the Cabinet reshuffle that followed, Lord Londonderry took Devonshire's post as the titular head of the Education Department ("like his predecessor", writes Halévy, "an aristocratic figurehead and with a less imposing personality"), while Sir John Gorst, who was unpopular with the Unionists (and others) was superseded by Sir William Anson.

3. The Fight Against the Bill Outside Parliament

The introduction of the Education Bill on 24 March sparked off a movement of intense opposition throughout the country which, rising to a climax in the autumn, only finally died away a decade later. Almost the entire Labour movement was solidly opposed, regarding the Bill as a profoundly reactionary measure directed against the working class. A mass conference of delegates representing over one million workers was called for 28 May to protest against the measure and many trades councils up and down the country actively opposed the Bill, calling meetings, passing resolutions, preparing petitions. But the approach of the Labour movement should be seen in the wider context of the Free Church or Nonconformist opposition, which was aroused to a high fighting level by the favoured treatment of the Church of England.

This movement was led by the redoubtable Dr. John Clifford and, in the north, by J. Hirst Hollowell. It was no sudden manifestation; for years the Nonconformists had watched with suspicion the attempts of the Church of England to strengthen its position. In 1896 the Northern Counties Education League had been set up to organise opposition to these moves and up to 1902, had challenged every step taken by the government or the Education Department to weaken the position of the School Boards.[1] Now the battle was really joined, and the Free Church movement threw itself into the struggle with tremendous energy.

"Three days after the introduction of the Bill," Hirst Hollowell's biographer has recorded, "the Northern Counties League met in Manchester, and the proposals of the Government were declared to be bad both in principle and machinery." Every clause was "considered and exposed". M.P.s "were called upon to reject the measure—amendment was impossible". There followed "strenuous opposition of every kind". Great meetings and demonstrations were held in the industrial

[1] The Northern Counties Education League was formed to prevent the 1896 Education Bill being passed. Its policy was:
  (i) To defend the existing Board School system in England and Wales against the attacks of Ecclesiastical parties.
  (ii) To demand that all Elementary Schools receiving Government grants or local rates shall be brought under popular control.
  (iii) To secure throughout England and Wales a Universal Board School system such as already exists in Scotland.
The activities of the League are described in W. Evans and W. Claridge, *James Hirst Hollowell and the Movement for Civic Control in Education* (1911), 48ff., from which the statement of policy is taken.

centres and elsewhere. "It is impossible," wrote Hirst Hollowell himself, "to enumerate the whole of the meetings held or addressed in the
northern and other counties during the agitation"; he personally
attended over 200, only a fraction of those organised during the year.[1]
"Meetings were held in every part of the country," writes Clifford's
biographer, "and he went up and down the land educating the public
as only he could. . . . Wherever he went halls were never large enough
to hold the throngs who went to hear him; he was hailed as the
champion of the hour."[2]

Clifford's aim was to get the Bill rejected; he felt that, should it
pass, there would be no hope of repeal by a future Liberal government, partly because of the powers of the House of Lords.[3] A pamphlet
he wrote against the Bill stirred his fellow Nonconformists to action
and had a "phenomenal" sale of several hundred thousands.[4] Demonstrations, especially in the north, reached a climax in the autumn with
a colossal turn-out on Woodhouse Moor outside Leeds. "Here on this
free moor of free Yorkshire," runs the description, "the greatest of all
English demonstrations against the Bill was organised. From 70,000
to 100,000 people attended, and the procession took two hours in
moving through the city of Leeds." Sixteen M.P.s were present,
speaking from six platforms, "the resolution being carried unanimously
at the sound of the bugle".[5]

Towards the end of July, a traditionally Tory constituency in Leeds,
at a by-election, returned by an overwhelming majority a Radical
candidate, a Baptist who had contested on the education question
alone.[6] This was followed by other reverses. Indeed, for the Liberal
party, controversy over the Education Bill appeared as a heaven sent
opportunity, enabling them to recruit forces in the country, overcome internal divisions, and prepare themselves for a struggle for
power. But, it has been suggested, it was not only for these reasons

---

[1] Evans and Claridge, op. cit., 84.
[2] Sir James Marchant, Dr. John Clifford (1924), 123.   [3] Allen, op. cit., 188-9.
[4] Ibid., 189; Marchant, op. cit., 125.
[5] Evans and Claridge, op. cit., 85. For this occasion Hirst Hollowell wrote the "Battle
Song of the Schools", beginning:

> England rouse thy legions
> Ere it be too late,
> Foes of right and foes of light
> Would storm the schoolhouse gate.

33,000 copies of this song were sold.
[6] Halévy, op. cit., 209; Allen, op. cit., 189. The Nonconformists had few representatives
in Parliament.

that the Liberal leaders "espoused the Nonconformist cause with such ardour"; it was also because they wished to counter-balance the growing agitation and organisation developing among the working class, in particular by socialists.[1]

The agitation outside Parliament was to some extent paralleled by the struggle in the House of Commons, particularly over the religious clauses of the Bill. It was in the course of this whole debate that Lloyd George, who characterised the Bill as a device for "riveting the clerical yoke on thousands of parishes in England",[2] sprang into prominence, threatening a movement of passive resistance if the Bill became law. Indeed all the leading Liberals—with the sole exception of Haldane, friend and supporter of Sidney Webb—fought the Bill clause by clause. The speeches of Sir William Harcourt combined irony and wit to great effect, and Asquith, Sir Edward Grey, Campbell Bannerman were among those in the fray; so also was the leading "educationist" in the House, James Bryce, onetime assistant commissioner to the Schools Inquiry Commission in the 1860s, Chairman of the Secondary Education Commission of 1894-5, who could speak with considerable authority. The fact that Balfour was compelled to use the closure so frequently underlines the strength of the opposition which, though unable to deflect the most unpopular measures, did succeed in winning certain amendments to the original Bill.[3]

It is within this context that the activities of the Labour movement must be assessed. We may first recall its organisation at this stage. By far the most important organisation was, of course, the Trades Union Congress, now in its thirty-third year of existence, covering all the leading trade unions and with an affiliated membership of 1,300,000. Its character had to some extent been transformed by the organisation of the unskilled workers in the 1890s, and it was, significantly, these unions, especially the Gasworkers, which took the lead in educational discussion and action. Linked with the T.U.C. were the local trades councils up and down the country.

In 1900 the Labour Representation Committee had been formed, specifically in order to organise Labour representation in Parliament. To this body were affiliated individual trade unions (representing

---

[1] Halévy, op. cit., 209-10. See also K. M. Hughes, "A Political Party and Education, Reflections on the Liberal Party's Educational Policy, 1870-1902", British Journal of Educational Studies, Vol. VIII, No. 2, 112-26.

[2] Hughes, op. cit., 122.

[3] Asquith and Grey accepted certain points in the Bill, but their overall attitude was one of opposition.

353,000 workers in 1900-1) as well as the I.L.P. and the Fabian Society. The S.D.F.. which had originally affiliated to the L.R.C., withdrew in 1901. Here, then, was an embryo political organisation, but at this stage the L.R.C. was mostly concerned with internal organisation, and devoted little time and energy to political discussion and activity. The more important political wings of the Labour movement, there-fore, were the I.L.P. and the S.D.F., both organised on the basis of local branches.[1] Finally, closely linked with the Labour movement, though not at this stage organisationally integrated, was the very widespread Co-operative movement.

The large proportion of the population represented in these organisa-tions was, of course, extremely under-represented in Parliament. The 1900 election had seen the return of two members sponsored by the Labour Representation Committee (Keir Hardie and Richard Bell). But these were the only two M.P.s who were in a position directly to reflect the attitude of the Labour movement as a whole. There were, however, in addition, a small group of Liberal working men M.P.s (Broadhurst, Cremer and the five miners' members), whose standpoint reflected that of the T.U.C. on particular questions.

In opposing the Education Bill, the Labour movement continued to fight on the main issues with which it had long been concerned: to prevent destruction of the School Boards, to avert clerical control and secure a secular education, and to extend secondary education. A number of other matters were raised, but in the main it was over these three issues, all closely interlinked, that battle was joined.

The Exeter Hall Conference held on 28 May, at which over a million workers were represented, placed the main stress on the fight for the School Boards. The unanimous resolution stated that, "as the Government Bill will destroy popularly-constituted bodies of educa-tion, this Conference expresses its dissent to the government policy on education; and further it is of opinion that the abolition of the School Boards will be detrimental to the interests of the education of the people, and will take away the advantages which the workers have in direct representation in the management of School Boards." The conference recommended all trade unions to send deputations to M.P.s urging them to oppose the Bill, while the T.U.C. Parliamentary Committee declared that steps should be taken to bring about the

[1] There were new divisions on the left at this time, members of the S.D.F., who regarded the leadership as reformist, seceding from it in 1903 to form the Socialist Labour Party whose main strength lay on Clydeside ,others seceding to form the Socialist Party of Great Britain.

defeat at the next election of all who failed to vote against it.[1]

In subsequent months all the organisations of the Labour movement, with the single exception of the Fabian Society, came out strongly against the Bill. The T.U.C., as we have seen, flatly rejected it. The I.L.P., at its tenth Annual Conference, passed a resolution moved by F. W. Jowett opposing the Bill "inasmuch as it withdraws education from public control".[2] The S.D.F. issued a striking Manifesto in October calling for outright rejection of the Bill; this, incidentally, characterised the conflict between Anglicans and Nonconformists as "contending for supremacy in the school", and called into question the motives of the Liberal party which, divided and "morally bankrupt", was fanning this strife to rehabilitate "its lost position".[3] The second Annual Conference of the Labour Representation Committee had met in February, before the introduction of the Bill, but the Committee took a definite line in favour of School Boards, decisively rejecting a Fabian amendment; this, moved by Pease, Secretary of the Fabian Society, and seconded by Snowden, mustered only fifteen votes.[4] The Co-operative movement also emphatically condemned the Bill "because it makes no adequate provision for secondary education or for the improvement of general education, and removes the whole question from the hands of the directly elected representatives of the people".[5]

The Fabians, therefore, won no significant support in the organised Labour movement, although there was a "definite trend" in the I.L.P. which tended to reflect the Fabian standpoint on the School Boards.[6] In general, however, the School Boards were invariably seen as democratically elected bodies enabling the working class to have some

[1] *35th T.U.C. Report*, 1902, 41.
[2] *10th I.L.P. Conference Report*, 1902, 24. At the previous annual conference the following resolution, proposed by Ramsay Macdonald, had been passed: "That in view of the possibility of a reconstruction of the educational administrative machinery, this conference declares that educational affairs should be administered from an Education Department by bodies specifically elected for that purpose". *9th I.L.P. Conference Report*, 42.
[3] *Justice*, 11 October 1902.
[4] The relevant part of the resolution adopted was in exactly the same words as that proposed by Macdonald at the I.L.P. Conference of 1901. It was Macdonald who opposed Pease and Snowden. *2nd L.R.C. Conference Report*, 1902, 25-6. It is worth noting here that the 1903 Conference did not discuss education.
[5] *34th Co-operative Congress Report*, 1902, 150.
[6] McCann, discussing the point, concludes that this may have weakened labour opposition; confusion was most evident and opposition to government policy least determined in the I.L.P., *op. cit.*, 433ff. Apart from articles mentioned later, printed at an early stage, the *Labour Leader* did not treat the Bill particularly seriously. In November and December, the climax of the affair, there is scarcely a reference to it, though long, rambling articles and reminiscences by Keir Hardie figure, the general impression is one of disinterest.

control over the education of their own children, and offering the possibility for a continuing upthrust into the fields of secondary and higher education.[1] To place the control of education in the hands of committees appointed by county or county borough councils, whose personnel was elected on other grounds than a concern with education—committees moreover which had power to co-opt non-elected members—seemed a retrograde step. It was, as the T.U.C. reiterated at its annual conference in the autumn of 1902, the "principle of direct representation" that they stood for.[2] In assessing this stand and its significance, it is essential to see it in terms of the contemporary situation, and of the issues that seemed to be at stake.

The most striking early attack on the Bill in the Labour press came from the pen of the Rev. Stewart Headlam, Fabian member of the London School Board, who, as we have seen, conducted a strong rearguard action in the Fabian Society in defence of the School Boards. After characterising the Bill as "the chief of several attacks which are being made on the people's schools" and detailing the various steps taken by the Board of Education over the past few years, he pinpointed the abolition of the School Boards as the main evil. Referring to the proposals of the original Bill which were to the effect that co-opted members would form the *majority* on education committees (it was stipulated that nominated members should outnumber the elected by one) he pointed out that education would cease to be controlled by elected people, that co-opted members would be "superfine people who will not offer themselves for election, but who are too good to

[1] It is interesting to note that a leader in *The Socialist* (organ of the Glasgow socialists about to found the Socialist Labour Party), although coming out very strongly against the Bill, queried whether it was politically correct to defend the School Boards on the ground that their abolition would be "undemocratic". School Boards, the writer claimed, *are* undemocratic, since proportional representation plus "plumping" allows cliques to gain representation. While it is true that the cumulative vote allows an occasional social-democrat to win a seat, he can do nothing on the Board except by favour of the "rate saving" middle-class representatives in the majority. For socialists who need a "clear and intelligible majority" the cumulative vote is an obstacle. The abolition of School Boards and the delegation of their powers to committees of the county councils would make them less subject to rate saving agitations—it would be a "step in the direction of national education". *The Socialist*, Vol. 1, No. 5, December 1902.

[2] The resolution states *inter alia*: "That, in order to secure the effective improvement and full extension of education in England and Wales, and especially with the view of securing economical administration and the provision of the various types of schools required by the special circumstances of different localities, as well as the prevention of unnecessary overlapping, it is essential that all grades of education should, in districts of suitable size, be under one local authority, directly elected, and elected solely for educational purposes, and that the Parliamentary Committee be instructed to oppose any Bill which does not provide for the election of such an authority." *35th T.U.C. Report*, 1902, 70-1.

be lost". Since the people would no longer manage their own schools, the Bill "is a straight, direct blow against democracy and municipal socialism". The new committees, not specifically elected for their interest in education, would be chiefly concerned to economise on education and so save the rates. Headlam also attacked other clauses of the Bill, as we shall see, and finished with a militant call for its defeat. "The Bill if carried," he writes, "will be carried by an unholy alliance between the bureaucrats and certain ecclesiastics—between Mr. Webb, of the Fabian Society, who welcomes the Bill as epoch-making—as epoch-making as the Act of 1870—and the Dean of St. Paul's, for years the leading spirit of the National Society, who says the School Boards have lowered the tone of morality and increased crime, and that his school board rate was given for the promotion of vice rather than the increase of virtue. It seems to me the duty of every loyal Churchman—every true citizen—to oppose the Bill to the uttermost."[1]

The approach of the I.L.P. to the School Boards was discussed in some detail in Keir Hardie's journal the *Labour Leader* by Philip Snowden, Ramsay Macdonald and others immediately after the introduction of the Bill. Two contributors, Fred Brocklehurst from Manchester and an anonymous teacher, on the whole supported the Bill, including the proposal to abolish School Boards, on the grounds that these attracted "faddists" and that the system of direct election tended to make religion an issue in the elections to the detriment of education. Snowden, in a long article which sharply attacked the Bill, ridiculed the claim that it created a single authority in education; instead it actually created additional education authorities, accentuating competition "between schools of the same grade in the same locality which remain under different management".[2] It destroyed "the principle of popular control while retaining the system of local taxation" and perpetuated sectarianism; the proposals for education committees were "reactionary and anti-democratic . . . every clause in the Bill betrays a distrust of popular control and popular education". After referring to other points Snowden characterised the Bill, in its general principles and in its details, as "anti-social, reactionary, and anti-educational. . . . It is a Bill of Bishops, parsons and middle-class schools, and so should be fought by all socialists." The logical and practical solution to the education question was: "one national authority; one local authority

---

1 *Clarion*, 23 May 1902.
2 Snowden claimed, with some justice, that seven authorities would be created instead of the existing two. *Labour Leader*, 19 April 1902.

of an area sufficiently large to contain every grade of school, below the university, which in co-operation—shall control and manage and support every school." Snowden did not, however, support the extension of the School Board system, suggesting that more "up to date machinery" was required. Ramsay Macdonald added his voice in calling for the defeat of the Bill for various reasons, one of which was that it placed education in the hands of committees which would be imperfectly controlled by a publicly elected body.[1]

While the Labour Representation Committee and the main body of the I.L.P. supported the School Board system, the T.U.C. fought much more strongly on this issue, as also did the S.D.F.—a differentiation within the Labour movement apparent before 1902 which continued for a considerable time. *Justice*, expressing strong S.D.F. support for School Boards as soon as the Bill was introduced, made the point that School Board administration may have been "very far from perfect" but the true line of reform was clearly to define and amplify powers, to extend the system to cover the country and to bring all education under popular control. "The very reverse of this policy has been presented by the government in this Bill."[2] This note recurs throughout the year, the Fabians being singled out for attack, to culminate in the Manifesto already mentioned.[3]

This then was one of the main points on which the Labour movement took its stand; the second, of perhaps more general significance, arose from the long traditional struggle of the working class for secular education; it involved the sharpest attack and exposure on those aspects of the Bill which, in its view, extended clerical control and influence on the schools.

The main point at issue was the provision that voluntary schools should come on the rates, and yet that they should remain "church" schools under the control of a majority of managers appointed by the foundation. In other words, denominational teaching was to be

[1] *Ibid.*, 26 April 1902.   [2] *Justice*, 29 March 1902.
[3] "It is true that the establishment of School Boards was a step in the direction of securing direct popular control and the subordination of the clerical influences; but the persistent hostility of the clericals to the School Boards, and the indifference of the people themselves, which has enabled the enemies of popular control, in many cases, to secure a predominance of representation upon the Boards, has done much to prevent the good which might otherwise have been accomplished.

"Instead, however, of perfecting direct popular control, the Government is seeking to abolish it altogether. The education authority in the towns is to be a mainly self-appointed committee, and in the rural districts a committee appointed by the County Council composed of parsons and squires having the least possible interest in the education of the children of the people, except to make them mere humble and obedient wage slaves." *Justice*, 11 October 1902.

subsidised and perpetuated. It was this that bulked large for the Labour movement; the fact that, in a sense, secular or lay control would also be enhanced was overshadowed by this issue. Thus the T.U.C. in its resolution raised the question of "no taxation without representation", holding that refusal to pay taxes was justified by these clauses. "Not a single member of the Managing Committees would be elected by popular vote," said Appleton in moving the resolution. "They threw the support of the schools on the rates but the ratepayers were to have no control over them. It was contended that control was given, but it was a sham control."[1] In addition ecclesiastical tests on the appointment of teachers were to remain. The religious difficulty would become more acute as a result of the Bill—it would be better to have no religion taught in school at all than this "squabbling" over the particular kind to be taught. He was sure of one thing, said Bowerman, in seconding, that the Bill "was designed to place their children in the fetters of clericalism".[2]

This note was struck in every expression of opinion by supporters of the Labour movement. The voluntary schools, wrote Headlam, would be in the hands of "managers". "The people are to pay and the parsons are to manage, we are told, and that is so."[3] "The placing of the sectarian schools entirely on the public purse is a barefaced endowment of sectarianism," wrote Philip Snowden, demanding a fully secular system. "For thirty years School Board education has been hampered by sectarian influences. So long as we recognise voluntaryism

[1] 35th T.U.C. Report, 1902, 7. This point of view was widely shared by Nonconformists and others. It is more fully elaborated in an editorial in the Contemporary Review reprinted in the Social Democrat (Vol. VI, No. 9, September 1902), which states that one of the main objects of the Bill is "the permanent fortification of the clerical schools, by throwing almost the last penny of their financial burden on to the public funds, while leaving them under ecclesiastical management; for the appointment by the public authority of one-third of the managers is practically insufficient either to secure fair play to the nonconformist children in the rural districts or to check the enslavement to the clergy of about half of the teaching profession . . . and this is done at a time when not only the dogmatic teaching of a large portion of the rectors and curates has become increasingly offensive to the general mass of the English people; but, apart from mere doctrine, the tendency of the rural clergy to assert exclusive rights for their Church, and separate themselves contemptuously from those who hold a different form of Christian religion, is sterner than ever." There were 5,600 districts, mostly in rural areas, where the only school available to the children was a Church of England school; the Bill seemed to perpetuate this situation.
[2] Ibid., 72.
[3] Clarion, 23 May 1902. The Labour attitude was well expressed in a Clarion leader: "The professed aim of the denominational schools, which are now to be thrown upon the rates, is the education of the poor in the principles of their various Churches, and it is preposterous that ratepayers should be compelled to pay an unwilling toll for the promulgation of a theology which they deny, coupled with a political propaganda which they most bitterly resent." Clarion, 1 August 1902.

in educational control, so long shall we have chaos and inefficiency. . . . The solution of the problem of educational organisation is the most obvious and simple of all the social questions demanding attention. Dissociate sectarianism from national education and the way of the education reformer would be easy."[1]

The Labour movement, incidentally, was particularly suspicious of the county councils. "The new education authorities," wrote *Justice* in May 1902, "will be whatever the squires and the parsons . . . choose to make them . . . our system of education is to be made a close preserve for clerical and obscurantist reactionists to whom educational progress and popular opinion is of no account whatever."[2] "Whatever the Bill may pretend, its real effect is to re-establish, to re-endow the parson," wrote Frank Colebrook in the same journal in September.[3] The price of Fabian unification would be "the absolute handing over of schools in about 8,000 parishes to parsons", for two-thirds of the managers would be Anglicans, who would appoint Anglican teachers. In the Manifesto issued in October, the S.D.F. once more made a clear call for secular education: "The interests of the children . . . demand that education in public schools should be secular, free from the teaching of any form of theological creed or dogma, and free from the influences of priest and parson. Religious belief is, and must be, a private matter, and to have any kind of religious teaching in our public schools is an infringement of religious liberty."[4]

While sharply attacking the Anglican attempt to enhance their control and influence at public expense, warning voices were raised within the socialist and Labour movement against becoming entangled on the side of the Nonconformists in what was seen as, partially at least, a purely sectarian struggle. As might be expected, it was particularly the S.D.F., the most consistent supporter of the secular solution,

[1] *Labour Leader*, 19 April 1902.

[2] *Justice*, 24 May 1902. Broadhurst pointed out in the House of Commons that the County Councils were not democratic; members had to be men of means with leisure. Bryce expressed the widespread suspicion of the Liberals about the intentions of the agricultural authorities (County Councils) as regards education: the attitude of the farmers had scarcely altered since 1868, when he acted as Assistant Commissioner to the Schools Inquiry Commission. *Hansard*, Vol. 109, cols. 895-6, 1446.

[3] *Justice*, 6 September 1902.

[4] An earlier paragraph ran: "Education in the past in this country has suffered in consequence of clerical influences, the insufficiency of direct popular control, and the absence of a properly coordinated system. The schools have been the happy hunting ground of priest and parson, much more interested in proselytising than in education; the whole administration of elementary education has been in the hands of the classes whose children do not attend our public elementary schools, and amid the din of contending religious factions and the clash of conflicting creeds, the interests of the children have been almost entirely disregarded." *Justice*, 11 October 1902.

that stressed the dangers; the attitude of the I.L.P., which included many Nonconformists, was less clear and militant. "The nonconformists are astir," wrote Colebrooke in *Justice* in September. "Between the churches and the chapels the comedy or tragedy of education may be a play with Education left out."[1] The longer the debate on the Education Bill goes on, wrote *Justice* in November, "the more clearly is the contest shown to be simply one between rival creeds, and the more fully is the need for a purely secular system of education demonstrated."[2] In the many meetings up and down the country on the Education Bill children were seldom mentioned. "Dr. Clifford, the stern, unrelenting High Priest of dogmatic Nonconformity, can declaim for hours and hardly mention the children. . . . Cardinal Vaughan rejoices as the Bill enables him to teach 'dogmatic Christianity', and the leader of the Hughligans, Lord Hugh Cecil, talks of a pathway leading from the Board School to the Church."[3]

In the same spirit is an ironic description in the *Labour Leader* (I.L.P.) of a Nonconformist-Liberal demonstration of 15,000 at Manchester. The organisers had attempted to draw in the Labour movement, "but trade unionists were conspicuous by their absence". Broadhurst and Hirst Hollowell spoke and, "as was only to be expected, a parson spoke from every platform, and they poured their vials of wrath upon their brother clerics for trying to do what they would do themselves—boss the schools if they got the chance"; they called also for a return of the Liberals as a means to the millennium.[4] "Fellow-workers," concluded the S.D.F. Manifesto, "turn a deaf ear to the cries of contending factions! Resist the attempt to cajole you into supporting one or the other of the capitalist parties! Nothing is further from their consideration than the cause of education. Strike out on a programme of your own; demand that all education shall be publicly supported and publicly controlled . . . in the interests of the children and the future of our class . . . we appeal to you to act now."[5]

The third major issue on which the Labour movement made a stand was secondary education, a question taken up to some effect by the

---

[1] *Justice*, 6 September 1902.   [2] *Ibid.*, 1 November 1902.

[3] *Justice*, 1 November 1902. The leading article goes on to warn against getting entangled with the Liberals in the fight against the Bill.

[4] *Labour Leader*, 18 October 1902.

[5] *Justice*, 11 October 1902. The S.L.P. also took this stand: as regards religious instruction "no choice can be made between Churchmen and Nonconformists. The latter insist just as strongly as the former on religious education in the schools". Unsectarian religious education was, as Lord Hugh Cecil maintained, nonconformist religion. *The Socialist*, Vol. 1, No. 5, December 1902.

Liberal opposition in the House of Commons. The Bill as originally drafted, said Steadman in his Presidential address to the T.U.C. in the autumn, did nothing whatever for secondary education, except express a pious wish. It had now been amended to enforce the maintenance of a certain standard of efficiency in secondary education, but this concession "gives no answer to the pressing question as to how secondary education may be brought within the reach of the industrial classes".[1] The resolution passed by the Congress once more demanded removal of the age limit fixed for the higher elementary schools, that no fees be charged "in any elementary, evening continuation, higher grade or technical schools" and the re-establishment of all grants to these schools "recently withdrawn or reduced". Free scholarships should be made available for all "anxious to continue the education of their children", the governing principle (as formulated a year earlier) being "that of intelligence and attainments of the child". Another resolution asked for a school leaving age of fifteen. In general, therefore, the T.U.C. once more pressed for an open road to secondary (or higher) education.[2]

Much the same point was made by Stewart Headlam who argued forcefully against the élitist scholarship system proposed by Sidney Webb: "What we want . . . is not the ladder for a dozen or so a year, but the broad staircase taking up a few thousands one floor higher in educational progress before they begin to earn their living"; for this, higher elementary schools with no age limit were needed.[3] Earlier, at the Labour Representation Committee's conference in February, Pete Curran had successfully moved an amendment urging the direct T.U.C. as opposed to Fabian policy: "that a liberal, non-competitive system of maintenance scholarships be established, in order that the fullest educational opportunities may be within the reach of every child."[4] Reference has already been made to the Co-operative movement's resolution which bore especially on this issue. Among the "sins of omission" of the Bill, according to the Glasgow socialists about to form the Socialist Labour Party, was the fact that no provision was made for secondary education worth speaking of. Elementary education was not enough; there should be free education up to the university.[5]

[1] 35th T.U.C. Report, 1902, 32.   [2] Ibid., 71, 76.
[3] Headlam also criticised the limitation of expenditure on secondary education to the product of a 2d. rate. Clarion, 23 May 1902.
[4] 2nd L.R.C. Conference Report, 1902, 25-6.
[5] The Socialist, Vol. 1, No. 5, December 1902.

Particular references to continued education do not, however, convey the full force of feeling in the Labour movement on this issue. It is essential to grasp that at this time the term "secondary education" did not carry the connotation it has today, indeed was rarely used except by those attempting to establish new and clear divisions; the government itself eschewed the term in favour of the phrase "other than elementary". In fact, a confusion of concepts prevailed in the field of "higher" education, the general term most frequently used, which reflected the haphazard growth of different types of institution; thus, besides grammar schools, there were "higher elementary" schools, "science" schools and so on, the latter providing what would now rank as secondary education but for obvious reasons not being allocated to any such category. The term "technical" education covered facilities of another kind but also some in the secondary field, relationships between the two being undefined. This confusion was reflected in the parliamentary debates on the second clause of the Bill.

The Labour movement was quite clear that the way to open up opportunities for "higher" education was to promote higher grade schools, evening continuation schools and similar developments. The grammar schools were, quite simply, class schools, regarded as quite alien, even if a few exhibitions had recently become available. Just as earlier administrative measures and the Cockerton Act of 1901 had been seen as a deliberate holding back of the tide of educational advance, so the present Bill was seen as another carefully planned step in a general offensive against popular education. This is why we find Steadman of the T.U.C. describing it as a "decidedly reactionary measure" because, as he said, "no provisions are made for any improvement in any way for elementary education"; wider opportunities for working-class children were only to be looked for in this direction. Though Morant, Balfour and others in the government were clear in their own minds about future policy—that, having successfully halted the upthrust from the elementary schools, they would build up a separate system on the foundation of the somewhat tenuous system of endowed grammar schools—this was not at all clear either to M.P.s, of whatever party, or at large.[1] It was only, as we shall see, after the

1 Though there had been some indications. For instance, on the day the Education Bill was introduced Balfour said that those who supported higher grade schools had no conception of the true nature of secondary education: "Many of them seem to suppose that by merely putting at the top of an elementary school a certain number of classes dealing with subjects higher than elementary, a system of secondary education was thereby immediately established." O. Banks, *Parity and Prestige in English Education* (1955), 26.

Education Act came into operation that, again largely through administrative measures, a new type of secondary system began to take shape under the guiding hand of Morant.

In Parliament Labour's voice could barely be heard, but outside it was a different story and local organisations up and down the country backed up the statements of their leading bodies with demonstrations and petitions. A month after the introduction of the Bill the Bradford Trades Council passed a resolution "protesting strongly" against it as "contrary to the principles of democratic legislation", and went on to organise a demonstration of more than 5,000 people against the Bill which declared decisively in favour of the School Board principle. It subsequently circulated three petitions, calling for "free, unsectarian education" under popular control, each signed by over a hundred members of trades councils representing in all 750,000 trade unionists. On 25 April the Federated Trades and Labour Councils of Yorkshire called a special protest meeting of all associated bodies at Leeds, and went on to prepare a petition to Parliament. The Lancashire Federation of Trades and Labour Councils also called a special meeting in April against the Bill, while the Bolton Trades Council also took action. The Birmingham Trades Council, true to its tradition of profound concern with education, passed a massive resolution and planned action. Many other trades councils took action along these lines.[1]

In October the T.U.C. sent out a circular to the trades "reminding them of their past action on education" and another asking all trades council members and voters in the local elections generally to vote only for those councillors who would press the government to withdraw the Bill: this also urged trade unions to put pressure on M.P.s, reporting a meeting with Radical and Labour M.P.s to strengthen the opposition.[2] Despite the doubts among socialists referred to earlier, supporters of the Labour movement participated in the great open-air protest meetings organised by nonconformists; for instance the President of the Manchester and Salford Trades Council spoke at the Manchester demonstration which drew 15,000 in October.[3] It seems evident that the most virile opposition in the Labour movement was centred in the north.

The Co-operative movement also organised meetings against the Bill, notably at Derby and Bristol, but the political wing, as represented in the I.L.P., does not appear to have been anything like so active

[1] McCann, op. cit., 417-19.   [2] 36th T.U.C. Report, 1903, 43.
[3] McCann, op. cit., 440-1.

as the trade union movement. A meeting with Keir Hardie and others speaking was organised in London on 25 November, where a rather colourless resolution was passed. The S.D.F. used the tactic, at that time an acceptable tradition, of moving amendments on secular education and free maintenance at Liberal and Radical meetings, while its local branches ran successful meetings, especially in London. Some 20,000 copies of the Manifesto against the Bill, published in October, were sold during that month alone.[1]

Despite all this opposition up and down the country, and the evident loss of political popularity by the Tories, the Bill was nonetheless passed to take its place on the statute book a week before the Christmas of 1902.

4. THE AFTERMATH—THE BOARD OF EDUCATION UNDER MORANT

The Education Act, 1902, with the London Act which followed a year later, created a new situation in certain important respects. By placing the church schools on the rates it secured their future and so brought into being a dual system of education locally financed. The struggle against the religious clauses of the Act was carried on in a militant manner by nonconformists, and the famous "Default" Act had to be passed before the Welsh county councils, bastions of nonconformity, could be brought into line.[2] A number of nonconformists were sent to prison as a result of their refusal to pay that proportion of the rates which, they calculated, went to support the church schools. In 1906, when the Liberals regained power, twice in 1908 and later, attempts were made to redress the balance in favour of nonconformists, while, as far as the Labour movement was concerned, the struggle for a strictly secular education was now carried on with renewed energy.

More important in the long run, however, were the administrative

1 McCann, op. cit., 420, 442-4. McCann refers also to the opposition organised by the National Labour Education League, which was set up in November 1901. This body, which was developed on the initiative of Mrs. Bridges Adams (a prominent member of the London I.L.P. and Labour member of the London School Board since 1897), is described as "the most interesting attempt to develop a positive labour educational policy". In April 1902, the League issued a statement on the Bill, criticising the proposals on secondary education as failing to bring it within the reach of the working class. It also forecast that most of the 2d. rate would be spent on middle-class education. It called on Trade Unions and Co-operatives to reject the Bill and stand by T.U.C. policy. The League, however, did not survive August 1902 as an effective body. Ibid., 423-4.
2 See E. Eaglesham, "Implementing the Education Act of 1902", British Journal of Educational Studies, Vol. X, No. 2, May 1962, 162-75, for a full analysis of this policy.

THE
BRISTOL CITIZENS' LEAGUE,

For securing Justice in the Management of the Schools of the People.

A Manifesto

Of those who intend to adopt "Passive Resistance."

To the CITIZENS OF BRISTOL.

We, being firmly persuaded that the fundamental rights of citizenship are endangered by the Education Act, 1902, have banded ourselves together as those who feel compelled on religious grounds to resist its working, in so far as it violates the principles of religious freedom and liberty of conscience.

The course we have resolved to pursue under the strongest compulsion of conscience, is to refuse to pay voluntarily the Education Rate, or at least that portion of it which is to be applied to denominationally managed schools, so far as it can be ascertained.

....

Therefore, with invincible determination, we reiterate the declaration made to the Prime Minister by the representatives of the Free Churches before the passing of the Act—

" To legislation which creates an ecclesiastical monopoly in the " schools of the people

"WE WILL NOT SUBMIT!"

Signed on behalf of the Committee.

D. J. HILEY, *President.*

W. F. PRICE, *Secretary.*

NONCONFORMIST OPPOSITION TO THE 1902 ACT: A BRISTOL LEAFLET
(The first and last pages of the four-page leaflet are reproduced; the dotted line indicates the break.)

measures carried out by the Board of Education, now under Morant's leadership as Permanent Secretary.[1] It should be made quite clear that the Education Act itself did not lay down what was to be the future direction of educational development. It merely empowered the new local authorities to subsidise education "other than elementary" out of the rates, requiring them to investigate needs and make plans for this development. It said nothing whatsoever about the nature of this education and its relation to that in elementary schools, nor, indeed, did the word "secondary" figure.

The solution of the key problem of the relation between elementary and secondary education—a solution that determined the basic structure of the educational system for the next half century and more—was decided by a series of administrative measures carried through by the Board of Education in the months and years immediately following the passage of the Act. Indeed it was Morant's aim, in the words of his biographer, to consolidate the Act as rapidly as possible "so that, whatever changes came, a permanent reconstruction would have been made which it would be difficult for any government, however powerful, to undo".[2] This reconstruction was guided and cemented by successive sets of regulations which (with their covering memoranda) strictly defined the respective spheres of elementary and secondary education, and controlled the development of the two types of school concerned.[3]

Morant, as we have seen, was a strong proponent of an *élitist* conception of secondary education, but of course in this he was not alone, since this, in essence, was a class question. The endowed grammar schools, with their links with Oxford and Cambridge and the new system of public schools, had, as a result of developments in the nineteenth century, become middle class schools, serving various sections of the middle class, and dominated by the literary tradition in education. From 1889, many of these schools had begun to receive public

[1] Morant was appointed Acting Permanent Secretary of the Board of Education in October 1902, Kekewich being told to resign six months earlier than he would normally have done. "By a meteoric rise of unprecedented rapidity," writes his biographer, "Morant became head of a great Department which he had entered seven years before as a junior official." Allen, *Sir Robert Morant*, 189-90. Morant's ruthlessness and determination has been the subject of much discussion. His unpopularity with the teachers, particularly the N.U.T., led to his transfer to another department in 1911.

[2] Allen, *op. cit.*, 204.

[3] The most important of these were the *Elementary School Code* and the *Regulations for Secondary Schools* both issued in June 1904. These were preceded by the *Regulations for the Instruction and Training of Pupil-Teachers* (1903) and followed by *Regulations for Evening Schools and Technical Institutes* (1904). All these were issued within eighteen months of the passage of the Act.

money through the Technical Education Committees of city and county councils. It was these schools and those connected with them, linked as they were traditionally with the Church and Tory party, that had felt themselves threatened by the developments in elementary education in the 1880s and '90s. The Headmasters' Association, as we have seen, fought strongly from its inception for a separate system of secondary schools.

This view was widely propagated just prior to the passage of the Act and formed the climate of thought of important sections of the governing class, whether Radical-Tory (like Sir John Gorst), Liberal (like Bryce and Michael Sadler) or "Collectivist" (Sydney Webb), as Olive Banks has shown in her study of this period. Thus the Bryce Commission (appointed by a Liberal government) held that only children of "exceptional ability" should be promoted from elementary to secondary schools, i.e. secondary education was something qualitatively different from what was required for the mass of the children. Indeed the fact that secondary education was *per se* unsuitable for the working class was advanced as the chief *educational* justification for confining it to the middle class: "While primary instruction should be provided for, and even enforced upon all," said Sir John Gorst, "advanced instruction is for the few. It is in the interest of the commonwealth at large that every boy and girl showing capacities above the average should be caught and given the best opportunities for developing these capacities. It is not in its interest to scatter broadcast a huge system of higher instruction for anyone who chooses to take advantage of it, however unfit to receive it."[1]

Following the passage of the Act there was, therefore, a general determination to develop a system of "genuinely secondary" schools alongside and parallel to, but qualitatively different from, the elementary schools—a system of education for the middle and lower middle class as distinct from a system of education for the working class. The way had been prepared for this by the Cockerton judgment and the administrative measures that followed it, cutting back the outgrowth from the elementary schools and strictly delimiting their development. Now was the time to firm up this differentiation, to clear away all

---

[1] Quoted in Banks, *op. cit.*, 51. Michael Sadler, the doyen of "Liberal" educationists, held that secondary education is "chiefly needed by pupils who look forward to a professional career, or to occupy posts of higher responsibility in industrial or commercial life". Or again: "Scholarships should be provided to draft [*sic*] to secondary schools—not later than twelve years of age—those . . . pupils with the kind of ability which a secondary school is best fitted to develop; but for the great majority of the pupils the higher elementary school will be the crown of their day school course". *Ibid.*, 52.

intermediary forms of education—or again to delimit them—and to impose within the state supported system of English education an hierarchic structure of schooling corresponding to social class divisions.

It has become the fashion to blame Morant personally for the long-term effects of this policy which, apart from perpetuating a class system of education, ensured that secondary schools carried on the tradition of a past age rather than taking account of the technical needs of twentieth century society. But, as we have seen, there were strong social pressures tending in this direction just as there were strong class reasons for stifling the more practical forms of education which had developed in higher grade schools. Morant was anything but an individualist, rather he was and felt himself to be a part of the engine which motivated the machinery of state. That machinery, it was the generally accepted view in the circles in which he moved, must purposefully shape measures of social reform. This is precisely what, with supreme confidence and conscious rectitude, Morant set out to do and his efforts were as warmly approved by a Liberal as by a Conservative government.[1] In other words the policy he operated was not so much a party policy, however many the political storms through which it passed, as a policy serving the interests of a class; of this, the T.U.C., standing out for the interests of the working class which this policy overrode, had shown itself acutely aware.

The first step necessary before secondary schooling could be developed was to establish the new local education authorities and, by the close of 1903, 240, two-thirds of the total, were in being. Since these had powers over both elementary and "other than elementary" education, and since schools recognised in either category would receive government grants on a different basis, it was essential to establish some general criterion of differentiation.

Elementary schools were, of course, already defined and operated under a distinct Code of Regulations. The 1904 issue of this Code was

[1] He was knighted in 1907, after the Liberal return to power. In a letter to a Liberal friend, dated 30 June, he wrote: "Though the 'K' in itself is but a symbol, I hope it means to some extent, and it clearly means in your case, that the government believe that I have done my best to serve *them* just as I did to serve the late government. More than this one cannot do, and less than this no civil servant would dream of doing. It is a platitude; and yet, as Education is so highly controversial, I have had the misfortune to rouse the suspicions or stimulate the hostility of many honest supporters of the government. Thus I do very deeply trust that the Prime Minister's chivalry in getting me my 'K' so soon may convince his supporters that *he* and his colleagues trust me: and perhaps this may revive the confidence of some, in the loyalty of the Civil Service, and its impartiality of service." From an unpublished letter to Alfred Emmott, M.P. in the possession of Joan Simon.

prefaced by a short introduction which attempted to set out the aims and purposes of the elementary school; and in this sense it marked a precedent. In essence, however, the introduction made it quite clear that the function of these schools was to provide the entire day school education of the mass of the children; an important subsidiary duty being "to discover individual children who show promise of *exceptional capacity* (my italics, B. S.), and to develop their special gifts . . . so that they may be qualified to pass at the proper age into secondary schools". As far as the majority of the children were concerned, they were fit only for elementary education. "Though their opportunities are but brief," continues the introduction, "the teachers can yet do much to lay the foundations of conduct."[1]

The definition of a secondary school, however, presented a very real difficulty, and was attempted in a "Prefatory Memorandum" to the *Regulations for Secondary Schools* issued in the same month as the *Elementary School Code* (June 1904). This pointed out that the term "secondary" was of French origin, connoting "that portion of the complete course of education necessary or desirable for the full intellectual development of the individual citizen which lay between Primary education, beyond which circumstances forbade the majority of the population to advance, and the Tertiary education which succeeded and completed it". In England, however, the term "primary" has been superseded by the term "elementary", while "the intermediate term of Secondary . . . has consequently been left in the air"— leading to "extreme vagueness" and "misuse". Pointing out that this term does not figure in the 1902 Act, the memorandum states that nonetheless the term secondary school "has come to have a recognised meaning in English education", and proceeds to define that meaning in a purely pragmatic way:

"For the purposes of these Regulations . . . the term 'Secondary School' will be held to include any Day or Boarding School which offers to each of its scholars, up to and beyond the age of sixteen, a general education, physical, mental and moral, given through a complete graded course of instruction of wider scope and more advanced degree than that given in Elementary Schools."[2]

---

[1] Quoted in Allen, *op. cit.*, 212; This introduction "was widely hailed as a welcome new departure", writes Allen, a great admirer of Morant. Its tone was "ennobling", since it set moral and intellectual ideals before the elementary school; this signalised that the Board of Education had ceased to be merely a financial and administrative centre and was now concerned with educational purposes and character formation.

[2] Allen, *op. cit.*, 216-17.

FREE CHURCH DEMONSTRATION AGAINST THE EDUCATION BILL, 1902

MARCH AGAINST BIRRELL'S BILL, 1906
WAITING FOR THE MARCH: BISHOP KNOX OF MANCHESTER

This definition well expresses the dilemma of the Board, seeking a rational justification for subsidising from public money a system of schools, running *parallel* to the "elementary" schools, but catering for a different social class; for secondary schools in fact took in children from the age of seven or eight.[1] The only possible definition was, therefore, along the lines given, that is in terms of something "wider" as well as "more advanced", something qualitatively different from what was provided in elementary schools. It was impossible to define secondary education as a definite stage, "end-on" to primary education, since it was precisely this concept that the Board, implementing a long standing policy, was determined to destroy. Secondary education was a *different* education—but the Board could not say it was a different education for a different class. Hence the purely pragmatic and indeed illogical definition offered. As we shall see, this memorandum hardly cleared up the situation as it claimed to do; it served, however, to cover the actual policy pursued, and, as such, it served its purpose.[2]

It was, of course, entirely up to the Board to determine which schools would be recognised as "secondary" for purposes of grant, and which rejected.[3] This raised the possibility of conflict with the more advanced local authorities several of which had a different, and more democratic, conception of secondary education than that officially held. The Board's policy, however, was clear enough, indeed it was the traditional one sanctioned by the Schools Inquiry Commission over thirty years earlier and subsequently operated: to develop effective secondary education it was essential to charge fees, so excluding all but a chosen few from the working class. "A fee of a substantial amount is desirable," it was stated in the Board's Regulations for Secondary Schools "both in order to ensure the financial stability of the school

---

[1] Some 12 to 15 per cent of children attending London's grammar schools in 1905 were under eleven. Flann Campbell, *Eleven Plus and All That* (1956), 9.

[2] Clearly Morant recognised the dilemma. His impatience with the logical meaning of the term (a product of the French Revolution embodying the conception of a graded system of education opening "la carrière aux talents"—as proposed by Condorcet and others) comes out in the rather petulant phrase in the memorandum, "That term ['secondary education', B. S.] is not exempt from criticism."

[3] The grants system to secondary schools after 1902 developed out of the old Science and Art Department grants which had been given originally on the basis of individual subjects and later to "Schools of Science". In 1901 Secondary Day Schools as such became eligible to receive grants from the Board. In 1902 and 1903 the Board of Education issued Regulations for Secondary Day Schools which classed the Schools of Science as "Secondary Day Schools (Division A)" and the grammar schools as "Secondary Day Schools (Division B)", both of which qualified for grants. In 1904 all grants for individual subjects were abolished, and a single grant given for an approved four-year course covering 12-16 or 13-17. See *Secondary Education with Special Reference to Grammar Schools and Technical High Schools* (1938) (The Spens Report), 66ff., for a summary of the situation.

and also to emphasise the fact that the education provided is of a superior kind, and consequently of a greater value to the scholars, than that in schools which, although they go beyond the ordinary elementary curriculum, do not aim at the higher standard and fuller course of an efficient secondary school."[1] To widen the educational ladder to "children of every class" would be to endanger standards. In general the Board insisted on a minimum fee of £3 a year—quite sufficient, in the circumstances of the time, to exclude working-class children with the exception of scholarship holders. But this was usually exceeded; an analysis by the President of the N.U.T. in 1907 showed that, of 685 secondary schools recognised in 1905-6, 607 charged more than £3, 46 exactly £3, 28 less than this figure while only 4 were wholly free.[2]

To plan secondary education as something quite different from elementary education, different, in particular, from what had been provided in the higher grade or science schools, inevitably meant resource to the academic tradition perpetuated in the grammar and public schools. Indeed "the Board took the existing Public schools and Grammar schools as their general *cadre* or archetype for secondary schools of all kinds."[3] Since all such schools were envisaged as middle-class schools taking only a small proportion of their pupils from elementary schools the Board naturally looked askance at the attempts of advanced local authorities to develop new municipal secondary schools—which were intended to and did take the *majority* of their pupils from elementary schools, once more taking active steps to prevent this development, or at least to keep it within bounds. Nottingham Education Committee, for instance, having advanced plans for four such schools and received permission to proceed with only two, accused the Board not only of "precipitate action" and "very harsh treatment" but also of discouraging "the demand of the people for increased educational facilities".[4] The leaders of the N.U.T.

---

[1] Quoted in Banks, *op. cit.*, 61. "Unless local circumstances can be proved to require exceptional treatment", it was stated in the 1904 Regulations for Secondary Schools, "the Board will not recognise a school in which no fees are charged".

[2] In presenting these figures the President said: "The whole policy of the Board tends to make a secondary school one which is not attended by the children of the people, unless they are scholarship holders." *The Schoolmaster*, 6 April 1907, 692. For a further analysis of the Board's policy on fees, Banks, *op. cit.*, 61-4.

[3] *Spens Report*, 72. The *Regulations for Secondary Schools* "were based wholly on the tradition of the Grammar Schools and the Public Schools"; *ibid.*, 66-7. The steps taken to implement this policy are described in Eaglesham, "Implementing the Education Act of 1902", *British Journal of Educational Studies*, Vol. X, No. 2, May 1962.

[4] Banks, *op. cit.*, 62.

thoroughly objected to the Board's refusal to recognise schools which did not charge fees. "We are bound to say," wrote Macnamara, a member of Parliament and editor of *The Schoolmaster*, "that we expected great things from the Act of 1902 in the direction of the establishment of public secondary schools—cheap, effective and democratically based. . . . The policy should have been to remember that, while class prejudices cannot be altogether put out of sight, they ought to be firmly subordinated . . . to the demands of a genuinely democratic and broadly based scheme of general education."[1] The Board, said the N.U.T. Executive, were interfering to "organise a system of secondary education for the middle classes as a thing apart".[2]

If the Board was to carry through its policy, then, the key issue was the strict delimitation of secondary education on the one hand, and elementary education on the other. But it was one thing to define differences and lay down procedure, the position in practice was extremely confused, precisely because of that upthrust from the elementary system which the Cockerton judgment and subsequent administrative action had sought to destroy, but which was necessarily endemic in the total situation and led then—as it does now—to perpetual struggle and conflict.

Since 1900, as we have seen, using the Cockerton judgment as a smokescreen, the Board had established a category of higher elementary schools with a strictly defined age limit as well as other conditions narrowly limiting their scope. The aim was clearly to provide a strictly delimited place for the higher grade schools which had developed and were pushing forward—to contain this movement within narrow limits and, above all, to prevent it moving into the field of secondary education. However, partly as a result of the Board's policy in refusing to recognise schools and departments proposed for this category (the London School Board's proposals for seventy-nine of its departments and schools were rejected *en bloc*), and partly because the category and indeed general conception of these schools was not popular with local authorities, by 1906 only 30 such schools existed in England and Wales. Actually 39 had been so recognised, but of these 8 had become secondary schools and 1 had reverted to elementary school status. Of the 39, 14 were conversions from higher grade schools.[3]

[1] *The Schoolmaster*, 11 March 1905, quoted in *ibid.*, 63.
[2] Banks, *op. cit.*, 63-4.
[3] *Report of the Consultative Committee upon Higher Elementary Schools*, 1906, 24.

However the higher grade schools as a whole did not become higher elementary schools in the period immediately following the Act. A few became secondary schools but for a few years this development appears to have been officially resisted, as indeed one would expect in view of the conception of secondary education that the Board fostered.[1] Meanwhile such schools were in an anomalous position; they could no longer receive grants from the Board at a higher rate than the normal elementary school, and the additional expense incurred for higher level work had to be borne by local authorities out of the rates.[2] Nevertheless they remained in existence and their aspirations continued to represent a threat to the Board's conception of a strictly isolated system of secondary education. There were in addition a variety of schools later described as "lower secondary schools"— small grammar schools, some higher grade schools converted to "secondary" schools after the Cockerton judgment, some higher elementary schools and even some elementary schools that had pushed upwards.[3] It was partly to clear up this situation that Morant asked the Consultative Committee to the Board of Education, in July 1905, to report on the whole question of the curriculum and nature of higher elementary schools.[4] The resulting report, as we shall see, provoked an outcry.

The position of the pupil-teacher centres—which also lay end-on to the elementary schools and gave what was to all intents and purposes a secondary education—was now also anomalous. Many of these by now had specially designed buildings, with assembly halls, laboratories, art rooms, and an experienced teaching staff; in short they provided with considerable success a secondary education for intending teachers. These not only constituted an important means by which working-

---

[1] Banks suggests that the higher grade schools developed naturally into municipal secondary schools (*op. cit.*, 53-4). This is true over a period of years, but in practice the Leeds and Manchester higher grade schools (central schools) were not recognised as secondary schools for several years. In 1911 Frank Goldstone, M.P., wrote: "At one time the excellent education given in the higher grade schools could be secured at very low fees weekly. Remarkable success attended their work and brought down upon their righteous heads the wrath of an undeserved 'Cockerton' judgment. Their subsequent development has been hampered, and it is not by reason of any generous encouragement they have received that many of them have now obtained the dignity and status of Secondary Schools, but by the determined resistance of some Local Authorities, who refused to be the puppets of reactionary permanent officials. When some of these Higher Grade Schools were transformed into secondary schools, fees in many cases were increased, and doubtless with the full approval of the Board of Education have sometimes reached as much as £6 p.a." *Socialist Review*, Vol. 7, No. 39, May 1911, 237.
[2] See *Report of the Consultative Committee upon Higher Elementary Schools*, 24-5.
[3] *Ibid.*, 25.
[4] The Consultative Committee was established by the Board of Education Act of 1899.

class children could gain a secondary education and enter a profession but also, since all pupils received grants, provided a precedent for maintenance grants for secondary education, a demand, as we have seen, advanced by the Labour movement.

It is easy to understand why, well before 1902, Morant regarded this development with suspicion; as yet another means whereby School Boards reached beyond the elementary field. The whole arrangement of these centres, he noted in a memorandum in 1901, grew up "as it were haphazard and unobserved, developed by the School Boards without any direct approval of the Education Department, just as was the case with the Higher Grade Schools". Until recently the Education Department "had not even any statistical information at all as to the extent of this development of School Board organisation and expenditure. Nor is it known, even approximately, to what extent School Boards are giving secondary education to any youth or girl who chooses to come and receive it, under the guise of probationers or pupil teachers, quite irrespective of the extent to which these individuals count, or are likely hereafter to count, towards the effective staffing of the elementary schools."[1]

It rapidly became clear after 1902 that the Board's policy was to block this avenue by closing down the centres or transforming them into secondary schools charging fees and taking pupils at twelve, at the same time insisting that the avenue of recuitment to the teaching profession should be through the secondary schools.[2] Already in 1900-1 the Board's policy was to prevent the establishment of further centres, as is now clear from research into the private papers of the Board of Education. Thus the Castleford School Board applied on 2 May 1901 for permission to build a new pupil-teacher centre. "If we allow small towns like Castleford, with a population of 14,000, to build what is practically a large secondary school at a cost of many thousands of pounds," noted the senior examiner at the Board, "what will be the effect in a year, or when Boards all over the country have indulged in similar undefined projects? Shall we not have a position and a confusion closely akin to the *Cockerton* position?" Another application, made on 8 October 1901 (by Handsworth) was greeted with the

[1] A. Shakoor, "The Training of Teachers in England and Wales, 1900-1939", unpublished Ph.D. thesis, University of Leicester (1964), 36-7.

[2] The Board of Education wanted elementary school teachers to be educated at secondary schools where they would come under the influence of secondary teachers (rather than the "uncultured" ex-elementary school teachers at the centres), and be given an education of an altogether different quality; cf. Asher Tropp, *The Schoolteachers* (1957), 184-91.

following remark. "This Board are rushing matters, and should, I think, be checked at once, in view of our policy of delay." The Chief Inspector of Schools noted in March 1902, "The Castleford School Board have been prevented from building a pupil-teacher centre by Whitehall."[1] Not only were School Boards denied permission to build such centres, but after the passage of the Act, between 1904 and 1907, many centres were closed and their pupils transferred to secondary schools. For obvious reasons this move was strongly resented both by the elementary school teachers and by the Labour movement.

In sum, the administrative measures applied in the years immediately following the Education Act of 1902 rigidly defined differences between elementary and secondary education. From now on there was to be no confusion; two systems, each with a distinct social function, were to run parallel to each other; any institutions crossing the lines must be swept away. In place of the higher grade schools which had offered quite new prospects of an upward development which might be extended to benefit all children, there was offered a competitive system of scholarships to transfer children from one set of schools, with an early leaving age irrevocably fixed, to a quite different system which alone offered the opportunity of advancement. When in 1907 the Liberal government introduced the requirement of 25 per cent free places in secondary schools, the selective system was fully established. From now on the pressure for secondary education for all inevitably took the form of a continuing attempt to open up the grammar schools—now the only secondary schools—to the working class.

[1] Shakoor, *op. cit.*, 141-5 (from Board of Education private papers, Public Record Office).

PART III

KEY EDUCATIONAL QUESTIONS
FOR LABOUR
1903–1920

Part II

SOME EDUCATIONAL QUESTIONS

FOR LABOUR

(1985-1991)

CHAPTER VIII

SECONDARY EDUCATION AND
SCHOOL WELFARE SERVICES, 1903-1914

DURING the twelve years between the passing of the 1902 Act and the outbreak of war the Labour movement evolved a clear educational policy, one which sought not only to gain immediate improvements but also to secure fundamental changes in the structure of the educational system as a whole. This growing clarity reflected an increasing strength and maturity; it reflected also the growing influence of socialist thinking.

The characteristics of the socialist movement in the early twentieth century have often been assessed. It had no recognised leadership but rather was still divided into a number of sects grouped around particular personalities—Hyndman and the S.D.F., Keir Hardie and the I.L.P., Blatchford and the *Clarion*—while the well organised Fabians at one extreme shaded off through Christian Socialists and Tolstoyans to Anarchists and other minor groupings. But whatever the differences and divisions, one objective was held in common and energetically pursued, to "make socialists" until there were enough of them to leaven the rest. "The deep passionate earnestness, the intense conviction, and the fervid exaltation with which we set about our self-appointed task of winning 'converts' for Socialism," writes one who was fully engaged in the movement, was shared by all groups.[1] This was the overriding impression of another participant who lived through this period in Glasgow:

"The period is one of intense propaganda for labour representation and the ideals of socialism. A veritable crusade was led throughout Scotland in those years with all the fervour and fanaticism of a new holy religion. In Glasgow and other towns street corner meetings, hitherto unknown and regarded with suspicion . . . by the more reserved and cautious workers, became more and more numerous. The villages in the countryside were visited by a corps of young men and women missionaries of the new faith, and colporteurs of its literature."[2]

[1] T. A. Jackson, *Solo Trumpet* (1953), 57; for a description of the position in the socialist movement, 51-7.
[2] T. Bell, *John Maclean* (1944) 7.

Propaganda for Labour representation was now being undertaken in a new situation. In 1902 there were only two members of Parliament who had been returned under the aegis of the new Labour Representation Committee to which only a minority of trade unions were affiliated. But as the Balfour government, not content with the Education Act, pursued a policy of direct attack on the unions, following on the Taff Vale judgment of 1901, feeling rose. That the funds and therefore the whole status and strength of the trade union movement had been jeopardised served to bring sharply into focus the need for action on the political plane, for independent representation in Parliament to legislate in the interests of Labour. Unions now hastened to affiliate to the Labour Representation Committee which was able to put up fifty-one candidates at the general election of 1906, twenty-nine of whom were elected.

At this election latent feeling in the country against the Tory administration came fully to light. The Liberals campaigned on a programme in which revision of the 1902 Education Act and legislation to regularise the position of the unions took a prominent place. Their victory was an overwhelming one; as one safe Tory seat after another fell, 377 Liberals returned to the House of Commons, many for the first time, accompanied by in all 53 representatives of Labour, while the Tory opposition numbered but 157.[1]

The Liberals had deliberately set out to harness not only what was a growing radicalism but also the developing Labour movement. Of the fifty-three Labour M.P.s returned, twenty-four were closely allied to the Liberal Party, while most of the remaining twenty-nine owed their seats to an electoral agreement which spared them Liberal opponents. In spite of this, the election results seemed to Balfour, who lost his own seat in Manchester, little short of a presage of revolution. Certainly the appearance for the first time of a body of Labour members, some declared socialists, on the floor of the House of Commons, signalised the arrival of the working class on the political scene at the centre of affairs. This created a new situation which called for new tactics, even a new political strategy. Whereas Robert Lowe had once stressed the need to teach newly enfranchised electors how to use their votes, the task that faced his successors was that of teaching newly elected Labour representatives how to govern the state. One course taken was to absorb those who showed aptitude into the governmental

---

[1] As there were also 83 Irish members, government supporters numbered over 500, giving a normal majority of 357; Roy Jenkins, *Mr. Balfour's Poodle* (1954), 6-7.

apparatus, a method which helped materially to draw the teeth of the Labour movement and separate leaders now in high places from the rank and file.[1] New approaches were also now made in the field of adult education.

It was in no spirit of abdication that Balfour had deplored the Liberal landslide; on the contrary, it was his determined purpose to ensure that "the great Unionist Party should still control, whether in power or whether in Opposition, the destinies of this great Empire",[2] and there was an instrument ready to hand which could be used to check all legislation. That the Liberal Party had increasingly courted radical opinion and taken steps to gain a hold over the Labour movement meant that its strength in the House of Lords had progressively fallen away. The huge Liberal majority in the Commons was, therefore, balanced by an overwhelming preponderance of Unionists in the upper house which acted, in Lloyd George's scathing phrase, as "Mr. Balfour's poodle". It had barely figured at all in the preceding years during which the most highly controversial piece of legislation had been the Education Act of 1902.[3] It was quite another matter when the Liberal administration introduced as its first piece of legislation in 1906 an Education Bill designed to revise a widely resented settlement; the Lords sent back the Bill, mangled beyond recognition, and when it was returned to them with their amendments ruled out *en bloc*, insisted on these anew. The resulting deadlock made withdrawal of the measure the only course and subsequently battle was joined between Commons and Lords to culminate in the Parliament Act of August 1911. It was, therefore, once more on the issue of education that major political conflicts came to be fought out. This was the context in which the Labour movement put forward its own policies for educational advance.

Once the way had been cleared, the Liberal administration—now headed by Asquith and including such men as Churchill and Lloyd

---

[1] A development acutely analysed by Halévy, *The Rule of Democracy, 1905-1914* (1961 edn.), 444-8. While socialist influence grew outside, the Parliamentary representatives of Labour progressively withdrew from a socialist position.

[2] Jenkins, *op. cit.*, 18-19.

[3] "The most controversial legislative proposal of these ten years was the Education Bill of 1902. It marked a sharp departure of policy on an issue which aroused very strong sectarian feeling; it was bitterly opposed by the Liberal Party (although supported by the Irish Nationalists); it was introduced against the known wishes of an important section of the government; and it was passed by a House of Commons in the election of which a discussion of the issue had played no important part. Yet the only reaction of the House of Lords was to insert into it an amendment, moved by the Bishop of Manchester, which made it a still more extreme and partisan measure." Jenkins, *op. cit.*, 18

George, Bryce and Haldane—went on to legislate for some of the social reforms promised to the electorate. These measures, long recognised as necessary in some circles, now seemed the more urgent with the growing militancy of the Labour movement, and many were modelled on Bismarck's legislation of the 1870s and '80s which had been specifically concerned to counter the growth of revolutionary socialism. With steps to introduce old age pensions, unemployment insurance, health services, the first foundations were laid of what is now called the "welfare state". Some of these measures directly related to the educational field.

All this, however, provided no answer so far as socialists were concerned, nor did it meet outstanding grievances among the workers at large; disillusion with the slow rate of reform led many to turn to syndicalism and industrial unionism, including the dynamic Tom Mann.[1] Though there were serious rifts in both the main political parties it seemed to such men that the hold of the capitalist class over Parliament was so complete as to be unbreakable; a feeling which spread the more as Labour representatives, responding to the overtures made, seemed to be falling in with other politicians rather than conducting the militant fight that had been expected of them in the Commons. As this was prosecuted with increasing vigour outside, industrial struggles became more bitter, to culminate in what has been called "the Great Unrest"—quelled only by the outbreak of war. But war, particularly a war so destructive of the nation's youth, acts as a midwife of social reform; and as that which began in 1914 ended, another Education Act was passed which marks the close of a distinct period of pressure to speed up the cause of educational advance.

1. THE DEMAND FOR EQUAL OPPORTUNITIES

"This Congress condemns the educational policy of the government, as laid down in the Act of 1902, and in all subsequently issued Minutes and Regulations," declared the resolution passed at the T.U.C. in 1905; "and demands the formulation of an educational programme based upon the principle of equal opportunities for all."[2] This was the

[1] In essence this was a turn away from Parliamentary politics. As Mann wrote in his letter of resignation from the S.D.P.: "I declare in favour of industrial organisation; not as a means, but as *the* means whereby the workers can ultimately overthrow the capitalist system and become the actual controllers of their own industrial and social destiny." *Social Democrat*, Vol. xv, No. 9, September 1911, 421. An industrialist Syndicalist Education League was formed to propagate syndicalism.

[2] *38th T.U.C. Report*, 1905, 142.

dominant note struck in the years immediately following the Balfour Act.

In the spring of the previous year the T.U.C. had taken the opportunity to press its policy on a wider public when elections to the London County Council took place. A circular headed "Education, Trade Unionism, and the Forthcoming L.C.C. Election", distributed in 100,000 copies, stressed that in future a committee appointed by the L.C.C. would control popular education; trade unionists should, therefore, see that candidates treated education with the attention it deserved. Setting out in detail the T.U.C. educational policy, including full popular control of all state aided schools, the abolition of fees in grammar schools, adequate maintenance grants for those staying on at schools, it stressed that now School Boards had been abolished the unions should not allow education to become a side issue swamped by religious controversy. In this connection the secular solution was advanced again as the only viable one. The state should teach *no* religion; *all* denominations should be free to impart, in their own way and at their own cost, such religious instruction as parents may desire. Higher education, including secondary and technical education, should be within the reach of all.[1] In common with other Labour organisations the T.U.C. had already set its face firmly against the developing scholarship system.

What was the position here? London, as we know, had for some years been actively developing under the leadership of Sidney Webb, Chairman of the Technical Education Board, a system of competitive entry to grammar schools. As a result of the Education Act of 1903, London was brought into line with the rest of the country and, in May 1904, an Education Committee of the London County Council took over control. In his *London Education*, as we saw in Chapter VI, Sidney Webb had stressed the importance of a rapid development of the scholarship system. He went on to outline the further steps needed. "Junior county scholarships" would now have to be considerably extended as a result of the Board of Education's new regulations concerning pupil-teacher centres. "The pupil-teacher of fourteen or fifteen as he exists today, is peremptorily abolished," wrote Webb. "The future teachers are henceforth to devote themselves exclusively to secondary education up to the age of, at least, sixteen; and their period of actual apprenticeship is limited to two years. . . . The whole of the regulations point to an intention on the part of the Board of

---

[1] *37th T.U.C. Report*, 1904, 68-9.

Education to make it impossible for the pupil-teachers of the future to be taken straight from the elementary school."[1] This would necessarily involve an expansion of secondary schools and the provision of up to 2,000 scholarships a year, half of which should be reserved for candidates undertaking to complete their pupil-teacher apprenticeship. Webb claimed that the scholarship system already provided for the cleverest children of the London wage-earners "a more genuinely accessible ladder than is open to the corresponding class in any American, French or German city". Its reform along the lines suggested "would organically connect the scholarship system with all the public elementary schools, instead of, as at present, only about a third of them; and would bring London's 'capacity-catching machine' to bear on every promising child".[2] This was, of course, the policy of the Board of Education, which, on requiring pupil teachers, after 1 August 1905, to be educated in future full-time to sixteen, where possible in a secondary school, urged a more liberal provision of scholarships "open to the cleverest pupils".

As already noted, the abolition of pupil-teacher centres was much resented by the Labour movement and by the N.U.T.[3] Some centres were now providing a full-time education to sixteen and achieving very good results—for instance in the London University matriculation examinations. The closing of this avenue meant that all teachers would in future be recruited from grammar schools, which were regarded as middle-class schools, even if a few elementary school children who had gained a scholarship were now allowed in. The selective machinery involved here was sharply criticised. The T.U.C. circular of 1904 referred scathingly to the "infinitesimally small" proportion of working-class children who achieved a secondary education through the L.C.C.'s competitive "scholarship ladder", and insisted that "the small number of scholarships gained is no measure of the ability which is lost to the nation by reason of the fact that so many young children

[1] S. Webb, London Education (1904), 24-6.

[2] Ibid., 26-8. He pointed out that London needed 2,000 pupil-teachers a year, but was getting only about 1,200 or 1,300. The deficiency was greatest on the male side, "the London boy has, in fact, nearly ceased to enter the teaching profession. In all London last year, with close upon five millions of people, the number of boys who became pupil-teachers in any kind of school did not reach two hundred." Ibid., 23.

[3] Thus the President of the N.U.T., at the 1907 conference, sharply attacked the Board's policy. Pupil-teachers now transferred to secondary schools were often made to work in separate classes from other pupils: in 48 cases they were taught entirely apart, in 27 cases mainly apart, and only in 10 schools were they taught together (The Schoolmaster, 6 April 1907). In 1904 there were 12 pupil-teacher centres in London with 3,710 scholars; by 1909 the L.C.C. had closed or converted to secondary schools 8 of these; the others were closed in the next few years.

leave school at so early an age". It was not an increase in the number of scholarships that was looked for. "The London 'scholarship ladder' must give place to a 'broad highway'—to a non-competitive system of maintenance scholarships, which will provide a secondary education scholarship for every child who can reach a certain standard."[1]

During the early years of the twentieth century the T.U.C. stated its policy for secondary education in slightly varying formulations, though the overall intention was the same as that expressed in the years 1897-9. In 1901 the Congress resolution asked for education for all to fifteen and the provision of scholarships, the governing principle of which should be the "intelligence and the attainment of the child". In 1903 the call was for free maintenance scholarships for all "whose usefulness would be enhanced by an extended education", but the 1904 circular was much more definite. In 1905 the Labour Representation Committee carried an important resolution, similar to that of 1902, insisting that secondary and technical education should be free and "placed within the reach of every child by the granting of bursaries or maintenance scholarships to all children".[2] The I.L.P. took the same line and the Trades Union Congress of that year held that the standard of capacity for secondary education "shall be judged by work previously accomplished and not by competitive examination". It was in 1906 that the T.U.C. came out with an unequivocal demand for secondary education for all, claiming that secondary and technical education was essential to the education of all children, and demanding a system of scholarships and maintenance grants to make it possible "for all children to be full-time day pupils to the age of sixteen". A resolution including a clause in these terms was carried annually up to the war.

These were years, up to 1906, of growing hostility to the government. In 1904 the attack on the trade union movement was broadened with the introduction of the Trades Disputes Bill. Annual congresses of the T.U.C. reflected the rising anger of the working class. No social legislation of any importance has been passed, declared the President in 1904, the government was concerned only with "the defence of property and capital".[3] "A worse government than the present one we could not possibly get," said James Sexton, President in the following year. An election was approaching and when the time

[1] 37th T.U.C. Report, 1904, 69.
[2] 5th L.R.C. Conference Report, 1905, 55.
[3] 37th T.U.C. Report, 1904, 48.

comes "let us not forget what we have to avenge", including the Education Act.[1]

There was little the Labour movement could do on a national level during these years other than to reiterate their standpoint, to clarify their policy, and to win support for its implementation.[2] In each of the years from 1903 to 1905 the T.U.C., as the leading body in the Labour movement, passed by overwhelming majorities a main resolution on education as well as others on subsidiary matters. The Labour Representation Committee, shortly to develop into the Labour Party, was mainly concerned with its own organisational affairs at its annual conferences; it only discussed education at all fully in 1905 and 1906, when the resolutions adopted paralleled those of the T.U.C.

In general T.U.C. policy was clear cut and simple, in line with the traditional demands of the Labour movement, and continuing to support what had been the principle behind School Boards, namely that all state-supported schools should be controlled and administered by "the directly elected representatives of the people". But if popular control, secular education and secondary education for all were the main planks of policy, other demands now began to figure; thus in 1905 the demand for maintenance grants to sixteen was extended to include the clause "that provision be made to continue the education of capable students through the university courses". There was also pressure for the expansion of teacher training facilities—the 1905 Congress proposed that these be established in connection with universities or university colleges, a proposal which, if implemented, would have prevented the development of teacher training on two levels. All these resolutions included a clause on the financing of education, and here increasingly strong references were made to school and university endowments, taken over during the nineteenth century by the middle and upper classes to finance their own, independent educational system. The full cost of education should be borne by the National Exchequer, out of revenue obtained by broadening the basis of taxation "and by the restoration and democratic administration of valuable misappropriated educational charities and endowments".[3] In 1906,

---

[1] *38th T.U.C. Report*, 1905, 52.
[2] On the local councils, however, there was some opportunity for action. Thus in 1904 "the Labour men on the Council increased", writes the humanist leader, F. J. Gould of Leicester, "and I acted as their secretary. . . . At the monthly Council meetings . . . we fifteen Labour men sat in a proletarian group in the curve of the horseshoe line of chairs." This group fought for free meals "for hungry school children", secular education, etc., F. J. Gould, *The Life-Story of a Humanist* (1923), 100ff.
[3] *38th T.U.C. Report*, 1905, 142.

Ben Tillett was calling for an enquiry into this matter. "The people have been robbed," he said. "If these bequests were looked into, we should take away from the middle and upper classes some of the schooling that really belongs to the poor."[1] But before this, in view of the approach of a general election—a much more important event than the L.C.C. elections of 1904 and one which might well be expected to bring in a new government—the T.U.C. decided to set the pace. It produced its own Education Bill.

2. THE T.U.C. BILL AND THE EDUCATION BILL, 1906

The comprehensive resolution on education adopted by the T.U.C. in the autumn of 1905 included a clause that the points made should be embodied into a Bill to be presented during the next session. No candidate was to be endorsed by the Parliamentary Committee unless prepared "to promote and accept" the educational policy set out. The Bill ran as follows:[2]

A BILL
TO PROMOTE THE IMPROVEMENT OF EDUCATION AND THE PHYSIQUE OF CHILDREN ATTENDING ELEMENTARY SCHOOLS

Be it enacted by the King's most excellent Majesty, by and with the advice and consent of the Lords Spiritual and Temporal, and Commons, in this present Parliament assembled, and by the authority of the same, as follows:

1. On and after the 1st day of January, 1907, all (Elementary) schools receiving Government grants shall be placed under the local education authority of their respective districts and boroughs.

2. The education authority shall be empowered to make such arrangements for the purchase or hiring of any denominational or privately owned school as may be mutually agreed upon, subject to the approval of the Education Department. Failing the making of such arrangement, the local authority shall provide a new school, and within one month of the opening of same, grants to the denominational schools shall cease.

3. The instruction in all State-aided schools shall be in secular subjects only, and no theological or denominational tests shall be applied to any of the staff or officers of the school or of the educational authority.

4. Provision shall be made by the local authorities for secondary

1 *39th T.U.C. Report*, 1906, 175.
2 S. Bryher, *The Labour and Socialist Movement in Bristol* (1929), Pt. III, 4-5.

R

and technical instruction for all who desire to avail themselves of it; and a sufficient number of free maintenance scholarships shall be provided by grants from the Board of Education, to enable all who have fitted themselves, by their previous work, to continue their studies at technical institutes or universities until they attain adult years.

5. Each education authority shall make suitable provision for the technical training necessary to complete the equipment of the teachers in State Schools.

6. The cost of carrying out the provisions of this Bill shall be met by grants from the Imperial Exchequer, and by the restoration of educational endowments.

7. Each education authority shall provide at least one free meal a day for children attending the schools in their respective areas.

8. Each education authority shall take steps to record the height, weight, and chest measurement of children attending elementary schools; and shall furnish the first returns thereon to the Board of Education not later than December 30th, 1906.

9. Each education authority shall appoint a medical officer, or officers, whose duty it shall be to medically examine, and to treat such children as the teachers may consider in need of medical advice.

This Bill shall be cited as the "State Education Act, 1906".

Before the close of the year Balfour had resigned and a Liberal administration had been formed which received the overwhelming support of the electorate in January 1906. This government was pledged to bring in a measure which would undo the damage caused by the religious clauses of the 1902 Act, in the interests of nonconformists in particular. It was in this situation that the T.U.C. Bill was circulated, and *Justice* wrote in February: "The Labour Party in the L.R.C. and the Trades Union Congress, in the House of Commons and in the constituencies stand for Secular education, pure and simple." This, the S.D.F. journal went on, is the principle to be fought for in the coming Parliament "and we can assure the Labour members of a vigorous agitation outside if they will only do their duty inside".[1]

A week later *Justice* was welcoming the resolution passed by the annual conference of the Labour Representation Committee (February 1906) where the T.U.C. policy was supported by a vote of 817,000 to 76,000; the minority which objected to the clause on secular

---

[1] *Justice*, 17 February 1906. The I.L.P. also strongly reaffirmed its demand for "a national system of secular education, with complete public control". *12th I.L.P. Conference Report*, 1904, 35.

education being led by Sexton, a Roman Catholic. An attempt to get the clause on secular education deleted had failed by 10:1, wrote *Justice*, a great victory for the secular principle and a clear mandate to M.P.s. After its expressions of sympathy for the working class the government could not afford to ignore this authoritative expression of opinion. "Every national working-class organisation has now expressed itself clearly in favour of secular education—what will Birrell do?"[1] The same number of the journal offered the new President of the Board of Education some guiding principles in an article by E. G. Maxted. All schools should be taken over and managed by the state; "this may be done either by confiscation or purchase, or a mixture of both." Since either all religions should be taught in schools or none, to teach none is "the only practical solution".

Will Thorne presented the T.U.C. Bill in the Commons on 2 April 1906;[2] on April 9 Birrell brought in the government Bill which sought to amend the more partisan clauses of the 1902 Act.[3] This was by no means a Bill for secular education, nor, indeed, did it deal with anything but the sectarian controversy; accordingly it was the target of much criticism from the Labour movement.

The annual conferences of both the I.L.P. and the S.D.F. were held in April so that both organisations expressed views almost immediately after the Bill had been published. Both opposed it. The I.L.P. recognised that it could mean increased public control of elementary education but expressed regret "that the sectarian controversy is not to be settled by a system of universal secular education at the cost of the Imperial Exchequer". The Bill was also castigated in the resolution for failure to provide for a national system of secondary and technical education "at the disposal of the working classes", and for other omissions.[4] The I.L.P. journal, the *Labour Leader*, had lost no time in pointing out

---

[1] *Ibid.*, 24 February 1906. Augustine Birrell, author and critic, was the first President of the Board of Education in the Liberal administration, to be followed in rapid succession by Reginald McKenna and Walter Runciman who were respectively responsible for the two Bills of 1908.

[2] *Hansard*, Vol. 155, col. 191. In view of developments this Bill was not proceeded with.

[3] Asquith described its main objects as "to put an end to the dual system created by the Act of 1902; to secure that every school maintained out of rates and taxes should be under the exclusive management and control of the representative local Authority; to abolish religious tests and the obligation to give denominational teaching, in the case of all teachers appointed by the Authority and paid out of public funds; to permit 'Cowper Temple' teaching in the 'provided' schools; and in the 'transferred' schools to give facilities for special denominational instruction, but not by the regular teachers." *Fifty Years of Parliament* by the Earl of Oxford and Asquith (1926), Vol. II, 43.

[4] *14th I.L.P. Conference Report*, 1906, 48.

that the Bill favoured Nonconformists, adding that if Birrell had declared for secular education, the forces in its favour would have been greatly strengthened.[1]

The S.D.F. reacted more sharply. The Bill was "a mere attempt by the Liberals to evade the real question at issue in the interests of Nonconformity". What was needed was "a complete system of thorough national education on a purely secular basis" from primary school to university, at national expense, including the free maintenance of children. The resolution was unanimous.[2] It was this note that found an echo at the T.U.C. later in the year. The Government Bill was "introduced to placate the denominations", said Appleton, opening the debate; it made no provision for secondary education nor for the T.U.C. policy that directly elected representatives should administer education. The resolution again demanded a national system of education under full popular control, free and secular from primary school to university.[3]

The T.U.C. subsequently called a conference of Labour M.P.s, after which this policy was clearly put by Keir Hardie in the Commons during the debate on the Lords' amendments in December. The House of Commons was discussing a working-class question, he pointed out, one on which working-class opinion had been clearly expressed. The T.U.C., with two million affiliated members, had four times in succession declared for a national system of education, under popular control, free and secular from primary school to the university. The great majority of members of the T.U.C., Hardie said, were, like himself, Christians, but they supported the secular solution owing to the impossibility of finding a common denominator that all would accept. The Bill settled nothing and pleased nobody. The government should have been logical and accepted the secular solution. There would have been one big fight but the religious difficulty would have been finished

---

[1] *Labour Leader*, 13 April 1906. Once again the *Labour Leader* devoted little attention to the Bill, by comparison with *Justice*. Two articles appeared in May by Margaret McMillan and the Hon. Charles Lister. The former held that the Bill was not a bad one but asked for the inclusion of provision for medical inspection and the appointment of a medical department at the Board of Education. Lister, a socialist Anglo-Catholic, pointed out that churchmen opposed the Bill (and "Birreligion"). Liberalism should cease to identify itself with Nonconformists. Secularism was the only just solution. *Ibid.*, 18 May 1906.

[2] *Justice*, 21 April 1906.

[3] *39th T.U.C. Report*, 1906, 175. The resolution itself did not directly refer to the Bill, and it appears that there were disagreements this year as to its formulation, since the resolution was referred back to a committee before it came before Congress, being taken on the agenda much later than usual. The disagreement may have been on the secular education clause.

ELECTORS !

❖◆❖◆❖◆❖◆❖◆❖◆❖

VOTE FOR HONESTY.

MR. BIRRELL, the new Education Minister, speaking of Church Schools, says that "he feels some difficulty but **THINKS** that he will not be wrong in saying that the Radicals will not take away any property without paying for it."—*Manchester Guardian, Jan. 5, p. 10.*

Do HONEST Men ever THINK or HESITATE to say whether they will take the property of other people without paying for it? What is taking the property of others without paying but **ROBBERY.** Mr. Birrell is not quite sure whether he and his friends will not **ROB.** Do not give them the chance.

VOTE FOR LIBERTY.

The rich man is allowed a choice of schools. At present the working classes have some choice: not as much as they ought to have : nor as much as the Act of 1902 would give them. The Radicals wish to take away all choice, and to compel parents to send their children to schools in which every one of the Teachers **MAY** be an Atheist. Why should not the **WORKING MAN** have the same liberty as the rich ?

HANDBILL USED IN SUPPORT OF THE TORY CANDIDATE IN
THE 1906 GENERAL ELECTION

with once and for all. "The bulk of the working class were indifferent on the subject of religious instruction, because they saw what little good had come to the country from the religious instruction of church and chapel alike." Supporting rejection of the Lords' amendments *in toto*, he said that Labour members had acquiesced in the Bill as a compromise. But if this Bill was to be rejected, the whole question must be reopened, and then there should be a fight to the finish so that "from the schools should be eliminated anything which could be called sectarianism".[1]

The S.D.F. had told Labour members that a stand in the House of Commons would be fully supported by an agitation outside, and they were as good as their word. On 8 April the first of a series of mass meetings was held at Bristol, called by the S.D.F. With James O'Grady in the Chair, the speakers included Hyndman, the Countess of Warwick, Mrs. Bridges Adams, Councillor Jack Jones and Will Thorne, M.P.; these were supported by the President and Secretary of the Trades Council, and representatives from the Bristol Socialist Society, the I.L.P., and the Clarion Fellowship. The meeting was called to support the T.U.C. Education Bill brought before the House of Commons in April, and in fact took place the day before the Government Bill was introduced.[2]

Large meetings of this kind were held throughout the summer, when the Bill was under discussion. Later in April the local S.D.F. branch at Stockport, together with the Trades Council, the Labour Church, and the local I.L.P. branch organised a successful demonstration with Will Thorne and Lady Warwick again among the speakers.[3] "Let every branch of the S.D.F. arrange large public meetings," wrote Frank H. Edwards in *Justice* at this time, "and without neglecting propaganda on behalf of our principles let every member of our organisation give the education question the special attention it deserves."[4] In May the I.L.P. ran a meeting in the Queen's Hall in London to advocate "the Labour Solution of the Education Difficulty", with Keir Hardie as Chairman, and J. R. Macdonald, Snowden, Will Thorne and Mrs. Cobden Sanderson (Cobden's daughter) as speakers. This, reported in the *Labour Leader* as a great success, passed a strong

---

[1] *40th T.U.C. Report*, 1907, 87–8.

[2] Bryher, *op. cit.*, Pt. III, 4–5. *Justice*, 14 April 1906.

[3] *Justice*, 28 April 1906.

[4] *Ibid.* At its conference in April the S.D.F. formed an education committee to watch the government's Education Bill and to arrange public meetings to propagate its educational policy. Thorne acted as chairmen and Mrs. Bridges Adams as secretary. *26th S.D.F. Conference Report*, 1906, 17.

resolution.[1] In June there was a great I.L.P. demonstration in Leicester, Macdonald's constituency, where the main speech was made by Keir Hardie.

The S.D.F. managed to fill the Free Trade Hall, Manchester, at the end of May for a meeting addressed by its own speakers, who called for free maintenance and secular education.[2] It was at this point that a crucial vote on an amendment in favour of secular education took place in Parliament; it was defeated by 477 to 63, the vast majority of Liberal members joining with the Conservatives in voting the proposition down. The nonconformists were bitterly denounced for this act by *Justice*, which claimed that they hated secular education and free maintenance because "their leaders gain power by stunting the minds and sweating the bodies of the children".[3] It was at this point that Stewart Headlam's popular pamphlet *Secular Schools, the only Just and Permanent Solution* was published.

In spite of the setback, the S.D.F. maintained its agitation, running a successful delegate meeting in London in June and, in July, a Trafalgar Square demonstration. *Justice* published a great deal of material on education at this time including long main leaders by Hyndman and others covering all aspects of the subject.[4] The Lords' discussions, however, dragged on, and the Bill was not returned to the House of Commons until late in the autumn. By then it was unrecognisable, and the government itself decided to reject it. This, commented *Justice* in December, is a good thing. The Bill in any case was "a miserable piece of makeshift . . . a wretched compromise"; owing to non-conformist pressure, the government had not dared propose the secular solution.[5] The final issue of the journal for 1906 agreed with Keir Hardie, the fight would have to be renewed; no tears need be shed for this particular Bill.[6]

[1] *Labour Leader*, 18 May 1906, 25 May 1906; *Justice*, 18 May 1906, 26 May 1906. The resolution, moved by J. R. Macdonald, asked for a national system of schools and training colleges under complete public control; for all schools to be free; for physical training, medical supervision and free meals to be available for all; and for teaching to be confined to secular subjects only.

[2] *Justice*, 2 June 1906.

[3] *Ibid*.

[4] See, for instance, *Justice*, 7 July 1906.

[5] *Ibid*., 15 December 1906.

[6] *Ibid*., 29 December 1906. See Marjorie Cruikshank, *Church and State in English Education* (1963), 90-103, for a full analysis of the progress of this Bill. The Conservative leaders, she writes, "did not want a peaceful settlement and it was they, rather than the Archbishop, who remained hard and uncompromising". Balfour, she adds, "with cool and ruthless cunning, was directing operations".

3. APPEAL TO THE PEOPLE AGAINST THE BOARD'S POLICIES

Birrell's Bill, then, was a failure, and we may note that this first attempted measure of the new Liberal government had contained no reference whatsoever to secondary education—no clause opening up in any way the secondary schools or rendering the developing system more democratic. The Liberal party, linked as it was with dissent and the great industrial centres, might have been expected to pursue a more democratic policy than the Tories but during their first year of office no change in the policy of the Board, still, of course, under Morant, was visible.[1] Indeed it appears that the Board at this time was insisting on *raising* secondary school fees, so making secondary education actually *more* exclusive. However in the country at large, and especially among the Labour movement, the elementary school teachers, and the more progressive local authorities, the movement of opposition to the Board's policy was building up a united strength that was to explode with considerable vigour in 1907.

This movement was triggered off by the Report of the Consultative Committee to the Board of Education on Higher Elementary Schools, published in July 1906, which confirmed all the worst fears about the outlook in governing circles in general—and the intentions of the Board of Education in particular. This document is unusual in that it is a completely frank statement of a class outlook in education, of the kind more usual in an earlier age before the extension of the franchise. The Committee's brief was to consider the role and curriculum of the schools concerned with a view to advising the Board about future developments. The general attitude of its members becomes clear in the first paragraph which states that evidence has been taken from administrators and teachers but also from "employers of labour with a view to determining what, in the employers' opinion, is the kind of product most to be desired".[2] The employers were unanimous in laying stress on the *moral* qualities of this product, in the opinion that

[1] The Board's Report for 1906 did, however, reveal "a mood of cautious surrender to democratic ideals" (Banks, *op. cit.*, 64). It referred to the two "types" of secondary school, the one "a difference of kind" (the old endowed grammar school type often with a preparatory department), the other "a difference of stage" (the new municipal secondary schools taking most of its children from the elementary schools at twelve). Both types were well established. Even to accept the concept of secondary education as a *stage* had positive implications. A class education, the Report admitted, "after the fashion of Plato's Republic is contrary to the essence of democracy [which] is naturally jealous of a privileged class; and one of the dangers that have to be guarded against is that this jealousy may restrict the province or contract the scope of higher education". *Board of Education Report*, 1905-6, 61.
[2] *Report of the Consultative Committee upon Higher Elementary Schools* (1906), 5.

"boys and girls in their service should possess habits of discipline, ready obedience, self-help, and of pride in good work for its own sake whatever it may be". While underlining the importance of "this ethical aspect", they added that their employees did not require knowledge so much as handiness. "The employers, like the Navy, want 'handy men'."[1]

To insist on employers' requirements was not illogical in terms of the Board's long established attitude to these schools. These were higher elementary schools—specifically *not* secondary schools; their purpose was to crown the *elementary* education of a small proportion of working-class children. This was quite clear to the Committee. The higher elementary school would provide education from the age of twelve for brighter children from the elementary schools "who will, as a class, complete their day school education at the age of fifteen, and thereupon go into the world to earn a living in the lower ranks of commerce and industry. For such children there must naturally be a kind of education that is likely to make them efficient members of the class to which they will belong." It followed that the first necessary step "is to discover what are the qualities wherein, in the eyes of employers and others . . . children of this class seem to be deficient".[2]

Throughout the report the desire to hive off this type of education, to separate it from any connection with the "liberal" purposes of secondary education, is clearly apparent. While it is accepted that the pupils should have a general rather than a vocational education, it is "obvious, of course, in the circumstances, that the range of subjects must be strictly limited", no more than "can be expected from a short course of instruction extending over three years at a comparatively early age".[3] A foreign language should *not* be taught except in "exceptional circumstances"; to do this, as some schools were doing, was to approximate "towards a 'secondary' education", a trend "that we shall have occasion to deprecate".[4] There were good reasons for this, again advanced by the witnesses of whom the Committee took most account: "Employers are said to be dissatisfied with much of the elementary education given, because the instruction, in so far as it is carried beyond the simplest elements, tends, if anything, to make a boy a little above his job."[5]

This committee was bound once more to attempt a clear definition of the difference between higher elementary and secondary education, to draw a distinct line of demarcation. Since its conclusions succinctly

[1] *Ibid.*, 7.   [2] *Ibid.*, 6.   [3] *Ibid.*, 9.   [4] *Ibid.*, 16.   [5] *Ibid.*, 20.

express the prevailing outlook, and so throw light on general policy, they may be given here in some detail. The main stress is laid both on the qualitative and on the structural differences between the two types of education. The higher elementary school is "end-on" to the ordinary elementary school, is "continuous" from it, both "are of the same gauge; they form a series". The secondary school on the other hand "is not continuous in the same way with the elementary school; its course is, normally, preceded by a course of primary education in a preparatory school or department; but this primary education differs in character and method from the elementary instruction which the Public Elementary School affords".[1] It was the first time this aspect had been so clearly emphasised. "The difference between the Higher Elementary School and the Secondary School extends downwards beyond the age of twelve, at which both schools admit pupils, and the difference is the same throughout the course." The two types of education are, therefore, qualitatively different.

Another main point of difference is the age of leaving. The maximum age-limit in higher elementary schools is fifteen (as fixed by the Board's regulations, of course). The secondary course extends from twelve to sixteen "but this leaving age is not, as in the other case, a maximum, but a minimum". Further, this course of four years is "only the core of the period of school life", so that "the plan of instruction may be laid out on different lines in the Secondary School". Whereas those leaving higher elementary schools at fifteen are "supposed to begin wage-earning at once", the secondary school leaver "may often be supposed to pursue his education further".[2] In sum, "the two types of school prepare for different walks of life—the one for the lower ranks of industry and commerce, the other for the higher ranks and for the liberal professions".[3] Each fulfils an entirely different social function.

It naturally followed that, in this Committee's view, a school drawing the bulk of its pupils from elementary schools was not a true secondary school at all; examples are given of some drawing up to 77 per cent of their pupils from elementary schools. A true secondary school is one cited (though the name is not given) where, of 341 pupils, only "ten are ex-elementary children".[4] Indeed the committee baldly state the logical conclusion from their premises, which is that a true

---

[1] *Report of the Consultative Committee upon Higher Elementary Schools*, 22. The different terms should be noted; in the preparatory departments of secondary schools (for which, of course, fees were charged), the pupil receives "primary education"; in the elementary schools he receives "elementary instruction".

[2] *Ibid.*   [3] *Ibid.*, 23.   [4] *Ibid.*, 26.

definition of secondary education is an education which is not suitable for working-class children. If the distinction between secondary and higher elementary education they have made is accepted, then it is obvious that the more nearly a lower secondary school "approximates to a secondary school of the real type the less it can be said to meet the needs of the class of children whose education is in question".[1]

The recommendations made were clear enough. Secondary education should be cut back; there were too many "pseudo-secondary" schools not doing genuine secondary work and the grants paid to them were "misapplied". The Committee had been given to understand "that the Board are at the present time taking steps to ensure that only schools that can fairly claim to be doing secondary work shall continue in receipt of grants at the Secondary School rate".[2] This was as it should be; schools not rising to the necessary standard should be warned for "defaulting" and the grant withdrawn. Local education authorities "must be discouraged from trying too long to raise the schools into the secondary rank".[3] Such schools must be developed as higher elementary schools with a different and specific purpose. The new push forward into secondary education must once more be rigidly cabined and confined.[4]

This Report, a clear expression of the actual policy pursued by the Board of Education since 1900, roused sharp opposition. In January 1907 the standpoint of the N.U.T. was crystallised in a pamphlet entitled *Higher Education and the People's Children*, subtitled "An Appeal to the People against the policy of the Secondary Schools' Branch of the Board of Education". The N.U.T. by now objected to the whole conception of higher elementary schools, seeing these as another means whereby the brighter children of eleven were to be siphoned off into another type of school instead of retained to raise the whole level of elementary education. But the pamphlet also expressed clearly the N.U.T.'s conviction that the establishment of higher elementary schools was part of "a deliberate policy on the part of the Board to discriminate against the children of the working classes". "One imperfectly concealed purpose—at any rate one effect—of the Report," says the pamphlet, "is to keep exclusive the secondary schools and set up higher elementary schools for the masses. Even the brighter children of the masses are to be kept apart, in what the Committee themselves

[1] *Ibid.*, 27.   [2] *Ibid.*, 30.   [3] *Ibid.*, 31.
[4] The Report made a number of proposals as to the nature of higher elementary schools. But as these were never widely developed they are peripheral to our purpose. The main interest of the Report lies in its analysis.

expressly consider a lower type of school. The Report looks at the workers' children from the standpoint of the employer of labour mainly. It regards such children as fitted to be what their fathers (often for lack of education only) have had to be in most cases".[1]

Suspicion, indeed repudiation, of both the Committee's and the Board's policy was vehemently expressed at the annual conference in April. "The administration of the Secondary Branch of the Board of Education is thwarting and hindering the higher educational interests of the children of the working classes," declared the President of the N.U.T. in his opening address. "Since the time of the Cockerton judgment endeavours have been systematically made to conserve the public supply of Higher Education as a social rather than a national provision." Although some good things had been done, yet there had also been "a deliberate attempt to 'fend off' from the secondary schools proper all but a few of the children of workers, and to secure the larger secondary grants for schools in most cases already charging a high fee, and not seldom endowed with money originally left for the education of the poor."[2] After delineating the various stages in the development of official policy, including the 1900 Minute ("an attempt to turn all higher grade schools into higher elementary schools with reduced grants and a narrower curriculum") and the imposition of fees together with restriction on scholarships, the President concluded that "the whole policy of the Board tends to make a secondary school one which is not attended by the children of the people, unless they are scholarship holders". As for the Consultative Committee's report, it was nothing but a "grotesque jumble of contradictory evidence and conclusions". There was *no place* for the higher elementary school; what was needed was a varied system of secondary schools.[3]

It was this point that was specifically taken up in the business of the conference, J. H. Yoxhall M.P., the general secretary of the union, emphatically protesting against the Report and demanding its withdrawal, in a resolution that was passed unanimously. In so doing Yoxhall called the N.U.T. to a "crusade", in which, in alliance with

[1] Quoted in Banks, *op. cit.*, 57-8.
[2] The example given was of the King's School, Warwick, an ancient grammar school, where the Board had urged the governors to raise fees, an action "which would have had the effect of excluding a large number of poor scholars in the future"—this in spite of the existence of a large endowment. The school, according to the Board, should be only for children entering the army, the professions and the ancient universities, all other boys should go to the Leamington Secondary School. This move was apparently defeated by the governors.
[3] *The Schoolmaster*, 6 April 1907, 692.

the leaders of the working classes "and other persons concerned in the uplifting of the working classes", the N.U.T. would "march to the conquest of a stronghold of class prejudice in the Secondary Branch of the Board of Education".[1] The higher elementary schools were a cul-de-sac, declared his seconder; moreover the workers were being robbed—"money which in the past had been set aside to them had been turned away to other demands and was now devoted to the education of the wealthy". If the well-to-do went to a secondary school at twelve, why should not the workers' children?[2] To read the N.U.T. debates of this period is to be impressed by the very general feeling of resentment and by the strength of opposition to the Board's policy that had been engendered, and the consequent readiness to join forces with the Labour movement.

It was in this year also (1907) that sudden and intensely strong feeling on the whole question of secondary education found expression at the T.U.C. This was sparked off by the Board's attempts to raise secondary school fees. Another representative conference, therefore, passed a unanimous resolution protesting strongly against the class prejudice and anti-democratic policy pursued by the Secondary Schools' Branch of the Board of Education, as well as against the action of local education committees in being party to the raising of school fees. The T.U.C. also objected most strongly to the abolition of payments to pupil-teachers aged 14-16, now determined on by the Board of Education. This policy was designed to close the door of the teaching profession against the workman's child. "We demand that the highest and most efficient form of secondary education be free and available to all children capable of taking advantage of it," ran the resolution on these two related issues. The Board was not only closing the door of the teaching profession to the workers, declared one speaker, it was also attempting to raise the wall higher to prevent their children getting into the secondary schools. Other speakers demanded an enquiry into the whole system of secondary education, asserting that the privileged classes had no monopoly of brain power. The discussion on this occasion revealed a new temper among the delegates. "The education of the children is by far the most important question before the workers of the country," declared the miners' leader, Bob Smillie.[3]

[1] Ibid., 705.　　[2] Ibid., 706.
[3] 40th T.U.C. Report, 1907, 188. There was a similar expression of view at the I.L.P. conference that year. "This Conference expresses its strong disapproval of the policy of the Board of Education in regard to Higher Elementary and Secondary Education," ran the

Something of this feeling found expression in the House of Commons early in 1907, when an attack was made on the policy of the Board of Education, in particular on the meagre system of scholarships, few of which, it was claimed, were actually won by working-class children. On this occasion McKenna, now President of the Board, while admitting that the system was not altogether satisfactory, defended the policy of fees.[1] But in May a renewed demand resulted in an important concession, that in future an increased grant (from additional money to be made available) would be given to secondary schools willing to offer 25 per cent of their places as free places to pupils coming from elementary schools. These children would have to pass an "attainment test", which was not intended (or so it was put) to involve a competitive entrance examination so that this method of entry would be distinct from winning a "scholarship". So the free place system was born, a step towards meeting the growing objections to heavy school fees for the secondary school. Its aim, as stated in the new Regulations for 1906-7, was "to secure that all secondary schools aided by grants shall be made fully accessible to children of all classes"; or, in the words of the Liberal Party's Blue Book *The Government's Record, 1906-13*, "to secure that all Secondary Schools aided by the State shall be accessible to all scholars who are qualified to profit by the instruction they give".[2] This was a notable change from the policy of reserving secondary schools to those of "exceptional ability".

As it turned out, however, intentions were not translated into

resolution, "inasmuch as that policy is directed at making the opportunities for Education beyond the Elementary school the monopoly of the middle classes." The resolution demanded increased grants to extend free education in secondary schools. *15th I.L.P. Conference Report*, 1907, 44-5.

[1] *Hansard*, Vol. 171, cols. 91ff. E. H. Pickersgill, M.P. for Bethnal Green, led the attack, criticising the "undemocratic spirit" of the Board of Education, the Consultative Committee's report, as well as the Board's policy of discouraging local authorities from providing secondary schools.

[2] p. 68. The new regulation made little immediate change in the position since, in May 1907, 24 per cent of pupils in grant-aided secondary schools paid no fees and had previously attended elementary schools. Most of these held local authority scholarships, about half being earmarked for pupils who had expressed the intention of becoming elementary school teachers. The proportion of free place scholars in grant-aided secondary schools in October 1907, after the first application of the new regulations, rose to 27 per cent; *Board of Education Report*, 1911-12, 10-14. "As originally conceived," continues the Report, "the 'free place' regulations were not framed with the intention of instituting a scholarship system for the intellectual *élite* of the elementary schools. The intention was rather to bring the advantages of higher education, so far as the limited funds at the disposal of the Board would permit, within the reach of children of the poorer classes, and to place them on the same footing as pupils whose parents were in a position to pay the school fees." The proportion of free places required could be reduced below 25 per cent by the Board "on sufficient grounds in the case of any particular school".

practice. As R. H. Tawney later noted, of 282,005 children in secondary schools in 1919-20, only 82,630 had free places. McKenna had stated that he "hoped" all secondary schools provided by local authorities would become free, but by 1913-14, when there were over 1,000 on the grant list, only six charged no fees.[1] "The truth is," wrote Tawney, summarising the situation, "that the free place system, though useful as making a break, if a small one, in the walls of educational exclusiveness, was really the product of an age in which secondary education was regarded as an exceptional privilege to be strained through a sieve, and reserved, so far as the mass of the people were concerned, for children of exceptional capacity."[2]

Nonetheless the thought that the trickle of elementary school children into the secondary schools might become a small stream aroused much foreboding. Sir William Anson, Parliamentary Secretary to the Board of Education in Balfour's administration, argued that the free place system "would risk the financial position of the secondary schools, would very likely lower their standard of teaching, and would not profit, but rather would very often fatigue and embarrass the unfortunate children who were sent up to occupy these places". Grammar school heads, entirely in accord with earlier policies, argued that the new system was turning "innumerable good artisans and domestic servants into very inferior and wretchedly paid clerks".[3]

Some grammar schools were not prepared to co-operate—for, writes S. J. Curtis, they "viewed with horror the idea of opening their doors to 'barbarians' from the elementary school and saw in the regulation a threat to their independence". These "preferred to forego the grant rather than submit to the new requirements". Others "were glad of the extra grant but adopted a suspicious, a supercilious or patronising attitude towards scholarship pupils. The writer well remembers," he goes on, "the attitude of the staff of an old foundation school to which, in 1904, he with five others was fortunate enough to proceed by means of a scholarship examination. They were constantly reminded by the masters that they were scholarship pupils, were looked upon in the light of poor relations. . . . This attitude passed over from the staff to the boys, who showed that in every way they regarded scholarship

---

[1] R. H. Tawney, *Secondary Education for All* (1922), 81-2, 84. Of the remainder, 242 charged up to 5 guineas a year, 623 between 5 and 10 guineas, 107 between 10 and 15 guineas, 47 over this sum.

[2] *Ibid.*, 83-4.   [3] Quoted in Banks, *op. cit.*, 67.

pupils as belonging to an inferior category."[1] This attitude was shared by parents. "I do not think we do right to ascribe the objection which the middle classes have to a democratised school all to snobbishness," said the head of Lincoln Grammar School in 1911. "A parent once said to me 'I want my boy to gain his first idea of *esprit de corps*, of what makes a gentleman, his manners and his language, from boys of his own class. If that is snobbish I am a snob!' That opinion is held widely and strongly enough to keep a large section of the population from sending their boys to a democratised school."[2] As far as concern for standards went the free placers, as a group, in fact stayed on longer at school than fee payers, so contributing to building up the sixth forms; they also achieved better examination results.[3]

As Tawney put it, the free place system made a break, if a small one, in the walls of educational exclusiveness. From this time on, while the Labour movement continued to put forward its conception of free secondary education for all to sixteen, and therefore stood for the complete abolition of fees, it devoted attention to maintaining, and if possible, extending the provision for 25 per cent of free places. Already in 1908 the I.L.P., at its annual conference, called for "the abolition of the present scholarship system", admission to secondary schools should be based on educational attainment alone and full maintenance grants provided.[4] In March, 1909, a T.U.C. deputation to Walter Runciman, President of the Board, urged abolition of fees, but welcomed the new regulations defining exactly what was meant by a free place, since many "so-called educationists, and many schoolmasters, who do not care for working class lads in the schools, have taken active steps to induce the Board of Education to withdraw the regulations".[5] A year later, moving yet another resolution urging the complete abolition of fees at the annual Congress, a delegate from the Blastfurnacemen stressed that local authorities were in fact increasing fees; the free place system he described as "largely a farce so far as

---

[1] S. J. Curtis, *Education in Britain since 1900* (1952), 62. "At the other extreme", he adds, "there were schools which hailed the new conditions as a means of deliverance from their financial difficulties, and it is no exaggeration to say that the institution of the free place system saved many grammar schools from having to close down."

[2] From a speech at the Annual Meeting of the Association of Headmasters, quoted in *The Socialist Review*, Vol. 7, No. 39, May 1911, 211-12.

[3] "It is the common experience both that they [the free placers] stay longer at school than other pupils and that they form a large proportion of the able pupils, with the result that in the higher forms they tend to predominate." *Board of Education Report*, 1923-4, 17.

[4] *16th I.L.P. Conference Report*, 1908, 62.

[5] *42nd T.U.C. Report*, 1909, 71-2.

working-class children are concerned", since they were won by children whose parents could afford to pay for coaching by teachers from the secondary schools. A fair opportunity for the worker's child meant free education. Fees were not being imposed because they provided a revenue for schools "but in order to establish their exclusiveness".[1] Much the same points were made in 1911[2] and again in 1912 when special resolutions were once more passed on this point. It was in relation to the need for a free secondary education and to break down grammar school exclusiveness, that the Labour movement was soon to raise anew, in a more militant way than in the past, the whole question of the misuse of educational endowments.

By 1914 the number of children attending grant-aided secondary schools was 187,000. Of every 1,000 pupils in the 10-11 age group in elementary schools only fifty-six found their way into secondary schools; the odds against such children gaining a free secondary education had been reduced but still stood at 40 to 1.[3]

4. THE SECTARIAN CONTROVERSY AND THE SECULAR SOLUTION

While continuing to call for an opening of the way to secondary education for all, as a main issue in education, the Labour movement also pressed for another important aspect of policy, the secularisation of the entire system of public education.

The failure of Birrell's Bill had, in the words of Harry Snell, "created a feeling of despair in the minds of educational reformers, and there arose an instant demand for the renewal of the policy of a secular education".[4] In February 1907 the Union of Ethical Societies called an open conference to determine on action, and as a result the Secular Education League was formed of which Snell became Secretary. The League, which insisted that "the teaching of religion was not the responsibility of the State", became a focus of activity, uniting representatives of the Labour movement and advanced liberal thinkers with that minority of Anglican and Nonconformist ministers who supported a secular solution.[5]

[1] 43rd T.U.C. Report, 1910, 167. This delegate, P. Walls, had been on a School Board for eleven years and on an Education Committee for six.
[2] 44th T.U.C. Report, 1911, 247-8. According to Frank W. Goldstone, M.P., of 957 secondary schools in receipt of the higher grant, 124 had been allowed to offer less than 25 per cent of free places. Socialist Review, Vol. 7, No. 39, May 1911, 235.
[3] G. A. N. Lowndes, The Silent Social Revolution, 113.
[4] Lord Snell, Men, Movements and Myself, 175.
[5] Ibid., 176. General Council members included Thomas Burt, M.P., Arthur Henderson, M.P., J. Ramsay Macdonald, M.P., Philip Snowden, M.P., J. M. Robertson, Sir Arthur

S

The formation of this new body signalised the greatly increased momentum gained by the movement for secular education in 1907-8.[1] The foundation of the Moral Instruction League in 1897 has already been mentioned; this sought to develop secular moral teaching in the schools and was, therefore, the educational counterpart of the secular movement generally. The leading figure, F. J. Gould, had gained his seat on the Leicester School Board on a platform of secular education and at this time became famous for his demonstration lessons in moral teaching and for his many publications on moral education.[2] The Secular Education League itself published pamphlets and leaflets and held demonstrations, becoming particularly active during the general election of 1910.[3] Necessarily it looked to the Labour movement as the only organised political force which stood consistently for the secular solution; in 1907 the T.U.C. and the Labour Party re-affirmed their position by huge majorities, though at both conferences the relevant clause was again opposed by James Sexton (representing the Liverpool dockers) and other Roman Catholics.[4]

In the following year the government made two further attempts to redress the balance in favour of Nonconformists. It would be tedious to describe the measures in detail—but in essence each Bill would have weakened the position of the Church of England considerably.[5] The first Bill, introduced in February, aroused no

Conan Doyle, Havelock Ellis, Frederic Harrison, George Meredith, J. A. Hobson, Rev. Stewart Headlam, Bishop Mitchinson, Eden Philpotts, Graham Wallas, H. G. Wells, Israel Zangwill. "Several hundred clergy and ministers either enrolled themselves as members of the League, or assisted its work in other ways." Snell was responsible for the League's executive and propaganda work until he became a member of the Labour government in 1931. (See his *Case for Secular Education*.)

[1] Among many publications were Joseph McCabe, *The Truth about Secular Education: Its History and Results* (1906), and *One Hundred Years of Education Controversy* (both published by the Rationalist Press Association); Snell wrote his *Case for Secular Education* about this time, and Headlam his *Secular Schools* (1906). A mass of articles on secular education appeared in the secularist and rationalist press: e.g. *Agnostic Annual and Ethical Review; Literary Guide and Rationalist Review; Fortnightly Review; Freethinker* (published by the Secular Education League); *Ethical World*, etc.

[2] Gould wrote fourteen lesson books and gave demonstration lessons to over 80,000 children in different parts of the world; F. J. Gould, *Life Story of a Humanist*, especially 92ff.; see also "The Moral Instruction League, 1897-1919" by F. H. Hilliard, *The Durham Research Review*, Vol. III, No. 12, September 1961, 53-63, and M. Sadler (ed.), *Report of an International Inquiry into Moral Instruction and Training in Schools* (1908).

[3] Benjamin Sacks, *The Religious Issue in the State Schools of England and Wales, 1902-14* (1961), 203. The contemporary arguments in favour of the secular solution, which covered a very wide field, are presented in detail in this book.

[4] At the T.U.C. the vote was 1,239,000 to 126,000; at the Labour Party Conference, 627,000 to 122,000. At the I.L.P. Conference in 1907 a resolution demanding the adoption of secular education was carried without opposition.

[5] The first Bill, introduced in February 1908, was a relatively strong measure withdrawing rate aid from voluntary schools and, in single school areas (this was the crux),

enthusiasm in the Labour movement; "it buttresses nonconformists and spikes the Church," proclaimed *Justice* of the original draft, and so it cannot stand. The secular solution was the only possible one, but the Liberal government had not got the moral courage to carry this through.[1] At this point Theodore Rothstein contributed a competent article analysing the situation. The Nonconformists were taking their revenge for 1902 since the Bill extended the privileges of dissent by requiring the teaching of undenominational Christianity in all rate-supported schools. In this situation Labour M.P.s should fight for the secular solution, he said, but many Labour leaders did not dare to propagate T.U.C. and Labour party policy to their constituents. "So much more is the pity, because apart from the purely educational aspects of this wretched religious wrangle . . . it is the minds of the children of the proletariat which are at stake in the unseemly game the two Christian bodies are playing."[2] At its April conference the S.D.F. came out strongly against the Bill, calling instead for "a national system of education, elementary and advanced, free and secular, and under complete popular control".[3] This standpoint was endorsed at the T.U.C. in the autumn when the call for a secular education was taken as a separate resolution and carried by the largest majority it was ever to receive, 1,433,000 to 131,000.[4] A "great vote", commented

---

providing for the compulsory transfer of voluntary schools to the local education authority. Voluntary schools in other areas could "contract out" and receive a direct exchequer grant—if "efficient". The second Bill, drafted after "protracted negotiations with the Archbishop of Canterbury" made certain important concessions to the Church. However, these finally proved unacceptable to the Church and the Bill was withdrawn. Cf.: *The Government's Record 1906-13* (Liberal Publication Department, 1913), 73.

[1] *Justice*, 29 February 1908.

[2] *Justice*, 7 March 1908. Rothstein held that the 1870 Act was a victory for the Non-conformists, and that the 1902 Act could be regarded as a restitution to the Church of England of the position thereby lost. He pointed out that, following the 1870 Act, "Nonconformist Christianity" could be taught at public expense in the board schools, and that when the 1902 Act made the same provision for the Church of England the Nonconformists then discovered their "conscience". *Ibid*. It was precisely to "Cowper Temple" teaching that Anglicans objected, regarding it as essentially Nonconformist; if this could be supported from the rates why not clerical schools teaching Anglican doctrine? Hence the violent resistance to the 1906 Bill.

[3] *Justice*, 25 April 1908. The I.L.P. also opposed the Bill, passing a resolution stating that "the only logical settlement of the education question lies in the adoption of secular education in all schools supported out of public funds". The resolution was supported by an Anglican minister, a Nonconformist minister, and by J. Larkin "speaking as a Catholic". *16th I.L.P. Conference Report*, 1908, 61.

[4] The resolution ran as follows: "This Congress urges the organised workers to continue their efforts to secure Parliamentary and Municipal recognition of the trade union education policy, which demands a national system of education under full popular control, free and secular, from the primary school to the university." *41st T.U.C. Report*, *1908*, 180.

Justice, achieved in spite of the efforts of clericalism in certain unions.[1] "We have no hesitation in rejoicing over the collapse of the Government's Education Bill," proclaimed the same journal in December.[2] Once more the failure of a Bill promoted largely to favour the Nonconformists provoked no tears from the Labour movement.

The Liberal Government, re-elected in 1910 with a reduced majority, made no further attempt to reverse the 1902 Act, although the question of secular education was made an issue in the election and the major obstacle, the House of Lords, was curbed by the Parliament Act of 1911. While support for the secular solution increased in the Labour movement, the Roman Catholic element, led by Sexton and James O'Grady, now fought the issue with increasing bitterness, claiming that it was divisive and should be excluded from discussion. At the 1910 Congress this minority demanded a ballot of the membership of all affiliated unions as to whether the demand for secular education should be retained, a motion which was rejected by only a small majority. But the usual resolution on secular education again gained an overwhelming majority (827,000 : 81,000), the mover stressing that it was more important than ever and illustrating how sectarianism retarded educational advance. A similar demand for a ballot was overwhelmingly defeated (810,000 : 99,000) after a tough debate at the Labour Party Conference that year when Arthur Henderson stressed that the secular standpoint was the only condition they could consistently adopt. "It must be of immense satisfaction to the Gasworkers' Union," he went on, "who in the days when the principle was not so popular brought it up year after year, to see the progress it now made."[3]

The Labour Party at this time published a two-page leaflet on "The Secular Solution". But the Catholic opposition was sedulously built up, and was to win some success. Analysing the position in the I.L.P. journal, *Socialist Review*, in April 1911, Harry Snell referred to the revolt "organised against this principle of civic equity by a small section of the trade union movement under the guidance of the prelates of a Church that is notoriously hostile to Socialism and to the working-class movement in every part of the world". Someone must give way, he added, and the majority cannot be coerced by the

[1] *Justice*, 3 October 1908.
[2] *Justice*, 12 December 1908.
[3] *10th Labour Party Conference Report*, 1910, 85; *43rd T.U.C. Report*, 1910, 175-7.

minority. The T.U.C. must remain loyal to its principles.[1] But in the same year a crisis was reached in the T.U.C.

Moving the main resolution on education, Will Thorne once more stressed the importance of the secular standpoint. He had been challenged, he said, as to whether he was prepared to go to the electors on the secular solution. He had done so in the election last year at West Ham, and this, he claimed, had done him nothing but good—he gained a majority of 5,000. This resolution had been on the agenda for sixteen years; it was not "his" resolution, it had been discussed at the Gasworkers biennial conference on every occasion, and the delegates to the T.U.C. Congress mandated. He went on to argue the case. This was too much for Sexton, who created what is officially described as a "regrettable scene of disorder". Amidst shouts and cries Sexton attempted to put the Catholic case. They had "no right to take the votes of Roman Catholics to thrust secular education down their throats". James O'Grady also attacked the motion but it was once more passed, although, significantly, the miners abstained.[2] At the Labour Party conference that year the normal motion went by default, as there was no mover when it was called.

In 1912, when Thorne was President of the T.U.C., the Catholic minority in effect prevailed. The Miners' Federation moved that the question of secular education be eliminated from discussions at any future Congress; it had already been eliminated from their own conferences since it led to such bad feeling. After a long debate this resolution just scraped home (952,000 : 909,000).[3]

This did not mean that the Labour movement ceased to support the secular solution; indeed one interpretation was that this was so much the settled policy of the trade union movement, that an annual resolution was unnecessary.[4] Nevertheless it necessarily removed it from

1 *The Socialist Review*, April 1911, 129-35. Snell stressed that support was growing rapidly. The Secular Education League had circulated recently a manifesto signed by 600 clergy and ministers of all denominations urging state neutrality, and had issued *An Appeal by Nonconformists to Nonconformists* and *An Appeal by Churchmen to Churchmen* written by well-known preachers. The Labour movement therefore should not renounce its principles.
2 *44th T.U.C. Report*, 1911, 243-6.
3 *45th T.U.C. Report*, 1912, 177-84.
4 This point was put by Ralph Morley in an article in *Justice* which claimed the Miners' resolution might be misconstrued: "The resolution in favour of Secular Education has always been carried at previous Conferences by overwhelming majorities, but the debate on the resolution has at times been marked by acrimonious discussion from certain quarters, and in order to avoid this in future, the resolution of the Miners' Federation in effect demanded that Secular education should be taken for granted as the settled policy of the trade union movement, and that, therefore, there would be no need to discuss the idea at future Congresses." *Justice*, 21 September 1912.

the scene. The Labour press continued to carry articles on the issue but the possibility of securing so fundamental a change seemed remote. There is probably also some truth in Rothstein's charge that some Labour leaders, Nonconformists themselves, feared to carry the fight for a genuinely secular education to the people, and were, perhaps, glad to let the issue drop. In any case the Labour Party and T.U.C. conferences from 1913 on no longer pressed the question. Though the preponderating opinion still held to what had been one of the main demands of the Labour movement since the days of the Chartists and before, this was one issue on which the Labour movement did not speak with a united voice.[1]

5. SCHOOL MEALS

During these years the Labour movement paid growing attention to ensuring that children were in a condition to benefit from their education. The low level of physical health among the mass of the people, which socialists had frequently emphasised, came to general notice during the Boer War. Over a third of the 700,000 recruits medically examined between 1893 and 1902 were found to be unfit for service but the inspector-general for recruiting put the rejection rate as high as 60 per cent, given that many more did not even qualify for inspection. These revelations led to the appointment in 1903 of an inter-departmental committee to enquire into "physical deterioration", and one of the recommendations of the report issued the following year was that local authorities be empowered to provide meals for hungry children. At the time they were unable to spend money from the rates for such purposes and, as described earlier, it was only voluntary bodies that provided free meals. Meanwhile fresh evidence of the appalling physical condition of many school children was accumulating.

The S.D.F. had consistently called for one free meal a day, as an aspect of full state maintenance, and continued to give prominence to this question. In so doing attention was drawn to effective school feeding arrangements abroad, as also to the work of the Mary Ward pioneer school in Tavistock Place.[2] Will Thorne, who had been the

---

[1] As the Labour party found to its cost later, the Education Bill of 1930 foundering on the opposition of the Catholics within the Labour party. Snell, *op. cit.*, 243-4.

[2] An article by Frederick Fletcher in *Social Democrat* describes an orphanage in California with very fine house and grounds, board and education provided; what an effect a few such institutions in England could have "taking our pale and starving slum children

first to raise this matter as a priority in the T.U.C., moved a resolution at the annual congress in 1904 embodying the S.D.F. policy; while making it clear that he personally stood for complete free mainten- ance, he emphasised that one free meal a day would represent a con- siderable advance at a time when twelve million people were living at or below the poverty line. The resolution, which also covered the employment of children, was carried unanimously.[1]

Branches of the S.D.F. gave considerable attention to this question. The records of the Hackney and Kingsland branch, for instance, which numbered among its members Theodore Rothstein and a local coun- cillor, show that the demand for state maintenance of school children was brought up at a Town's Meeting in 1903, and at a special public meeting with trade unionist speakers in 1904; local support was mobilised for a Trafalgar Square demonstration that summer and there were further activities in 1905.[2] It was, however, the I.L.P. at Bradford which carried on the most effective campaign and made the most important break-through at this time.

Here the movement for school feeding and child welfare had received a tremendous impetus in the late 1890s from the work of Margaret McMillan as a School Board member and from Robert Blatchford's initiative in founding the Cinderella Club movement which systematically fed and clothed slum children. But, writes Coun- cillor J. H. Palin, in his description of this movement, the one meal a week that was voluntarily provided was totally insufficient—even cruelty. The worst cases were, therefore, sorted out and fed at the Club's premises and in schools in the poorer districts five days a week. This was carried on for several winters.

Margaret McMillan's most essential point was, of course, that it was impossible to educate starving children, and although she left Bradford in 1902, the I.L.P. decided, a year later, to place child feeding in the forefront of their municipal programme and to force the city

and returning them a few years later healthy and well-developed, young men and women. This would awaken the masses to something better than they enjoy today; there are plenty of places on our coasts"; Vol. 9, 1905. See also articles in Vol. 5, 1901; Vol. 8, 1904; Vol. 11, 1907.

[1] 37th T.U.C. Report, 1904, 119.

[2] Andrew Rothstein, "An S.D.F. Branch, 1903-6", Our History, No. 19 (1960). Accord- ing to the secretary of the S.D.F. (H. W. Lee) the Trafalgar Square demonstration was "unquestionably the greatest gathering" that had been held there since such meetings had been permitted again in 1892. The 1904 conference of the S.D.F. had decided on "a vigorous agitation" on state maintenance, including "public demonstrations in every industrial centre of the country". These were assessed as highly successful in 1905. 24th and 25th S.D.F. Conference Reports, 1904 and 1905.

authorities to face up to the position. A report drawn up by two I.L.P. members working in the Cinderella Club showed that some 2,000 Bradford children were insufficiently clothed and underfed, many going to school without breakfast. Voluntary help could never solve the problem.

The report produced a sensation. As a result of the wide publicity given to it by the I.L.P. the City Council was forced to take action and called a conference of leading citizens. This was a very representative meeting, which heard the truth about the children's condition from the lips of the teachers. "No one present at that meeting unless made of stone could listen unmoved. The scene will never be effaced from my memory as long as I live," writes Palin. "They told us it was not merely a winter question, or one that was very much affected by good or bad trade; in summer they had children falling from their seats and fainting from want of food; they also incidentally told us very modestly of their own heroic efforts to deal with the worst cases out of their own slender means, and we came out of that meeting ashamed to look each other in the face."

The opponents of school feeding, however—the Liberal majority on the Council—did not share this feeling, continuing to refuse assistance on the grounds that to provide meals for children would be to reduce parental authority and responsibility. Although appearing to make a concession immediately before the 1904 municipal elections, this was rescinded immediately after. At the crucial meeting of the Education Committee, which extended from 3 p.m. to 2.25 a.m., Jowett, Hayhurst and others made a strong appeal for action by the local authority but were defeated by 47 to 29. The course taken was to hand the children over to the Poor Law Guardians who alone could provide meals financed out of the rates. Such meals as were then provided, partly from a Mayor's fund, and partly by the Guardians, consisted, according to Palin, of a stale bun, a banana, and "milk".

During 1905 the battle continued, especially at the time of the elections; the existing system was exposed by Jowett and others and some slight improvements secured. In that year Jowett was elected a member of Parliament, and, in 1906, came the "never to be forgotten day when the fight was transferred to the floor of the House of Commons".[1] Bradford was to become a pioneer authority in the school meals service; but nothing effective could be done locally—in the face

---

[1] This account of the Bradford struggles is taken from J. H. Palin, "The Feeding of School Children, Bradford's Experience". *The Socialist Review*, Vol. I, 1908, 207-19.

of the opposition that existed—without an Act of Parliament. Partly because of the Bradford agitation, but also because of the movement all over the country this step was at last becoming a possibility.

Late in 1904 the movement for school meals received a great impetus from the publication of the report of the committee on Physical Deterioration. This had taken evidence from a large number of witnesses who revealed clearly the actual conditions of the school children. "With scarcely an exception," reported the committee, "there was a general consensus of opinion that the time had come when the State should realise the necessity of ensuring adequate nourishment to children in attendance at school; it was said to be the height of cruelty", they added, "to subject half-starved children to the processes of education." Over 120,000 children in London alone were shown to be underfed—in Manchester and elsewhere the proportion was similar (15 to 16 per cent).[1] The Labour movement moved rapidly into action. In January 1905 the T.U.C., together with the London Trades Council and the S.D.F., organised a conference at the Guildhall to consider state maintenance of children, the Chair being taken by one often regarded as an enemy, but an ally in this context, Sir John Gorst.[2] In the same month the Labour Representation Committee organised a conference on "The Provision of Meals for School Children at Public Expense" with Arthur Henderson in the Chair, and among speakers J. R. Macdonald, Keir Hardie and four leading trade unionists—John Hodge representing the steel smelters, Ben Turner the weavers, Will Thorne and Pete Curran the gasworkers. The resolution insisted that "the time has come for the provision of meals for school children at public expense" and asked Labour M.P.s to introduce a Bill next session "giving effect to the demand". It also called on Labour councillors to urge that Councils allocate money for this purpose at once, "pending a final settlement of the question by Parliament".[3]

The T.U.C. kept up the pressure and, at its Congress in 1905, passed

---

[1] "The only witness who appeared absolutely to dissent from that view," reported the committee, "was the Bishop of Ross, who, while admitting an enormous number of underfed children in Ireland, deprecated any steps being taken to remedy the evil, on the ground that it would weaken the sense of self-respect and self-reliance both of parent and child." Report of the Inter-Departmental Committee on Physical Deterioration (1904), Vol. 1, 66-7, 69.

[2] See his The Children of the Nation. How their Health and Vigour should be promoted by the State (1906).

[3] 5th L.R.C. Conference Report, 1905, 69-71. Thorne proposed an amendment in favour of full state maintenance of children but this, opposed by J. R. Macdonald, Sexton, and Mrs. Pankhurst of the I.L.P., was defeated.

a resolution moved by Thorne which referred to the Committee's report and again declared "in favour of the principle of State mainten-ance of children". This covered not only one free meal a day but also a call for free medical advice and inspection and physical training for all; it was stipulated that the administration of these services should be completely disassociated from charity and the Poor Law—a very important point.

In the General Election campaign of January 1906 the issue was kept well to the fore by Labour and socialist candidates. The S.D.F. made it the main priority in its Election manifesto. "State maintenance of school children is the most valuable stepping stone to social re-organisation", it claimed, it was essential in order to enable children to take full advantage of free education, "and to grow up strong and capable citizens".[1]

During the first session of Parliament, W. T. Wilson, a new Labour M.P. returned for Westhoughton, introduced a Bill providing for the feeding of necessitous school children, and this was given a second reading (without a division) in March. In an important sense the Bill introduced a new principle in social legislation—it implied acceptance by the community of responsibility for poverty. This point was seized on both by those in support and those opposed. "Those who ventured to criticise and oppose the Bill," wrote H. W. Lee in *Justice*, "laid stress upon the fact that State action, when once entered upon, would not stop at feeding. Books and clothing, ventilation and sanitation of homes, and communal care in other directions would inevitably follow. That is what makes the outlook so encouraging for us." The Bill was "a matter for sincere congratulation".[2] The Select Committee which now considered the Bill attempted to hedge it round with every kind of restriction, drawing up a series of nine points; one of these ran that "only in extreme and exceptional cases—where neither parental resources nor local voluntary funds are sufficient, and after the consent of the Board of Education, a local authority may use the rates to pay the cost of the actual food, the rate not to exceed $\frac{1}{2}d.$ in the pound".[3]

In the meantime pressure in favour of the Bill was kept up by the Labour movement outside Parliament. The I.L.P. conference, held in April, sharply criticising Birrell's Bill, noted that it made no adequate provision either for medical inspection or school feeding and called on the government "to give facilities for the passing of the Feeding of

[1] *Justice*, 6 January 1906.   [2] *Ibid.*, 10 March 1906.
[3] *39th T.U.C. Report*, 1906, 78-9.

Children's Bill, which has been introduced and read a second time on the initiative of the Labour members".[1] Similar resolutions were moved at large meetings at Birmingham and elsewhere called by the S.D.F.[2] During the subsequent debate in the House of Commons, Keir Hardie, Jowett, Will Crooks and others spoke. The Bill eventually passed and received Royal Assent on 21 December 1906.

Local authorities were now empowered to spend money out of the rates on feeding necessitous children (the Act was permissive only); it remained to see that they did so. By 1908-9, the number providing meals under the Act was 85, by 1910-11 it had risen to 100, considerably less than a third of the total. At one time it seemed doubtful whether the L.C.C. would make use of the new powers. A letter to *The Times* by Hyndman, H. W. Lee and others, sent also to all members of the L.C.C. in December 1907, launched an S.D.F. campaign which culminated in a mass meeting at Queen's Hall in London "on behalf of starving children". Victor Grayson, who had won a great victory at a by-election in Colne Valley in July, was the main speaker, supported by Hyndman, the Countess of Warwick, Mrs. Bridges Adams and two other M.P.s, Thorne and O'Grady.[3] The L.C.C. was castigated for its niggardly approach and continued appeals for charity at a time when it not only had powers to act but its own Education Committee had concluded that 47,000 children were in need of meals.[4]

---

[1] *Justice*, 21 April 1906.

[2] *Justice*, 10 March 1906. At the Birmingham meeting the resolution supporting the Bill on School Feeding was moved by Lady Warwick and seconded by James O'Grady, M.P.

[3] *Justice*, 28 December 1907, 4 January 1908, 25 January 1908. The S.D.F. had strongly supported Grayson's election campaign, Mrs. Bridges Adams and others working for him. Of his victory *Justice* remarked: "Especially to be noted was the reception accorded to all references to the 'immediate' Socialist proposals on behalf of the children. We are sometimes told that Lancashire and Yorkshire workpeople would laugh at and reject with scorn our proposals for raising the school age of children to sixteen, and providing them with free maintenance. But the working-class electors of Colne Valley didn't laugh. They cheered these proposals to the echo, and what is more they went and voted for them at the poll. Victor Grayson's victory was a victory for the children." *Justice*, 27 July 1907.

[4] The S.D.F. launched a "strenuous agitation" in London to force the L.C.C. to operate the relevant section of the Provision of Meals Act, since, if this was successful, London's example would be widely followed, reported the secretary to the 1908 conference. A petition to this effect gained 21,000 signatures in three hours, but the Education Committee of the L.C.C. had refused to receive a deputation. Many public and Town's Meetings had been organised throughout London and resolutions carried that the Act's provisions should be made compulsory, that the $\frac{1}{2}d$. limit on rates should be removed, and that a grant should be made from the exchequer towards the cost of providing food; *28th S.D.F. Conference Report*, 1908, 22. The I.L.P. also took this up, publishing in 1909 *London's Children—how to feed them and how not to feed them*, a pamphlet by Margaret McMillan and A. Cobden Sanderson. "In London itself, all is dire confusion," they wrote, "the feeding is haphazard and insufficient, and the conditions under which it is often carried out are demoralising." The pamphlet contained a very strong indictment of the L.C.C. and of the attitudes of those concerned.

Elsewhere a fight often had to be made to get the Act implemented. In Bradford, socialist pressure continued to meet with opposition, a leading Liberal (the President of the Free Church Council) opposing public aid on the grounds that private charity was not exhausted. But in November 1907, the Education Committee finally took over from the Guardians and made good the delay. It opened new feeding centres, greatly increased the numbers fed and provided a nourishing and varied diet under pleasant and civilised conditions. Initial experiments in systematic feeding showed that the children gained weight remarkably. The numbers receiving meals rose from 609, taken over from the Guardians in November, to 1,658 four months later at the end of February. Bradford had shown what could be achieved under the 1906 Act, in spite of the limitations which hedged it around.[1]

While a progressive authority could, therefore, make a definite impact on under-nourishment there was no obligation on others even to operate the Act. Right up to the war the Labour movement pressed for an amending Bill to make provision compulsory, and Jowett succeeded in introducing a Bill in 1912, but it failed to pass. Meanwhile both the S.D.F. and the I.L.P. continued the campaign for full services, frequently arguing the case for boarding schools and other facilities at meetings, in the journals and in pamphlets.[2] The call for state maintenance remained for many years the first clause of the T.U.C.'s all-embracing resolution on education. This was a specifically socialist demand and it is, perhaps, of some significance that Margaret McMillan's resolution on this matter at the Labour Party Conference of 1909 was defeated for the first time owing to the opposition of two Parliamentarians, Keir Hardie and J. R. Macdonald. Hardie's view was

---

[1] Cf. J. H. Palin, *loc. cit.* and Alderman E. R. Hartley, *How to Feed the Children* (1908), a pamphlet headed "Bradford's Example", which includes the original menus. Palin describes the method of central cooking and distribution, and refers to a report to the Education Committe on meals which was adopted. This proposed that (1) children whose parents were willing to pay should be fed as well as necessitous children; (2) the dining halls should be clean and tastefully arranged with flowers, etc., so that the meal served an *educational* function; (3) teachers should supervise the meals; (4) the children fed should be clean and individual attention be given to each child. The teachers in Bradford volunteered to take full charge of the service.

[2] E.g., J. Hunter Watts, *An Appeal for the Children* (1908) which kept alive a more generous vision of what education might be: "On sandy stretches by the sea shore, on the beautiful waste spaces of heather-clad uplands which are natural playgrounds for the children, the workers must build capacious boarding schools." See also "The State and its School Children" by Margaretta Hicks, *Social Democrat*, Vol. XIV, No. 5 and No. 6, May and June 1910, which describe what is done for the children in different European countries; "The Feeding and Clothing of School Children", by G. M. Hale, *ibid.*, Vol. XIV, No. 7, July 1910, and "State Maintenance" by Zelda Kahan, *ibid.*, Vol. XV, No. 2, February 1911.

that, while food and clothing should be provided where necessary, "he declined to have himself committed to a vague and indefinite phrase which might mean anything—as most often happened, nothing of a practical kind".[1]

The 1906 Act, then, marked the only practical achievement during this period. In his memoirs published in 1911, Hyndman, whose wife had earlier played an important part in furthering the voluntary movement to provide meals for London's school children, summarised the movement in characteristic vein. Looking back to the early 1880s and the success of the Paris Municipal Council under the impetus of the nine socialist members in establishing free school meals, he recalled the deputation he had led to Acland on the issue in 1892. "Nineteen more years have gone by," he wrote, "and the utmost we have extracted from the reactionary capitalist-ridden House of Commons is a permissive Act, allowing the Municipalities to impose a halfpenny rate to go towards feeding necessitous children. In the overwhelming majority of cases, our precious Bumbles of the Municipalities have, of course, declined to adopt the measure at all."[2]

6. MEDICAL INSPECTION

In securing at least a measure of free school feeding the Labour movement had spoken with a united voice to some effect. But many realised that a great deal more was needed, chief among them Margaret McMillan, that pioneer in education, who understood the needs of the children so well. Not greatly interested in the demand for secondary education, or what she described as "the inevitable ladder from primary school to university", she insisted with all her force that "the bottom rungs are rotten"—8 per cent of children were deformed, 25 per cent anaemic, 10 per cent backward and dull, all this was a result of evil physical conditions.[3] "The greatest need of the age is to see to the proper health and proper development of all the bodily and mental faculties of the child," she told the I.L.P. conference in 1906, deploring the fact that the party had not a more constructive policy and calling both for medical inspection of school children and effective physical education. Margaret McMillan spoke with deep emotion, runs one report, "and her address was heard with the deepest silence and respect".[4]

---

[1] 9th Labour Party Conference Report, 1909, 77. The voting was 712,000 : 248,000.
[2] H. M. Hyndman, The Record of an Adventurous Life (1911), 301-3.
[3] Labour Leader, 18 May 1906. [4] Ibid., 20 April 1906.

The matter had already been taken up in the T.U.C. when, in 1905, Will Thorne won support for his resolution demanding free meals, free medical advice and inspection, and efficient physical training for all children. This resolution also requested that the Board of Education establish a statistical department to collate and publish statistics concerning the health and mortality of school children, and asked that the Parliamentary Committee incorporate these proposals in a Bill for the next session.[1] In accordance with this last proposal, the Bill comprising the whole T.U.C. educational policy which was drawn up for presentation to Parliament, included relevant clauses. As we have seen, it was intended "to Promote the Improvement of Education and the Physique" of children in elementary schools, and one clause required that local authorities record the height, weight and chest measurement of all children, and appoint school medical officers to examine and treat school children. Though the Bill was withdrawn, in the summer Birrell, as President of the Board, finally accepted the principle of medical inspection of school children.[2] This was eventually given effect in the Education (Administrative Provisions) Act of 1907, but not before there had been further agitation on this issue. The relevant section of the Act came into force on 1 January 1908.

The original proposals brought before the Commons were criticised as unsatisfactory in a manifesto issued by the National Union of Gasworkers and General Labourers, signed by Will Thorne, in the spring of 1907. Whereas the T.U.C. had asked for scientific physical education as well as medical inspection, the keeping of health records and skilled medical attention for all children requiring it, a much less comprehensive measure was being discussed. This should be amended, notably to ensure a properly staffed Medical Department at the Board of Education as well as payment of an adequate grant from the exchequer to cover the cost of inspection.[3]

Immediately after the issue of this manifesto there took place what *Justice* described as "a most remarkable meeting" at Canning Town,

---

[1] *38th T.U.C. Report*, 1905, 151. The Inter-Departmental Committee on Physical Deterioration had come out very strongly for "systematised medical inspection of children at school"; it was "emphatic in recommending" that this "should be imposed as a public duty on every school authority," a contribution to the cost being made out of the Parliamentary vote; *Report* (1904), Vol. I, 91. A further Inter-Departmental Committee (on Medical Inspection and Feeding of Children attending Public Elementary Schools), reporting in 1905, reinforced these findings.

[2] Cf. *Justice*, 21 July 1906, where Birrell's "forced acceptance" of this principle is referred to.

[3] *Justice*, 20 April 1907.

CARTOON BY WALTER CRANE FOR THE GASWORKERS' UNION'S
CELEBRATION OF CHILDREN'S SUNDAY

organised by the Gasworkers' Union. Called to consider medical inspection, it brought one of the "leading medical scientists of the day",
Sir Victor Horsley, F.R.S., "face to face with the West Ham proletariat". At the meeting, which opened with the singing of "England
Arise" and closed with the "Red Flag", Sir Victor declared his adhesion
to the educational policy of the T.U.C. and Labour Party, and made a
lucid statement on the medical needs of school children. According to
Thorne, Reginald McKenna, now President of the Board, had set his
face against individual medical inspection; he was, therefore, arranging
a similar meeting in McKenna's constituency, at which Horsley offered
to speak.[1]

The Act of 1907 did in fact set up a Medical Department in the
Board of Education, the first Chief Medical Officer being George
Newman, who issued a remarkable series of annual reports covering
every aspect of child health. It also provided for the medical inspection
of children twice during school life, on entering and leaving school.
In 1912 medical treatment was also permitted—to be made compulsory
in 1918.

Once again the passage of an Act was only the accomplishment of a
first stage; attention turned to getting it implemented and the provisions extended.[2] Bradford was the first to take advantage of one
clause to establish the first General School Clinic for treatment in the
country. By the close of 1908 there were three other general clinics
but one, in London, was connected with a single school. This last
owed its inception to Margaret McMillan, who had moved there
from Bradford in 1902. In 1910 Margaret McMillan opened her
pioneering clinic at Deptford which served a number of schools; this
was run by the "Independent Labour Party Committee for the Physical
Welfare of School Children", and not yet provided by the L.C.C.[3]

Systematic medical inspection now revealed most starkly the actual
physical condition of the mass of the children. "Millions of children

---

[1] *Justice*, 11 May 1907.

[2] The Act did include certain extended clauses, giving power to local authorities to
make certain arrangements for attending to the health and physical condition of school
children. These included (a) the employment of school nurses for treatment purposes,
(b) the provision of spectacles, (c) contribution to hospitals, (d) establishment of school
treatment clinics, (e) establishment of dental clinics.

[3] See Albert Mansbridge, *Margaret McMillan, Prophet and Pioneer* (1932), 73-86, where
the work of this clinic, together with its effect on the children, is described. At the 1909
conference of the I.L.P. Margaret McMillan moved a resolution pressing for the early
establishment of school clinics—this was agreed unanimously after considerable discussion and support. *17th I.L.P. Conference Report*, 1909, 81. Her pamphlet, *The School
Clinic Today*, was published in 1912 by the I.L.P.

WILL THORNE IN 1890

THE FIRST SCHOOL FEEDING, BRADFORD, 1907

are robbed of their earliest days of happiness, underfed, badly housed, without space to run or play, badly clothed and without medical oversight, sometimes till death is in sight," wrote Dr. Kerr, who had assisted Margaret McMillan at Bradford and moved to London to work for the School Board in 1902. "This is the lot of the majority of pre-school children all the time and of many school children most of the time."[1] A statement commented on in the *Social Democrat* in 1910 showed that the physical condition of London's 750,000 children was deplorable. There was a prevalence of dental, eye, ear, nose and throat troubles; no systematic dental examination was carried out, but probably more than 100,000 children were in need of immediate dental care, while 60,000 needed attention to their eyes. According to Dr. Kerr, 7,500 suffered from discharging ears while, in the previous year, 1,179,934 attendances were lost owing to ringworm. Hospital and dispensary treatment was inadequate and bad but Dr. Kerr's request for school clinics had been turned down by the Education Committee on the grounds of cost; despite expert advice the Committee preferred to arrange treatment in hospitals, thus incurring, incidentally, a strong protest from the British Medical Association. The article concluded with a call to socialists to take this matter up at the L.C.C. elections, and to bring the medical aspect to the fore on socialist platforms.[2]

The health of the school child continued to figure in resolutions and discussions at T.U.C. and Labour Party conferences. The Labour Party, stressing the need to establish school clinics and free treatment, asked as well for open air schools and school baths, the beneficial effect of which had been strikingly shown at Bradford and in London by Margaret McMillan and Dr. Kerr. In 1912, a resolution moved by Dan Irving at the S.D.F. conference included a long section on physical development.[3] While the machinery for medical inspection developed rapidly—over 900 medical officers were engaged in the school medical service by 1911 though not all were full-time—the provision of facilities for treatment in school clinics lagged; there were still only 30 by 1913 and only 16 dental clinics (by comparison with 70 treatment centres in London alone in 1930). Nevertheless the first important steps had been taken, steps to ensure that children in the schools should enjoy the physical health necessary to enable them to benefit from full-time education.

1 *The Fundamentals of School Health* (1926), 632, quoted in Mansbridge, *op. cit.*, 62. Kerr was now employed as Medical Officer to the L.C.C.
2 *Social Democrat*, Vol. xiv, No. 1, January 1910, 27-32.
3 *Justice*, 25 May 1912.

T

7. CHILD LABOUR AND THE RAISING OF THE LEAVING AGE

Little progress was made during these years in the matter of controlling child labour, a question vital to the effective raising of the leaving age both in terms of lengthening elementary schooling and extending secondary education. Whereas the Factory Acts had been the first to enforce a measure of education for children in the earlier years of the century, these subsequently operated to exclude children from the benefits of the 1870 Education Act. The position was amended by the Elementary Education Act of 1876 and especially that of 1880 which strengthened the provisions for compulsory attendance at school, overriding the Factory Acts by requiring that no child between the ages of ten and thirteen be employed without a certificate showing that he had passed through the minimum standards in school or put in a certain amount of attendance; but this only enforced a school leaving age of ten. The Cross Commission, reporting eight years later, recommended the raising of the leaving age to eleven but not until 1893 did another short Elementary Education (School Attendance) Act enforce this; one of the consequences was a drop in the number of children employed as half-timers.[1] In 1899 a private member's Bill which received official support amended the 1893 Act to raise the leaving age to twelve without exemption and a year later School Boards, as we have seen, were permitted to make by-laws raising the upper age of attendance in their area from thirteen to fourteen, but, by statute, all such by-laws had to contain some provision for either total or partial exemption below fourteen. The half-time system, therefore, remained embedded and between 1906 and 1907 the number of children so employed, which had fallen to a low level, nearly doubled.[2] Meanwhile an allied evil had come under investigation, the number of schoolchildren employed before and after school hours in a variety of occupations.

The effect of such employment was brought to general notice in 1901 by publication of the report of an Inter-Departmental Committee on the Employment of School Children, together with detailed

---

[1] The following figures, giving the number of half-timers, show the decline was slow but continuous over this period:

      1876   201,284
      1890   175,437 (52·46 per cent of whom were in Lancashire)
      1897   110,654 (54·27 per cent in Lancashire)

Graham Balfour, *The Educational Systems of England and Wales* (1898), 49.

[2] In 1906 the number of half-timers was 47,360, in 1907, 84,298. *42nd T.U.C. Report*, 1909, 91-2.

minutes of the evidence presented (published in 1902). This cited striking examples of the actual working hours of children employed, not only as half-timers, but also as street sellers, in shops, on milk delivery and other jobs, and calculated that 300,000 schoolchildren were so engaged. The outcome was the Employment of Children Act which came into force on 1 January 1904, to be described in the *Social Democrat* as a partial and tardy recognition of the duty the community owes to its citizens, a piecemeal restriction of child slavery.[1] The T.U.C. of that year called for rigid enforcement of the Act and for its extension so that children under fourteen "shall not be employed at any calling before and after school hours".[2]

Four years later the half-time system was made the subject of another official enquiry by a departmental committee appointed to consider the working of the Employment of Children Act. Its report, issued in July 1909, recommended total exemption from employment below thirteen. By this time the matter had been taken up again by the Labour movement though there was still opposition among textile workers. The S.D.F., however, had always fought this question and continued to do so. "What is the reality?" asked a factory worker in *Justice*. "Here in Lancashire, the infamous home of child labour, where parents live upon their children's earnings, thousands of children, tall, short, weak and strong, turn out of their beds from all kinds of homes to answer in person the call of the factory bell."[3] The T.U.C. congress of 1908, overcoming earlier divisions, expressed a strong and unanimous opinion that the time has "long since arrived for the total abolition of the 'half-timer'"; the system was "cruel and unjust to the children and future citizens, absolutely wasteful both morally and financially, and a standing blot upon our professed civilisation".[4] The following year the departmental committee's recommendation to abolish the system was welcomed and in 1910, noting that nothing had yet been done, the T.U.C. urged the government to introduce a Bill giving effect to this recommendation. "These little children going into work in the early hours of the morning is a survival of barbarism," said the mover of the resolution. "There is not a public man to-day who would dare to defend the half-time system." There were, however,

---

[1] The article describes the Act and the responsibilities of local authorities, *Social Democrat*, Vol. VIII, 1904, 3–4. In foregoing issues there had been discussion of the evidence presented to the Inter-departmental Committee; *ibid.*, Vol. VII, 1903, 465ff.

[2] *37th T.U.C. Report*, 1904, 119. For the effect of full and part-time employment of children below fourteen see Robert H. Sherard, *Child Slaves in Britain* (1904).

[3] *Justice*, 22 February 1908.   [4] *41st T.U.C. Report*, 1908, 183.

members of the textile unions still unprepared to see it go and in these years a minority vote was again registered.[1]

With the passing of the Parliament Act in the summer of 1911 the powers of the House of Lords were reduced and the way cleared for some measures of social reform. During the previous two years there had been a great wave of activity on the industrial front, the cotton workers, miners, railway and shipbuilding workers striking for union recognition and better wages and conditions. But it was before the passage of the Parliament Act, in May, that the government brought in a Bill to abolish the half-time system and raise the leaving age from twelve to thirteen; a Bill which also provided that after that age children should either remain at school to fourteen (or fifteen if the local authority so determined by by-law) or attend continuation classes until the age of sixteen. In the circumstances this measure, forecasting the later one of 1918, was withdrawn without discussion "owing to pressure of time";[2] it was not to be revived as attention turned to questions of unemployment and health insurance. The T.U.C. stood for a school leaving age of sixteen and at the 1911 congress H. H. Elvin moved a resolution expressing disappointment with the government Bill.[3] Later there was pressure for the introduction of another measure but, though a pledge had been made to proceed with a similar Bill, the government took no further step before the fatal summer of 1914.

8. THE GREAT UNREST AND EDUCATIONAL DEMANDS

"The past year has been one of fierce conflict between capital and labour," said Ben Turner, in a militant address from the Chair to the Labour Party conference of 1912. "The increased cost of living, the lack of wage improvement, the outward evidence of waste riches on the part of the capitalist class, and the keener poverty of the people,

[1] In 1909 Marsland, of the Cotton Spinners, reported that his union had held a ballot on raising the age of exemption to thirteen; of 185,000 who recorded a vote, 151,000 were opposed but he was trying to educate the membership on this matter. In 1911, Ben Turner, with other representatives of the textile unions, stressed that a reform movement was growing and in 1912 he seconded the resolution.

[2] *The Government's Record, 1906-13*, 73-4. The background to this Bill is given in *Final Report of the Departmental Committee on Juvenile Employment in relation to Employment after the War* (The Lewis Report, 1917), Vol. I, 4-6. Reports which dealt in detail with the question of child labour included the Majority and Minority Reports of the Poor Law Commission, the Report of the Consultative Committee on Continuation Schools and the Report of the Inter-departmental Committee on Partial Exemption from School Attendance, all of which were published in 1909.

[3] *44th T.U.C. Report*, 1911, 165.

made it impossible for the workers to remain quiet any longer." Scores of thousands had been out on strike, only prepared to return to work when agreements had been reached "that meant more wages, less hours, better regulations, and a greater share of the comforts of life. In town after town the same unrest evidenced itself." This had been met with the use of troops in 1910 and 1911 but the tide had not been stemmed. The workers were on the move.[1]

In subsequent years it was not only the more highly organised industrial workers who took action but some of the most backward sections, those in the Black Country, clay workers in Devon and Cornwall, unskilled operatives in the Yorkshire woollen industry, semi-skilled engineers in the midlands. The outcome was a great rise in union membership extending to clerical workers and women workers: the T.U.C. claimed affiliated bodies representing 2,300,000 workers in 1909, nearly 4,000,000 in 1914 when miners, railwaymen and dockers were organised in a powerful "triple alliance". By the summer of 1914, in the well-known assessment of the Webbs, British trade unionism was "working up for an almost revolutionary outburst of gigantic industrial disputes".[2]

Such struggles naturally sharpened class feeling and it is significant that in the same address Ben Turner characterised the educational system as one designed to provide elementary schools for the working class, secondary schools for the middle class "and Universities for rich people's sons". Despite a few scholarships the path from elementary school to university "is a thorny and narrow one". The urgent need was to remove barriers, to open up and free the road to education. At the Trades Union Congress Will Thorne, as President, once more stressed how much remained to be done to achieve equal opportunities for all.[3] It is said there is a class war in the economic and industrial field, wrote H. J. Lowe in the I.L.P. quarterly, *Socialist Review*, but there is also a class struggle, quite as bitter and far more insidious, in the educational field. Nowhere was equality of opportunity to be found, education was stratified into three grades, elementary, secondary and university, each the monopoly of a different class, while the public schools were also class schools. In secondary schools there was one teacher to every seventeen children, in elementary schools the ratio was 1 to 50; the Board insisted that the secondary school must have

---

[1] *12th Labour Party Conference Report*, 1912, 62.
[2] S. and B. Webb, *The History of Trade Unionism* (1920 edn.), 690.
[3] *45th T.U.C. Report*, 1912, 51.

four classrooms for every 100 children, none to be designed for over thirty children; no such mandate existed for elementary schools except that none should be planned for more than 50 to 60 pupils "except in special cases". The financial grants for each type of school differed enormously.[1]

It was at this time that the Labour movement began persistently to call for a Royal Commission to enquire into the misuse of educational endowments, especially those supporting the public schools and ancient universities. The first call for such a Commission had been made at the Trades Union Congress in 1909. It was well known, Will Thorne had then affirmed, that many endowments, left solely for the education of poor children, were being used for the education of children of the middle and upper classes—a full enquiry would be "a revelation of a startling character".[2] The proposition having been flatly rejected by the President of the Board of Education, the T.U.C. returned to the matter in 1910 and made out a detailed case. There were two good grounds for such an enquiry, first, the increasing cost of education "due mainly to the demand which organised labour is now making on behalf of the children", and second, "the increasing value and notoriously undemocratic administration of the wealthy university and public school endowments". A Royal Commission should enquire into the finances of universities and public schools and issue a report making clear the history and present value of endowments originally intended for the poor. It should also go into the conditions governing scholarships and other means of financial aid to scholars, the relations of these institutions with the schools, and into the whole question of the government of the ancient universities and public schools. The Commission should make recommendations to show "how these institutions may be brought under full public control".[3]

This was a direct attack at a key point, since the endowments of the public schools and ancient universities were the essential basis of their "independence". In moving this resolution, Thorne went out of

---

[1] *Socialist Review*, Vol. 9, No. 51, May 1912, 201-6. Grants to secondary schools were at the rate of £2 per capita for pupils of 10-12, £5 for pupils of 12-18; elementary school pupils rated 13s. 4d. per capita when under 5, 21s. 4d. when aged 5-15, though in particular circumstances they could rise to a maximum of £2.

[2] *42nd T.U.C. Report*, 1909, 194. The point had been canvassed in the preceding years, in the press and at large, and in July 1907 Bishop Gore had called in the House of Lords for a Royal Commission to enquire into the endowments, government and teaching of the universities of Oxford and Cambridge and their constituent colleges.

[3] *43rd T.U.C. Report*, 1910, 173-4.

his way to stress that he did so "as a revolutionary, class conscious Trade Unionist and Social Democrat". The President of the Board had rejected the proposal, saying "it was rather a tall order and he could not see his way to grant it". What he was really saying, declared Thorne, was that "his own class would be involved in the charge of receiving education from the grants for endowments originally left to the poor of the country". The annual value of these amounted to several millions a year,[1] this was not private income but a public responsibility. It is interesting to note that the argument is similar to that advanced by Gladstone and others in the 1850s and '60s when the concern had been to turn these endowments to the use of education for the middle class.[2]

Both the T.U.C. and the Labour Party continued to press this demand in subsequent years, the latter insisting particularly on investigation of the finances of Oxford and Cambridge. In 1913 the Labour Party appointed a deputation to bring this request before the Prime Minister. There was another blank refusal to parley; Asquith would not even receive the deputation.[3] On this issue nothing was to be conceded.

As the nation moved towards the catastrophe of the First World War, the class issues in education were being more sharply raised than ever before. At its annual conference in the spring of 1914 the Labour Party accepted an overall programme of educational advance but the T.U.C. still had the clearer and more decisive approach. The previous year it had instructed its Parliamentary Committee to conduct an organised campaign for educational advance in the industrial centres, where other active battles were now under way. In the circumstances of the time the Labour movement was beginning to see, almost as clearly as the Chartist movement had once done, the link between education and political and economic emancipation.

[1] A detailed return made to the House of Commons by the Charity Commissioners in 1892 showed that educational endowments in England available for secondary education alone amounted to £697,132 per annum exclusive of "property of an incalculable value in the form of sites and buildings for schools". An official investigation in 1876 had found a total gross income for all charities of £2,198,464, which greatly increased during the remainder of the century as a result of a rise in the value of land, particularly in the cities. G. Balfour, *The Educational System of England and Wales*, 162, 164.

[2] B. Simon, *Studies in the History of Education, 1780-1870*, 305.

[3] *13th Labour Party Conference Report*, 1913, 39; *14th Labour Party Conference Report*, 1914, 42.

CHAPTER IX

DEVELOPMENTS AND CONFLICTS IN ADULT
EDUCATION, 1900-1920

THE new interests of the organised Labour movement, and the aspirations of socialists within it, became manifest in the field of adult education after the Liberal landslide and Labour successes of January 1906. If there were some who hoped to educate the new generation of Labour leaders to continue to throw their weight behind the Liberal party and the cause of gradual social reform, there were many in the Labour movement who now began to see matters from quite another point of view. Rather than win some slight improvements within the existing social structure, these now looked to a fundamental transformation through the introduction of socialism; in their view the great need was to educate men to understand the necessity for social change and the means to bring it about. In these circumstances there evolved two quite different concepts of the function of adult education, and the resulting conflict became a motive force in the development of new educational activities during the second decade of the century, activities that continued during the war years.

These new developments arose in the context of the wider educational movement (described in chapters one and two) which comprised activities organised by the working class, in which socialist groups were particularly prominent, and those organised for the working class by other institutions and individuals. After 1900, these two approaches were to some extent brought together in the work of a new body, the Workers' Educational Association, which quickly came to the fore, to be challenged in due course by another organisation concerned to promote education exclusively under working-class control—the Labour College movement. There developed, then, two trends in the movement for adult education.

1. THE SEARCH FOR KNOWLEDGE AND MARXIST STUDIES

Socialist ideas were already making a strong appeal among the young in particular at the turn of the century. In 1903 a Labour

Representation Committee was formed in Sheffield whose leading figures contrasted strongly with the "Lib-Lab leaders" of the Trades Council, "elderly men who never succeeded in shedding their Victorian solidity and respectability". These were "a vigorous group of young men, many of them still in their twenties, full of fighting spirit, developing an amazing range of activities and interests, delighting in discovering new horizons in themselves and in the working men they led, avid for action and change, experimenting with new ideas, forming and breaking friendships with bewildering rapidity, and, for their recreation, following their new secretary . . . and his Clarion Ramblers into the Derbyshire hills on their free Sundays."[1] These young men, in Sheffield and elsewhere, were new candidates for educational classes and study groups, purchasers of journals and such books as were to be had bearing on the political and social problems of the time.

The Labour press greatly expanded at this time, the three main national journals—*Labour Leader*, *Justice* and *Clarion*—being supplemented by a wide variety of regional papers and local sheets.[2] But books were also increasingly sought after, and the most advanced workers now explored current philosophical, economic and political literature much more broadly than was possible in the past. In 1902 the Rationalist Press Association launched a series of 6d. reprints in large editions, making such works as *The Origin of the Species*, the polemics of Huxley and Tyndall, Haeckel's *Riddle of the Universe* available to a wide readership; these gave an impetus to the secularist movement which was receiving renewed popular support. To a large pamphlet literature published by the socialist movement—the writings of William Morris and Blatchford, such books as Bellamy's *Looking Backward*—there were now added translations of some of the works of Marx and Engels, of Bebel and Lafargue, Bernstein and Plekhanov; many of these, made available by the socialist publishing house in Chicago, Kerr and Co., were widely circulated in Britain.[3]

Socialist groups, active in many places, were particularly lively in Scotland at this period, carrying the "new gospel" of socialism and

1 S. Pollard, *et. al.*, *Sheffield Trades and Labour Council, 1858-1958* (1958), 53.
2 For a survey of the Labour press at this time, T. A. Jackson, *Solo Trumpet* (1953), 62-3.
3 The works available are listed by Jackson, *op. cit.*, 59-60, 67, see also T. Bell, *Pioneering Days* (1941), 260. They included the *Communist Manifesto*, *Wage Labour and Capital*, *Poverty of Philosophy* and the first volume of *Capital* by Marx, *Socialism, Utopian and Scientific* by Engels, *Woman* by Bebel, *Evolution of Private Property* by Lafargue, essays and speeches by Plekhanov, Bernstein, Vandervelde, Guesde. Engels' *The Condition of the Working Class in England in 1844* was also available. Kerr & Co. contributed Lewis H. Morgan, *Ancient Society*, Engels, *The Origin of the Family* and Feuerbach, Marx, *Critique of Political Economy* and other pamphlets.

literature of all kinds to the mining villages of Lanarkshire, Ayrshire, Fife, and the Lothians. "The sale of pamphlets and books, socialist, labour, rationalist, and scientific, was enormous," writes Tom Bell in his biography of John Maclean, one of the key figures in Scotland. "The adherents of the respective groups read, studied and discussed things with a seriousness that caused some heart-burnings to the custodians in those days of the bourgeois order. Victimisation and blacklisting became all too frequent; but only spread the movement to new and hitherto untouched places. It was a period of confidence, of high optimism and enthusiastic conviction on the part of the militants in the certainty of victory, and of a new socialist society."[1]

In these circumstances the reading and study undertaken by individual workers equalled in extent the earlier efforts at self-education of a Francis Place or a Thomas Cooper. Many must have experienced the same intellectual excitement as Arthur McManus and Tom Bell: "We had dabbled in the dialectical philosophy of Josef Dietzgen, in Bergson's philosophy, and Sorel's application of Bergson to Syndicalism, and the deification of intuition as opposed to reason. Nietsche, Bernard Shaw, Ibsen, Hauptmann and Strindberg added their weight to our intellectual challenge to all existing social standards and conventionalities. We read feverishly, discussed fiercely, and walked the streets, often after midnight, in an effort to sort out for ourselves the problem of man and the universe. We experimented psychologically on everything and everybody and eagerly watched for the results."[2]

The socialist movement was now producing its own tutors to guide studies and organise classes or study groups of the kind fostered by Tom Mann and others from the 1890s. Those run by the S.D.F. concentrated on Marxist works. "It was our practice . . . to form classes for the study of Marx's economics," writes T. A. Jackson who joined the S.D.F. in 1900 and was later to play a leading part in Marxist education. As a young man of twenty-one, employed as a compositor, he attended a class on *Capital* taken by "very nearly the best-read man I have ever met"; this was Jack Fitzgerald, an Irishman settled in London, one of those who had moved from secularism to socialism as a direct outcome of the famous Hyndman-Bradlaugh debate.[3] It was, however, Scotland, Glasgow in particular, that was the main centre of Marxist education. Here, where there was a tradition of independent working-class study, classes run by branches of the S.D.F.

---

[1] T. Bell, *John Maclean* (1944), 8.   [2] T. Bell, *Pioneering Days*, 97.
[3] Jackson, *op. cit.*, 60.

were often attended by all members. Among tutors who developed what has been described as a "network of study circles" was the stone-breaker, William Nairne—described as "the founder and pioneer of the S.D.F. in Scotland"—up to his death in 1901; others were John F. Armour, a stonemason, and George Yates, an engineer, employed by Glasgow University as a technician in the science laboratories.[1]

It was Yates's economics class that the young Tom Bell joined in the winter of 1902, to be led "direct to the sources of the knowledge I desired. He put into my hands the basic theoretical works of Marxism and the writings of the great masters of science and general literature." Here was a tutor who could read and speak French and German and was well versed in "economics, history, philosophy, logic, literature".[2] The texts he used in his class that winter included Marx's *Wage Labour and Capital*, and *Value, Price and Profit*, the first nine chapters of *Capital*, Thorold Rogers's *Six Centuries of Work and Wages* (which had reached a sixth edition by 1901), J. L. Green's *A Short History of the English People;* he also gave readings from Shakespeare and lessons in English grammar and logic. Each class lasted for two and a half hours, including discussion, and guidance was given for reading at home to be examined at the next class.[3]

A considerable impetus was given to this educational work when the Socialist Labour Party came into being in 1903, formed by members of the S.D.F. who differed with Hyndman on questions of strategy and sought a more militant policy. The S.D.F. itself had withdrawn from the Labour Representation Committee in 1901 after the failure of a resolution calling for clear socialist aims; the S.L.P. was, perhaps, more sectarian in some respects, but at the same time particularly concerned to study and propagate Marxism in a more concentrated way than in the past.[4] According to T. A. Jackson, who was closely involved, "the whole movement of Independent Working-Class Education was a by-product of our *Impossibilist* revolt against Hyndman, and our drive for a more firmly based as well as a more militant Marxism". He

---

1 T. Bell, *John Maclean* 10, 128; For Nairne see H. W. Lee and E. Archbold, *Social Democracy in Britain*, 140.

2 Yates was a delegate to congresses of the second International; he came into promin-ence in 1900 when he opposed Hyndman and Kautsky on the question of socialist partici-pation in bourgeois governments; Bell, *Pioneering Days*, 36-7.

3 *Ibid.*, 38-9.

4 The breakaway took place when Yates and others, expelled from the S.D.F. at the annual conference in 1903, immediately formed the Glasgow Socialist Society, to estab-lish the Socialist Labour Party in August with James Connolly as national organiser and Neil Maclean as secretary; Bell, *Pioneering Days*, 40. A number of S.D.F. branches in Scotland went over to the new party.

adds: "We 'impossibilists' ran our own study classes religiously as part of the process of giving ourselves and others a more extended, as well as a more profound, grasp of Marxist theory."[1]

The tradition of regular economics classes continued, therefore, in Glasgow under the auspices both of the newly formed S.L.P. and the S.D.F. in the intervals of active political work. The campaign run during the municipal elections of 1904 once over, writes Tom Bell who joined the S.L.P., "we began our winter sessions of Economics classes, which we maintained with unfailing regularity until 1920". These S.L.P. classes, he adds, "apart from the economic and social conditions, played an important part in gaining the Clydeside the reputation for being 'Red'. Every year produced new worker-tutors. Classes sprang up in a number of ship-yards and engineering shops. In the great majority of these classes the tutors had come through the S.L.P. parent groups."[2] Similar study classes were held and tutors trained at Edinburgh, Leith, Falkirk, Kirkcaldy and Aberdeen in Scotland, and farther afield at Manchester, Newcastle, Reading and London.

The method used in the "parent groups" involved intensive study and it is this aspect of the work that, in Bell's words, "produced a crop of competent class tutors, who led classes inside the factories". As he outlines it, the procedure bears a remarkable resemblance to that used in the classes organised by the Corresponding Societies in the 1790s, the first organised study groups of workers described by Francis Place.[3] Each session opened with a preliminary survey of the ground to be traversed and the textbooks to be used. The class then studied "a series of definitions of terms used by Marx", which were thoroughly discussed during the first four meetings and moved on to *Wage Labour and Capital*, which the students studied at home. In class, writes Bell, "we would read it over paragraph by paragraph, round the class. This practice aimed at helping the students to speak fluently and grammatically. At the following class meeting questions would be put and answered, and the points raised thoroughly understood by everyone, the results of each lesson being summarised by the leader." Students, therefore, learned to express themselves clearly, as well as

---

[1] Jackson, *op. cit.*, 145. Bell also says that Marxist education was carried on "with greater intensity in the Socialist Labour Party after the split in 1903". *John Maclean*, 128.

[2] Among the most outstanding of these worker-tutors, according to Bell, were William Paul, T. Clark, J. W. Muir, J. McClure, Arthur McManus, John Wilson and John McBain. *Ibid.*

[3] B. Simon, *Studies in the History of Education, 1780-1870*, 180-3.

grasping the content of the book studied. Later the class turned to industrial history, using the same method and as textbooks, H. de B. Gibbins' *Industry in England*, Buckle's *History of Civilisation* and Marx's *Capital*, afterwards going on to historical materialism and formal logic. As a result, writes Bell, every worker who went through the whole session of six months "came out a potential tutor for other classes".[1]

This kind of activity was as revolutionary in its implications as had been that of the Corresponding Societies in an earlier age. The works of Marx, used as textbooks, advanced the proposition that it is the historic role of the working class to "expropriate the expropriators", to put an end to the capitalist system and introduce socialism. Marxist economics was concerned with explaining the nature of the exploitation of labour at one pole as the source of profits at the other. At a time when there was conspicuous waste in high society many workers still experienced conditions approximating to those described in detail in *Capital*, which also set out to explain how this situation had come about and the forces that made for change. This was scientific, as opposed to utopian, socialism, as Engels argued, giving due weight to the contribution the English working class had made in demonstrating the power of organised struggle since the days of the Chartists. Such an approach, which appeared to meet the actual experience of the working class and show the way to socialism, made intrinsically difficult subjects of absorbing interest and the effort to master them worth while.

"We seized every occasion for discussion," writes Tom Bell who, in 1904, was working in a Glasgow foundry. "During meal hours we would sit in a group and argue. After the cast, when we had run about with ladles of boiling metal till we were bathed in perspiration, it was a union rule to take a rest of fifteen minutes to cool down. Then we would collect together, and if we cooled our bodies we didn't cool our ardour, for we pitched into one another in fine style. By dint of perseverance in discussion, and by means of pamphlets and books I won over a goodly number to my side. Workers would come to my house to get references for points raised in our discussions. Soon I was able to suggest we start a study circle. This we did, and a study circle was formed on Marxism and Industrial History."[2] This kind of activity in factory, foundry and pit, laid a firm foundation for the network of study circles, promoting on the ground floor study by workers and

---

[1] T. Bell, *Pioneering Days*, 57.   [2] *Ibid.*, 63.

led by workers in close relation to current activities in the industrial and political field.

The S.D.F. contribution of this time is well summed up in the work of one of its most active supporters, John Maclean, a school teacher who had graduated at Glasgow University. Maclean joined the S.D.F. in 1905 and was soon involved in acting as a tutor in Glasgow; an ardent co-operator, he also made use of the opportunities offered by the Education Department of the Co-operative Societies, so carrying the socialist message to wider circles. During the long summer vacations he devoted much time and energy to political and educational activities and by 1907-8 was taking Marxist classes well outside Glasgow, in Gourock, Falkirk, Pollokshaws. His methods differed from those of the S.L.P. tutors, consisting more usually of lectures rather than intensive study by the class, but his popularisation and exposition of Marxism by this means began at this time to make a considerable impact, as he himself was later to do in the wider field of politics.[1]

In the early 1900s, therefore, Marxism was beginning to make a serious impact in the working-class movement, providing a new alternative to the generalised appeal of such socialist works as Blatchford's *Merrie England* and *Britain for the British*. But while the S.D.F. and the S.L.P. drew on Marx, leaders of the I.L.P. were drawing primarily on the works of continental social democrats such as Bernstein, Vandervelde and Jaurès whose efforts were directed at the revision of Marxism and the development of reformist politics. In 1905, J. R. Macdonald, who dismissed Marxism as being out of date, published his *Socialism and Society* as one of a library of books ("The Socialist Library") under the editorship of himself and Philip Snowden. Here he drew on Darwinian ideas of evolution to advance the conception of a gradual development of society from a lower to a higher stage, free of revolutionary breaks. This series of books, in Tom Bell's view, was prepared to arm members of the I.L.P. with ideas that would provide an antidote to Marxism, as taught in the economics classes, since these "were having a disturbing influence on the I.L.P."[2] This conflict of ideas acted as a further stimulus to reading and discussion.

These activities of the still small though well organised political

---

[1] Bell, *John Maclean*, 10, 131. Examples of his very lively teaching methods are given in *ibid.*, 128-9. "Maclean's method had the merit of popularising economic study amongst large numbers of the workers, but had the defect of becoming a propaganda lecture. The S.L.P. method was more intensive and produced a crop of competent class tutors, who led classes inside the factories." No such tutors emerged from Maclean's classes except later from the Scottish Labour College; Bell, *Pioneering Days*, 56.

[2] Bell, *Pioneering Days*, 81-2.

groups in the socialist movement—primarily of the Marxist groups since there is little evidence of organised systematic study in the I.L.P.—must be seen in the framework of the much wider cultural and educational activities described earlier. This was the period when the Clarion movement reached its highest development, while the social and cultural activities of the co-operative movement were now taking on a broader aspect. Linked to these was the Labour Church movement, primarily educative and social, and, perhaps of particular significance, the Socialist Sunday Schools, which now formed a national organisation. All these went to make up a whole complex of institutions reflecting the outlook and aspirations of the working class and under their own control. But it was the socialist groups that made the greatest impact in terms of organising classes for sustained study, and introduced a new factor into the situation by concentrating study mainly on Marxist works.

2. UNIVERSITY EXTENSION AND THE WORKERS' EDUCATIONAL ASSOCIATION

There were other indications at the turn of the century of a new, even passionate, interest in education. One of the most striking was the sudden revival and spread of the Adult School movement, which took even those engaged in it by surprise. Here the midlands, and especially Leicestershire, was the spearhead. The year 1899, wrote a participant, "saw the flood-tide of extension break in the county". The first school to feel the effect was that at Mountsorrel, an industrial village outside Leicester; within six months it had outgrown two different buildings. "Early in February," Gilbert continues, "a school was opened at Market Harborough, an entirely new side of the county as far as Adult School work was concerned. Driving home after the initial meeting, one of the committee remarked: 'January, Mountsorrel; February, Market Harborough; why not a school for March?' 'Why not a school for every month of the year?' was the rejoinder, and thus the slogan 'a school a month'—which ran through the movement from end to end—was born." By the close of the year, sixteen new schools had been opened in Leicestershire and the following year the movement spread well beyond the midlands: "In the autumn of 1900 Tyneside was the scene of much enthusiastic extension. Schools were opened in rapid succession in all the townships along the river."[1]

[1] G. Currie Martin, The Adult School Movement (1924), 158-63.

In response to a new demand Adult Schools now greatly extended their scope to provide, in place of the elementary teaching of an earlier age, a much broader education covering historical, political, literary as well as religious topics. This phenomenal development doubled the number of students to a peak of over 100,000 organised in nearly 2,000 schools by 1909-10.[1]

By contrast the University Extension work which, as we have seen, failed to attract significant working-class support in the 1880s and '90s, was making little headway. Nevertheless it was the link established by this work between university men and working-class audiences— in which such men as Michael Sadler and Hudson Shaw were engaged —and the similar link through the Settlement movement led by Canon Barnett that formed a new growing point for adult education. Its leaders and active workers among the middle and professional classes were, then, educationists, conscious of the social problem, seeking a means to social harmony, motivated sometimes by a sense of guilt and by sympathy with the aspirations of labour. All shared a liberal-humanist outlook: education was good for its own sake, the workers deserved all that the university could offer in the form of extra-mural teaching; education would spiritualise their lives. This implied a desire to provide a broad, humane, comprehensive, above all, an impartial education, one rising above, and so enabling students to rise above the ephemeral and material struggles of the time: "The appeal of the hour to trade unionists and co-operators is that they make political strokes, promote Bills, register protests, and send deputations to responsible ministers," wrote Albert Mansbridge, in 1903. "The true appeal is that they lift themselves up through higher knowledge to higher works and higher pleasures, which, if responded to, will inevitably bring about right and sound action upon municipal, national, and imperial affairs; action brought about without conscious effort—the only effectual action."[2] This, in essence, was the outlook of the new organisation that came into being at this time, the Workers' Educational Association.

The outlook described seems at first sight entirely opposed to the socialist approach outlined earlier, but the two groups concerned had more in common than might appear on the surface. Both rejected the idea of education as a means of "getting on" in life, of material advancement. Both held that the educated worker should not separate himself

[1] T. Kelly, *A History of Adult Education in Great Britain* (1962), 260.
[2] A. Mansbridge, *The Kingdom of the Mind* (1944), 2.

from his class; he should remain with and of it so that through his influence the working class as a whole might profit. On the other hand one group saw education as a means towards transforming society, the other wished to direct it to transforming the individual. There was here a fundamental divergence of purpose, even though leaders of the W.E.A. showed sympathy with the active working-class struggle.[1]

Albert Mansbridge was a young co-operator with Christian socialist tendencies, enthusiastic for education, who had attended University Extension classes at Toynbee Hall and elsewhere. The co-operative movement, which sponsored a wide range of educational activities, acted as a base for the establishment of extension classes. Unlike the trade unions it was, of course, open to all classes and some extension lecturers and organisers were themselves co-operators and attended the annual Congresses. It was at the 1898 congress that J. A. R. Marriott, who had succeeded Michael Sadler as Secretary of the Oxford Extension Delegacy, and Hudson Shaw, one of the leading tutors, first met Mansbridge who took the opportunity of advocating a new development of extension work in the movement to further the study of history and citizenship. University teachers, from Oxford in particular, had for some time been concerned about the state of University Extension classes and were themselves seeking a way to establish new relations with working-class organisations. Mansbridge was invited to develop his theme at a conference organised at Oxford in 1899 during the University Extension summer meeting, a conference which served to air the matter and arouse further interest. It was raised again at the co-operative conference in 1900 when one of the Extension organisers present offered increased assistance in co-operative educational activities. "You have gone a long way to find a solution of one of the most difficult of all social problems—the relation of capital and labour," he said, but with the help of extension lecturers more could be done; these were men carefully trained in various schools of thought, for "in a university you are comparatively free from political influences".[2]

The idea matured during succeeding years, and, in January 1903,

---

[1] Thus in 1910, at a time of growing labour unrest, Bishop Gore declared at the Annual Meeting of the W.E.A.: "All this passion for justice will accomplish nothing, believe me, unless you get knowledge. You may become strong and clamorous, you may win a victory, you may effect a revolution, but you will be trodden down again under the feet of knowledge unless you get it for yourselves; even if you win that victory, you will be trodden down again under the feet of knowledge if you leave knowledge in the hands of privilege, because knowledge will always win over ignorance." H. P. Smith, *Labour and Learning* (1956), 59.

[2] *32nd Co-operative Congress Report*, 1900, 17.

there appeared the first of three articles by Mansbridge in the official University Extension journal. These developed the ideas he had put forward previously. In the meantime Mansbridge, who had already formed a Christian Economic Society with a group of like-minded workmen, went on to launch his "Association to Promote the Higher Education of Working Men" with the support of representatives of the Labour movement and adult clubs and societies. From this moment events moved fast. In July a provisional committee constituted on these lines, which included two members of the T.U.C. Parliamentary Committee, met at Toynbee Hall. In August the new association, formed "to construct a working alliance between university extension and the working-class movement", took part in the annual summer meeting of the University Extension Delegacy, at a special conference presided over by the Bishop of Hereford and the Dean of Durham and attended by members of both universities and by manual workers and clerks.

Mansbridge, of course, already had an entry at Oxford through his acquaintance with Marriott, Hudson Shaw and others. Perhaps even more important, however, was his friendship with Bishop Gore whom he had sought out as a young man and whose outlook greatly influenced him. It was probably the latter who helped Mansbridge to gain further support from the Church, so enabling him to launch his new association at the Oxford conference under the auspices of leading churchmen.

There were many at Oxford who saw in this new association a means to cement new relations between classes, much as settlements had earlier set out to do, and their support greatly contributed to the success of the Workers' Educational Association, as it soon came to be called. According to Mansbridge none did more to help the movement in its first stages than Sir William Anson, Warden of All Souls, Parliamentary Secretary to the Board of Education in the Balfour administration and a close ally of Morant. "This keen little man," wrote Mansbridge later, "conservative to the finger tips, was ever ready to welcome working-class students to Oxford. Under his influence, All Souls took at the outset a real and unflagging share in the work. The dignified fellows of an earlier day would have rubbed their eyes in disapproving astonishment at the sight of a Warden, near to midnight, keeping time to 'Auld Lang Syne' with hands clasping those of the burly trade unionists on either side of him." The W.E.A., claimed Mansbridge later, referring to Anson's assistance, "has united in one body, without conscious difference, men of all experiences—

the peer's son rejoices in the fellowship of the miner's son, and the casual labourer in the friendship of the don. . . . Education unites and does not divide."[1]

This mixture of social classes was, perhaps, one of the most striking features of the early Oxford meetings of the W.E.A., Mansbridge himself acting as the catalyst. "Perhaps the most interesting gathering of all," wrote an Oxford don of this time, "was that which met at Mr. Mansbridge's lodgings at Wellington Square on the evening of the conference. The bishop and a number of workmen were staying in the house, and they were joined by one friend after another who dropped in for a talk. Most branches of education were represented: Whitehall (which sat on the window-sill), Cambridge, in the person of a fellow of Trinity, the Oxford professoriate, and the elementary teacher; there was capital in the shape of a London banker, and there was labour galore (in both sexes)."[2]

Mansbridge held the view that higher education for the working class should be concerned fundamentally with their spiritual development and not with immediate political or practical issues, that its function, in fact, was precisely to raise the workers from material considerations; these would right themselves in the end, he thought, although in his published writings he tends to use large and general phrases which left the actual process of change vague. Education, he wrote, in his University Extension articles (1903)—or rather "deep draughts of knowledge"—will "divert the strong movements of the people from the narrow paths of immediate interests to the broad way of that rightly ordered social life of which only glimpses have yet been seen even by the greatest of the world's seers".[3] The working class, he claimed, was the only class which did not subordinate education to "materialistic ends". "There are miners and factory hands in the north who don't care tuppence about increasing their wages or living in bigger houses or wearing finer clothes, but who can discuss Greek history with men like Alfred Zimmern, Greek poetry with men like Gilbert Murray, and Greek philosophy with men like W. H. Hadow."[4]

This evangelical humanism, as it has been called, together with Mansbridge's evident success in winning support, commended itself to Oxford. This association "in which the initiative has been taken by the working men themselves," reported the University Extension

[1] Quoted in Smith, *Labour and Learning*, 45. [2] *Ibid.*, 68.
[3] Mansbridge, *The Kingdom of the Mind*, 6. [4] Smith, *op. cit.*, 15.

Delegacy, outlining the 1903 conference, ". . . contains the promise of much usefulness in the future, and . . . it may do much to rally the working classes to the further support of an educational movement which, largely initiated for their benefit, has already won a large measure of their confidence."[1]

From this moment the work of the W.E.A. began to branch out, the seal of Oxford and Church approval helping considerably. In 1904 the first local branch was established, that at Reading based on former educational activity, which received the full support of the Principal of the University College and the local Director of Education.[2] In 1904 and again in 1905 the Association organised conferences at Oxford during the Summer Extension meeting. The 1905 conference was, in effect, the first national conference of the W.E.A., the name being changed shortly after. Presided over by the Dean of Christ Church, and with nearly 1,000 present, it was this conference that formulated the demand for compulsory attendance at evening (or continuation) school. This was followed by what Mansbridge claimed as the first working-class deputation to the Board of Education (led by Will Crooks) to press the demand.[3] It was on this occasion, incidentally, that William Temple, later Archbishop of Canterbury, looking in on the conference, made his first acquaintance with the W.E.A., of which he became a leading member and the first President.

The next two annual conferences took the work further, indeed laid the basis for the whole future development of the W.E.A. That of 1907, on the topic "What Oxford can do for Working People", was presided over by Bishop Gore and attended by 400 delegates. Among these was Morant of the Board of Education. From this conference, which took place shortly after Bishop Gore had raised the demand for a Royal Commission on Oxford and Cambridge in the House of Lords, came the initiative in setting up a committee of fourteen—seven representatives of the Labour movement nominated by the W.E.A., and seven university representatives—"to devise a scheme whereby the University may be brought into closer contact

[1] Smith, op. cit., 66-7.
[2] M. Stocks, The Workers' Educational Association (1953), 30-1; Smith, op. cit., 42, where it is said that the local S.D.F. branch co-operated in establishing the W.E.A. branch.
[3] This proposal arose partially from the co-operative movement's experience of running such schools in the 1890s. The Consultative Committee of the Board of Education reported on the question of attendance ("compulsory or otherwise") in 1909. See Mansbridge, An Adventure in Working-class Education (1920), 16-17; and his article "Working Men and Continuation Schools" in M. Sadler, Continuation Schools in England and Elsewhere (1907).

with the working classes of the country".[1] It was at this conference also that Morant, who had developed close relations with Mansbridge, promised official support for the developing alliance between the university and the W.E.A. "The Board of Education," he announced, "is looking for guidance from such an association as is represented here today, to show us the way in which adult education can best be furthered. In particular we believe it is to small classes, and solid, earnest work that we can give increasingly of the golden stream."[2]

With the approval and support of church and state, of Oxford dons and leaders of the Labour movement, the W.E.A. was well and truly launched. Its annual meetings, held in industrial cities, were now impressive occasions. That held in 1911 at Manchester, attended by "leaders in all departments of the life of the city" and representatives of 120 labour organisations, drew an audience of 3,000 who, in Mansbridge's words, "evinced such enthusiasm for education as to give the meeting all the qualities of a spiritual revival".[3] At Sheffield two years earlier, 3,000 were present half an hour before the meeting was due to start, an overflow hall was filled and many turned away; representatives from eighty societies were present while the main speakers included the Archbishop of York, Arthur Henderson and Margaret McMillan.

In the meantime further developments were taking place on a local level up and down the country—new branches and area, or district, committees coming into being; the Midlands district, for instance, was inaugurated in October 1905 at a meeting of "intense fervour" attended by 600 delegates and 400 visitors.[4] But it was at Rochdale in Lancashire, and at Longton in Staffordshire, that "solid earnest work" first developed.

Rochdale, with its radical co-operative tradition, had for many years been the centre of various forms of educational activity. Here Hudson Shaw could attract large audiences of working men to his Extension lectures, particularly those on John Ruskin. It was here that one of the

---

[1] Smith, *op. cit.*, 24, Mansbridge, *op. cit.*, 38. During the discussion on this question, J. M. MacTavish, a shipwright from Portsmouth (later to be General Secretary of the W.E.A.), made his famous speech insisting that Oxford could do nothing for the working class unless it opened its doors widely to the people, transformed the content of its education—especially in history and economics—and inspired its students "not with the idea of getting on, but with the idea of social service". This militant speech "stole the thunder of the left". It is printed in full in A. Mansbridge, *University Tutorial Classes* (1913), 194-7.

[2] *Ibid.*, 46. See *Report of the Board of Education*, 1906-7, 91-2, for this development. Mansbridge was made a member of the Consultative Committee in 1907, an "exceptional event". *Ibid.*

[3] Mansbridge, *An Adventure in Working-class Education*, 58.   [4] *Ibid.*, 17-18.

first branches of the W.E.A. was formed, called the Rochdale Educational Guild, which rapidly organised a variety of educational and social activities.[1] The workers' desire for more intensive study than was possible on the Extension lecture pattern was manifest. "After long reflection," writes Mansbridge, "I came to the conclusion that the best thing to do would be to ask Rochdale to get thirty students to pledge themselves to make every attendance for two years and to write regular essays. If they would do this we would get the best tutor in England." The Rochdale students did pledge themselves in this way, and R. H. Tawney, at that time lecturing in Economics at Glasgow, agreed to become tutor. "In this way," writes Mansbridge, "a pioneer experiment was initiated, of far reaching consequence for the education of the workers."[2]

Before the Rochdale class started a similar one was organised at Longton, an area which also had a long tradition of working-class educational activity, and, too, a particular connection with Oxford. Tawney undertook to tutor this class as well, beginning work in January 1908.[3] Such was the beginning of what might be called intensive educational work by the W.E.A. These tutorial classes demanded a high standard of work by the students, in reading, the writing of essays, and in attendance. Approximately half of each two hour weekly session was set aside for discussion. The tutorial classes represented the new educational form that had been sought, one closely linking the universities to working-class organisations and meeting an expressed need.

After the 1907 Summer Extension Conference at Oxford, where the demand for such classes had crystallised among W.E.A. delegates, an Oxford Tutorial Classes Committee was set up to develop this new approach with Temple acting as secretary for the university and Mansbridge for the W.E.A. Various Oxford colleges were approached with some success for financial aid, and in a short time, eight tutorial classes were in existence. The personnel of these classes, wrote Temple in the committee's first annual report, "may be said to be recruited almost entirely from the younger and more energetic members of the manual working classes, who are keenly alive to civic questions and desire to improve their knowledge of them by impartial study".[4]

[1] For the first year's work of the Guild see *ibid.*, 36-8; see also Smith, *op. cit.*, 70.
[2] Mansbridge, *op. cit.*, 37.
[3] Smith, *op. cit.*, 70. The Longton class met on Friday evenings, the Rochdale class on Saturday; the former was, therefore, the first actually to start.
[4] *Ibid.*, 25, 71-2.

This was the means, then, by which the growing demand of the Labour movement for an extension of university facilities was immediately met. The W.E.A. classes proved a popular way of providing education, of a high standard and in the liberal tradition, for the working class, even if they did not involve any transformation of the ancient universities themselves. The "impartial" study of historical and economic questions so fostered was something very different from the Marxist studies promoted by socialist groups which had inherited the earlier Socialist League slogan: educate—agitate—organise. Nevertheless there was one institution at Oxford in which these two conceptions of education for the workers came dramatically into conflict.

3. RUSKIN COLLEGE AND THE OXFORD REPORT

Ruskin College was a working men's college on the doorstep of the university but independent, founded in 1899 by two American philanthropists, Walter Vrooman and Charles Beard. The founders originally supported students but after their departure in 1902 the college looked for financial support to two sources, the trade union movement and wealthy individuals. By 1906 a considerable proportion of the student body were selected by various labour organisations and there were some fifty in residence. Ruskin College was the only institution of its kind, bringing together relatively mature and experienced working-class students—young men in their late twenties for the most part—for a two-year course of study, in the main of economics, sociology and politics. By 1908 the student body was frankly socialist in colour, predominantly Marxist in outlook, and a thorn in the side of the university.

"Most of us were socialist of one party shade or another," writes W. W. Craik, one of the students entering in 1908—from the I.L.P., S.D.F., Clarion, and one from the S.L.P. "We were, however, soon made aware that the socialism of the second-year men was hewn from more solid and durable stone than ours." Accordingly, "zealous for the conversion of the local working people to the cause of Labour", they aired "their socialist views out of doors".[1] The matter is put somewhat differently by an historian of the W.E.A., that the Ruskin students seized every opportunity to display their faith holding "open-air meetings at the Martyrs' Memorial almost daily to attack Oxford or to provoke it".[2] It was Ruskin students who provided the stewards

---

[1] W. W. Craik, *The Central Labour College* (1964), 40, 52. [2] Smith, *op. cit.*, 52.

and bodyguards for Arthur Henderson and Keir Hardie when Oxford students attempted to break up their meetings.[1] Sanderson Furniss, a young tutor appointed to Ruskin in 1907, found the students "were practically all socialists of one brand or another, and there were amongst them some of the wildest and most revolutionary young men in the country".[2]

Although some university men had, from the inception of Ruskin College, associated themselves with its work and even formed the majority of its governing body, in fact, writes Craik, the College was treated with "cold indifference" by the majority of Oxford dons, or at least regarded as "an undesirable intrusion". However, the atmosphere perceptibly changed after the Labour victories of 1906, and that year and the next concerted moves were made by university representatives towards subsuming the college under the university. The outlook and behaviour of the students hastened this process, but they for their part resented the intrusion and attempts to undermine the independence of the college. This policy came clearly to light with the publication of *Oxford and Working Class Education* in December 1908, the report of the joint committee of W.E.A. and university representatives set up in 1907.[3] This report covered the whole field indicated in its title, but it made specific propositions about Ruskin and it was these, together with the actual trend of events at the college, that aroused deep hostility among the Ruskin students.

The Oxford Report, together with Lord Curzon's *Principles and Methods of University Reform* published the following year, must be seen in part as a reaction to mounting criticism of the ancient universities not only from the Labour movement but more generally. In July 1907, as we have already seen, Bishop Gore had initiated a debate

---

[1] Craik, *op. cit.*, 68.

[2] Lord Sanderson, *Memories of Sixty Years* (1931), 86.

[3] The university representatives on the committee were: T. B. Strong, Dean of Christ Church and Chairman of the Extension Delegacy; H. H. Turner, Savilian Professor of Astronomy; A. L. Smith, Fellow of Balliol College (and later Master); S. Ball, Fellow of St. John's College; J. A. R. Marriott, Secretary of the Extension Delegacy; H. B. Lees Smith, Chairman of the Executive Committee of Ruskin College and Professor of Economics at University College, Bristol; A. E. Zimmern, Fellow of New College. Those nominated by the W.E.A. were: W. H. Berry, Assistant Secretary of the Working Men's Club and Institute Union, representing the Educational Committee of the Co-operative Union; C. W. Bowerman, M.P., representing the Parliamentary Committee of the T.U.C.; Richard Campbell, representing the National Conference of Friendly Societies; J. M. MacTavish, Labour member of the Portsmouth Town Council (later Secretary of the W.E.A.); Albert Mansbridge, Secretary of the W.E.A.; D. J. Shackleton, M.P., representing the Parliamentary Committee of the T.U.C.; Alfred Wilkinson, Labour member of the Rochdale Town Council. The Committee issued an Interim Report in May 1908.

in the House of Lords asking for the appointment of a Royal Commission "to enquire into the endowment, government, administration, and teaching of the Universities of Oxford and Cambridge and their constituent Colleges, in order to secure the best use of their resources for the benefit of all classes of the community".[1] "Previously to this debate," writes Curzon, "the subject of such changes had been much discussed in the press and elsewhere, and Bishop Gore's speech lent form and authority to criticisms that had already obtained a wide circulation."[2] That the university was becoming sensitive to such criticisms is evident from the Oxford Report, which states at the outset that Oxford "is in the main the University of the wealthier classes". The Report specifically draws attention to the growing working-class demand for entrance to the universities "as a matter of right". It stresses that "workpeople will not be content with any substitute for University education, however excellent, which assumes they will be unable to enter the Universities themselves", quotes the T.U.C. resolution demanding "a national system of education under full popular control, free and secular, from the primary school to the University", and refers also to I.L.P. and S.D.P. support for this programme.[3] The Report also draws attention to the claim that the "poor", or working-class, scholar has been excluded from the university in so far as college endowments, originally left to assist "poor" scholars, have been appropriated by the wealthy. Though rejecting (or appearing to reject) this accusation, the report recognises that this idea is widely held among the working class so that, in their view, "in demanding a larger share in the endowments at the disposal of Oxford, they are asking, not for an innovation, but for a restoration of old advantages".[4] The committee assessed the net receipts from endowments as £265,000 p.a. They found also (although they did not juxtapose the two figures) that the total cost to the university of Extension work in 1907 was £535.

The main burden of the Report is that the working class should have direct access to the university through a developed system of university tutorial classes on the lines of those functioning at Rochdale, Longton,

[1] Lord Curzon, *Principles and Methods of University Reform* (1909), 9. Curzon was Chancellor of Oxford University.   [2] *Ibid.*, 9.

[3] *Oxford and Working Class Education* (2nd edn. 1909), 22, 46.

[4] *Ibid.*, 22-3. The Report quotes the West London Council of the I.L.P. which held that the funds requisite for organising higher education for the working classes "should be met by grants from the Imperial Exchequer, and by the restoration of educational endowments, which, primarily intended for the education of the poor, have in the course of time become appropriated by the richer members of the community".

and elsewhere,[1] that provision should be made for students who had completed these courses satisfactorily at each college, at Ruskin, and as non-collegiate students, and that special two-year Diploma courses be established in Economics and Political Science, for which the students should study. University Extension, the Report claimed, has been a *substitute* for university education; its true function should be to *prepare* men for it.

The stated object of these somewhat radical proposals was twofold. First, the working-class demand for access to the university would be, to some extent, met at a time when it was important to educate leading members of this class; second, the presence of outstanding working-class students at Oxford would enable the university to guide their general outlook. "The demand that the Universities shall serve all classes derives much additional significance from changes which are taking place in the constitution of English society and in the distribution of political power," writes the committee. Pointing to the increase in the number of Labour M.P.s and councillors, "the great increase in the membership of political associations", and the movement towards political action by the trade unions, the committee add that their effect "has certainly been both to foster a ferment of ideas in classes where formerly it did not exist and to make it imperative that they should obtain the knowledge necessary to enable them to show foresight in their choice of political means".[2]

It was particularly the function of the ancient universities ("though, of course, not to the exclusion of the new") "to train men for all departments of political life and public administration". This now needed a new interpretation. "The Trade Union secretary and the 'Labour member' need an Oxford education as much . . . as the civil servant or the barrister." "It seems to us," the report continues, "that it would involve a grave loss both to Oxford and to English political life were the close association which has existed between the University and the world of affairs to be broken or impaired on the accession of new classes to power." Precisely because of the social changes, Oxford education should be made more generally available; "we are strongly of opinion that recent political developments make it imperative that

---

[1] By the time the second edition of the Report was prepared (August 1909), tutorial classes had been started at Chesterfield, Glossop, Littleborough, Oldham, Swindon and Wrexham as well as at Rochdale and Longton; in October 1908, these functioned under a committee consisting of working-class members and Extension Delegacy representatives in equal numbers. *Oxford and Working Class Education.*, iv-v.

[2] *Ibid.*, 47.

in her own interests, as much as in the interests of workpeople, it should be made possible for a far larger number to turn to her for teaching than have done so in the past".[1]

This would tend greatly towards social harmony. Modern life and living tends to a growing separation of classes, making it increasingly difficult for each to understand the circumstances and aspirations of other sections of the community; there is "little that brings them together". The leaders of "every class" should have the opportunity of developing "a wide outlook on the historical development and economic condition of the whole English community, such as is given by a University education"; or, as it is put in a passage by an Oxford member of the committee (Sydney Ball) quoted in the report, "of obtaining the synoptic mind which, as Plato says, is desirable in governors".[2] The inference is that workers with a "wide outlook" and a "synoptic mind" will not be tempted to put class interests first.

So the university should be accessible to every class. The workers should share the benefits of what Curzon called the "indescribable glamour" of collegiate life; their education at the university should be "liberal", giving "a broad reasoned view of things and a sane measure of social values". Over and above this, the university should concern itself closely with educational and social developments generally: "it has become incumbent upon Universities to watch carefully every sign that a new class is ready to receive their guidance, in order that the seed of University culture may be deposited wherever it has suitable material on which to work."[3]

The first step, then, was the organisation of university tutorial classes, and here the committee drew on the experience of those already existing. The report here stresses the need to co-operate with the workers "in their efforts to obtain what they want, instead of providing, without consulting them, what the University thinks they ought to want". The latter had, of course, been the tradition of university Extension lectures as of all earlier approaches by the middle and professional class to workers' education. This committee, however, was very conscious of the suspicion with which sections of the working class regarded the universities and significantly quoted a resolution from

[1] *Ibid.*, 48.
[2] *Ibid.*, 48-9. Workers' representatives are now hampered in industrial bargaining by lack of knowledge. "The education which Oxford can give, by broadening his knowledge and strengthening his judgment, would make him at once a more efficient servant of his own society, and a more potent influence on the side of industrial peace." *Ibid.*, 83
[3] *Ibid.*, 53.

the Barry branch of the Amalgamated Society of Railway Servants which sent a delegate to the 1907 Summer conference: "That it is inexpedient for the Working Classes to cultivate a closer relationship with Oxford by University Extension Lectures, or any other methods, until the teachings of the Universities are radically altered, so that a truer view of social questions may be taught, and that it is inadvisable to send working men students to colleges unless the curriculum is made suitable for the training of Labour leaders."[1]

This leads on to recognition of the fact that workers "are sometimes inclined to suspect teachers of displaying . . . an unconscious class bias".[2] It is to meet this criticism that the Report stresses the need for a form of workers' control: "The whole history of the University Extension Movement shows that higher education cannot be imposed upon workpeople from above, but must be organised and managed by men who belong to themselves, and whom they have learned to trust in other capacities. This is, in our opinion, a fundamental axiom, the neglect of which will be followed by certain failure." If "the management and organisation of the class should be mainly in the hands of workpeople, the selection of curricula and guidance in reading must be the duty of the University acting in co-operation with workpeople"; that is, the *content* of education, as indeed inevitably in such a scheme, would be largely a university responsibility, once the class has chosen a particular course.[3]

The Report includes as appendices a number of model syllabuses drawn up by a sub-committee on economics, history, politics and literature.[4] The key subject here is, of course, that of economics, in so far as the working-class outlook, when it tended to Marxism, differed profoundly in method and approach from that of the university. This is recognised in the report, both directly and obliquely. In a section on "the Duties, Qualifications and Status of the teacher" it stresses that the teacher should have a good knowledge "of working-

---

[1] *Oxford and Working Class Education*, 57-8. Sanderson Furniss, a tutor at Ruskin College from 1907, stresses the hostility of working men to the universities at this time; this, he says, "was partly due to the universities themselves". Only a sprinkling of working-class children reached the universities; those who did so moved into the professional class "and gradually drifted away from their own people". There was also "much truth in the criticism that the education at Oxford was bourgeois and middle class. It was, at any rate, 'class' education and in some respects narrow . . . undergraduates at that time left Oxford, as I had done myself, in almost complete ignorance of the working class and of working-class thought." Sanderson, *Memories of Sixty Years*, 107-8.

[2] *Oxford and Working Class Education*, 57.   [3] *Ibid.*, 58-9.

[4] Members of this sub-committee included R. H. Tawney, Graham Wallas, Ernest Barker, H. A. L. Fisher, L. T. Hobhouse, Ramsay Macdonald, and others.

class life and habits of thought" so that he can understand "the lines along which students have reached their conclusions, and see the unstated assumptions from which their questions start". Too often a teacher "fails almost entirely when confronted with a working-class audience, because he has started from a point of view so different from theirs as to make it impossible for the minds of students and teachers ever to come into real contact with each other". The teacher—and this is almost certainly a reference to Marx—may never have "read the books through which alone they have approached the subject"; he has, therefore, "never really touched the problems upon which their minds are exercised". "Every teacher of economics, for example, who has lectured to a working-class audience must have been for the moment at a loss when confronted with unfamiliar formulae on the lips of men to whom they seem exactly to answer all their problems. In the same way, working-class audiences who listen for the first time to economics being taught by a University man have an uncomfortable feeling of being played with by a clever dialectician."[1]

The matter is dealt with in more detail in the syllabus on economics where the strength of the Marxist appeal is admitted and advice given on how to cope with it. After the study of "Descriptive Economics" (using Marshall's *Economics of Industry* as a textbook) and of economic history, the class should turn to economic theory. "If many members of the class have socialistic views, it would be well to preface this part of the subject" by reading the first nine chapters of Marx's *Capital*, or, since "the style is rather difficult", Hyndman's *Economics of Socialism*. The teacher who adopts this course "must, however, be very sure that the criticism of Marx, implicit in the ordinary textbook, is equally carefully explained", the "best direct statement of this criticism is in Böhm-Bawerk's *Capital and Interest* and in the same writer's *Karl Marx and the Close of his System*". Following this the tutor should go on to the theory of value showing the different way the problem is tackled by Marx and "orthodox economists". From this point a textbook by an "orthodox economist" should be carefully studied, preferably Marshall's *Principles of Economics*; although this is "not easy for beginners" the tutor should "at any rate eventually take the class through Marshall, as he does much to show working men that a scientific economist can be a human being".[2]

The Report makes a number of proposals for the organisation and extension of tutorial class work, and for the admission of working

[1] *Oxford and Working Class Education*, 65.   [2] *Ibid.*, 111-13.

men from these classes to the university itself. It also makes two specific recommendations about Ruskin. First, that residence in the college for one year, together with a certificate from the college supported by two university representatives that the student's work had been satisfactory, "should be accepted as satisfying the requirements of the University that he has received a good general education and is qualified to pursue the study of Economics". Second, that "under any scheme of Scholarships or Exhibitions for working men, a certain number of such Scholarships or Exhibitions should be placed at the disposal of the Council of Ruskin College for second-year students who have qualified for admission to the Diploma course in Economics or Political Science".[1] The intention is clear, to change Ruskin from a Labour college into a college preparatory to university studies, involving a transformation of its whole ethos and purpose.[2]

Lord Curzon, welcoming this report, spoke more clearly to the same end, advocating that Ruskin should be inside the university, not independent of it. "There is always a danger," he wrote, "that a Working-men's College, outside the University, and subject neither to its influences nor its discipline, may develop into a club dominated by the narrow views of particular political or economic schools, recruiting itself solely from one party, and out of touch with many of the best elements in academic life." The poor man to be encouraged was definitely not "the man who comes to Oxford merely in order to obtain a sketchy acquaintance with political problems, or to practise the arts of the popular speaker. I do not think that Oxford is a proper palaestra for such exercises."[3]

In order to understand the response of Ruskin students to these pronouncements and proposals, a reaction which led directly to the development of a new organisation to promote working-class education, it is necessary to turn to the situation inside the college at the time.

4. THE RUSKIN STRIKE AND THE CENTRAL LABOUR COLLEGE

Ruskin College was governed by a body composed of members of the university and leading trade unionists, among the latter Richard Bell of the Railway Servants and David Shackleton of the Weavers' Union. But it had a very unusual Principal, appointed by one of the

[1] *Oxford and Working Class Education*, 89-90.
[2] A long and critical review of the Report appeared in *Justice*, 19 December 1908.
[3] Curzon, *op. cit.*, 63-4.

original founders. An Oxford graduate, ordained in the Church of England in 1878, Dennis Hird ten years later became a socialist and, as a curate in Battersea, "was soon preaching socialism inside the Church at the time when John Burns was preaching it outside".[1] A few years later he joined the S.D.F. and continued as an open exponent of socialism—his lecture on "Jesus the Socialist" selling 75,000 copies—and in 1896 renounced 'orders' after being excluded from a country living he then held. In charge of Ruskin since its inception, Hird had strong convictions about the nature of the college and how it could best serve the Labour movement; he was a man who, in matters of conviction, took a firm stand.

The college had recently obtained increased financial support from the trade unions, and connections with the Labour movement were becoming closer. In 1907 the T.U.C. issued an official appeal for support: "Now that Labour is showing that it is determined to take its rightful position in the country," ran a key passage, "it more than ever needs the knowledge and training necessary to maintain that position."[2] It was, however, just at this time that the university began a series of approaches to the college.

In fact Ruskin was being pulled in two directions. Some of the unions sending students were among the most militant; most of the students reaching Ruskin were inclined to socialism, believed in the existence of the class struggle, and wanted an education that would prepare them for active service in the Labour cause. On the other hand university dons on the governing body or lecturing at the college, and several of the staff (predominantly liberal in outlook), shared the outlook of the Oxford report, that the approach should be "non-partisan". It was because this aim was canvassed that appeals for financial support had brought donations from such figures as the Dukes of Fife and Norfolk, Lords Avebury, Crewe, Monkswell, Ripon, Rothschild, Tweedmouth, Northcliffe, Rosebery, Wolverhampton, as well as from leading politicians of both main parties including A. J. Balfour and Walter Runciman. The very fact that financial aid was forthcoming from such sources was sufficient proof, the militant students later proclaimed, that "non-partisan" education meant in practice "simply an inculcation of governing-class ideas".[3]

[1] W. W. Craik, The Central Labour College, 37.
[2] The Burning Question of Education (2nd edn. 1910), 2; this pamphlet, subtitled "An Account of the Ruskin College dispute, its cause and consequences", was published by the Executive Committee of the "Plebs" League.
[3] Ibid., 5.

Already in 1907 students were paying less and less attention to lectures, with the single exception of those on sociology given by the Principal, and turning instead to the organisation of Marxist study groups. It was in this situation, when proposals to link Ruskin more closely with the university were already in the air,[1] that a sub-committee of the Ruskin executive proposed that Hird should cease teaching sociology and logic and in future confine himself to the subjects of literature and temperance. The students' reaction was immediate. With one dissentient they signed a petition "protesting most emphatically against any such change being made, and threatening to leave the College instantly were it made operative".[2]

This proved to be only the first move in a sustained effort to change the character of the college. The various steps cannot be followed in detail here,[3] but in the autumn of 1907 the students were approached by A. L. Smith, fellow of Balliol and member of the Oxford committee. If the university assisted with money, he asked the students, and opened its doors to some of them, would they approve? The students' answer was that although the college needed funds they were not prepared to sacrifice its independence to this end.[4]

A few weeks later the Chancellor of the university paid a visit, speaking to the students and again raising the question of a closer relationship with the university. This meeting between Curzon, recently Viceroy of India, and the socialist Principal and students has been graphically described by one of the participants.[5] In reply to Curzon's statement, Hird said, in substance, "My Lord, when you speak of Ruskin College you are not referring merely to this institution here in Oxford, for this is only the branch of a great democratic movement that has its roots all over the country. To ask Ruskin College to come into closer contact with the University is to ask the great democracy whose foundation is the Labour movement, a democracy that in the near future will come into its own, and when it does will bring great changes in its wake." The clear inference was that a closer

---

[1] Those set out in a document entitled "Notes for the consideration of the Joint Committee on the possible relations between Ruskin College and the University", submitted in 1907 to the committee that produced the Oxford Report.

[2] Craik, op. cit., 48.

[3] They have been fully described in W. W. Craik, The Central Labour College (1964); see also The Burning Question of Education, and the "Plebs" Magazine, Vol. I (1909). Material bearing on this episode is to be found in Sanderson, Memories of Sixty Years, 82–112; The Story of Ruskin College (1949); J. F. and Winifred Horrabin, Working-Class Education (1924), 43ff.; Eden and Cedar Paul, Proletcult (1921), 53ff.

[4] The Burning Question of Education, 9–10; Craik, op. cit., 49.

[5] In The Burning Question, 10–11.

THE FOUNDATION OF RUSKIN COLLEGE, TOWN HALL MEETING AT OXFORD IN 1899

THE RUSKIN STRIKE: STUDENTS MOVE OUT

relationship with the university as it was, was not desired; the students present supported their Principal, and Curzon "without another word . . . turned on his heel and walked out, followed by the remainder of the lecturing staff". From this point it was crystal clear that the Principal stood with the students for the independence of the college.

About this time new members were appointed to the staff without consulting Hird, while Lees Smith, already Chairman of the governing body, was appointed Director of Studies. In various ways, Hird's authority as Principal was diminished. Matters now moved fast to a crisis as the governors' determination to link the college with the university became increasingly clear; the students, for their part, particularly in view of the changing nature of the teaching, now began increasingly to hold the view that a Labour college could not be neutral. The key issue was the question of the *content* of education and especially of economics, whether Marxist economics should be taught or merely ignored or refuted.[1] There was a clear move in the latter direction;[2] the introduction of an examination in the summer of 1908, which aimed to crystallise this direction of the teaching, was strongly resisted by the students who regarded it as a means of approximating the curriculum to that of the university.[3] Deputations to the trade union members of the governing body met with no success. It was in this unsettled situation, in the autumn of 1908, that the Oxford Report appeared making definite propositions for the transformation of Ruskin College into an institution preparatory for university studies, effectively therefore under university control.

The students decided that a determined effort must be made to inform and arouse the trade unions, and in October formed an organisation, The Plebs League, into which they soon drew many ex-students; its object, "to bring about a more satisfactory connection of Ruskin College with the Labour Movement".[4] To propagate their views about the true nature and requirements of independent working-class education a journal was launched entitled The *"Plebs" Magazine*. The first number, published in February 1909, set out clearly the dangers that would attend absorption of the college by the university, and called on the trade unions for action to ensure the control of Ruskin

---

[1] Cf. T. A. Jackson, *op. cit.*, 149-52.

[2] Thus Sanderson Furniss, appointed tutor at this time, describes his course of lectures as "undoubtedly very critical of the socialist position . . . I was chiefly occupied in refuting Marx's theory of value . . . which I regarded as absolute nonsense." Sanderson, *op. cit.*, 94.

[3] Craik, *op. cit.*, 54.   [4] *The Burning Question*, 15.

W

by the workers and so to bring about a new era in the annals of the Labour movement.

The Secretary of the League was George Sims, a carpenter, a man of immense energy. "We were very optimistic young men," writes W. W. Craik, who edited *Plebs* at this time, "and so confident of the soundness and convincing power of our cause that, come hell or high water, we were going to see it through, whatever the cost."[1] There was reason for confidence in that ex-students of Ruskin were already, at the beginning of 1909, setting up branches of the Plebs League in South Wales, the midlands and the north. Some of these began to run study classes from their inception, a development fostered by *Plebs*.[2]

Meanwhile work at the college continued in an atmosphere of unease. The formation of the Plebs League was naturally regarded with considerable disfavour by the governing body, a sub-committee describing it as "capable of being an organisation whose object would be to force the Executive to move in a direction in which it would not be desirable to go". The governors were further alarmed at the support for the journal and its views among the trade unions. Suspecting that Hird was involved (although apparently he was not) they ordered him to sever any connection he had with the League. Then suddenly, at the end of March, they dismissed him from the post of Principal for "failure to maintain discipline". In effect, Hird was asked to resign and given no opportunity of appearing before the relevant committee (the Council) to state his case.[3] The student body went on strike.

Hird was dismissed, writes Craik, "because of his attitude as a socialist towards the take-over of the education at Ruskin College by the University"; thus, "for the third time in his life, he was made to pay for his principles with the loss of his job". It was the main demand of the students that the Principal's resignation be withdrawn.

The Ruskin College strike, which lasted a week, hit the headlines; nothing like it had been known before. Among the fifty-four students there were only ten described as "wobblers", not more than two of whom were holders of trade union scholarships. A rigid discipline was maintained and selected students replaced the lecturers.[4] Since distorted accounts were appearing in the national press, particular efforts were made to get across to the Labour movement, and particularly to the rank and file of the organised workers, the real issue at stake, that the students had struck in defence of Hird because "the Principal

[1] Craik, *op. cit.*, 66.   [2] *Ibid.*, 66.
[3] *Ibid.*, 63, 74-5; *The Burning Question*, 16.   [4] *The Burning Question*, 16.

stood for a principle". The strikers were successful in this and followed up the advantage. Forced to give up the hope of winning Ruskin College for the Labour movement against mounting odds, they organised a referendum vote in favour of a new departure; as a result, in Craik's words, "the great majority of the ex-students and the students then in residence at Ruskin started, through the Plebs League and its organ, a country-wide campaign for a new and genuine Labour College".[1]

As the week's strike came to an end, the authorities closed the college for a fortnight, perhaps to allow tempers to cool. In fact the former strikers, thoroughly warmed up, and now dispersed over the country, contacted trade union branches and other Labour organisations, and canvassed the new aim. The moving spirit was George Sims, member of the S.D.P., who had helped in the conduct of Marxist classes at the college and taken a leading part in the strike as secretary of the Plebs League.[2] Sims was, in fact, victimised as a result of it, his scholarship, privately awarded by Dr. Salter of Bermondsey, being withdrawn as a result of a letter from the secretary of the college. He was, therefore, free to begin and continue an intensive campaign in the Labour movement for the new objective of the Plebs League: "To assist in the formation of a Central Labour College in Oxford and similar institutions elsewhere, to be controlled by organised Labour bodies."[3] During the three months following the strike an immense amount of spadework was done to prepare the ground for a conference planned for early in August to launch the movement for the Labour college.

This movement, directed largely by *Plebs*, succeeded in arousing considerable interest in the Labour movement. "Young as we were," writes Craik, "and despite all our own theoretical immaturities, we were full of fight and fire against what we were firmly convinced was not a type of education capable of equipping the working-class movement with the knowledge about capitalist society it badly needed in order to change that society."[4] In South Wales the Plebs League issued a circular to local Labour organisations. "Perhaps there never was, certainly there never was in education, a movement which has commanded such enthusiasm and energy in so short a time as has this movement for pure Labour education," it began. "In the space of a

[1] Craik, *op. cit.*, 75, 78.
[2] For Sims, see *ibid.*, 79–80 (the S.D.F. had changed its name to the Social Democratic Party—S.D.P.—in 1908).
[3] *Ibid.*, 78–80.   [4] *Ibid.*, 81.

few months an incredibly large number of classes for the study of
economics and history from the workers' standpoint have been formed
in many localities in every industrial area. This means that a demand is
being created, a new demand for a new kind of education." The
workers need, as well as industrial and political organisations, their
own, independent *educational* organisation "to give both of these a
constant supply of vitality and ideas". This required "the establishment of a network of Labour Colleges through the country . . . a
huge educational structure entirely devoted to the interests of the
working class".[1]

Early in August 1909, there took place the first Annual Meeting of
the Plebs League, attended by "some two hundred trade union representatives, students and ex-students", which brought into being the
Central Labour College. Already two houses for the use of the college
had been rented at Oxford and a provisional committee formed. The
conference declared that the time had arrived "when the working class
should enter the educational world to work out its own problems for
itself".[2] The working class, declared Sims, must see that the new
educational organisation was put in such a position as "to supply the
movement with men and women thoroughly equipped theoretically
for the part that the history of the ages has assigned to the modern
working class, namely, the abolition of all classes, and all that this
implies for the uplifting of our common humanity". On 8 September
1909, the college opened with Dennis Hird as Principal (unpaid) and
twenty students. The new Labour college stood, therefore, in the
words of the Plebs League, as a "declaration of Working Class Independence in Education".[3]

Others among the strikers besides Sims had later been forced to
leave Ruskin, including Ben McKay and W. W. Craik. There was
later a progressive withdrawal of trade union sponsored scholars.
Already by October 1909, writes Craik, "district units of the South
Wales Miners had decided to withdraw their scholarships from Ruskin
and transfer them to the Central Labour College. By an overwhelming
majority the Amalagamated Society of Railway Servants had decided
to do likewise".[4] Steps were now being taken to place the Labour

[1] *The Burning Question*, 17.
[2] The *"Plebs"* *Magazine*, Vol. I, No. 8, September 1909; this number contains a detailed
report of the conference. The main resolution was moved by Noah Ablett of the South
Wales Miners' Federation—an ex-student of Ruskin—and seconded by Mrs. Bridges
Adams (S.D.P.).
[3] *The Burning Question*, 22.   [4] Craik, *op. cit.*, 85.

college under a board of management fully representative of the Labour movement.

But the formation of a Labour college was not the sole aim. Branches of the Plebs League were also organising classes in the localities with the aim of "demonstrating the need for, and the value of, the new Labour education", particularly, as Craik puts it, "the need to meet and counter the W.E.A. on this front". This was an integral part of the scheme. "Our purpose is not completed with the education of the few," wrote *Plebs* in January 1910. Labour college education "is to serve essentially as a means for the education of the workers throughout the country", the aim was to inaugurate "a systematic provincial scheme of working-class education". From the college men would go out into the industrial world "to train their fellow-workers", so giving the Labour movement "the intelligent discipline and solidarity it so much needs".[1] It is the principle of the parent-groups and worker-tutors, applied on Clydeside and elsewhere, now applied in terms of an organised educational institution.

With the establishment of the Central Labour College the local classes already initiated by the Plebs League were extended and co-ordinated on a district and divisional basis. It is significant that one of the first districts was based on Rochdale where the W.E.A. had established its pioneer tutorial class. Already in September 1909, a Ruskin striker set to work organising the Rochdale and District Labour College classes with considerable success and W. W. Craik followed up this work in the winter of 1910, acting as tutor to five weekly classes held in Rochdale, Bacup, Bury and Preston.[2] Thus the challenge of the Labour college movement providing independent working-class education based on Marxism to the university sponsored "non-partisan" education of the W.E.A. was immediate and direct.

By the winter of 1909, then, the two major trends in working-class education had assumed both organisational and institutional form. On the one hand the W.E.A., now in its sixth year, had developed a new type of relationship with the university and, as a result, was now assured of official support from the Board of Education and local

---

[1] *Ibid.*, 86-7.
[2] *Ibid.*, 92. There is a certain irony in the fact that, according to Craik, the ex-Ruskin student who pioneered the Rochdale Labour College classes had been a W.E.A. supporter, and sent by the W.E.A. to Ruskin as a student. "I recall the arguments that some of us had with him in his early weeks at Ruskin in 1909," writes Craik. As a result of his experiences there he became a strong supporter of the Plebs League and its outlook.

authorities.[1] On the other hand the Central Labour College had now come into existence supported by the Plebs League with its journal and local organisation. The differences between the two organisations, in terms of the purpose of working-class education, the content of teaching, organisation and finance were fundamental. Almost a century earlier a classic struggle at the London Mechanics' Institute had been fought on similar issues, to lead in turn to a proliferation of working-class educational activities which kept themselves independent of patronage and ultimate control by representatives of the middle and upper classes. The Labour college and the Plebs League were carrying on this tradition at a time when the working-class was more homo-geneous and more highly organised than it had been at this earlier phase. The effect of this breakaway was, therefore, the more far-reaching.

5. DEVELOPMENTS IN WORKING-CLASS EDUCATION, 1910-20

The new pattern of working-class education took further shape in the four years that remained before the war. These were the years of the "Great Unrest", but with the outbreak of war, the Labour move-ment was thrown into disarray—the leadership in the trade unions and Labour Party, after a brief anti-war campaign, expressing support; even the British Socialist Party (which now united the former S.D.P. and other smaller socialist societies), under the influence of Hyndman's imperialism, publicly stating its desire "to see the prosecution of the war to a speedy and successful issue". This was to leave aside the policy agreed at the Basle Conference of the Second International in 1912, to which the Labour Party was officially committed; that militarism and war were instruments of the capitalist class and that the duty of social democrats was to rouse the workers to fight against the war peril, or, should war break out, to use the resultant crisis "to accelerate the fall of the bourgeoisie". In fact in May 1915, Arthur Henderson was found a place in Asquith's all-party government and during the war years, in the words of the Webbs, the trade union apparatus became recognised as "part of the social machinery of the state", implying a fundamental "transformation of the social and political standing of the official representatives of the trade union world".[2] This deepened already apparent divisions between the

[1] Though the recommendation of the Oxford Report, that students should proceed direct from tutorial classes to a university course, had no effect, classes certainly increased in number. Ruskin College remained under its former governing body.
[2] S. and B. Webb, *The History of Trade Unionism* (1920 edn.), 635.

leadership and the rank and file and when in 1916 mounting grievances among the workers led to renewed industrial unrest the more militant socialist groups threw off their leadership and came out in opposition to the war.

It will be clear that these developments bore closely on the position in adult education, where differences of approach were already marked. In this field two trends had now become so firmly established that they may well be considered apart, though, as will appear, they now came increasingly into competition.

(i) *The Expansion of the W.E.A.*

The W.E.A. had grown rapidly since its inception in 1903 and the industrial and political conflicts of the pre-war years only gave a new impetus to development. It was at this time that the great annual meetings in industrial towns were held which sometimes took on a Messianic quality. The number of branches increased from 13 in 1906 to 179 in 1914 while individual membership also rose and affiliated organisations numbered over 2,500 by 1914, many of these being trade union branches and local co-operative societies.[1]

W.E.A. branches organised a wide variety of educational and recreational activities, including short-term classes and weekend schools on various topics, reading circles, lecture courses, and so on. But the pride of the movement was undoubtedly the university tutorial classes; these expanded rapidly after the formation of the Oxford joint committee in 1908. By the autumn of 1909 the universities of Birmingham, Cambridge, Leeds, Liverpool, London and Manchester had all followed the lead and in that year the Central Joint Advisory Committee on Tutorial Classes was established. In 1913-14 students in these classes totalled 3,234 and the vast majority were working class.[2]

Since tutorial classes had official subvention, they were open to inspection. In 1909-10 the Board of Education, which now had its own Inspectors of adult education, arranged for a full inspection producing a special report which assessed the work of the classes in the highest terms.[3] In the same year the Board of Education issued Regulations defining a tutorial class as a three year course of study according

---

[1] *Final Report of the Adult Education Committee* (Ministry of Reconstruction) 1919, 38-9.

[2] *Ibid.*, 44, gives an occupational analysis of 3,035 of these students. Non-working-class categories were: teachers, 308; insurance agents, etc., 59; foremen and managers, 26. All the rest are classified as working class.

[3] Smith, *op. cit.*, 73. The report was drawn up by Professor L. T. Hobhouse and J. W. Headlam, H.M.I.

to a syllabus approved by a university body and under a tutor appointed by it; if these conditions were fulfilled an official grant would be obtainable.

One of the great successes of the pre-war W.E.A. occurred among the miners of North Staffordshire, where a movement for higher education snowballed very rapidly between 1911 and 1914. The connection between Oxford and North Staffordshire was already of long duration, and in 1912 E. S. Cartwright, a miner from Longton, became organising secretary of the Oxford Tutorial Class Committee.[1] The movement spread from Tawney's original tutorial class which, in its third and final year in 1911, determined to carry their enthusiasm for learning into the mining villages surrounding the Potteries towns. A meeting held in the School of Mining at Stoke-on-Trent in May was addressed by Tawney, and it was at this meeting that the North Staffordshire miners' higher education movement was established. Already a month later fourteen applications for classes in mining villages were received and in the winter ten of these were established—lack of teachers being the limiting factor. By 1913 twenty-four tutorial classes were functioning in the area with 520 students—most of these in mining villages with populations varying between 800 and 3,000.

These classes did not, of course, operate the full tutorial class system—most of the courses were of twelve lectures followed by discussion, held at fortnightly intervals because of shift work. The teaching was undertaken largely by past and present tutorial class students—of the first twelve classes, eight were taken by members of Tawney's tutorial class all of whom, of course, were working at their jobs.[2] Seventy per cent of the students were miners. The main subjects studied lay in the field of economic and social problems, history, literature and politics. From the first meeting in 1911, this movement was affiliated to the W.E.A.[3]

In Yorkshire and some other areas there was also something of a break-through to the working class, the main initiative coming from the localities. To men such as A. E. Zimmern the classes in the Potteries were a sign of a new educational renaissance; were Erasmus to come

[1] Smith, op. cit., 84.
[2] Their occupations were: 1 miner, 1 colliery weighman, 1 potter's engineman, 1 potter's decorator, 1 railway booking-clerk, 1 elementary school teacher, 1 secretary and 1 municipal clerk.
[3] Final Report of the Adult Education Committee, 296-309, for a full description of this development.

to England again to consort with the new learning, he would go to North Staffordshire to find it.[1] It was, however, Tawney who best summarised the objectives he and others set before the W.E.A. at this period. Its aim, he wrote in 1914, "is to articulate the educational aspirations of Labour, to represent them to the proper authorities, to stimulate into activity, when it exists, the organisation through which they can be satisfied, and create it when it does not". The object must be "to build from within, to help men to develop their own genius, their own education, their own culture"; above all the W.E.A. must lay the "smiling illusion" that culture is the perquisite only of the wealthy and meet the workers' demand for the knowledge that was denied them. "It is, perhaps, not fanciful to say," concludes Tawney in a characteristic passage, "that the disinterested desire of knowledge for its own sake, the belief in the free exercise of reason without regard to material results and because reason is divine, a faith not yet characteristic of English life, but which it is the highest spiritual end of Universities to develop, finds in the Tutorial Classes of the Workers' Educational Association as complete an expression as it does within the walls of some University cities. To these miners and weavers and engineers who pursue knowledge with the passion born of difficulties, knowledge can never be a means, but only an end; for what have they to gain from it save knowledge itself?"[2]

Work, even expansion, continued during the war though necessarily at a reduced rate.[3] In 1917 the W.E.A. issued a statement of aims and objects which illustrates how central the tutorial classes and the policy set out in the Oxford report now were to its whole approach. Members of the W.E.A., it is stated, are "united by the desire to bring within the reach of the whole community the Higher Education which has hitherto been too much the privilege of the few". Besides co-ordinating existing agencies the association "devises fresh means by which people of all degrees may be raised educationally step by step, until they are able to take advantage of the facilities which are and may be provided by the universities. It is a missionary organisation

[1] Smith, *op. cit.*, 80, summarising A. E. Zimmern, "Education and the Working Class" *The Round Table*, March 1914.

[2] R. H. Tawney, "An Experiment in Democratic Education", *The Political Quarterly*, May 1914, 72-4, 81-2 (reprinted in R. H. Tawney, *The Radical Tradition* (1964)). I do not know if any follow-up has been done of the membership of Tawney's original classes. One, A. P. Wadsworth of the Rochdale class, became editor of the *Manchester Guardian*.

[3] Between 1914 and 1918 the number of W.E.A. branches increased from 179 to 209; of affiliated bodies from 2,555 to 2,709, of individual members from 11,430 to 14,697; Mansbridge, *An Adventure in Working-Class Education*, 67.

working in co-operation with the education authorities and working-class organisations. It is definitely unsectarian, non-political and democratic."[1]

(ii) The Plebs League and the National Council of Labour Colleges

The Plebs League by contrast was a frankly political organisation with a partisan rather than an impartial approach to education. Here the perfection of individual culture was not the aim; this could be made available to all after the socialist revolution, not merely to some hundreds of workers engaged in individual study. Meantime the task was to equip the working class as a whole with the knowledge that would aid their fight against capitalism and lighten the road to socialism. From this point of view the W.E.A., however devoted and self-sacrificing its leaders, seemed to be providing a diversion, to be weakening rather than advancing the working-class cause. Here was a juxtaposition of views similar to that in the 1840s between the National Charter Association led by Feargus O'Connor and the "knowledge" Chartists led by William Lovett. The first essential, O'Connor had consistently argued, is the winning of political power; from this all else will follow. The first essential, said the Plebs League, is to work towards the socialist revolution. The matter is summed up in a statement of the aim of the Central Labour College which, in contrast to the W.E.A. view of knowledge as an end in itself, clearly sees knowledge as a means:

"The Labour College teaches the workmen to look for the causes of social evils and the problems arising therefrom in the material foundation of society; that these causes are in the last analysis economic; that their elimination involves in the first place economic changes of such a character as to lead to the eradication of capitalist economy."

For this reason, it is added, the college "lays no claim to being non-partisan or non-political. As it exists for a partisan movement it must be opposed to all those in opposition to that movement. But its partisanship is a consequence of the actual facts which it scientifically unfolds."[2]

It was, then, no accident that students and supporters of the Labour

[1] The Highway, February 1917, No. 101. This statement ends by saying the W.E.A. "is a Federation consisting at present of 2,150 organisations".
[2] From a statement by the sub-warden of the college quoted in Final Report of the Adult Education Committee, 222-3.

college took a leading part in the formation of industrial unions during this period of increasing militancy. Several, including Noah Ablett, were involved in the formation of the Industrial Democracy League in South Wales which fought for the reform of the South Wales Miners' Federation on more centralised and democratic lines, and which produced the policy document *The Miners' Next Step* in 1912. A similar campaign in which Labour college ex-students were active led to the establishment of the National Union of Railwaymen in the spring of 1913. These, the first two industrial unions, were also the first unions to give official support to the Central Labour College. As Craik comments, "A new kind of trade union organisation became identified with a new kind of trade union education".[1]

Things did not, however, go smoothly for the new Labour College; indeed it can well be argued that it had a greater importance at this time as a symbol of independence and defiance than in terms of the number of full-time students passing through it. In 1911 the college moved to London, and the years up to the war saw a hard struggle for survival and for a measure of official support. The Railwaymen and South Wales miners now sent their students there, and these were joined by other unions including the Notts and Forest of Dean miners, but in 1913-14 there were only twelve in residence and debts were mounting. There was little sympathy for the college and indeed for the whole conception of independent working-class education among the leadership of the T.U.C. and individual unions. The T.U.C. itself was already committed to the support of Ruskin, and Bowerman and Sexton were its representatives on the governing body. The Labour College had been forced from the first to appeal to the rank and file— to win majorities at trade union conferences against the platform, and so gradually gain the official support of the unions. In this the college had powerful support from the newly founded *Daily Herald* under the editorship of George Lansbury. But it was not until 1915 that the management of the college could finally be vested in the two unions that gave it its main support and that the T.U.C. at length conceded that the Labour College had "the same claims upon our regard as Ruskin College". From that date it enjoyed the official recognition of the T.U.C.[2]

[1] Craik, *op. cit.*, 94.
[2] In 1911 protests were made at the annual Congress against treating Ruskin as if it was the official college of the T.U.C. because it had two members on the Board; in 1913 a resolution, moved by Bowerman, which would have given Ruskin the official endorsement of the T.U.C., was lost by a large majority amid cheers, in spite of a violent speech

The Plebs League, which had brought the central college into being, was now actively engaged in forming local classes on the lines of those already established at Rochdale. Soon after the Labour college arrived in Kensington, writes Craik, "it began to conduct evening classes, both within and without, for working men and women in the district, and to extend their range. Not many years were to pass before there was hardly a suburb in Greater London without one or more Labour college classes at work in it." Many of these were taken by the staff of the college and by second year students as part of their training.[1] Elsewhere classes were organised with the support of trade union bodies, or of branches of the I.L.P., the British Socialist Party and S.L.P. Two articles contributed by George Sims to *Justice* describe classes in the north-west at Bury, Oldham, Waterfoot, Radcliffe, St. Helens, Warrington, Wigan, Liverpool and Birkenhead.[2] In 1913 *Plebs* reported that provincial classes with "an aggregate membership approximating 1,000" were being carried on in the North-East Lancashire District, the Rochdale District, the Rhondda Valley, Barry, Bradford, Halifax, Birmingham and Edinburgh.[3]

The official Plebs classes, however, were not the only examples of independent working-class education being carried on at the time; neither the Plebs League nor the W.E.A., for instance, made much impact in Scotland at this time—the educational activities of the S.L.P. and S.D.P. met the needs of the more advanced workers. In the circumstances, free-lance socialist propagandists could earn a living, if a scanty one, by lecturing on Marxism to local socialist societies, many of which were still independent of any organisation. Thus T. A. Jackson, who gained his own education in study classes, describes how he was invited to do a month's lecture tour in the Bristol area in the spring of 1910 at thirty shillings a week. "My stay in Bristol was extended, and led to an engagement in Newport, Mon., where my stay was extended from a week to a month, then for three months, and then for a six-months' engagement. From Newport as a centre," he adds, "I toured all the Welsh valleys."[4] It was during these years

by Sexton opposing the Labour college. A card vote was demanded but instead the Parliamentary Committee suggested a reference back for twelve months to allow for an enquiry into the Labour college. This was accepted and led to the official endorsement of the Labour college in 1915 (there was no Congress in 1914). Cf. Craik, *op. cit.*, 109–11 and T.U.C. reports.

[1] Craik, *op. cit.*, 100–1.   [2] *Justice*, 24 February and 2 March 1912.

[3] *Final Report of the Adult Education Committee*, 223. In addition classes were formed for study on a system of "lectures by post", chiefly in N.U.R. branches (at Wolverhampton, Shrewsbury, Wellington and Carlisle).

[4] Jackson, *Solo Trumpet*, 90.

that a young member of the B.S.P., Harry Pollitt, was regularly attending classes in industrial history and economics on Sunday mornings at the Socialist Hall in Openshaw,[1] and his experience was shared by many others up and down the country.

It is difficult, if not impossible, to estimate the extent of such classes; but the strength of the Labour college movement, at a time of disillusion with the leadership in unions and in Parliament, lay in its appeal to the militants in the rank and file of the Labour movement. Sometimes there was a conflict of interest when both the W.E.A. and the Plebs League had classes running in the same locality. In Sheffield, for instance, the Trades and Labour Council, which had long taken an interest in education, affiliated to the W.E.A. in 1910. In 1914 a large group of its members went over to the support of the Central Labour College and determined to form a Labour college in the city. This movement was based on a Labour college class started by the Sheffield Education Committee of the N.U.R.[2] So, in the centres of industry, the key question as to the nature and purpose of working-class education was fought out on a local basis; the final decision resting on the balance of forces within the organisation concerned.

The war years brought setbacks in some quarters but further developments in others. The Central Labour College was forced to close down for the duration late in 1916, soon after it was taken over by the two trade unions which had supported it from the start. The provincial classes it had sponsored with the Plebs League, however, continued, and it was here that the most striking developments were to take place. The outbreak of war had itself given a certain impetus to educational work. "It set workers thinking about the causes of things political as they had never thought before," writes T. A. Jackson, who conducted Plebs League classes in Leeds and Bradford during the war.[3] Nevertheless, for the first eighteen months or so there was no appreciable development. It was in 1916 that a change became apparent. During the next two years an important thrust forward was to be made in different parts of the country, but particularly in South Wales, the north-east mining areas, Lancashire, Yorkshire and Scotland.

South Wales had been a centre of educational activity since the formation of the Plebs League in 1909, activity closely linked with the

---

[1] Harry Pollitt, *Serving My Time* (1940), 33.
[2] S. Pollard, *The Sheffield Trades and Labour Council, 1858-1958*, 75.
[3] Jackson, *op. cit.*, 153-4.

miners' trade union organisation. Noah Ablett, A. J. Cook and others fully engaged in industrial struggles were among the foremost supporters of the Labour college—both these were taking educational classes in the Welsh valleys in the early stages of the war. According to one observer, some 300 miners were attending Plebs classes in the Rhondda Valley alone in 1915, I.L.P. influence was waning and the W.E.A. had not "caught on". "The South Wales Plebs, although comparatively small numerically, has probably exercised a more profound influence on miners' trade unionism than any other external agency."[1]

In 1916, when grievances in the pits came to a head and there was a renewal of the bitter struggles which had marked the pre-war years this work began to attract official attention. The Welsh miners struck work and held out for a prolonged period. In November that year *The Times* carried an article characterising South Wales as "the industrial storm centre of Great Britain".

The causes of disaffection in South Wales, wrote *The Times*, were two-fold. In the first place "seething discontent" was promoted by the mining industry itself which was no more than a "de-humanised, commercial machine for the extraction of gold out of labour". Second, to the "fiery temperament" of the Celts, there was added "a degree of education which would astonish some of their absentee employers. There are scores of men working in the Welsh pits who could pass an examination in Ibsen or Shaw or Swinburne, or could hold their own in an argument on economics or politics with the average member of Parliament." These men owed their training "not to the state or the municipalities" but to the educational facilities provided by the I.L.P., the Central Labour College, and the Plebs League. "For years past free evening classes in economics, industrial history, and similar subjects have been held in I.L.P. branch rooms in the various mining centres"; another educational movement, the Central Labour College, was centred in the Rhondda where ex-students took classes and were making special efforts to extend their work throughout the district, "chiefly by lectures in the workmen's institutes and co-operative society rooms". The Plebs League aimed to educate workers by classes in sociology, industrial history and Marxist economics. "Not only do hundreds of young miners absorb their teaching", but others had gone to the college and returned to preach what they had

[1] The assessment occurs in an article in a Cardiff monthly, *The Welsh Outlook*, quoted in *Plebs*, Vol. VIII, No. 9, October 1916.

learned. Men so educated attended Lodge meetings so that decisions were taken by a handful of extremists; to a large extent the Miners Federation "has been captured by men of advanced and even revolutionary views".[1]

The same points were made by the Commission of Enquiry into Industrial Unrest which reported on South Wales in August 1917. Independent working-class education was again assessed as an important factor, the Commissioners estimating that up to 500 students were being educated in C.L.C. classes; they added that the number had largely increased since March. The trades councils "have become centres of *educational* work from which lectures and classes on political and social subjects have been organised, and secondly, they have become centres of *social* and *political* activity more potent, perhaps, than any other of the social movements of the community". On the other hand university Extension work, the teachings of "the younger school of Oxford democrats", had no direct appeal to the Welsh workers; "the closely-packed valleys of Glamorgan have been given over to propagandist work of a political nature" and thereby "the essential spirituality of education" had been forgotten. The Commissioners pressed the need for education, pursued in the spirit Tawney had outlined as a moving spirit in the W.E.A., to further "not knowledge in the narrow, limited sense of equipment, but knowledge sought in the spirit of truth and pursued for its own end". The point was forthwith taken up from the employers' side, an article in the *Colliery Guardian* advocating that the university take over all educational work.[2] The attention given to the educational work in South Wales was probably justified; with the exception of Clydeside, there was no district where it was so integrally connected with Labour movement organisation. In December 1917 nearly forty classes in the area were listed by *Plebs*, A. J. Cook (who took three classes), Mark Starr and W. H. Mainwaring being particularly active.[3]

---

[1] *Plebs*, Vol. VIII, No. 11, December 1916, quoting *The Times*, 22 November 1916.
[2] It added, "We would suggest that courses of lectures on Marxian sociology should be given in every industrial centre. Few people who talk and write upon the relation of Capital and Labour are really familiar with the absurdity of the views advocated by Karl Marx." *Colliery Guardian* 10 August 1917; *Report of the Commission of Enquiry into Industrial Unrest*, No. 7 District, Wales and Monmouthshire, quoted and commented on in *Plebs*, Vol. IX, No. 8, September 1917.
[3] A. J. Cook, an ex-student of the Labour college, was Secretary of the Miners' Federation of Great Britain at the time of the General Strike; Mark Starr was a leading supporter of the C.L.C., writing their first textbook *A Worker looks at History*. A. J. Mainwaring, another ex-student of the Labour College, later joined its staff. He was Labour M.P. for the Rhondda Valley from 1933 to 1959.

In the mining districts of Northumberland and Durham, where, as we have seen, there was a long tradition of working-class education, Will Lawther and Ebby Edwards, later leading figures in the Miners' Federation, were the moving spirits, starting classes on economics for miners at Chopwell and Consett in 1915,[1] and in May 1916, calling a conference at Newcastle at which W. W. Craik put the case for the Labour college and its provincial classes to union delegates. From this point steps were taken to start classes in various centres, and a determined effort made to get union support for them, Lawther publishing an Open Letter to the Durham Miners prior to their Annual Conference. "Last month the editor commented on our 'big push'," reported Lawther to *Plebs*, "we have now turned it into a 'big offensive' and it augurs well."[2]

At this stage a clash developed with the W.E.A. which had received a £50 grant from the Durham miners and was seeking the official support of the Northumberland miners union, a clash which gave rise to something of a pamphlet war. The Central Labour College was now also establishing regional associations and in March 1917, a conference was held to consider the formation of one in the north-east, comparable to that established in South Wales; Lawther presided and Edwards was one of the speakers. Afterwards Edwards, a member of the executive committee of the Northumberland Miners' Union, challenged the secretary of the W.E.A. to a debate on the aims and nature of working-class education and this subsequently took place in Newcastle at a great conference organised by the W.E.A. The speech given on this occasion by Ebby Edwards was printed by his supporters and widely circulated; this, *A Plea for a Real Working-class Education*, drew from the W.E.A. the response *What is Real Democratic Education?* a reprint of Edwards' speech with a foreword and reply by MacTavish, the W.E.A. secretary. In July the Plebs League entered the field with a lively, popular pamphlet *What does Education mean to the Workers?* by J. F. and W. Horrabin which sold out a first edition of 10,000 in two months; this again put the case for an independent organisation and was in part a reply to an earlier pamphlet by MacTavish *What Labour Wants from Education*.[3]

Meanwhile the north-east division of the Central Labour College

---

[1] *Plebs*, Vol. VII, No. 11, December 1915.
[2] *Ibid.*, Vol. VIII, No. 4, May 1915; Vol. IX, No. 11, December 1916. At this time three classes were being run at Newcastle, and three elsewhere in the area (Consett, Chopwell, South Shields).
[3] *Ibid.*, Vol. IX, No. 2, March 1917; No. 3, April 1917; No. 6, July 1917.

THE PIONEER W.E.A. TUTORIAL CLASS AT ROCHDALE, 1907

Harold Pershouse
Eugene Tiernan
John A. Lee.
Henry Hill
Bingford
Thomas W. Price
Thos. W. Ormerod.
Charles H. Pearce
Leonard Plant
Thomas McLean
Eleanor Hatshaw
Arthur Shore
Wallis L. Stafford
Alfred Sutcliffe
Fanny Taylor
Frederick Turner
Alfred P. Wadsworth
James Warburton
Alfred Wilkinson
Albert E. Wilson
Joseph Wormald.

Tom Bailey
Joseph Binns
Harold Briggs
Albert Butterworth
John Clegg
Arthur Collinge
Joseph Dyer
Stanley Dawson
John Dowbes.
Roy Duckworth
Harry Forrest
Frederick Greenwood
George E. Greenwood
Lawrence V. Gill
Fred Hall
James Kernighan
Chas. H. Miller
Richard Heyes
Charles Heartle
James E. Fell—
Esther Vanhear

A. Tawney.

had been formed, with Lawther as president and Edwards treasurer, and by the close of 1917 there were some fifty trade union branches affiliated and sixteen classes running; the Northumberland Miners' Union had accorded financial support (by a vote of 35 to 14) and the Durham Miners were considering a £50 grant. Before the end of the war, then, the Labour college movement had taken firm roots among the miners of the north-east.

Once more, however, it was on Clydeside, where John Maclean had lectured widely for the S.D.F. and the S.L.P. had held organised classes over many years, that the link between Marxist education and disaffection was the closest, expressed in a growing movement against the war which combined open air meetings and demonstrations with study classes and "sustained discussions and literature sales in the factories".[1] Maclean, now a member of the British Socialist Party which had superseded the S.D.P., was the leader of this movement. "His energy and activity surpassed anything we had seen before," writes William Gallacher. "Breathing hatred for the capitalist class and the destruction which it threatened humanity, he went about the streets of Glasgow rousing the workers to a fury of anger against the war and the warmakers."[2] Clydeside was soon "a seething cauldron of unrest" but it remained also a centre of study. The outbreak of war "in no way interrupted the general educational work," writes Bell in his biography of Maclean. "On the contrary the urge among the workers, towards reading, study and propaganda steadily increased." Classes began to be formed in the workshops to study economics and industrial history, during the dinner hour on the day shift, and during the night shift break between 1 a.m. and 2 a.m. But these efforts were "largely spontaneous and unco-ordinated"[3] until the Plebs League took root in Scotland and moves were made on the initiative of Maclean to found a Scottish Labour College

Before the meeting called to consider the latter question took place Maclean had been arrested, to be sentenced to a three-year term of imprisonment of which he served fifteen months.[4] But his speech was

---

[1] A. L. Morton and G. Tate, *The British Labour Movement* (1956), 260.

[2] W. Gallacher, *Revolt on the Clyde* (1936), 20.

[3] Bell, *John Maclean*, 132.

[4] It was stated at the British Socialist Party conference in April 1916, during discussion of a resolution of protest against the arrest of Maclean and others, that "it was because of the educational side of the B.S.P. work that it had been attacked. In Glasgow they had the largest economics class in the world . . . Macdougall (also arrested) had also carried on tremendous educational work, and had numerous speakers' classes. The six men who had been deported to Edinburgh had also been associated with education in working class organisations." *5th B.S.P. Conference Report*, 1916.

read to a conference attended by 500 delegates from trade unions, co-operative and socialist organisations held in Glasgow on 12 February 1916, presided over by the miners' leader, Bob Smillie. Maclean made the case for independent working-class education drawing on a long experience of conducting it. The workers "must establish and maintain their own Colleges to equip themselves for their own specific tasks as a class". At a Labour college "economics must be taught fundamentally from the Labour standpoint . . . our students must make the writings of Marx and Marxian scholars the basis of their studies; otherwise the college becomes an expensive tragedy". The teaching of history must also be based on Marxism. Trade unionism and the co-operative movement deserved special study, while general subjects such as literature and mathematics demanded attention. "That there is a need for a college is proved by the success which has attended the voluntary classes . . . and by the size of this conference today," he concluded. "The workers, if they are successfully to resist increased exploitation, and to make progress towards freedom, can only do so if they utilise their resources wisely for the training of leaders and the diffusion of essential knowledge amongst themselves."[1]

A resolution gave unanimous approval to the proposal and appointed a provisional committee to run the college; but in Maclean's absence progress was at first slow. Meanwhile the Plebs League began to take root in Scotland for the first time, fostered mainly by the Socialist Labour Party which was active at this time in publishing Marxist works. Soon Tom Bell, now employed at a Glasgow steel works, found as many as 200 workers attending his lectures on Marxism at a study circle which had grown up since the war; in 1917 and 1918 he was running special economics study circles for foundry workers, moulders, iron dressers and labourers.[2] A Glasgow branch of the Plebs League was set up after a conference convened by the S.L.P. and attended by representatives from union branches, workshop groups and a variety of socialist bodies (the S.L.P., I.L.P., B.S.P., Industrial Workers of the World). Maclean, fearing a clash between this body and the Scottish Labour College, opposed this step and for a few months the two organisations functioned separately. In the winter of 1917, according to Bell, the new Plebs organisation was running twenty classes while the Scottish Labour College, which organised classes in many different cities, claimed an aggregate attendance of

[1] Bell, *John Maclean*, 133-5.
[2] Bell, *Pioneering Days*, 129-30, 147.

1,500 students.[1] The two organisations were eventually merged, a conference in March 1918, attended by over 400 delegates, establishing a constitution for the Scottish Labour College, John Maclean being appointed as one of its paid tutors.

There had been a new vigour in this work after the revolutions in Russia in 1917 which evoked wide enthusiasm among all sections of the British Labour movement and brought new support to the left wing. Lancashire and Yorkshire now developed as centres of activity and conferences were held to further developments in Manchester, Liverpool, Sheffield and Halifax as well as in London and Durham. When the war ended seven provincial divisions were established or in the making, textbooks were now being produced, the circulation of *Plebs* had risen and well over a hundred classes were running.[2] If the greatest strength of this movement lay in West Scotland and South Wales it had also made a mark in the industrial centres of England.

When, after the armistice, the Central Labour College in London reopened, a fresh impetus was given to work in the provinces and some local colleges were now established with full-time teachers. The term "Labour college" otherwise covered all the individual classes organised in a particular area which, to maintain the principle of working-class control, were governed by a body made up of area representatives of trade unions, co-operative and other societies providing the funds and support. By 1920 it had become evident that national co-ordination was now called for and the National Council of Labour Colleges came into being in 1921 with an executive committee elected from the local organisations. This set out to gain affiliation from trade unions at the national level offering to provide educational schemes for their members.

The W.E.A., which was still engaged in extending its relations with the trade union movement, now also set up a national body to this end, the Workers' Educational Trade Union Committee. During the next four or five years the T.U.C. general council attempted to work out a scheme, acceptable to all parties, which would co-ordinate the

---

[1] Tom Bell, *John Maclean*, 136-7. *Final Report of the Adult Education Committee* (1919) states that the provisional committee of the Scottish Labour College organised seventeen classes in economic and political subjects in the winter of 1917-18, with 1,500 students enrolled. The Glasgow Plebs League organised nineteen classes, "in which about 1,000 students were enrolled" (p. 291). Many of these classes were tutored by Maclean, others by J. F. Armour, now Secretary of the Scottish Labour College, and William Gallacher. *Plebs*, Vol. IX, No. 11, December 1917.

[2] *Plebs*, Vol. X, No. 8, September 1918.

work of the two organisations and bring them under T.U.C. control. Throughout these negotiations the N.C.L.C. and the Central Labour College (now standing as an independent body controlled by the N.U.R. and the S.W.M.F.) firmly insisted on one guarantee—that the teaching organised through these bodies, or whatever superseded them, should continue to be based on Marxism. This condition was accepted by the general council of the T.U.C. In the outcome, however, the protracted negotiations ended in failure.[1] Subsequently the N.C.L.C., engaged in promoting education for different unions and controlled by an executive representing a variety of local organisations, itself moved gradually away from this standpoint, in particular after the general strike of 1926.

Meanwhile the Plebs League remained active on its own account providing, through its journal and classes, a centre for Marxist discussion and education. In 1920, however, many of its members joined the Communist Party, which incorporated also former members of the B.S.P., S.L.P. and other socialist societies. Although Communists continued to participate in the work of the Plebs League, inevitably the Communist Party found it necessary to develop its own, independent educational activity. It was in this context that Marxist education developed anew, once more in direct connection with the political movement. This, it may be said, represented continuation of the tradition of independent working-class education, which had always been pursued as an integral aspect of the struggle for political and economic emancipation and latterly with a determination not only to maintain working-class control but also to promote teaching based on Marxism.

A whole phase of development thus came to a close at this time. From the first upsurge of socialism in the 1880s there had been a proliferation of educational activity organised by the working class for the working class, first in small circles but then reaching out more widely into a Labour movement embracing a wide variety of organisations concerned with educational and cultural activities. There had also been, for humanitarian, philanthropic and political reasons, a growing provision of education for the workers by other organisations—the adult school movement, settlements and clubs, the universities. Some efforts were more successful than others, at a time when the demand for education was growing, and teaching was sponsored at various

---

[1] The Central Labour College was forced to close in 1929. For the post-war years of the college and the negotiations with the T.U.C. see Craik, *op. cit.*, 112-53.

levels. Then, in 1903, the Workers' Educational Association brought the universities more closely into contact with working-class organisations to provide a new basis for development. Classes were successfully established which aimed to provide a higher education leading on to university work, but this aim was not achieved; the universities remained as exclusive as ever and it was only when scholarship holders from the secondary schools began to find their way up in the 1920s and 1930s that working-class children at last began to have access to university education on a small scale.

The education provided for workers remaining in their jobs thus increasingly appeared not as a means of transforming society but rather as a means to personal cultivation. The W.E.A. rapidly expanded but was soon challenged by the Labour college movement which grew out of the Ruskin College strike; a strike directed immediately against the plan to subsume a working men's college under the university but which led to the launching of a general movement to renew and extend facilities for working-class education under working-class control. The long-term gain of this movement in terms of an educational organisation was the National Council of Labour Colleges, supported solely by the trade union and Labour movement and receiving no official grants of any kind. In response, pursuing its own policy, the W.E.A. also entered the field at a national level, to provide through the allied Workers' Educational Trade Union Committee a form of service to the unions which left to them control of the actual education given in classes.

These organisations, as they became settled, took the leading part in providing organised education for the working-class by comparison with the settlements, clubs and schools of an earlier decade. Consequently the Labour movement itself paid less direct attention to promoting educational work at a time when other ancillary organisations—such as the Clarion movement and the Labour Churches—tended gradually to lose their former wide appeal and influence. It remained once more for the left wing of the political movement to promote anew the conception of independent working-class education and attempt to spread it. But during these years, as the trade union apparatus itself established a new relationship with the machinery of state, a foundation was laid for general acceptance of the idea that education must essentially be non-partisan, above the battle. It would later seem reasonable enough that a major part in promoting adult education should be taken over by the educational system, if still in co-operation with outside organisations. Although the trade union and co-operative movement continued to promote educational activities on the part of their members, the Labour movement as a whole now made no further move towards founding institutions designed to teach from a specifically Labour standpoint.

CHAPTER X

THE FIRST WORLD WAR AND EDUCATIONAL REFORM

FOR over a year from May 1915 to October 1916 a representative of the Labour movement, Arthur Henderson, held the post of President of the Board of Education in the Asquith administration. But this was a token of lack of concern for education rather than otherwise, for Henderson, brought into the government to deal with labour relations, was simply awarded the office as a resting place. Unable to give any attention to the work of the Board he complained that he appeared to his own party and in Parliament "principally as the defender of the reactionary policies inherited from his predecessor".[1] The matter was amended when the Asquith government fell and Lloyd George succeeded as premier. War weariness was spreading, industrial unrest and disaffection growing, while socialist agitation against the war had reached alarming proportions on Clydeside. Lloyd George determined on a fresh approach. Vigorous prosecution of the war would be coupled with plans for all-round reconstruction, education would have priority as a chief means of promoting in social life that equality of condition with which men now faced death on the battlefield. As evidence of sincerity he appointed H. A. L. Fisher, Vice-Chancellor of Sheffield University, as President of the Board, accorded him a seat in the cabinet and gave "an undertaking that money would be found for ambitious educational measures".[2]

The pressure for educational change came from various sources—particularly from working-class organisations, teachers, and certain Liberal groups. At the same time the higher level of German education was seen as a continuing threat, and this incentive played its part. But there were, of course, other reasons why some advance in education was considered desirable—especially in a period of mounting industrial struggle: it was seen as an effective antidote to social unrest. The war might end, "and find us unprepared for new developments as in 1815," wrote the leading educational journal. Continuation classes from 14-18 were essential to "carry on the moral and disciplinary

---

[1] Mary Agnes Hamilton, *Arthur Henderson* (1938), 106.
[2] David Ogg, *Herbert Fisher* (1947), 62.

influence of the elementary schools".[1] "If industrial harmony is to take the place of social unrest," said A. L. Smith, now Master of Balliol, "education, on the moral and social side must be taken up in a way that had hardly been experimented upon as yet. . . . Unless we educated our democracy there would be the greatest social and political trouble as the outcome of the war."[2] Education, said Fisher, in a speech at Newcastle, "dispels the hideous clouds of class suspicion and softens the asperities of faction." It is encouraging to observe, he added, that "the sense of the value of education as an end in itself, as one of the constituent elements in human happiness, is now widely spread among the manual workers of the country".[3]

Different views were, however, finding expression in the Labour movement where the establishment of a highly structured system of education was still seen as the consolidation of class divisions in a new form, directed by those interested in maintaining these divisions. "The whole system is rotten," declared a speaker at the 1916 congress of the T.U.C., "and since University men have been established at Whitehall, the line of partition between the middle and working classes is greater than ever." Hundreds of thousands of pounds were paid over by the government towards the education of the middle classes in schools outside popular control. "I was a member of a School Board as far back as 1890, and we fought for the establishment of the system of free higher primary schools. We were successful in that fight, and then we saw the introduction of secondary schools. We understood that the secondary schools were schools to which our children would advance, but we have been bitterly disappointed . . . We cannot get our children to the secondary schools, because our people cannot afford it."[4]

Working-class children were excluded from secondary schools not only by high fees but also because only enough places were provided to educate a small proportion of each age group, those who were to

---

[1] *Times Educational Supplement*, 19 April 1917; 5 April 1917.
[2] *Ibid.*, 4 January 1917.
[3] *Ibid.*, 7 June 1916. Some believe that education is a source of discontent and unrest, he said, but education does not breed discontent, it heals it. A similar point is stressed by Fisher in his preface to *Educational Reform*, a collection of his speeches published early in 1918; here Fisher notes the connection between the provisions of the Education Bill and the Representation of the People Act. Men and women, he says, must be rescued from "the dumb helplessness of ignorance". "In these columns," noted the *Times Educational Supplement*, "we have repeatedly declared that the new franchise and the new education are supplementary things. Without education, Bolshevism, or syndicalism run mad, indicates the unconscious goal. Labour has nothing to gain from such madness." *Ibid.*, 28 February 1918.
[4] *48th T.U.C. Report*, 1916, 370-1.

be groomed to rise out of the manual working class. This opinion was expressed by the Professor of Education at Manchester University, J. J. Findlay, when he said that the secondary school was by tradition a "class" school "largely designed to enable its pupils to escape from a democratic environment and to play their part as members of a directing and governing class".[1] Over and above this longstanding grievance, conditions in the schools, for the children generally, had greatly deteriorated during the first two years of the war. Summing up the situation in the spirit of 1917, the *Times Educational Supplement* recalled that four years earlier Haldane had declared education to be the most urgent of the great social problems with which the government had to deal. A wide range of proposals had then been discussed, from raising the leaving age to fourteen to the establishment of new universities. The government had promised legislation but nothing had been done. With the outbreak of war child labour had been "revived and intensified", the estimates of local authorities slashed, "but the government gave no sign. The teachers were to be patriotic and go on as best they could." War had since absorbed more and more attention, education less and less.[2]

"In directing attention during a crisis of the war to the need for vast schemes of social reform Lloyd George was rightly interpreting the mood of the nation," writes Fisher's biographer assessing the situation from another angle.[3] There was certainly a growing determination that after the war things would be different, social evils and injustices abolished, and a brave new world emerge from the years of frustration, horror and mass slaughter. Fisher himself vividly depicts one expression of this feeling during the campaign for his Education Bill. "Everywhere the halls were packed and the audiences enthusiastic", but the most surprising occasion was a meeting of dockers in a theatre in Bristol: "I have never encountered such enthusiasm. They did what I have never seen before or since, rose to their feet two or three times in the course of my speech, waved their handkerchiefs, and cheered themselves hoarse. The prospect of wider opportunities which the new plan for education might open to the disinherited filled them with enthusiasm." Writing at a later date he is, however, bound to add an epitaph: "Alas for these good folk. They expected from an Education Bill what no Bill on education or anything else can give, a new Heaven and a new Earth."[4]

[1] *Times Educational Supplement*, 19 April 1917.   [2] *Ibid.*   [3] Ogg, *op. cit.*, 62.
[4] H. A. L. Fisher, *An Unfinished Autobiography* (1940), 106-7.

In the outcome the Fisher Act, passed in August 1918, was the only major measure of social reform placed on the statute book before the war ended, a pattern in due course to be repeated with the Education Act of 1944.

1. The Bradford Charter

The Labour movement receives no mention in the *Times Educational Supplement* among those contributing to the stream of "schemes of educational reform, amounting in fact to educational revolution" pouring in to the press in the spring of 1917; though it enumerates every variety of educational body, "statesmen and cranks, experts and amateurs, headmasters and assistant masters, directors of education, education committees, associations of teachers, and leagues of reformers and reactionaries, humanists and men of science, Montessorists, Froebelians, bishops, priests, and the dwellers in America".[1] Yet the programme which became known as "the Bradford Charter" had already been formulated, published and commented upon in October 1916.

Up to this time the T.U.C. had been concentrating on three main issues in the effort to arrest the deterioration in conditions: the economy drive and its effect on education, the extension of child labour and the tendency to reduce the already meagre provision of free places in secondary schools. Each of these was seen as an attack on popular education, on gains hardly won, and on each strong opinions were expressed. In 1915 the T.U.C., which had not met the previous year, passed a long resolution on traditional lines demanding a widely ranging educational advance and requested the President of the Board to receive a deputation. They received a dusty answer. The matters raised would require legislation "often of a highly contentious character" as well as "substantial grants of public money". The President doubted whether discussions would be fruitful. No perspective for any reconstruction planning or legislation was held out: "it is clear that both legislation and additional State aid for education are out of the question so long as the war lasts"—what could be achieved after it was over would be determined by the financial situation. The letter, signed by an official (G. M. Young), concluded by saying that the President was inclined to think "it would be sufficient that the desiderata of the Congress should be placed on record" for later consideration.[2]

---

[1] *Times Educational Supplement*, 4 January 1917.
[2] *48th T.U.C. Report*, 1916, 82.

Henderson did, however, receive a deputation on the question of child labour, a matter to which the T.U.C. returned at the 1916 congress protesting emphatically against the increased employment of children in agriculture as well as in the factories. The Treasury policy of retrenchment in educational expenditure was also denounced as "false economy and prejudicial to the ultimate welfare of the nation". At this Congress, Henderson's complacency as President of the Board was sharply criticised by several delegates, H. H. Elvin moving a resolution arguing that local authorities were simply "taking advantage of the call for economy to deprive children of adequate educational facilities". New school buildings were being delayed, classes increasing in size, and the position generally deteriorating.[1]

The I.L.P. conference this year also entered "an emphatic protest against the actions of many Education Authorities in curtailing expenditure on education.[2] There was also a new ally in the W.E.A., one of whose aims was "to articulate the educational aspirations of Labour" and represent them to the proper authorities, and it was perhaps chiefly at the conferences sponsored by local W.E.A. branches that growing feeling in the matter was expressed. Well placed to organise meetings, since they could call on a variety of affiliated bodies, W.E.A. branches did so with effect during 1916 at Bristol, Rugby, Durham and elsewhere. But one of the most influential conferences was the first held that year, in January, called at the Memorial Hall, Faringdon Street; it drew 550 delegates from different organisations to protest against a proposed cut of £362,000 in the educational expenditure of the L.C.C. The annual conference of the W.E.A. could, therefore, summarise a great deal of opinion when it resolved that:

> "Any reduction in National Expenditure on education would be both false economy and gravely prejudicial to the welfare of the nation . . . the whole educational resources of the nation—rates, endowments and taxes—should be so administered and expended as to secure that the children of the poor do not suffer as compared with the children of the well-to-do."[3]

It was, however, not to complain of present discontents but to discuss a comprehensive programme for education after the war that the Bradford Trades Council called a conference in October 1916. The initiative may have come from the Labour Party—the Southampton Trades and Labour Council held a similar conference at this

---

[1] Ibid., 365-9.   [2] 24th I.L.P. Conference Report, 1916, 92.
[3] The Highway, Vol. 8, No. 86, November 1915, 26-7.

time and also produced a programme—but the proposals set before
the conference, which was attended by delegates representing 60,000
organised workers, had been formulated by local trade unionists. The
conference unanimously adopted this far-reaching programme and it
was then forwarded to other trades councils which in turn lent support. It
was, therefore, with the backing of thirty or more trades councils that
the Bradford scheme came before the annual conferences of the I.L.P.
and the Labour Party in 1917, to be adopted as the Labour programme.[1]

The plan drawn up by Bradford trade unionists embodied points
which had featured regularly in earlier policies advanced by the Labour
movement but took them a stage further, envisaging a wide ranging
educational advance. The central feature of the programme is "universal, free, compulsory secondary education" involving the raising of
the leaving age to sixteen and no exemptions for part-time employment. Abolition of the dual system is implied in the proposal that all
schools, colleges and universities should become a public responsibility. All higher forms of education, both technical and university,
should be "entirely free" to pupils who wished to follow these courses
and fully co-ordinated. A sound foundation of general education for all
is envisaged; only in the final year of the secondary course should
there be any technical, professional or commercial bias, and then as
part of a continuing general education.

In short, the Bradford scheme proposed, within the framework of
a unified national system of education, a common secondary school;
this is what the abolition of all forms of competitive entry and the
emphasis on a general education for all implies. "No longer ought
education to be administered on the assumption that only a minority
are fit to be educated, or that education is for the few," declared
W. Leach who proposed the programme. This also called, as was
proper coming from Bradford, for a great extension of medical
services to children and expectant mothers, for gymnasia, swimming
baths, playing-fields for elementary schools, extension of the school
meals service and many other items.[2] Claiming as a right for the
working class the kind of facilities long enjoyed by the wealthy, the
Bradford scheme constituted a charter of educational advance.

[1] *Labour Party Conference Report*, 1917, 135.
[2] Including an increase in the number of maintenance grants, improvement of hygienic
conditions in elementary schools, a scheme of physical education for young people aged
16-20, higher salaries and a better standard of equipment for teachers, reduction of the
size of classes in elementary schools, acceptance of the principle of the open-air school.
Times Educational Supplement, 19 October 1916.

It received a bad press. The scheme represented a doctrine of education "that had played its clear part in the downfall of Germany", said a leader "Labour and Education" in the *Times Educational Supplement;* the state is made "an all-powerful superhuman personality" whereas what is really important is the "individuality" of every child.[1] The essence of the Bradford scheme, however, was its firm insistence on secondary education for all. This, in the next decades, was to become and to remain the key issue. It is only necessary to compare the Bradford scheme with others now being put forward to recognise its importance.

In November and December 1916 three representative bodies put forward their plans for educational reform: the W.E.A., the National Union of Teachers and the Educational Reform Council. Each gave an important place to secondary schooling but none advocated secondary education for all.

The W.E.A. called for a large increase in the number of secondary schools to which children should be admitted who "have reached an approved standard of education"; secondary schools should be varied in type, providing a "more variable" curriculum to meet the interests of individual pupils. This was the first clear statement of a policy which later found expression in the Hadow and Spens Reports. Further the W.E.A., in contrast to the Bradford scheme, stressed the need for compulsory part-time education for all to eighteen. The school leaving age should be raised to fifteen without exemptions within five years, but local authorities should be allowed to make by-laws raising the age to sixteen.[2]

The National Union of Teachers appears to have drawn up proposals hurriedly for it issued a pedestrian document; this, too, advocated that schools "other than primary" should be of "different types" and that admission to them "shall depend on capacity to take advantage of the courses of instruction given therein"—the formula used in introducing free places in 1907.[3]

The Education Reform Council, founded in April 1916 at a conference in London called to discuss educational reconstruction, was the province of liberal educationists of a similar background to Fisher; its programme was signed by Gilbert Murray, Michael Sadler, Percy Nunn, A. N. Whitehead, William Garnett, Henry Miers among others.[4] This, rather than envisaging secondary education for all,

---

[1] *Ibid.*, 26 October 1916.   [2] *Ibid.*, 14 December 1916.
[3] *Ibid.*, 28 December 1916.   [4] *Ibid.*, 30 November 1916.

suggested that elementary schools be divided at eleven into junior sections (5-11) and senior sections (11-14). At eleven some should be transferred, by means of scholarships and free places, to secondary (grammar) schools and to selective higher elementary schools. The Council worked out proposals for the examination at eleven in some detail. Here, then, the idea that elementary and secondary schools are of different kinds is explicitly perpetuated by comparison with the W.E.A.'s emphasis on providing a variety of secondary schools to meet the interests of different groups of children beyond the age of eleven. But in practice, given the system already in existence, both policies tended towards the same end and shades of meaning did not greatly count. The programme of the Education Reform Council was, in fact, that implemented in the 1920s and '30s.

Other schemes advanced often called for an expansion of secondary education, including an increase in the number of scholarship and free places and variation in the types of school established. But nearly all shared another common feature in advocacy of part-time continued education up to sixteen or eighteen. This proposal had been reported upon by the Consultative Committee in 1909; it had figured in the abortive Education Bill of 1911 and was thereafter widely taken up. The danger, of course, was that it might be seen as an alternative to the raising of the school leaving age. Only the Bradford scheme, taking up what had for years been a key point of T.U.C. policy, insisted squarely on full-time secondary education up to a leaving age of sixteen. Before the close of 1917 this had become the official policy of the I.L.P. and the Labour Party.[1]

2. THE PASSAGE OF THE EDUCATION ACT, 1918

In the early spring of 1917, as advice accumulated, Fisher was working out his proposals; they had been discussed and accepted by the Cabinet by the end of February.[2] Meanwhile on 15 February, the President of the Board, receiving a deputation from the T.U.C., said that he looked to the unions to direct public opinion. In April the W.E.A.'s views were pressed by a deputation headed by William Temple, President of the association, which included Ernest Bevin, representing the Bristol dockers who were shortly so to touch Fisher's

[1] At the Labour Party conference the resolution on education, comprising the full Bradford programme, was moved by F. Titterington, of the Bradford Trades Council. *Labour Party Conference Report*, 1917, 135.

[2] *Times Educational Supplement*, 1 March 1917. The Cabinet's discussion of Fisher's proposals "was over in less than half an hour". Fisher, *An Unfinished Autobiography*, 103.

heart; it was given a pat on the back and a somewhat pompous lecture to the effect that the W.E.A. should encourage a greater interest in education in the Labour movement.[1]

Attention became focused at this point on the vital and related question of child labour by the publication in April of the Report of the Departmental Committee on Juvenile Employment (the Lewis Report). *The Times Educational Supplement*, which had frequently drawn attention to the worsening of conditions since the war, affirmed that hitherto child labour had been "deliberately fostered by the state"; to permit exemption from school attendance (as was statutorily necessary) made it "certain that, in manufacturing districts, every child will leave at thirteen", and they would become half-timers at twelve. There had been no inducement for local education authorities to move when the Board of Education was forced to allow its great name to sanctify "by-laws as iniquitous as they were disastrous". To raise the leaving age to fourteen without exemptions would mean that "the whole rout of industrial provisions contained in various Labour Acts will go", and the authorities will be able for the first time to provide fairly for the children's education.[2]

It was in much the same spirit that the Lewis Report, criticising the exemption clauses of previous Acts and the consequent continuance of half-time schooling, as well as the chaos reigning in the field of apprenticeship and the conditions of child labour, stressed the need for a complete change of attitude. "We do not think it necessary to detail once more the arguments in favour of bringing to an end the present detestable system of half-time exemptions below the age of fourteen," stated the committee; the dominating influence on young people between the ages of twelve and eighteen must be educational. Great emphasis was put on the need for part-time continued education, the committee recommending a leaving age of fourteen, with no exemptions, followed by attendance for not less than eight hours a week or 320 hours a year at continuation classes up to the age of eighteen. The conception of the juvenile "as primarily a little wage-earner" must give place to the conception of him "as primarily the workman and citizen in training".[3]

---

[1] *Ibid.*, 19 April 1917. Fisher often returned to the theme of lack of interest in education among the working class.

[2] *Ibid.*, 1 March 1917. See also review of Spurley Hey's *Development of the Education of Wage Earners*, "responsibility lies with successive governments who have deliberately fostered the use of child labour". *Ibid.*, 8 March 1917. Spurley Hey was Director of Education at Manchester.

[3] *Final Report of the Departmental Committee on Juvenile Employment* (1917), Vol. I, 5, 8.

The T.U.C. pressed for immediate implementation of the recommendations of the report, regarding these as a minimum; but since they were clearly limited in scope and proposed no change in the class nature of the educational system, expressed "intense dissatisfaction" with them.[1] It was shortly after this, at the end of April, that Fisher made his first important intervention in the Commons with a two hour speech on the Education Estimates. His announcement of a substantial increase in expenditure to a total of nearly £4 millions—a move supposed "out of the question" a year earlier—received a general welcome in the House. There was, however, some disappointment that he devoted little time to reconstruction, only sketching the outlines of a policy.[2] That policy was enunciated four months later.

The Bill Fisher brought before the Commons on 16 August 1917, incorporated, among many minor measures, two main proposals. All children should remain at school until fourteen, implying an end to all exemptions below this age and the abolition of the half-time system. All who did not receive full-time education up to sixteen should have part-time continued education up to eighteen for eight hours a week during forty weeks, or a total of 320 hours a year as recommended by the Lewis Report. In addition the Bill provided for the establishment of nursery schools for children under five, improvement of the school meals service, as well as of baths, playing-fields and games centres. There were proposals to develop higher forms of elementary education, to abolish fees in elementary schools and consolidate grants to these, and for making a general survey of educational provision including developing a closer relation between private institutions (the public schools) and the national system. Other clauses strengthened administration by giving more powers to the Board of Education.[3]

One point may be noted at the start—the Bill contained no religious clauses whatsoever: the settlement of 1902 was to be left undisturbed. This did not mean that either the churches on the one hand, or the secularists on the other, were satisfied. The Bradford scheme, as we have seen, demanded the overthrow of the 1902 Act, and full public control over all schools. The supporters of sectarian education felt that their schools were at a disadvantage. They did not, however, feel that this was the time to prosecute sectarian ends. "A great scheme of

---

[1] *49th T.U.C. Report*, 1917, 355.
[2] *Times Educational Supplement*, 26 April 1917.
[3] *Ibid.*, 16 August 1917.

educational reform" had been unfolded "in which there was no mention at all of religion", said the Bishop of Oxford in May. The reason why it was shelved by Fisher "was to be found in the attitude of the working classes. It was not that the working classes were irreligious, but that they had such bitter memories of the losses that had been sustained by education through religious controversy, and they were determined that religious controversy should no longer be allowed to pervert or disturb or stop educational reform. It was all part of the humiliating alienation of the workers from the churches of the country." Educational reform should continue unimpeded by controversy. Afterwards, the Church of England and Nonconformists should unite together and consider the whole question of religion.[1] In July Convocation came out in support of Fisher's reform proposals, "but resolved that so soon as such action can be taken without hindrance to those proposals a united effort should be made to secure that adequate religious instruction be an essential part of the education given".[2] The Church of England was waiting in the wings.[3]

How was the Bill received? Described as a "great Bill" by the Liberal press, it seemed at first as if it would win general support. In the early summer Fisher set out on his "educational campaign" during the course of which he met the Bristol dockers. Starting in Yorkshire he worked his way through Lancashire down to the Midlands and Wales, stressing in particular the need to put an end to the exploitation of child labour. Here he expected opposition and got it; the Lancashire cotton manufacturers launched an attack on the Bill, claiming that the abolition of the half-time system would disrupt the textile industry.[4]

Meeting in the autumn, the T.U.C. did not pass any resolution directly supporting the Bill and in the course of the conference failure to raise the leaving age to sixteen was strongly criticised. The reforms proposed "were overdue before the war", said one speaker, F. F. Riley of the Postal Clerks; certain improvements were advocated "but it is too much to suggest that the Bill can be accepted as a proper settlement of Labour's requirements in the direction of education".[5] Once

1 *Ibid.*, 17 May 1917.   2 *Ibid.*, 12 July 1917.
3 "The friends of religious teaching in our schools," said Fisher, "should be profoundly grateful that there is no mention of religion in the Bill, and that for once there is a chance of a great measure of educational reform being discussed without any stirring of sectarian passion." Ogg, *op. cit.*, 72. "After a few years' experience," writes Fisher's biographer, "he had to admit that the old dualism impeded any far-reaching measure of educational reform." In 1920 Fisher brought in a Bill which sought to modify the settlement of 1902. *Ibid.*, 73, 80.
4 *Times Educational Supplement*, 10 October 1917.
5 *49th T.U.C. Report*, 1917, 355.

Y

again there was a different response from Labour representatives in Parliament; Philip Snowden described the Bill as "the greatest attempt to reform and improve our system of National Education . . . since Mr. Forster's Education Act of 1870".[1] The Labour Party had no meeting at this time but in January 1918 described the Bill as falling "far short of the minimum that is adequate to the needs of the country and the opportunity before it".[2] The W.E.A. immediately remarked on its limitations: "The Bill is really a measure abolishing half-time," ran a statement issued in September which stressed the leaving age of fourteen and the limited plans for part-time continued education, "our members will naturally be disappointed with it. It prescribes a standard of universal education much below that which the Association has laid down as practical and necessary at the end of the war."[3] Fisher, who was free with his criticisms of the Labour movement for lack of interest in education, was disappointed by this general response; but it was lack of enthusiasm for a measure which failed to deal with matters in which Labour was interested.[4]

Towards the end of October it became clear that the Bill was running into difficulties and it was announced that it could not be passed before Christmas. The objections were various. "The fact is that the opposition to the Bill from certain Northern manufacturers, from certain groups of voluntary schools in the North-West of England, and from various education authorities (opposed to the increased power of the Board of Education) has made it clear that this is not an agreed measure," wrote the Times Educational Supplement.[5] There was an immediate and strong public reaction to withdrawal of the Bill, prompted by fears of strong pressure behind the scenes from

[1] Labour Leader, 25 October 1917.

[2] Labour Party Conference Report, January 1918, 122.

[3] The Highway, Vol. 9, No. 108, September 1917, 198.

[4] See, for instance, the severe criticisms of the Education Bill by the North-Western District of the W.E.A., Times Educational Supplement, 27 September 1917. It was Ernest Bevin's view, as expressed at a dockers' conference in 1918, that "the desire that the children shall have a better chance than their parents is inherent in the working class. The bolder the Minister of Education is in his proposals, the bigger the response he will get from the people." Alan Bullock, The Life and Times of Ernest Bevin (1960), I, 84-5. The Lewis Committee held the same view: "We have been impressed with the conviction of some of our witnesses as to the extent of the support which a vigorous educational policy would command amongst working men." The majority of the bodies affiliated to the London Trades Council, for instance, "are in favour of a leaving age of sixteen". Final Report of the Departmental Committee on Juvenile Employment, Vol. I, 6-7.

[5] 25 October 1917. "Protests poured in from different quarters," writes Fisher, referring to local authority objections. "The Bill, we were given to understand, was good enough, if the administrative provisions could be amended." Fisher, op. cit., 107.

long-standing enemies of educational advance.[1] Leicester Trades Council was one body to pass a resolution of protest in November, taking the opportunity to urge on the government a great increase in grants to provide for "a hundred thousand scholarships, to enable children of ability in the Elementary schools to proceed with their education to the age of twenty-one".[2] To allay disquiet it was announced that a revised Education Bill would be taken as the first business when the Commons resumed their sitting on 14 January.

The new Bill turned out to be the same in all essentials as the first; beyond minor changes it was only the administrative clauses, giving more powers to the Board, which had been excluded.[3] There had, then, been a concession to objections from the local authorities against more central control but none to the Lancashire manufacturers. These were to come. Like the Church of England the Lancashire employers did not feel that too much outright pressure for sectional interests would meet the case in the prevailing climate. But they nonetheless organised opposition, attempting also to rally the workers in the industry,[4] and received solid support when the Federation of British Industries issued a memorandum in January 1918 opposing the provision of compulsory continued education to eighteen, claiming that "in every industry this proposal is viewed with great alarm". The chief danger to the Bill, warned the Times Educational Supplement, "is and was the secret opposition of a powerful group of employers who are determined to retain child labour for the industries in which they are interested"; it foretold that the tactic would be to get spokesmen in the Commons to support a second reading and then attempt to modify the relevant clauses.[5] The outcome was as prophesied: the introduction

[1] Many letters of protest from organisations and individuals figure in the *Times Educational Supplement*, 8 November 1917; 15 November 1917.
[2] *Leicester Pioneer*, 9 November 1917. I owe this reference to Mr. J. C. Jones.
[3] The differences between the two Bills are analysed in *Times Educational Supplement*, 24 January 1918.
[4] A meeting was organised in February to oppose part-time continued education, which brought together all employers' and operatives' associations; *Ibid.*, 14 February 1918.
[5] The point is made as an accompaniment to a violent attack on the F.B.I. memorandum, including exposure of the attempts to win Labour for the employers' point of view; *ibid.*, 28 February 1918. The memorandum argued openly for a strictly stratified system of education, as well as for a restrictive educational policy. It expressed the view, wrote R. H. Tawney in a contemporary article, that the aim of education "is to reflect, to defend, and to perpetuate the division of mankind into masters and servants. . . . The Bourbons of industry who drafted it," he adds, "have learned nothing and forgotten nothing. Europe is in ruins; and out of the sea of blood and tears the Federation of British Industries emerges jaunty and unabashed, clamouring that whatever else is shaken, the vested interest of employers in the labour of children of fourteen must not be disturbed by so much as eight hours a week." *Daily News*, 14 February 1918, reprinted in R. H. Tawney, *The Radical Tradition*, 47-51.

and acceptance of an amendment which postponed for seven years part-time continued education between the ages of sixteen and eighteen. Without this amendment, wrote Fisher later, "the Bill would not have passed".[1] Finally, on 8 August, nearly a year after the first Bill had been introduced, the Education Act, 1918, reached the statute book.

It aroused no more enthusiasm in the Labour movement as an Act than it had done as a Bill. At its conference in January 1918, the Labour Party had urged amendment of the Bill to make it "a complete Charter of National Education from the Primary School to the University" and some delegates had expressed the hope that Labour M.P.s would fight for the "Bradford Charter".[2] This was the conference which acclaimed enthusiastically an address by an official representative of the Soviet government, brought to power by the socialist revolution of the previous October—at a special conference in June the Labour Party accepted socialism as its aim and fundamentally overhauled its constitution. On this occasion resolutions were put covering the whole field of reconstruction, the comprehensive one on education being moved by Sidney Webb. The most important of all measures of social reconstruction, it urged, is "a genuine nationalisation of education which shall get rid of all class distinctions and privileges".

This resolution, no doubt drafted by Sidney Webb but reflecting the feelings of the hour, was something of a manifesto. The Labour Party, while appreciating the proposals in the Education Bill, "cannot be satisfied with a system which condemns the great bulk of children to merely elementary schooling with accommodation and equipment inferior to that of secondary schools, in classes too large for efficient instruction, under teachers of whom at least one third are insufficiently trained . . . and which, notwithstanding what is yet done by way of scholarships, for exceptional geniuses, still reserves the endowed secondary schools, and even more the universities . . . to the sons and daughters of a small privileged class, whilst contemplating nothing better than eight weeks a year continuation schooling up to eighteen for 90 per cent of the youth of the nation." What was needed was "a systematic reorganisation of the whole educational system from the nursery school to the university on the basis of (a) social equality,

[1] Fisher, op. cit., 108.
[2] Labour Party Conference Report, January 1918, and adjourned conference 26 February 1918, 122. The resolution was moved by George Isaacs.

(b) the provision for each age—children, youth, adults—of the best and most varied education of which it is capable, (c) educational institutions, irrespective of social class or wealth to be planned, equipped and staffed according to their several functions up to the same high level for elementary, secondary or University teaching, with regard solely to the greatest possible educational efficiency, (d) recognition of the teaching profession, without distinction of grade, as one of the most valuable to the community."[1]

In September the T.U.C. called once more for a wide expansion of secondary and higher education with full maintenance, as the only means to realise that equality of opportunity "which the organised workers demand as theirs by right". The school leaving age should be raised to sixteen, all fees in secondary schools abolished, the curriculum needed complete revision especially in history and allied subjects; the establishment of nursery schools should not be permissive but obligatory. A Royal Commission should enquire into the universities—their constitution, endowments, colleges—and the Board should report regularly on the value, control and expenditure of the income from all endowments for schools and colleges. Whereas the Labour Party made a general statement, the T.U.C. particularised.[2] There was a need to open up perspectives again; to formulate precisely objectives not yet gained.

3. A STAGE IN EDUCATIONAL ADVANCE

The Fisher Act did not mark a stage in educational advance. As one provision after another fell victim during the years of post-war crisis it merely operated, much as the W.E.A. had suggested in the first flush of disappointment in 1917, as a measure to abolish the half-time system. In 1920 the school leaving age was raised to fourteen but there was neither compulsory part-time continued education after that age (except at Rugby) nor full-time secondary education for the great majority. In 1926 the Consultative Committee to the Board of Education produced the Hadow Report (*The Education of the Adolescent*) whose recommendations were partly put into practice amid the difficulties of the 1930s. Twelve years on again, in 1938, the Spens Report (*Secondary Education with Special Reference to Grammar Schools and Technical High Schools*) produced further plans for post-primary

---

[1] *18th Labour Party Conference Report*, June 1918, 71-2.
[2] *50th T.U.C. Report*, 1918, 303-4.

education but there was no time to implement these before the second world war broke out. Time was then once more found to pass an Education Act and in 1944 it was finally recognised in principle that there should be secondary education for all.

Nonetheless a new stage of development was reached in the 1920s, if in the politics of education rather than in terms of education itself. In particular the "coupon" election of 1918, and the coalition government consequently established under the wartime premier, spelt the demise of the great Liberal party; the two governments which briefly broke the spell of conservative rule were Labour governments, even if they were dependent on Liberal support. It was the end of a long road and the beginning of another.

To look back over the previous half-century is to find that during these years an educational system began to come into being, but one that was developed in a direction contrary to the expressed interests of the working class. From the moment that the foundations for a national system was laid by the 1870 Act, the efforts of the Labour movement were directed towards consolidating and extending the scope of schools providing for the workers' children. These efforts met with considerable success during the era of the School Boards, notably in the main industrial centres, only to be cut off by a policy directed to establishing anew the barriers between elementary schooling and any form of secondary education. The policy pursued could be defended on the grounds that it was essential to impose order on chaos, that development had been piecemeal and uncontrolled, that it must in future take place on lines and on a scale that it would be beyond the scope of local School Boards to administer—arguments which, it might be added, applied equally well to the methods of management of voluntary schools but were not there used. But the measures taken operated to remove administration of elementary education from the authorities which had done most to encourage upward development.

The seal was set on this policy in 1902 when all available forces were mobilised to ensure the sweeping away of School Boards. This necessarily implied heavy concessions to the Church—the granting of permanent forms of aid from public funds to deteriorating voluntary schools. The penalty paid was the firm establishment of a dual system of elementary education, controlled and financed on the one hand by the new education authorities and on the other by bodies of managers administering what were essentially sectarian, initially in the main Anglican, schools. This step, which resulted immediately in a decade of intense bitterness and strife, created on a long term view a brake on educational advance which could be operated at will by the Church.

The 1902 Education Act thus achieved two main objectives; it rescued the voluntary schools from certain inanition to create a divided system of elementary education, and it cleared the way for the consolidation of secondary schools quite separately from this system. Passage from elementary to secondary schools was strictly controlled by the award of scholarships and free places on a limited scale, but secondary schools remained open to children whose parents could pay fees. The measures necessary to this end were rigorously enforced during the years after 1902 under the guidance of Morant. These included new forms of grant aid which, while an advance to the old and discredited system of payment by results, allocated a great deal more per head in respect of pupils in secondary schools than for children in elementary schools. Whatever might be said in later years about providing "higher" forms of elementary education, the hard fact remained that higher grants were not available.

In objecting strongly to these policies the Labour movement saw them as part of a general intention strictly to circumscribe the education of working-class children while providing increasing facilities for the development of subsidised forms of secondary and higher education for the middle and upper class. Here the question of educational endowments was a key one, consistently evaded and beclouded by administrators, for it was indeed with the aid of funds left for the education of the poor and of local children that such schools as Harrow, Rugby, Oundle and many another edged out of the category of grammar schools and into that of public schools. The more the ordinary schools were brought under some form of control, the more urgent the efforts of public schools to contract out of any "state system", to establish, despite continued use of endowments which had once been looked on as a public responsibility, the right to independence of any form of public control. This state of affairs was consistently exposed and opposed by the T.U.C. and other organisations of the Labour movement when calling for a Royal Commission to investigate the finances and government of both universities and schools.

The cementing of the public school system, under the guidance of the Headmasters' Conference, introduced a new and powerful factor on the educational scene, providing also a rallying point for the remaining endowed grammar schools which were passing through difficult days. It was the combined pressure of such interested bodies that ensured the establishment of a secondary schools department of the Board of Education when this came into being in 1899; that department, staffed by ex-public school and university men, was responsible for administering the regulations governing all other secondary schools to which the Labour movement and the N.U.T. so strongly reacted. In the circumstances, in accordance with the whole policy which had motivated the Balfour-Morant Act of 1902, these regulations imposed both on the grammar schools and on newly developing municipal secondary schools the academic tradition of education that had been given a new lease of life in public schools. By the same token, efforts to promote a different form of post-primary education with a more scientific and technical content, of the kind favoured in higher grade and science schools, now met with considerable difficulties.

It was, in a sense, in the effort to revive this conception and counter the move towards a predominantly literary form of education that such bodies as the W.E.A. subsequently pressed for a variety of forms of secondary education to meet varying interests and needs. Only the T.U.C. adhered steadfastly to the conception of secondary education for all, specifying that there should be no vocational bias in the secondary course before the age of fifteen. Meanwhile there still reigned in hard fact a system which divided post-primary schooling from the age of eleven into two quite different kinds of education, elementary and secondary. Yet it was, increasingly, over the question of the form secondary schooling should take, on the educational rather than the social plane, that future arguments would be formulated.

Much the same occurred in the field of adult education with the establishment of new forms of co-operation between the universities and voluntary bodies to promote serious study; the aim of opening a way into the universities for mature students from the working class receded into the background while attention concentrated on developing an extra-mural form of further or higher education regarded as complete in itself. The idea that education is valuable for its own sake, an idea born of the very real desire for knowledge on the part of the working class and the idealism of those who set out to realise it, paradoxically enough contributed powerfully to limiting horizons. It was not to get on in life, to escape from their class, that these workers sought knowledge, but rather to enhance their own cultivation without wish or hope of entering either a university or politics. The universities themselves were well content to support this solution rather than opening their doors to the working-class student. As soon as Ruskin College began to develop into a centre of higher education, meeting the immediate needs of labour, it was regarded as a foreign body to be tamed and, if possible, absorbed. Working-class education, as many of the rank and file of the Labour and socialist movement conceived of it, could only be furthered outside this orbit in close connection with industrial and political activity directed to winning rights for labour in a wider field.

During a period of often bitter industrial struggles the organised Labour movement began once again, as earlier militant working-class movements had done, to regard access to education as one of the main keys to political and economic emancipation. What shines through the T.U.C. programmes and discussions at this time is the claim not merely for this or that provision but for education as a human right, recognition of which must inevitably imply a genuine equality of opportunity. At the same time efforts were directed to developing the services that had been gained, not least those essential welfare services without which children could not begin to profit from teaching. While campaigns on these issues met with considerable success, the consistent demand for a secular education and exposure of sectarian wranglings was also not without effect; it was a victory, if a limited one and not to be repeated, that the Education Act of 1918 passed without interference from the Church.

Achievement, however, could bring its own penalties in terms of losing sight of wider aims. As the day-to-day struggle to extend existing facilities—on local councils and in Parliament—tended to overtake the larger aim of transforming the educational system as a whole, Labour programmes began to approximate more nearly to those of other bodies concerned to promote social reform. This marked an important change, paralleling wider political developments—in particular the rise of Labour past the stage of representation in Parliament towards that of government itself. This evolution, and the change in outlook that accompanied it, may in a sense be regarded as the triumph of a more general educational initiative, that which had been consciously directed to training Labour to rule in the interests of the nation rather than, as socialists pressed, in the interests of the working class. Labour representatives in Parliament had from the first been responsive to this approach, but there were also sections of the organised Labour movement at large, notably the Fabians, whose outlook had been fixed in this direction. Socialists flatly rejected it, claiming, as the Ruskin students had once done, that a non-partisan approach meant in practice leaving aside the interests of Labour and the ultimate aim of socialism in favour of maintaining the *status quo*. But though socialist groups formed up anew on the left of the Labour movement during and immediately after the war, and there were many active struggles to come, opportunities for breaking through again into the movement at large were less favourable than in an earlier day. Following the General Strike the trade union leadership, with some exceptions, drew back from militant struggle while the Parliamentary Labour Party also sought social harmony. The debacle of 1931, the formation of the National Government and the massive unemployment of the '30s forced the Labour movement on to the defensive.

It was against this background that plans for educational reform now began to be argued predominantly on educational grounds. In a book which set out what had now become accepted Labour policy, *Secondary Education for All* (1922), R. H. Tawney ridiculed the conception that "the mass of the people, like anthropoid apes," have "fewer convolutions in their brains than the rich". Yet in the years to come, as the pressure for secondary education for all increased, the newly developed theories derived from intelligence testing were used to justify provision of different types of education for different children. There was now less stress on the need for elementary and secondary education to be different in kind, more and more on the different levels of "intelligence" inherent in children's minds from birth, making it necessary in their own best interests to provide varying educational fare, particularly after the age of eleven. This was a key argument advanced to support the main recommendation of the Hadow Report (*The Education of the Adolescent*, 1926): that elementary schools be divided into junior and senior departments, and that while all schools taking children from eleven upwards should be regarded as secondary, grammar schools must remain separate and parallel to the other types of school, reserved for the intelligent few, as Morant and others had designed they should be from 1900.

In all the circumstances the call for different types of secondary school to meet different needs, advanced by the W.E.A. in 1917 and later by Tawney on behalf of the Labour Party, proved to be the Achilles heel of Labour's post-war educational policy. To insist on this point was in practice to join forces with those who were concerned to maintain fundamental divisions in education beyond the elementary stage; it was a clear retreat from the position that the Bradford Charter had mapped out, and the T.U.C. and the Labour Party itself earlier accepted—that the only way to move towards equality of opportunity is to provide secondary education for all in a common school. The result is spelt out in the evolution of the educational system over the forty years after 1918, from Hadow reorganisation after 1926 to tri-partitism after 1944—no matter what was decided in principle about the need for secondary education for all.

It should be recalled that it was not until 1945 that fees in maintained secondary schools were abolished, forty-eight years after the T.U.C. first advanced this demand. Meanwhile, from 1902 onwards an increase in provision for secondary schooling meant only an increase in grammar school places, many open only to fee-payers (it is only by forgetting earlier history, and the methods whereby they were brought to the fore, that old-established grammar schools can claim a long tradition of educating the clever child). Not until the 1960s did there develop a clear trend towards the comprehensive—or common—secondary school, based on the pioneering work of certain progressive local authorities and teachers in the previous decade. This at length created the conditions for the merging of two separate traditions in English education —the elementary and the secondary.

In sum, developments during the half-century after 1870, surveyed from the standpoint of the Labour movement, present a scene very different from that usually depicted in histories of education. No doubt there was, in one sense, a "silent social revolution" at this time, but the changes brought about in the educational system were ultimately the outcome of battles fought out amid much noise and dust. This is not merely a story of philanthropy and growing enlightenment, resulting in a continuous upward curve of development but rather a history of breakthroughs and retreats from which the lesson to emerge for the Labour movement was that nothing is gained (or retained) without persistent and determined pressure. Even this may fail to avert severe setbacks. There can be no doubt that, in the eyes of organised Labour, the Education Act of 1902—so often hailed for its statesmanlike qualities—appeared as an extremely retrograde measure. Equally, whatever the realisation that Fisher was doing what he could, the Education Act of 1918 was a severe disappointment. During these years the Labour movement evolved a consistent outlook on education going far beyond what could be achieved through current legislation, formulated its objectives and campaigned for them. In an important sense it made the running. The main issues at stake, however, remained to be fought out in changing conditions during the years to come.

BIBLIOGRAPHY

This bibliography covers the main books, and other materials, used in this study.

BOOKS

ADAMSON, J. W., *English Education, 1789-1902* (1930)

ALLEN, B. M., *Sir Robert Morant* (1943)

ARCH, JOSEPH, *Joseph Arch, the Story of his Life* (ed. Countess of Warwick, n.d.)

ARMYTAGE, W. H. G., *A. J. Mundella, 1825-97* (1951)

BALFOUR, GRAHAM, *The Educational Systems of England and Wales* (1898)

BANKS, OLIVE, *Parity and Prestige in English Education* (1955)

BARNETT, S. A., *Canon Barnett, His Life, Work and Friends* (1921 ed.)

BELL, E. A., *A History of Giggleswick School, 1499-1912* (1912)

BELL, TOM, *John Maclean* (1944)

—— *Pioneering Days* (1941)

BINGHAM, J. H., *The Sheffield School Board, 1870-1903* (1949)

BINNS, H. B., *A Century of Education* (1908)

BIRCHENOUGH, C., *History of Elementary Education* (1914)

BROCKWAY, FENNER, *Socialism over Sixty Years* (1946)

BRYHER, S., *The Labour and Socialist Movement in Bristol* (1929)

BULLOCK, ALAN, *The Life and Times of Ernest Bevin*, Vol. I (1960)

CAMPBELL, FLANN, *Eleven Plus and All That* (1956)

CARPENTER, EDWARD, *My Days and Dreams* (1916)

CHURCHILL, W. S., *Lord Randolph Churchill*, Vol. I (1906)

CLARK, G. KITSON, *The Making of Victorian England* (1962)

COLE, G. D. H., *The Second International, 1899-1914* (1956)

COLE, M. I. (ed.), *Beatrice Webb's Diaries, 1912-24* (1952)

COTGROVE, S. F., *Technical Education and Social Change* (1958)

CRAIK, W. W., *The Central Labour College* (1964)

CRUIKSHANK, MARJORIE, *Church and State in English Education* (1963)

CURTIS, S. J., *Education in Britain since 1900* (1952)

CURZON, LORD, *Principles and Methods of University Reform* (1909)

DOLLING, R. R., *Ten Years in a Portsmouth Slum* (1897)

DRAPER, W. H., *University Extension, 1873-1923* (1923)

DRURY, J. F. W., *Manual of Education* (1903)

EAGER, W. McG., *Making Men* (1953)

EAGLESHAM, ERIC, *From School Board to Local Authority* (1956)

EDWARDS, D. L., *A History of King's School, Canterbury* (1957)

EVANS, W. and CLARIDGE, W., *James Hirst Hollowell and the Movement for the Civic Control of Education* (1911)

FISHER, H. A. L., *Educational Reform* (1918)

—— *An Unfinished Autobiography* (1940)

FITZROY, SIR ALMERIC, *Memoirs*, 2 vols. (1926)

GALLACHER, WILLIAM, *Revolt on the Clyde* (1936)

GAUTREY, THOMAS, *School Board Memories* (n.d., *c.* 1937)

GORST, SIR JOHN, *The Children of the Nation, How their Health and Vigour should be promoted by the State* (1906)

GOULD, F. J., *The Life-Story of a Humanist* (1923)

GOURLAY, A. B., *A History of Sherborne School* (1951)

GREAVES, C. DESMOND, *The Life and Times of James Connolly* (1961)

HABAKKUK, H. J., *American and British Technology in the Nineteenth Century* (1962)

HALDANE, VISCOUNT, *Education and Empire* (1902)

—— *The Universities and National Life* (3rd ed. 1912)

HALÉVY, E., *Imperialism and the Rise of Labour, 1895-1905* (1961 ed.)

—— *The Rule of Democracy, 1905-1914* (1961 ed.)

HALL, B. T., *Our Fifty Years* (1912)

HAMILTON, MARY AGNES, *Arthur Henderson* (1938)

HARRISON, J. F. C., *Learning and Living, 1760-1960* (1961)

HARRISON, S., *Alex Gossip* (1962)

HOBSBAWM, E. J., *Labouring Men* (1964)

HOLMES, EDMOND, *In Quest of an Ideal* (1920)

—— *What is and What Might Be* (1911)

HORRABIN, J. F. and W., *Working-Class Education* (1924)

HOWARD, C. H. D. (ed.), *Joseph Chamberlain; a Political Memoir, 1880-1892* (1953)

HUTTON, A. W., *Cardinal Manning* (1892)

HYNDMAN, H. M., *The Record of an Adventurous Life* (1911)

INGLIS, K. S., *Churches and the Working Classes in Victorian England* (1963)

JACKSON, T. A., *Solo Trumpet* (1953)

JENKINS, ROY, *Mr. Balfour's Poodle* (1954)

KEELING, FREDERICK, *Child Labour in the United Kingdom* (1914)

KEKEWICH, G. W., *The Education Department and After* (1920)

KELLY, T., *A History of Adult Education in Great Britain* (1962)

KNAPP, JOHN M. (ed.), *The Universities and the Social Problem* (1895)

KNOX, E. A., *Reminiscences of an Octogenarian* (n.d. 1935?)

LEE, H. W. and ARCHBOLD, E., *Social Democracy in Britain* (1935)

LEESE, JOHN, *Personalities and Power in English Education* (1950)

LIBERAL PARTY PUBLICATION, *The Government's Record, 1906-13* (1913)

LORD, MIRIAM, *Margaret McMillan in Bradford* (1957)

LOWNDES, G. A. N., *The Silent Social Revolution* (1937)

MACDONALD, ALEC, *A Short History of Repton* (1929)

MACK, E. C., *Public Schools and Political Opinion since 1860* (1941)

MACKAIL, J. W., *The Life of William Morris*, 2 vols. (1911)

MACLEAN, A. H. H., *The Public Schools and the War in South Africa* (1903)

MAGNUS, SIR PHILIP, *Educational Aims and Efforts, 1880-1910* (1910)

MANN, T., *Memoirs* (1923)

MANSBRIDGE, ALBERT, *University Tutorial Classes* (1913)

—— *An Adventure in Working Class Education* (1920)

—— *Margaret McMillan, Prophet and Pioneer* (1932)

—— *The Kingdom of the Mind* (1941)

MARCHANT, SIR JAMES, *Dr. John Clifford* (1924)

MARTIN, G. CURRIE, *The Adult School Movement* (1924)

McMILLAN, MARGARET, *The Child and the State* (1911)

MILLIS, C. T., *Technical Education, its Development and Aims* (1925)

MILNER, LORD, *Arnold Toynbee* (1895)

MORRIS, WILLIAM, *On Art and Socialism* (ed. Holbrook Jackson, 1947)

MORRISON, A., *A Child of the Jago* (1896)

MORTON, A. L. and TATE, G., *The British Labour Movement* (1956)

NETHERCOT, ARTHUR N., *The First Five Lives of Annie Besant* (1961)

NEWSOME, DAVID, *A History of Wellington College* (1959)

—— *Godliness and Good Learning* (1961)

OGG, DAVID, *Herbert Fisher* (1947)

OSTROGORSKI, M., *Democracy and the Organisation of Political Parties* (1902)

OXFORD AND ASQUITH, EARL OF, *Fifty Years of Parliament*, 2 vols. (1926)

Oxford and Working Class Education (2nd ed. 1909)

PARKYN, G. R., *Life and Letters of Edward Thring* (1900 ed.)

PAUL, EDEN and CEDAR, *Proletcult* (1921)

PEACOCK, ROGER S., *Pioneer of Boyhood* (1954)

PEASE, EDWARD R., *History of the Fabian Society* (1916)

PEERS, ROBERT, *Adult Education, a Comparative Study* (1958)

PELLING, H., *The Origins of the Labour Party* (1954)

PERCIVAL, ALICIA C., *Youth Will be Led* (1951)

PILKINGTON, E. M. S., *An Eton Playing Field* (1896)

PIMLOTT, J. A. R., *Toynbee Hall* (1935)

POLLARD, S., et al., *Sheffield Trades and Labour Council, 1858-1958* (1958)

POLLITT, HARRY, *Serving my Time* (1940)

REYNOLDS, E. E., *Baden Powell* (1942)

RICHTER, MELVIN, *The Politics of Conscience, T. H. Green and his Age* (1964)

ROBB, JANET H., *The Primrose League, 1883-1906* (1942)

ROBERTS, R. D., *Eighteen Years of University Extension* (1891)

ROSCOE, H. E., *The Life and Experiences of Sir H. E. Roscoe* (1906)

RUSSELL, C. E. B., *Lads' Clubs* (1932 ed.)

SACKS, BENJAMIN, *The Religious Issue in the State Schools of England and Wales, 1902-14* (1961)

SADLER, MICHAEL (ed.), *Continuation Schools in England and Elsewhere* (1907)

SANDERSON, LORD, *Memories of Sixty Years* (1931)

SEMMEL, B., *Imperialism and Social Reform* (1960)

SHAW, BERNARD, *Fabianism and the Empire* (1900)

SHERARD, ROBERT H., *Child Slaves in Britain* (1904)

SIMON, BRIAN, *Studies in the History of Education, 1780-1870* (1960)

SIMON, SHENA D., *A Century of City Government* (1938)

SMILLIE, ROBERT, *My Life for Labour* (1924)

SMITH, FRANK, *A History of English Elementary Education, 1760-1902* (1931)

SMITH, H. P., *Labour and Learning* (1956)

SNELL, LORD, *Men, Movements and Myself* (1936)

SNEYD-KYNNERSLEY, E. M., *H.M.I., Passages in the Life of an Inspector of Schools* (1908)

SOLLY, HENRY, *Working Men's Social Clubs and Educational Institutes* (1867)

SOUTTER, F. W., *Recollections of a Labour Pioneer* (1924 ed.)

STEWART, W., *J. Keir Hardie* (1925 ed.)

STOCKS, M., *The Workers' Educational Association* (1953)

STORR, F., *Life and Remains of Quick* (1899)

TAWNEY, R. H., *Secondary Education for All* (1922)

—— *Education, the Socialist Policy* (1924)

—— *The Radical Tradition* (1964)

THOMPSON, E. P., *William Morris, Romantic to Revolutionary* (1955)

THORNE, WILL, *My Life's Battles* (n.d.)

TILLETT, BEN, *Memories and Reflections* (1931)

TORR, DONA, *Tom Mann and his Times* (1956)

TROPP, ASHER, *The School Teachers* (1957)

TURNER, BEN, *About Myself* (1930)

WALKER, WILLIAM GEORGE, *A History of the Oundle School* (1956)

WEBB, BEATRICE, *My Apprenticeship* (1926)

WEBB, SYDNEY, *The Educational Muddle and the Way Out* (Fabian Tract No. 106, 1901)

—— *Twentieth Century Politics* (Fabian Tract No. 108, 1901)

—— *London Education* (1904)

WEBB, SYDNEY and BEATRICE, *The History of Trade Unionism* (1892)

WELBOURNE, E., *The Miners' Unions of Northumberland and Durham* (1923)

WILLIAMS, J. E. D. HODDER, *The Life of Sir George Williams* (1906)

ARTICLES

EAGLESHAM, ERIC, "Planning the Education Bill of 1902", *British Journal of Educational Studies*, Vol. IX, No. 1

—— "Implementing the Education Act of 1902', *British Journal of Educational Studies*, Vol. X, No. 2

GOSDEN, P. H. J. C., "The Board of Education Act of 1899", *British Journal of Educational Studies*, Vol. XI, No. 1

HILLIARD, F. H., "The Moral Instruction League, 1872-1919", *Durham Research Review*, Vol. III, No. 12

HUTT, ALLEN, "The Hours of Labour", *Marxist Quarterly*, Vol. II, No. 1

JENKINS, H. and JONES, D. CARADOG, "Social Class of Cambridge Alumni", *British Journal of Sociology*, Vol. I, No. 2

JUDGES, A. V., "The Educational Influence of the Webbs", *British Journal of Educational Studies*, Vol. X, No. 1

HUGHES, K. M., "A Political Party and Education, Reflections on the Liberal Party's Educational Policy, 1870-1902", *British Journal of Educational Studies*, Vol. VIII, No. 2

PALIN, J. H., "The Feeding of School Children, Bradford's Experience", *The Socialist Review*, Vol. I.

ROGERS, ALAN, "Churches and Children—A Study in the Controversy over the 1902 Education Act", *British Journal of Educational Studies*, Vol. VIII, No. 1.

STANSKY, PETER, "Lyttleton and Thring: a study in nineteenth-century education", *Victorian Studies*, Vol. V, No. 3.

z

THESES

McCANN, W. P., "Trade Unionist, Co-operative and Socialist Organisations in relation to Popular Education, 1870-1902" (University of Manchester, 1960)

SHAKOOR, A., "The Training of Teachers in England and Wales, 1900-1939" (University of Leicester, 1964)

TAYLOR, A. F., "Birmingham and the Movement for National Education, 1867-77" (University of Leicester, 1960)

JOURNALS

Clarion
Commonweal (Socialist League)
Fabian News
The Highway (W.E.A.)
Justice (S.D.F.)
The Labour Annual (1896-7)
Labour Leader (I.L.P.)
Labour Prophet
National Reformer (National Secular Society)
The "Plebs" Magazine
The Schoolmaster (N.U.T.)
Social Democrat (S.D.F., monthly)
The Socialist (S.L.P.)
Socialist Review (I.L.P., monthly)
Times Educational Supplement
The Young Socialist

REPORTS

Co-operative Congress Reports, 1900-2
Independent Labour Party Conference Reports, 1893-1920
Labour Representation Committee Conference Reports, 1901-1905
Labour Party Conference Reports, 1906-1920
Social Democratic Federation Conference Reports, 1894-1907[1]
Social Democratic Party Conference Reports, 1908-1911
British Socialist Party Conference Reports, 1912-1918
Trade Union Congress Reports, 1881-1920

---

[1] The 14th annual conference of the S.D.F., held in 1894, was the first that was followed by a printed report of the proceedings. Earlier reports may be found in *Justice*.

GOVERNMENT PUBLICATIONS

1864 Royal Commission on Public Schools ("Clarendon"); report and evidence

1868 Schools Inquiry Commission (Royal Commission, "Taunton"); report and evidence

1884 Royal Commission on Technical Instruction; report and evidence

1884 Report to the Education Department upon the alleged over-pressure of work in public elementary schools

1887-8 Royal Commission on the Elementary Education Acts ("Cross"); report and evidence

1895 Royal Commission on Secondary Education ("Bryce")

1904 Inter-Departmental Committee on Physical Deterioration; report

1905 Inter-Departmental Committee on Medical Inspection and Feeding of Children attending Public Elementary Schools; report

1906 Report of the Consultative Committee upon Higher Elementary Schools

1917 Departmental Committee on Juvenile Employment in relation to Employment after the War; report

1918 Adult Education Committee (Ministry of Reconstruction); final report

1926 Report of the Consultative Committee on the Education of the Adolescent ("Hadow report")

1938 Report of the Consultative Committee on Secondary Education with Special Reference to Grammar Schools and Technical High Schools ("Spens report")

1944 The Public Schools and the General Educational System ("Fleming report")

Annual reports of the Committee of Council on Education; 1890-1898
Annual reports of the Board of Education; 1899-1920
Hansard; 1902, 1906

INDEX